Building Basic
Competencies in
Social Work Research

Building Basic Competencies in Social Work Research

An Experiential Approach

Reginald O. York
East Carolina University

Allyn and Bacon
Boston • London • Toronto • Sydney • Tokyo • Singapore

Series Editor, Social Work: Judy Fifer
Editor in Chief, Social Sciences: Karen Hanson
Editorial Assistant: Mary Visco
Marketing Manager: Quinn Perkson
Editorial/Production Service: Chestnut Hill Enterprises, Inc.
Manufacturing Buyer: Megan Cochran
Cover Administrator: Suzanne Harbison

Library of Congress Cataloging-in-Publication Data

York, Reginald O., (date)
  Building basic competencies in social work research : an
experiential approach / Reginald O. York.
      p. cm.
  Includes bibliographical references and index.
  ISBN 0-205-19357-9 (pbk.)
    1. Social service—Research—Methodology. 2. Social service—
Research—Problems, exercises, etc. I. Title.
  HV11.Y56 1996
361.3'2'072—dc20   96-10977
                                                          CIP

Printed in the United States of America

Contents

LEVEL I: Understanding Social Work Research   39

3   Understanding Explanatory Research: Does Gender Explain Social Work Salaries When Position Level Is Controlled?   68

Preface

This is a book that will help the reader to develop skill in the execution of the tasks involved in social work research. In the pursuit of this goal, you will be given exercises in which you will be called on to evaluate alternative ways to complete each task and to make certain decisions in the process of conducting research. This text differs from other texts in several important ways.

First, it is presented within a developmental framework in which the learner encounters simple tasks in one stage of learning before moving to more complicated ones in later stages of learning. Second, these stages of learning are presented holistically, in that the reader uses examples which address each of the major phases of the research process at the simple level before moving on. With few exceptions, the chapters in this text cover the entire research process from A to Z.

A third major way this text is different lies in its emphasis on the purposes of research rather than the various subjects of research. For example, the reader examines knowledge regarding the achievement of a given purpose for a research study, such as the evaluation of a social work intervention, rather than focusing inordinate attention on one specific task such as measurement, sampling, research design, and so forth. Each of these tasks in the research process, of course, is examined in this text, but it is done within the framework of the purpose of a study. Thus, specific tasks are examined within the framework of a given purpose. With the typical research textbook, the reader must focus attention on a myriad of questions revolving around one task, with the idea that they will exit this lesson with a substantial knowledge of a given task such as sampling. It is assumed that the learner will be willing to delay the gratification of applying that knowledge until all the tasks have been thoroughly mastered and the complete picture comes into focus. This process can be rather frustrating to the typical social work student.

Fourth, this text is predicated on the model of adult learning in which the reader is actively engaged in the research process and is constantly called on to make decisions or demonstrate an understanding of why things were done the way they were. It rests on the assumption that the teacher can gain little meaningful ground by saying "Learn this because I say it is something you need to know." Adult learners are mature people who need to be able to make use of knowledge in a way that is meaningful to them.

Finally, the reader will encounter a great deal of reinforcement of lessons previously addressed. I assume that the typical learner needs such reinforcement. Lessons about such concepts as sampling or statistical significance or validity will not normally be retained by the social work student unless lessons are reinforced through new examples.

The Developmental Framework

The building of skills in this text is undertaken within a developmental framework. This framework rests on the assumption that learners must master each task in the research process at the elementary level before they are ready for the intermediate level, which must be mastered before engaging in tasks or concepts considered to be more advanced. To put it simply, you must learn how to crawl before you can walk.

This perspective has grown from my experience as a research instructor for graduate and undergraduate social work students. It became increasingly obvious that the average social work student was easily overwhelmed when confronted with the typical presentation of research knowledge in most research texts, knowledge which seems to many students to be much like the learning of a new language. But instead of being treated to exercises which present lessons in simple terms before moving on to more complex concepts or tasks, the reader of the typical textbook on research is expected to understand, for example, the difference between criterion validity and construct validity on the first encounter with an explanation, and to grasp this distinction in the same chapter which introduces a myriad of new information of a rather technical nature. Often, the student loses the forest for the trees, and soon forgets even the trees.

There are three stages, or levels, in this developmental framework: understanding research, using research, and conducting research. In the first stage, the learner develops an appreciation of why the research process unfolds as it does. At the completion of this stage, the reader will have an understanding of the spirit of scientific inquiry, the steps in the research process, and some of the basic concepts in research, such as theory, study sample, study variables, validity, and statistical significance, among others. An understanding of the four major purposes of social work research is also acquired.

At the completion of the second stage, the reader is prepared to critically evaluate published research. This requires an understanding of the alternatives available for defining problems, measuring variables, analyzing data, and drawing conclusions. For example, the learner will develop the ability to analyze whether a given knowledge base would tend to guide one toward the development of a quantitative means for measuring variables or a qualitative method of doing so. This provides the learner with the ability to evaluate whether an existing study utilized an optimal means of measurement, given the knowledge base and the study purpose.

The third stage of learning prepares the reader to conduct each of the tasks in the research process. This agenda is the focus of other texts, but is addressed in the last chapter in the present text. In that chapter, the student becomes both a researcher and a study subject. A study I designed uses the student as a study subject. Students respond to questions and combine their answers with their classmates and undertake an analysis of the results. The student then draws conclusions regarding the research question.

An Emphasis On the Entire Process of Research

These levels of learning are acquired through case examples in research in which each of the phases of the research process are examined. The first chapter in this process (Chapter 2 in this book), for example, examines the goal of describing the opinions of the clients of a hypothetical family service agency. In this chapter, the reader is taken through the research phases of problem formulation, research methodology, data analysis, and conclusions. A number of very basic research concepts are introduced in this endeavor.

The next chapter utilizes a new example which is in a different category of research. While this chapter is also in the first stage of learning, the developmental framework is further utilized in that the learner is introduced to several new concepts in research. The same can be said about the third and fourth chapters in this first section of the text. In fact, the reader will discover that this developmental focus undergirds the entire text.

An Emphasis On the Purposes of Research

In this text, examples are used which fit into each of the four major categories of research when research is organized according to purpose. These purposes are description, explanation, evaluation, and exploration. In the first major section of the text, there is one chapter which illustrates descriptive research, one which illustrates explanatory research, one in which the learner examines evaluative research, and one which illustrates exploratory research. This is repeated in the second major section of this text.

Descriptive research simply attempts to describe a given phenomenon. Examples include the level of satisfaction of clients of an agency or the demographic characteristics of social work students. If you want to know what proportion of social workers are female, or of hispanic origin, you are talking about a descriptive study. However, if you want to determine if salary is explained by gender when position level is taken into consideration, you are referring to an explanatory study. An explanatory study is used to explain a given phenomenon. This usually takes the form of an examination of the relationships among a set of study variables, such as salary, gender, and position level.

C h a p t e r *1*

Introduction

In this chapter you will be introduced to several key themes in research. After you review a definition of social work research, you will examine the uses of research in social work, the nature of scientific inquiry, the process of research, and the four major purposes of research in social work. You will then confront a few of the many basic principles that will eventually guide your efforts as a social work researcher.

In keeping with the orientation of this book, this treatment of research will be rather basic, because it is designed to be your first major lesson in research. Thus, you will not confront a large number of terms with which you are not familiar. For this reason, you will not find a glossary of terms at the end of this chapter as you will with many of the chapters that follow. You will find that this chapter will provide examples of research for you to apply your learning, and will offer you a set of assignments for your completion in preparation for class discussion.

Objectives

At the completion of this chapter, you will be able to:

1. Distinguish between examples of knowledge building that are and are not consistent with the spirit of scientific inquiry;
2. Identify whether a given example of research is in the category of descriptive research, exploratory research, explanatory research, or evaluative research;
3. Identify the basic sequence of the steps in the research process;
4. Identify six basic principles of research;
5. Apply the above objectives to three examples of research: the full moon; service options for the abused wife; stress among social work students.

The Nature of Social Work Research

Social work research is a means of gaining relevant knowledge through the use of the scientific method. If an example of an inquiry into a problem or question is to be labeled as social work research, it will, of course, be relevant to the mission of the social work profession. It will also employ a method of inquiry that is orderly and objective. An inquiry that is designed to prove a point is not an example of social work research. An inquiry that is incomplete or illogical also fails to qualify as social work research.

The scientific method is orderly and systematic, and is designed to reduce human error in observation. It moves from one phase of inquiry to another in a logical sequence of activities. For example, researchers must have a clear idea of what they want to find out before they select a means of doing so. They must know what they will be observing (or measuring) before they select subjects for study, because some groups of subjects will not provide them with the opportunity to measure what they wish to measure. Before they can draw conclusions about their research question, researchers must collect and analyze data relevant to it, and they must do so in a manner that provides them with the opportunity to find that their previous expectations about reality are not supported, as well as having the opportunity to find support for their expectations. Selective observations, biased by preconceived notions of reality, are outside the bounds of the spirit of scientific inquiry.

The most important reason that social workers should understand social work research methods is that this knowledge can be used to improve social work practice. All professions are founded upon a systematically collected body of knowledge which guides practice. While that body of knowledge is more incomplete in some areas than others, it is imperative that a reasonable body of knowledge exists in order for a line of work to qualify as a profession. Research methods provide the means by which the social work knowledge base is developed and refined.

Professions are also guided by a code of ethics. In social work, the code of ethics requires that the professional social worker employ methods that are effective to the extent that such knowledge is known. Practice that is clearly out of the bounds of the standard body of knowledge of a profession is the primary basis for a malpractice suit. And failure to know that body of knowledge is not a suitable defense for the practitioner. Thus, if you wish to become a professional social worker or to continue in this profession, you must maintain your knowledge of what is more or less effective in practice. To do otherwise is to remove yourself from the ranks of those who are truly professional.

Research methods can be used to test certain assumptions you have acquired in practice or questions which you have developed. When your perceptions are supported by your research efforts, you can have more confidence in their accuracy, and, perhaps, you will learn something in this process which will refine your understanding. When your expectations are not supported by your research results, you can be stimulated to further growth by your efforts to rethink the problem under study. As you continue in this growth and validation of practice principles and methods, you will be in a better position to meet the challenges of accountability that have been increasing in recent decades.

The Purposes of Social Work Research

In this text, research will be classified into four general categories according to the purpose of the study. One purpose is description. Sometimes researchers want to describe something in detail so that they understand it better, and call this type *descriptive* research. Examples include the description of the characteristics of the clients of the Hopewell Mental Health Clinic, or the health needs of the homeless people of Jones County. In the next chapter, you will examine the process of describing the extent to which the clients of a family service agency express satisfaction with the services they have received.

Sometimes researchers want to test an explanation of what causes things to be the way they are. In this type of research, called *explanatory* research, they examine the relationships among a set of variables to see if their expectations about causation are supported. In a research study described later, you will examine the question of what influences the helping person's tendency to emphasize economic independence rather than interpersonal dynamics in the provision of services to an abused wife.

In the third chapter of this text, you will examine whether gender is related to salary when position level is taken into consideration. There is evidence from previous research that female social workers receive lower salaries than male social workers. Females are also less likely than males to be found in management positions. Is the relationship between gender and salary explained by position level? In other words, do females receive lower salaries primarily because they are in lower positions? If this proposition is true, perhaps efforts toward gender equity should focus upon advancement more than salary equalization between men and women in the same positions. But if female managers are found to receive lower salaries than male managers, the evidence will provide an argument for a different priority in the quest for equity.

A third general purpose of social work research is the evaluation of the extent to which a social work intervention was effective in reaching its goals. This type of research will be referred to as *evaluative* research. In the fourth chapter, you will examine whether an inpatient treatment program in a hospital was effective in reducing the depression level of its clients.

The fourth general type of social work research is *exploratory*. This type of research has the purpose of generating new theories about social behavior or new conceptions of the way things are. It is useful when knowledge of a given subject is limited. An example given in this text is the work of John Powell, who studied the experience of being adopted by interviewing adults who had been adopted as older children and could remember the experience. What is it like to experience being adopted? This was the basic question he explored.

The Process of Social Work Research

In this text, the process of social work research is divided generally into four phases: (1) problem formulation, (2) study methodology, (3) data collection and analysis, and (4) conclusions. To put these steps into familiar language, when research efforts are complete, the following questions will be answered:

1. What did you want to do (or know)?
2. How did you do it (or how did you go about the task of finding out)?
3. What did you discover?
4. What conclusions did you draw?

The phases of the research process can be divided into many steps or few, depending upon how detailed you wish to be. In this book, I will divide it into four major phases, each of which contains several tasks. Having described these phases in common language, let's learn a little about each phase.

The first phase is *problem formulation.* I call this phase "problem formulation" because researchers must analyze their problem area before they can fully develop an intelligent research question. In this phase, they identify an area of concern for which they wish more knowledge, and examine the existing literature for answers to various questions which they might have regarding this topic. From their analysis of this subject, they develop a research question, one that is not well answered from previous research.

Armed with their research question, they enter the second phase of research—*study methodology.* Essential to this phase is the selection of a means of observation (measurement) and the selection of study subjects. The structure of research methods (sometimes referred to as the research design) is another critical task in this phase.

Sometimes researchers choose to measure variables precisely, and employ an instrument for doing so. At other times, their purpose is better served by a more flexible means of observation such as an interview with general questions or direct observation of behavior.

Sometimes researchers select their study subjects at random from their study population so that they can better generalize their findings from the study subjects to a broader population of people. Sometimes this is not feasible, so they have to be more careful in making generalizations.

In some studies, researchers may measure study subjects on certain variables at one point in time to see if there is a relationship between them. In other studies, they may introduce an intervention and measure their subjects at two points in time to see if there is a change that might be attributed to the intervention.

In each of these critical tasks in the design of a study, there are many more options than mentioned above. These options were presented as examples to illustrate the process of research.

The third phase of the research process entails the *analysis of data.* What was found? Was the average salary of males and females different? If so, how different? Were clients found to have a lower level of depression after treatment than before? If so, was this difference significant? What did graduate students say in their interviews about the ways that they had experienced stress and the ways they had coped with it? What topics were mentioned by more than one student?

In the final phase of research, researchers *draw conclusions* about their research question. Was the intervention effective enough for them to publicize their treatment model to others? How might they speculate on the things which might explain their findings? If social support was not found to be related to stress among social work students, was it because these students were found to have such high levels of support that this variable was rendered meaningless as a method of testing the research question? If there is not a meaningful number of students with low levels of support to compare to those with high support, they cannot very well test their question about the relationship between support and stress.

Some of the questions to be addressed in each phase of the research process are presented below.

PROBLEM FORMULATION
What was the subject of study?
Why did we want to study this subject?
What was already known about this subject?
What was the research question that emerged?

STUDY METHODOLOGY
How were critical concepts measured in this study?
How were people selected for this study?
How were data collected?

DATA ANALYSIS
What kinds of people were included in the study?
What did the data reveal about the study question?

CONCLUSIONS
What conclusions were supported by the results?

On the next page, you will find the first of many assignments in this book. These assignments are designed to help you to review the material that has been covered in the past few pages of the text. You should respond to the questions from this assignment and be prepared to present your answers for class discussion. You will find that space is available to write your responses in this book. Students have found this to be an effective means of reviewing material and testing their understanding of it. Class discussion should help you to see the strengths and limitations of your own reflections on the content you have been covering.

ASSIGNMENT 1–A [FOR CLASS DISCUSSION]

1. Is it necessary that professional social workers develop skills in the use of research? Explain your response.

_____

_____

_____

_____

_____

_____

2. Is it necessary that professional social workers develop skills in the conducting of their own research? Explain.

_____

_____

_____

_____

_____

_____

3. One of the types of research, classified by the purpose of the study, is known as descriptive research. Give an example.

_____

_____

_____

_____

_____

4. What are the other three types of research?

    1. _____

    2. _____

    3. _____

5. Classify each of the following studies according to type.

_____   This study will seek an understanding of the process whereby social workers develop a level of stress that has come to be known as "burnout." What, for example, are the typical stages of movement toward burnout?

_____   This study will collect information on the characteristics of social work students, such as gender, age, ethnicity, and so forth.

_____   This study will examine whether a group of abused wives have higher self-esteem after they have participated in a support group than before they had this experience.

_____   This study will examine whether economic dependence upon the spouse is more influential than self-esteem in determining whether an abused wife returns to her husband.

6. There are two sets of statements below. For each set, select the one that comes first in the research process and place (1) next to it. Then select the one that comes next and place (2) by it. The final item will be (3). These sets, of course, do not cover all phases of the research process. Your task is to identify the proper sequence among these three statements in each of the two sets.

Set Number 1

_____   **A.** It was found that the stress scores for males and females did not differ significantly.

_____   **B.** Stress was measured by the Stress Sub-Scale of the Stress–Arousal Checklist.

_____   **C.** The evidence from the study reported in this paper fails to support the conclusion that gender influences one's level of stress.

Set Number 2

_____   **A.** The persons to be included in this study will be the students currently enrolled in two sections of a research course in one school of social work.

_____   **B.** Stress is a topic of importance because other researchers have found that persons with high levels of stress are more likely than others to have health problems.

_____   **C.** Students with high levels of social support were found to have lower levels of stress than did students with low levels of social support.

An Examination of a Few Basic Principles

There are many basic principles of scientific inquiry that should guide you in your efforts with research. In keeping with the basic approach of this text, I will start with only a few. In the next few pages, you will examine the following fundamental principles that will serve as your first lessons in research:

1. Social research entails a process of discovery, not justification.
2. Don't reinvent the wheel.
3. Don't put the cart before the horse.
4. Two heads are better than one.
5. Some things happen just by chance.
6. When you wear the research hat, you should be very careful with your conclusions.

In the next section, you will examine each of these fundamental principles and then apply it to an example in research.

1. Social research entails a process of discovery, not justification.

Researchers do not engage in research efforts for the purpose of justifying their preconceived ideas about reality. They do so because they want to find out whether certain ideas are supported by facts. If the scientific approach is taken seriously, the discovery that certain explanations of reality are not supported by relevant facts will lead you either to change your mind about that reality or to seek other relevant facts or both. As researchers seek more facts, they must do so in the spirit of scientific inquiry, which means that they will not select their facts according to their biases about the subject. They will consider all relevant facts and will try to place them into perspective so that their inquiry will be a carefully guided one.

The concept of bias is critical to this first principle. A bias is a mental leaning or inclination or a prejudice about a given subject. Sometimes people have made up their minds about a certain reality and are not prepared to accept contradictory information. Often this bias will be caused by their personal interests in a subject. If I am trying to sell you my used car, I will naturally have a bias about the value of it because I stand to gain by a perception that my car is worth top dollar. Thus, I am not in the best possible position to determine the true value of my car.

An important type of bias for the researcher is known as the social desirability bias. This is the bias someone might have because of the desire to express ideas that are socially desirable rather than ideas that truly reflect conceptions in their fullest representation. Are you always completely honest when you respond to the question "How do you like my new dress?" The desire to express ideas to others that will be agreeable to them is a very important bias that researchers must control if their efforts to gain new insight into reality are to progress.

Sometimes biases are the result of a limited experience with a given reality. Only one side of the story may be known. To be scientific, researchers must seek information on all sides of the story.

2. Don't reinvent the wheel!

In the history of human inquiry, there has been an enormous amount of social research that has been undertaken. When researchers develop a question, they usually find that there is a great deal of guidance that can come from an examination of the literature. Often, they find a suitable answer to their question from this review and will not find it necessary to undertake a new study of the subject. Even when they do not find a suitable answer to their question, they find much guidance from the literature on what aspects of the question have been left more or less unanswered, and find assistance with the conceptualization of their study and the measurement of social phenomena required to answer their question.

It is not reasonable to expect a novice researcher to do an exhaustive review of the literature on a given subject. There is a wide range of knowledge that has been written in places that are not well known or easily accessed. However, novice researchers can be expected to delve into the most available and best known literature on the subject of inquiry, so that they can avoid repeating the mistakes of early work on the subject, or failing to contribute anything of substance about the topic.

While there is normally a wide array of research that has been undertaken on any given subject, there is usually a good deal of research that needs to be added. Often what is needed is the use of a different type of person as the study subject or a different way of conceptualizing or measuring the phenomena under inquiry. Thus, you are not likely to encounter a situation in which the research you wish to undertake is substantially redundant. The greater reason for examining the previous literature is to help you avoid the mistakes of the past. You might find that the way you wish to undertake your study has been done many years ago and failed to provide a good means of addressing the research question. Later researchers will have corrected for these mistakes in their research methods.

3. Don't put the cart before the horse!

The research process follows the same basic path as good problem solving. Good problem solving starts with the identification of the problem and the objectives to be achieved by solving it. Methods of solving the problem are identified and used.

Then, the results are evaluated in order to determine if the problem has been solved. One of the common pitfalls in basic human problem solving is stating a problem in terms of only one solution. In so doing, people are starting with a solution rather than with the identification of the human condition to be addressed.

Social research begins with the formulation of the problem resulting in the articulation of the research question. After the question has been clearly identified, researchers determine the methods to be used in the pursuit of the answer to their question. One of the mistakes commonly made by the novice researcher is to begin a process of inquiry that starts with a research instrument. It is not uncommon for a student of research to review a set of research instruments that measure certain psychological conditions and become especially interested in the use of a certain instrument in some kind of research.

The process of research conceptualized in this book starts with problem formulation and moves logically to research methodology, then to data collection and analysis, and ends with conclusions. Obviously, you should not start with conclusions about the research question. I have covered this mistake in my examination of the purposes of scientific inquiry (discovery rather than justification). Likewise, it is not logical to start with data and formulate a research question that fits the data. (However, it is legitimate to use an exploration of data as a springboard for focusing a set of questions which guide the investigation of the literature.) Furthermore, as mentioned above, you would not start the process with the selection of study methods.

4. Two heads are better than one.

Because objective reality is so difficult to discover in the field of human behavior, researchers must rely upon a method of inquiry that reduces human error in observation. One such method is for researchers to ask for more than one observation of a given phenomenon in order to become confident that they have a true picture of it. In research, it is assumed that reality is more likely to be discovered when different people perceive things in the same light. Of course, it is possible that one person who is in the minority has the true picture while those in the majority are incorrect. But, in view of the fact that there is so little truly "hard" evidence of reality about human behavior, researchers make the assumption that their best bet is to go with the consensus of many people rather than the unsupported opinion of one person. And they have developed many ways to test the dependability of a given method of measuring their subjects of study. Thus, this principle serves as one of the assumptions of scientific inquiry.

5. Some things happen just by chance.

The fact that I had eggs for breakfast this morning does not necessarily mean that I prefer eggs over cereal for breakfast in general. It could be that I have eggs half the time and cereal half the time and I just happened to have had eggs this morning. If you observed me at breakfast several times and noted that I had eggs each and every time, you would have more reliable evidence that I prefer eggs for breakfast. The more observations, the more confident you would be in your conclusion that I prefer eggs for breakfast.

I am referring to a thing called "probability." I will deal with some of the technicalities of this concept in future chapters of this book, but for now, I will only address the concept in a very general way. Logic would suggest that there is a 50 percent chance of getting a heads on a given flip of a coin because there are only two possibilities—heads and tails. When people roll a die with six sides, they have one chance in six of rolling any one of the numbers from one to six. But let's suppose that someone said that there was one coin in a set of coins that was rigged to land on heads more often than tails because of the distribution of the weight of the coin. You pick out one coin and you want to know if this is the one that is rigged. Let's suppose that you had the following results when you flipped this coin eighteen times.

Flip Number	Results	Percentage of Heads
1	Heads	
2	Tails	50%
3	Tails	
4	Tails	25%
5	Heads	
6	Heads	50%
7	Tails	
8	Heads	50%
9	Heads	
10	Tails	50%
11	Heads	
12	Heads	58%
13	Tails	
14	Heads	57%
15	Tails	
16	Heads	56%
17	Tails	
18	Heads	50%

After four flips of the coin, you might wonder if this coin was rigged to land on tails more often than heads. But you would more likely realize that four flips of the coin are not very many flips. So, you continue to flip the coin in the pursuit of an answer to your question. After the sixth flip, your coin has landed on heads exactly fifty percent of the time, so you have little reason to believe that you have selected the rigged coin. But you might want to go further in your inquiry. After twelve flips you have 58 percent heads, but you will notice that the percentage of heads moves back to the 50 percent rate after eighteen flips. Now, you would probably be somewhat confident in concluding that you had not found the rigged coin. However, more flips of the coin would provide even more evidence to support your conclusion. If you had found 60 percent of the flips had landed on heads, you might be suspicious that you had selected the rigged coin, but a finding that 70 percent had been heads would be even more conclusive. Thus, you have two things to consider in your analysis: the number of flips and the percentage of heads. The more flips of the coin, the more confident you can be in your conclusion. The higher the percentage of heads, the more confident you can be in your conclusion. If you had a large number of flips *and* a very high percentage of heads, you could be very confident that you had found the rigged coin.

Now, let's put this same lesson to use with a more practical example. Let's suppose that you want to know whether males and females differ in their satisfaction with instruction in research courses. Are females higher or lower than males in their level of satisfaction? You could ask a given group of students if they are generally satisfied with their research instruction, with the options of YES or NO. You could then compare the proportion of those females who answered YES with the proportion of those males who answered YES. What if you found that 63 percent of females were satisfied and that 65 percent of males were satisfied? Does that mean that you can conclude that there is truly a difference between males and females? If so, would you be prepared to bet a large sum of money that a new study of this subject would result in males having a higher level of satisfaction? I doubt that you would, because you would realize that this small a difference between males and females could be easily explained by chance. If you had found 60 percent of females were satisfied as compared to only 40 percent of males, you would be more likely to see this difference as noteworthy. However, such a difference with a sample of only ten students would likely make you wonder if you should take these results seriously. A sample of a hundred students would make that difference more significant.

Those of you with previous training in research and statistics will recognize this discussion as being related to the concept of statistical significance, which will be examined later in this book. As you will see later, methods have been developed for estimating the likelihood that a given set of data results could be explained by chance.

6. When we wear the research hat, we must be very cautious with our conclusions.

Due to the limitations inherent in social research methods, researchers normally are cautious in the conclusions that they draw from their data. Their methods of measurement may not be optimal. Their study subjects may not be representative of others. Thus, a repeat of a study may provide different results.

As professionals, social workers are called upon to wear many hats. They might wear the hat of client advocate, in which case they are committed to the organization of information that advances the cause of their client. When they wear the research hat, they accept the norms of the scientific community and the spirit of scientific inquiry. This obligates them to pursue their interests with as much objectivity as they can muster, with the goal of advancing knowledge.

When researchers conduct a research study, they pursue a given research question. After data is collected and analyzed, they draw conclusions about their research question. Their data might provide strong support, or weak support, or no support for a given explanation of their study subject. Often the results are not entirely conclusive, and they might conceptualize new avenues of inquiry which might better illuminate the subject. The critical point here, however, is that they must avoid the temptation of drawing conclusions based upon prior understandings about their study subject which are not supported by the data they collected. They are, of course, at liberty to maintain any kind of personal opinion about their study subject which they believe to be true. But they must not pretend that this view is supported by the study if this is not true.

When social workers wear the research hat, they view study results as tentative. They seldom are in a position, after a single research study, to draw definitive conclusions about their research questions. They do not speak of proof or disproof, but, instead, of how the data either supports or fails to support a particular theory or conclusion.

ASSIGNMENT 1–B [FOR CLASS DISCUSSION]

1. John is a graduate social work student who learned how to conduct telephone surveys in a research course at the undergraduate level. When given the assignment of conducting a research project in a research class, he decides that he wishes to conduct a telephone survey. He then begins to think of topics which he might study using this study methodology.

   What is wrong with this approach? What basic principle is violated here?

   _____

   _____

   _____

2. A group of researchers decides to examine the effects of certain working conditions upon work production of persons in a sheltered workshop who are assembling the parts of a plastic toy for sale. The researchers want to know such things as whether lowering the lighting in the workshop will reduce productivity or if lowering the heat will do the same. They wish to discover the optimal working conditions. They select a par-

ticular workshop for their study. They bring the workers together and announce that they will be asked to participate in a special study about working conditions that will be of benefit to the design of similar workshops all over the country. In their efforts to stimulate participation and reduce any anxiety about the experiment, they decide to use regular group meetings with the workers to discuss any problems they will be having. They learn to their surprise that the productivity of the workers continually goes up even as they are reducing the lighting and the heat. Did the reduction of the lighting and the heat actually cause *more* productivity rather than less?

This would seem like a strange result, but what these hypothetical researchers did not know was that a similar experiment was undertaken many years ago in what came to be known as the Hawthorne Experiment. That study led to the conclusion that the behavior of people will be affected by the mere fact that they are the center of attention and have been viewed by others as being in a special situation. This condition seems to stimulate motivation. In that study, it was not concluded that lowering of lights increases performance, but, instead, that giving people special attention will increase motivation.

Which one of the basic principles is illustrated by this story?

_____

_____

_____

_____

3. Which one or ones of the following statements of the purpose of a research study would you consider to be acceptable according to one of the basic principles of research?

   a. The purpose of this study is to challenge the criticism that social workers have been inattentive to the needs of the elderly.
   b. The purpose of this study is to prove that females are being discriminated against in the administration of salaries.
   c. The purpose of this study is to examine whether males and females differ in their level of interest in the pursuit of a career in social work administration.
   d. The purpose of this study is to demonstrate that social work services are effective in meeting client needs.

   Explain your choice or choices.

_____

_____

_____

_____

Which basic principle is illustrated in this question?

_____

_____

4. A social worker with experience working with adolescent parents decided to conduct a study of the relationship between various sources of social support and psychological well-being for these parents. A study was undertaken in which various sources of social support were measured for a group of teenage parents. It was found that teenage mothers with a positive relationship with the father of their child had a more positive sense of well-being than those without such a positive relationship. It was found that those with stronger support from their maternal grandmothers did not differ from those with lower support from this source in regard to their levels of psychological well-being. It was also found that those who participated in support groups had more positive psychological well-being than those who had not had such group experiences.

   In the conclusions section of this study, the following statement can be found: "A professional service plan that effectively incorporates maternal grandmothers, male partners, and self-help groups appears to offer the best possibilities for reducing the distress of teenage mothers." What is wrong with this statement? What basic principle has been violated?

_____

_____

_____

_____

5. David is a new member of a group. When he first meets them he announces that he can determine whether each member is right-handed or left-handed by looking intensely into their eyes. They challenge his skill. He looks intensely into the eyes of one member and says "You are right-handed." The member responds "Yes, I am." David says "See, I told you I could do this."

   What basic principle is illustrated by the above?

_____

_____

6. Martha is a social worker who is providing marital therapy for Sam and Louise. They have made the mistake of allowing negative feelings to go unresolved for long periods of time, which eventually causes explosive fights. They are working on the strategy of not going to bed without reaching closure on disagreements they have had that have led to negative emotions of a significant level. Martha asks Louise to record the number

of nights when this happens as a means of monitoring progress with this problem. What is the limitation of this procedure? What basic principle is illustrated?

_____

_____

_____

_____

_____

Applying the Basic Principles: Does the Full Moon Make People Act Differently?

Let's apply what you've learned about these principles with regard to a research question. I will use one that is simple, and may even be fun. Have you ever heard someone say "It must be the full moon" when they witness strange behavior? When I have asked whether the full moon affects the behavior of mental health clients, I have often received an affirmative response from social workers. Some social workers seem convinced that the full moon has such an effect.

What is the purpose of this study? Is it to prove that the full moon does cause strange behavior in people? Is it to prove that it does not cause strange behavior? Or, is our purpose better stated as an attempt to find out whether or not there is a relationship between the existence of the full moon and the existence of strange behavior? You should have no difficulty recognizing the last statement as the best statement of the purpose of this study. If researchers seek to prove a point, they will naturally fall into various traps that will hamper their pursuit of knowledge about a subject. Remember that research is a process of discovery, not justification. The process of inquiry should be designed to provide an objective appraisal of the research subject. The reduction of the potential of human bias is key to this accomplishment.

With these thoughts in mind, let's consider several ways to collect information regarding the research question. The following list suggests several such methods:

1. Ask a group of mental health clinicians to record the strange things they observe during the full moon. In other words, ask them to stop at the end of the day when there is a full moon and record the strange things they have observed from their clients that day. Explain that you are asking them to record these behaviors on this day because it is the full moon and you are seeking information on whether the full moon makes people act strange.

2. Ask a group of mental health clinicians to record the number of things that meet certain qualifications for being out of the ordinary for each client for a

given day, but do not tell them that you are asking for this information because there is a full moon on this particular day. Use these data about the incidence of strange behavior during the full moon as the basis for your conclusions.

3. Ask a group of mental health clinicians to give their opinions about whether the full moon makes people act strange. Use this as the basis for drawing your conclusions.

4. Ask a group of mental health clinicians to record the number of things that meet certain qualifications for being out of the ordinary for each of several clients for two designated days. One of these designated days will be when the moon is full and one will be when the moon is not full. Do not tell them that you are comparing behavior during the full moon with behavior when there is not a full moon. Compare these data for these two days as the basis for your conclusions.

Can you rank order these four approaches in regard to the extent to which they fit within the spirit of scientific inquiry? Look back over this list with this task in mind before continuing with the material presented below.

The proper order for these approaches to the study is as follows: (4), (2), (1), and (3). Option (3) has great potential for bias and does not ask for the systematic collection of data at all. Option (1) calls for the collection of data but provides the basis for a bias because those making the observations know that the study is about the full moon. This may tempt them to interpret many behaviors as strange simply because their attention has been drawn to this issue. Option (2) has the advantage that the observers have not been informed that the subject of study is the full moon, so they may not be tempted in the same way as those in option (1). However, with this option, you do not have information when the moon is not full to use for a comparison. Option (4) provides you with this information. With this option, you compare the rate of strange behaviors during the full moon with the same when there is not a full moon.

The second principle tells you to avoid reinventing the wheel. You can best apply this principle by examining the literature. I will return to this principle later, but for now, let's examine some of the other principles.

According to the third principle, you should not put the cart before the horse. That is, you should not start your study process with the discovery of an instrument for measuring strange behavior, but with the question which has to do with the relationship between the full moon and strange behavior. However, as you will see in later chapters, the research process can start with observations which arouse your curiosity. A researcher's perception of the nature of a research problem or question normally starts with some form of observation.

The fourth principle states that two heads are better than one. If you believe this statement, you will want to assess the dependability of your method of measuring strange behavior. Do your clinicians know what strange behavior is? Are they likely to be consistent in recording this behavior from one situation to another? Are clinicians likely to be consistent with one another in their observations? You can assess these questions by such methods as having two clinicians working together record their observations independently. You could then compare these observations to see if they are consistent. If not, you will have less confidence in your use of their observations as a means of measuring strange behavior. The more that different people agree in their observations, the more confidence you can have that you have accurately measured the thing you are trying to measure. If you cannot have confidence in your means of measuring strange behavior, you will have a weak method of testing your research question.

The fifth principle acknowledges that things sometimes happen just by chance. What if you found that the proportion of patients in a mental hospital who were observed to act stranger than usual was 37 percent during the full moon and 31 percent when there was not a full moon? Could this difference be something that you could write off to chance? If so, you would not conclude that there was a relationship between the full moon and strange behavior. This means that you would be unlikely to bet your money on the discovery of a relationship between the full moon and strange behavior if you had the opportunity to repeat this study.

What if you found that 68 percent of these patients acted stranger than usual during the full moon while only 24 percent did so when there was not a full moon? In this case, you would be less likely to write off these differences to chance. You would be more likely to conclude that you had found a legitimate relationship between the full moon and strange behavior. There are ways to estimate the likelihood that a given set of results would occur by chance, but I will deal with that topic later.

The final principle reminds researchers to be cautious in drawing conclusions when they are wearing the research hat. For example, you should be very careful to insure that study conclusions are consistent with the data that you analyzed. If you had applied a statistical measure to your data and found that the likelihood that your results would occur by chance to be high, you would be reluctant to conclude that you have found a legitimate relationship between the full moon and strange behavior. This principle is easily applied to this example because it is a rather simple one. But more complex examples would provide a better challenge. However, before you complete all the material and exercises in this text, you will confront published research in which there appear to be study conclusions taken seriously by study authors in situations in which the results can be easily explained by chance.

When you examine the literature, you will find that different researchers have found many methods for studying this research question. The results are not always consistent. Thus, you should treat the results of any one study cautiously.

I have discussed a few questions about how you might go about finding out whether the full moon makes people act strange or different. Before you venture into your own research on this question, you should examine the literature to see what others have found. Perhaps the answer to the question already exists in the work of others.

There have been numerous studies of this question. One such study was conducted of attempted suicides (Mathew, et. al, 1991). The records of the Accident and Emergency Department of a large urban hospital were examined to determine if the rate of suicide attempts which came to the attention of this hospital were different during the full moon than other times. The number of suicides attempted for each day of one month were recorded. The full moon fell on day 15. On that day, a total of 19 suicide attempts were recorded. The largest number of suicide attempts (23) were recorded on days 3 and 17, one of which was close to the full moon but the other was at a great distance from it. The number of attempts on the day of the full moon was slightly higher than the average for the entire month, but the difference was determined to be nonsignificant. When you research this question, you might also want to compare the three days when the moon is fullest with the three days in which it is least full. If the full moon causes suicide, you would expect the three days of the full moon to be significantly higher. For the data from this study, the average number of suicide attempts during the full moon period was 18 compared to 17 for the new moon period (the three days when the moon is least full). This would clearly not be considered to be very significant.

Well, you might say that this is only one study. And you would be wise if you exhibited such caution in your conclusions about this research question. But there have been many other studies. In one such study, a set of researchers examined the records of a psychiatric hospital to determine if dangerous behavior of patients was more prevalent during the full moon than other times. Dangerous behavior was defined as "erratic behavior which was assessed by qualified mental health professionals as dangerous to self or others to the extent that isolation (seclusion) or restraints were necessary to prevent harm to self or others" (Durm, Terry, & Hammonds, 1986, p. 988). Data for three years (1982, 1983, & 1984) were collected. The average number of such incidents of dangerous behavior was actually higher (13.17 per day) during the period that the moon was not full than it was during the period of the full moon (11.61 per day).

Are you convinced yet? Well, perhaps a certain degree of caution is still warranted because I have only mentioned two studies. But, I can go further. The best bet in this investigation now is to examine a reference in which a large number of published studies has been reviewed. Such was the case in an article by Byrnes and Kelly (1992). They reviewed twelve studies which examined the relationship between the lunar cycle and such things as crisis calls to police stations, poison centers, and crisis intervention centers. Their conclusion from this review was that "there is no evidence whatsoever for the contention that calls of a more emotional or 'out-of-control' nature occur more often at the full moon" (Byrnes & Kelly, 1992, p. 779).

Another review of many studies was undertaken by Rotten and Kelly (1985). A total of thirty-seven published studies were included in their review. They also concluded that there was little evidence to support the theory that the full moon affects people's behavior. This pattern of findings of nonsignificant differences between behaviors during the full moon and other periods is found in a review of other sources. But one study claimed to have found a relationship between the full moon and behavior. That study was conducted by Hicks–Casey and Potter (1991). They found that there were more aggressive acting-out misbehaviors in a sample of twenty developmentally delayed women during the full moon than other times. However, the analysis of their data was challenged by Flynn (1992).

Is a study of the effect of the full moon on behavior still worthwhile? This review of the existing literature suggests that this question has been substantially answered already. Do you want to spend your time reinventing the wheel?

An Example for Class Discussion: Service Options for the Abused Wife

When Sara Bentzel was a graduate social work student, she decided to pursue her interest in services to abused women in a research project. She had noticed that the array of services available through a shelter could be classified into two major categories—those that focused on independence (empowerment) and those that focused on interpersonal relations between the clients and their mates. In the empowerment category were such services as financial assistance, employment counseling, legal assistance, and support groups. In the interpersonal category were such services as marriage counseling and family therapy. This researcher had worked with a shelter for abused women and had noticed that the volunteers who worked with the clients of this shelter had a tendency to focus attention on services that tended to improve the client's social and economic independence (empowerment).

Bentzel reviewed the literature and found a body of knowledge that tended to criticize social workers for placing too much emphasis on interpersonal dynamics in their approach to the problem of spouse abuse. Such an emphasis, according to the feminist literature, tended to suggest that the woman was partly to blame for the problem rather than being a victim of a crime. Bentzel wondered if volunteers were different from social workers in their orientation to this problem. Could it be that professional social workers tended to emphasize interpersonal dynamics while volunteers tended to emphasize empowerment? The review of the literature resulted in the discovery of no studies which compared these two groups on this question.

Bentzel was interested in the relationship between professional status (whether one was a shelter volunteer or a professional social worker) and emphasis on empowerment in work with abused wives. However, further analysis of this issue led to the identification of feminism as a potentially important variable. Perhaps it was agreement with a feminist philosophy about spouse abuse that was the cause of emphasis on independence rather than professional status (i.e., whether one was a professional social worker or a volunteer). Both social workers and volunteers were capable of agreeing or disagreeing with this philosophy. Maybe feminist social workers and feminist volunteers were more likely to emphasize independence than the nonfeminists in these two groups.

It had been noted that many persons who volunteer for this work had been drawn to it from their special concern for women's issues and that such persons were more likely than others to embrace a feminist philosophy. However, it was not likely that all volunteers were feminists. But perhaps there was a higher proportion of feminists who were shelter care volunteers than feminists who were social workers. If volunteers were found to be more likely than social workers to emphasize independence, perhaps this was because they were more likely to be feminists rather than because of something inherent in the role of volunteer. If so, the variable of special concern was perhaps feminism rather than professional status.

A study was undertaken to examine this question. Social workers from throughout one state were drawn from the membership list of the National Association of Social Workers for this study. Volunteers from four agencies were also asked to participate. **Professional status** was measured by whether the study participants were in the category of professional social worker or volunteer. **Emphasis on empowerment** was measured in the following way: Study participants were asked to review a hypothetical case of an abused wife and to indicate the extent to which they would place emphasis on each of several services; their score reflected the degree to which their emphasis was greater for services in the empowerment category than the interpersonal dynamics category. **Feminism** was measured by one's degree of agreement with a set of statements drawn from the feminist literature.

If was found that the majority of both social workers (72 percent) and volunteers (63 percent) placed greater emphasis on empowerment than interpersonal dynamics, and that the differences between these two groups was slight. For the overall sample of study subjects, there was only a slight difference in emphasis on empowerment for those high on agreement with the feminist perspective on spouse abuse and those low on agreement with this perspective. However, when the social workers were analyzed separately, it was found that those high on agreement with the feminist perspective were significantly more likely to emphasize empowerment than those low on agreement with this perspective. (For more details, see Sara Bentzel and Reginald York, Influence of feminism and professional status upon service options for the battered woman, *Community Mental Health Journal*, 24, 1988, pp. 52–63.)

This study illustrates the basic steps in the research process. Recall the steps enumerated in the previous section on the process of research. The following is a breakdown of the flow of the study by Bentzel in this same format.

PROBLEM FORMULATION
A feminist view of spouse abuse focuses on the empowerment of the abused wife.
Professionals are criticized for emphasizing interpersonal dynamics over empowerment.
Women's shelter volunteers are perceived as placing emphasis on empowerment.
Are volunteers more likely than professionals to emphasize empowerment?
Are feminists more likely than non-feminists to emphasize empowerment?

STUDY METHODOLOGY
A questionnaire was mailed to a group of women's shelter volunteers and a group of social workers.
Feminism was measured by a scale on the questionnaire.
Emphasis on independence was measured by a set of questions on the questionnaire.
Professional status was measured by whether the helping person was a volunteer or social worker.

DATA ANALYSIS

Both volunteers and social workers were found to place greater emphasis on empowerment than interpersonal dynamics, and the difference between the two groups was not significant.

Feminist social workers were found to be more likely to place emphasis on empowerment than nonfeminist social workers.

CONCLUSIONS

Helping persons of various kinds (social workers and volunteers; feminists and nonfeminists) tend to place greater emphasis on empowerment than interpersonal dynamics in their work with abused wives. The feminist concern that social workers tend to de-emphasize empowerment was not supported by these data.

ASSIGNMENT 1–C [FOR CLASS DISCUSSION]

1. Examine each of the following statements of the purpose of the study of service options for the abused wife. Indicate whether each statement is consistent with the spirit of scientific inquiry.

   a. The purpose of this study is to demonstrate that social workers and volunteers are different in their orientations to services to the abused wife.
   b. The purpose of this study is to determine whether volunteers and professional social workers differ in their orientation to services to the abused wife.
   c. The purpose of this study is to prove that social workers are just as likely as volunteers to emphasize empowerment in their work with abused wives.
   d. The purpose of this study is to challenge the criticism that social workers are not sufficiently sensitive to the importance of empowerment for women.
      Which of the six basic principles of research enumerated in the previous section are illustrated by the above statements?

---

2. Is there evidence that Bentzel has or has not made the mistake of attempting to reinvent the wheel in her research?

_____

_____

3. Examine the following list of steps in the research process and place (1) next to the first logical step in this process, (2) by the second step, (3) by the next, and (4) next to the last step.

_____   Service emphasis can be measured by questions which ask respondents to review a hypothetical case of an abused wife and indicate the extent to which each of several services in the empowerment category should be emphasized and the extent to which each of several services in the interpersonal dynamics category should be emphasized. The score for level of emphasis on services in the interpersonal category can be subtracted from the score for level of emphasis on empowerment services to derive a score for emphasis on empowerment. Respondents who are volunteers in domestic violence shelters can be compared to respondents drawn from the membership list of an association of professional social workers.

_____   The proportion of professional social workers who emphasized empowerment was 72 percent compared to 62 percent of the volunteers.

_____   The research question asks whether volunteers and social workers differ in their tendency to emphasize empowerment vis-à-vis interpersonal dynamics in their work with abused wives.

_____   It was concluded that these data had failed to support the idea that volunteers were more likely than social workers to emphasize empowerment in their work with abused wives.

What basic principle is relevant to this question?

_____

_____

_____

_____

4. Select a basic principle of research not illustrated above and briefly discuss its application to this study.

_____

_____

_____

_____

5. What type of study was undertaken by Bentzel?

_____	Descriptive	_____	Evaluative
_____	Explanatory	_____	Exploratory

6. In your opinion, what is the most important finding of this study?

_____

_____

_____

_____

_____

_____

A Research Exercise on the Study of Stress among Social Work Students

Now that you have examined some of the basic principles of research as well as the process of research, you will be given the opportunity to participate in an example of research. You will be asked to respond to a set of questions on the next page. These same questions were presented to a group of graduate social work students. After responding to the questions which follow on the next page, you will be able to compare yourself with this group of social work students. Then, you will look at some of the data from that group of students in the consideration of some research questions. Thus, you will become a little more involved in the research process yourself by being both a research subject and a researcher.

Now, turn the page and respond to the questions which follow.

PRELIMINARY TASK: RESPONDING TO THE SURVEY

Your first task in this exercise on research is to respond to the instrument below. This instrument will be employed in a study in which you will serve as one of the study subjects. This will provide you with an initial example of social work research which you can personalize.

*1. The words below describe different feelings and moods. Please indicate how often each word characterizes the way you have been feeling in the past few months by using the following scale: 0 = Seldom or Never   1 = Some of the Time   2 = Often   3 = Most of the time

_____	1. Tense	_____	7. Relaxed	_____	13. Restful
_____	2. Apprehensive	_____	8. Bothered	_____	14. Worried
_____	3. Cheerful	_____	9. Dejected	_____	15. Nervous
_____	4. Uneasy	_____	10. Peaceful	_____	16. Calm
_____	5. Pleasant	_____	11. Uptight	_____	17. Jittery
_____	6. Distressed	_____	12. Contented	_____	18. Comfortable

2. Do you engage in aerobic exercise (running, biking, swimming, vigorous walking, etc.) for a minimum of 20 minutes at least 3 times a week (i.e., a total of at least 60 minutes)?

_____   Yes   _____   No

3. To what extent have you experienced illness (colds, the flu, etc.) in the past few months?

_____   To a great extent   _____   To some extent   _____   Not at all

*The items for this question are taken from the stress portion of the Stress-Arousal Checklist by Dr. Tom Cox, Department of Psychology, University of Nottingham, Nottingham, U.K. Used with permission.

Phase 1: Problem Formulation

The previous questions were employed in a study of stress for a group of graduate social work students in a rural section of a southern state in 1994. In this exercise you compare your responses to those from this study and examine some of the results of that study. If the opportunity arises, you may even be able to collect data from your classmates on these questions and analyze several study questions with your class members as the study subjects.

In this endeavor, the question, "What is stress?" must be addressed first. Most people probably feel that they know what this term means, but it is easy to see that there are many shades of difference in what that term means. In research, you must be specific in your use of concepts so that others can properly interpret your findings.

The second question is "Why should we study stress?" While the satisfaction of idle curiosity may be appropriate as a rationale for research in some disciplines, you must keep in mind that social work is a profession with a mission that should guide all social work endeavors. Thus, you should address the contribution that your research may make.

The third question is "What do we want to know about stress?" In other words, what are your research questions? This issue logically follows from the previous one. If you are studying stress because it affects the performance of social workers, you would logically want to know either the causes or the consequences of stress. There will always be a myriad of potential questions that can arise from the study of a given social topic. One of the tasks of the researcher is to select one or more for the present study and leave the others for other studies to address.

What Is Stress?

When they use the word *stress,* most people will have a general idea of what they are talking about, but definitions will vary. Most people think of stress as an uncomfortable condition caused by demands that are made upon their lives by work and family responsibilities. Feelings such as tense, uptight, and anxious are frequently associated with the concept of stress. Often, people recognize certain physical symptoms as being associated with stress, such as sleeplessness, headaches, and an increase in minor illnesses such as colds and the flu. Some writers define stress as environmental conditions rather than psychological feelings (see, for example, Shinn, et al., 1984).

For this study, *stress* is defined as a condition of psychological tension that is exemplified by such feelings and moods as apprehension, uneasiness, and nervousness, and contrasts with such feelings and moods as cheerfulness, relaxation, and contentment. Thus, you are focusing upon the psychological dimension of this concept rather than environmental conditions such as job demands, parental responsibilities, or life events such as divorce or the death of a close family member. These environmental conditions can influence stress as it is defined here, but they are considered to be separate conceptually. You might refer to these conditions as stressors rather than stress.

Stress is a condition of the individual rather than the environment. But the environment can cause stress to occur. For example, high caseloads of abused children to serve can cause social workers to be stressed. If most people with high caseloads are found to have high stress while most people with low caseloads are found to have low stress, it is possible that there is a relationship between stress and caseloads. But everyone with high caseloads will not necessarily have high stress and everyone with low caseloads will not necessarily have low stress. There are other things that can potentially influence stress and can explain these exceptions to the rule.

Researchers should be careful to define their terms in research because many people define them differently, and they want others to understand what they mean when they say something like "Students who engaged in regular aerobic exercise were found to experience lower levels of stress than students who did not."

Why Should We Study Stress?

Stress is important for at least two major reasons—it can lead to health problems and to poor work performance. The work of Hans Selye (1982) and many others has been instrumental in bringing attention to the fact that persons suffering from life events which lead to stress have more health problems. In the social work field, the problem of burnout has received widespread attention. Burnout is a condition which results from prolonged or intense stress and is characterized by emotional exhaustion, cynicism about the clients and the nature of the work being performed, and a desire to terminate employment. These conditions logically can be considered to have a negative effect on work performance (see Maslach and Jackson, 1981).

What Do We Already Know about Stress among Social Work Students?

While social work faculty members have undertaken informal studies of stress among students for decades, few studies have been published which present hard data on this topic. Among those that do is a study by Munson (1984) who surveyed the students in one school of social work. Munson found that approximately one-third of these social work students experienced symptoms of stress in class, but a lower percent experienced these symptoms in the field. Munson did not find significant differences in stress levels for males and females, nor did he find differences between married and single students. But he did find higher levels of stress among first-year than second-year students.

What Do We Want to Know about Stress?

There are many fruitful avenues of inquiry about stress. Much research has been done on the causes and consequences of this condition. You will take a rather limited journey down this trail of research by examining stress for yourself and for other social work students. The first question is "What is my level of stress and how does it compare to others?" For this question, you will be able to compute your own stress score and compare it to a study which was done of one group of social work students in one school.

The second and third questions deal with things that might be related to stress. You will examine whether persons who engage in regular aerobic exercise have lower levels of stress than those who do not. You will also examine whether persons with higher stress have a greater tendency to have minor health problems such as headaches, insomnia, and so forth. Neither of these questions was pursued in the study of stress among social work students by Munson.

Phase 2: Study Methodology

What Are the Research Questions?

You have examined the nature of stress, the key research concept. You have some guidance on how to measure it and what else to measure in order to answer the following research questions:

1. How does my stress score compare to others?
2. Does stress lead to health problems?
3. Does exercise alleviate stress?

How Will I Measure My Study Variables?

There are three things that must be measured in order to pursue the research questions—stress, exercise, and health. For this study, stress is measured by a combination of responses to all the items in Question (1) from the preliminary exercise. These items constitute the Stress Scale of the Stress–Arousal Checklist (Mackay and Cox, 1978, as cited in Corcoran and Fischer, 1987). Exercise is measured by Question (2) and health problems by Question (3).

Who Will I Study?

The data for this study are drawn from a survey conducted of one group of second-year students in a graduate school of social work. A total of thirty-seven students in three sections of a second-year social work specialization practice course responded to the questionnaire in the spring of 1994. This group of students constituted approximately 90 percent of the students enrolled in these three courses.

You will examine some data from that survey. You will be given the opportunity to compare your stress scores to those from that school and to consider data regarding stress and health and stress and exercise. If you are highly ambitious, you may want to consider collecting data from your class and comparing your class to that one and examining the relationship of stress with health and exercise for your own class. But that probably will require the help of a research assistant.

The next step in the process is to compute your score for stress. The instructions for this task are contained in Exhibit 1.1.

EXHIBIT 1.1:   Measuring Your Level of Stress

Adding Your Score for Negative Items on the Scale

You were asked to assign either the number 0, 1, 2, or 3 to each of 18 words in Question 1. Many of the words on the scale were negative in that they were indicative of stress. These items are presented below. Add the points you have assigned to each of the items:

_____	1. Tense	_____	6. Distressed	_____	11. Uptight
_____	2. Apprehensive	_____	8. Bothered	_____	14. Worried
_____	4. Uneasy	_____	9. Dejected	_____	15. Nervous
				_____	17. Jittery

For these negative items, my total score is_____.

Adding Your Score for Positive Items

Each of the words in the above list indicates stress. The more you experienced it, the higher your score for stress. The other words were in opposition to the above words, so they must be scored differently. For example, if you indicated that you felt cheerful "most of the time," you should receive the lowest score for stress, because this state is in opposition to stress. So your score would be 0 rather than 3. Thus, you must reverse the scoring for the items listed below. If your response to Cheerful was 2, you would give yourself a score of 1 for stress. In the instructions below, you are given a coding scheme for converting your responses to a stress score that will reverse the scores. Draw a circle around your score for each of the seven words that follow. Then add these scores together.

Cheerful	0	1	2	3	← If this was your answer
	3	2	1	0	← Then this is your score
Pleasant	0	1	2	3	← If this was your answer
	3	2	1	0	← Then this is your score
Relaxed	0	1	2	3	← If this was your answer
	3	2	1	0	← Then this is your score
Peaceful	0	1	2	3	← If this was your answer
	3	2	1	0	← Then this is your score

EXHIBIT 1.1 *Continued*

Contented	0	1	2	3	← If this was your answer
	3	2	1	0	← Then this is your score
Restful	0	1	2	3	← If this was your answer
	3	2	1	0	← Then this is your score
Comfortable	0	1	2	3	← If this was your answer
	3	2	1	0	← Then this is your score

For these positive items, your score is _____.

Now combine your scores for positive and negative items to obtain your total score for stress. Your score can range from a low of 0 to a high of 54.

Total Stress Score is _____.

Phase 3: Examining the Study Results

How Does My Stress Score Compare to Others?

The instrument for measuring your level of stress is the Stress Scale of the Stress–Arousal Checklist developed by MacKay and Cox (see Corcoran and Fischer, 1987). On this instrument, the higher your score, the more stress you are experiencing. To check this scale for accuracy, the authors studied whether people's scores on this scale went up when they were subjected to situations thought to be stressful. They found that scores were higher when people were exposed to such conditions. This gave them confidence that their scale actually measured the thing they wanted to measure.

This instrument was given to a group of graduate social work students in one school of social work. The results are given in Table 1.1. This table displays the number and percent of students with each score as well as the cumulative percent (i.e., the current percent plus the percent of those with lower scores).

As you can see from this table, there was one student with a score of 7 and this was the lowest score obtained by any of these students. This one person represented 2.7 percent of the total group of students. There was one student with a score of 12, which was the next highest score. When this student's percent of the total is combined with the previous student, we can see that 5.4 percent of these students had scores of 12 or less (as reflected in the Cumulative Percent column). Moving on down the table, you will notice that three students (8.1 percent of the total) had a score of 18 and that 24.3 percent of these students had a score of 18 or less.

TABLE 1.1 **Stress Scores for a Sample of Graduate Social Work Students (N = 37)**

Score	Number of Students with this score	Percent with this score	Cumulative Percent
7	1	2.7%	2.7%
12	1	2.7	5.4
13	2	5.4	10.8
15	1	2.7	13.5
16	1	2.7	16.2
18	3	8.1	24.3
19	2	5.4	29.7
20	3	8.1	37.8
22	3	8.1	45.9
24	4	10.8	56.8
25	1	2.7	59.6
26	1	2.7	62.2
27	2	5.4	67.6
29	1	2.7	70.3
30	1	2.7	73.0
31	1	2.7	75.7
32	2	5.4	81.1
33	1	2.7	83.8
36	1	2.7	86.5
43	2	5.4	91.9
45	2	5.4	97.3
48	1	2.7	100.0

From this table, you can see where you stand in comparison to this group of social work students. If your score was 31, you can say that 73 percent of these students had a score for stress that was lower than your score (see the Cumulative Percent figure for the next lowest score of 30).

What are the Consequences of Stress?

It has been suggested by research on stress among persons in the general population that stress is related to illness. Is this true for social work students? Are students with high stress more likely to experience minor illnesses such as colds, the flu, and so forth? For the students reported in this exercise, the answer can be found in Figure 1.1.

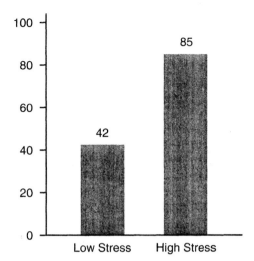

**FIGURE 1.1   Percentage of Students
with Minor Recent
Illnesses Divided by
Level of Stress**

For this analysis, students were divided into the categories of High and Low for stress. If one's score on the Stress Scale was 22 or below, they were classified as Low for stress while scores of 23 and above were classified as High. These students were asked to indicate the extent to which they had recently experienced minor illnesses. They were classified in the affirmative if they responded as either "to some extent" or "to a great extent." They were classified in the negative if their response was "not at all." As you can see from Figure 1.1, 85 percent of those who were high for stress had experienced illnesses recently. This compares to only 42 percent of those with low stress. (While we will not discuss the concept of statistical significance in this chapter, those of you who are familiar with this concept will be interested in knowing that this difference was statistically significant at the .05 level.)

In the first part of this exercise, you were asked to indicate whether you had experienced illnesses in recent months and you were given the stress scale. Were you high for stress (i.e., above 22 on the Stress Scale)? Have you experienced illnesses in recent months? If you fit the pattern indicated by the students in the study reported in this exercise, you will be in the category of HIGH for stress and YES for illness, or you will be in the category of LOW for stress and NO for illness.

If this is not true, you did not fit this pattern. (In other words, you would not fit the pattern if you are in either the category of LOW for stress and YES for illness, or if you were HIGH for stress and NO for illness.) If you did not fit the pattern and had been in that study, you would have been an exception to the rule. In social research, there are always exceptions to the rule. The more exceptions in a given analysis, the less important the discovery. For example, if 75 percent of those low on stress had experienced illnesses rather than the 42 percent that was found, the data would be less noteworthy because those low on stress would not have been very different from those high on stress. Instead, the results of 42 percent for those low on stress and 85 percent for those high on stress represent a rather noteworthy difference.

Does Exercise Alleviate Stress?

The students in this study were asked the following question: "Do you engage in aerobic exercise (such as running, biking, swimming, vigorous walking, and so forth) for a minimum of 20 minutes at least 3 times a week (i.e., a total of 60 minutes)? They answered either YES or NO. Approximately one-half answered YES (47%) and approximately one-half answered NO (53%). The mean Stress Score was computed for each group. The mean for those who did not exercise was 29, while the mean for those who did exercise was 22. These data are displayed graphically in Figure 1.2. (This difference was statistically significant.)

Did you fit the pattern established by the students in this study? If your stress score is around 29 or higher and you also engage in regular aerobic exercise, you do not fit this pattern. If you do not exercise and your stress score is around 22 or lower, you also do not fit the pattern. In either of these cases, you would be an exception to the rule. On the other hand, if you have low stress scores and you exercise, you would fit the pattern. Likewise, if you have high stress scores and you do not exercise, you would fit the pattern.

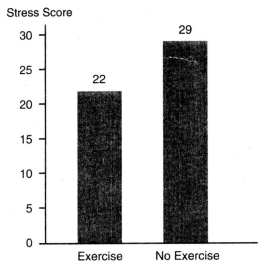

FIGURE 1.2   Mean Stress Scores and Exercise

Phase 4: Conclusions

When researchers conduct social work research, they obtain evidence regarding their research questions. Seldom can anyone claim to have secured proof regarding the answers to these questions because of the myriad of potential errors in any one research study. Data from one group of study subjects may be different from that of another group. Is it possible to generalize from one group to others? There are also potential errors in the way they choose to measure things. For these and other reasons, the results of one study are considered to be evidence in support of a given conclusion.

What about your questions? Did you find evidence that stress might lead to health problems? Did you find evidence that exercise might reduce stress? Did you find that you were more or less stressed than others?

If you were to conduct this study with another group of people, how might you improve it? Would you include a larger group of study subjects? Would you measure things differently?

ASSIGNMENT 1–D

1. What is the research question for the stress study?

_____

_____

_____

_____

2. How would you characterize the purpose of this study?

_____

_____

_____

_____

3. Identify one of the basic principles of research and apply it to the stress study.

_____

_____

4. How should the stress study be classified?

   _____ **a.** Exploratory   _____ **c.** Evaluative

   _____ **b.** Explanatory   _____ **d.** Descriptive

5. What types of persons were the subjects of this study?

6. How was stress measured in this study?

7. Did this study produce evidence that would support the conclusion that stress leads to an increase in minor illnesses?

8. Did this study produce evidence that female students are more stressed than male students?

_____

_____

_____

_____

_____

9. Did this study produce evidence to support the conclusion that exercise can reduce stress?

_____

_____

_____

_____

_____

Summary

You have had the opportunity to see how research works and to gain some knowledge about stress, a subject of much concern to social work students and the profession in general. You have seen that this process starts with a major concern about a topic. This topic is placed into perspective by reference to the work of others. A literature search provides some focus to the major concern about the topic, and facilitates conceptualizing a research question. To pursue an answer to the question, researchers determine how to measure the variables in their research question and select a group of persons from whom data is drawn. They analyze that data to determine the answer to their question.

As you continue with the chapters ahead, you will come back to this process over and over again. And you will see repetitions of definitions in different examples because many of the concepts in research are rather technical to social work students and require much reinforcement. The next chapter is in the typical format for almost all of the remaining chapters. You will be given a research example that will serve as the focus of the chapter. Various concepts and tasks in research will be reviewed with this example in mind. You will periodically be stopped and called upon to respond to questions about the example at hand as a test of your understanding of what has been covered. Your responses to the questions in the assignments can be used for class discussion.

References

Benzel, S. & York, R. O. (1988). Influence of feminism and professional status upon service options for the battered woman. *Community Mental Health Journal,* 24, 52–63.

Byrnes, G., & Kelly, I. W. (1992). Crisis calls and lunar cycles: A twenty-year review. *Psychological Reports,* 71, 779–785.

Corcoran, K., & Fischer, J. (1987). *Measures for clinical practice.* New York: Free Press.

Durm, M. W., Terry, C. L., & Hammonds, C. R. (1986). Lunar phase and acting-out behavior. *Psychological Reports,* 59, 987–990.

Flynn, M. (1991). Critical comment on Hicks–Casey and Potter, "Effect of the full moon on a sample of developmentally delayed, institutionalized women." *Perceptual and Motor Skills,* 73, 963–968.

Hicks–Casey, W. E., & Potter, D. R. (1991). Effect of the full moon on a sample of developmentally delayed, institutionalized women. *Perceptual and Motor Skills,* 72, 1375–1380.

Maslach, C., & Jackson, S. E. (1981). The measurement of experienced burnout. *Journal of Occupational Therapy,* 2, 99–113.

Mathew, V. M., Lindesay, J., Shanmuganathan, N., & Eapen, V. (1991). Attempted suicide and the lunar cycle. *Psychological Reports,* 68, 927–930.

Munson, C. E. (1984). Stress among graduate social work students: An empirical study. *Journal of Education for Social Work,* 20 (3), 20–29.

Rotten, J., & Kelly, I. W. (1985). Much ado about the full moon: A meta-analysis of lunar–lunacy research. *Psychological Bulletin,* 97 (2), 286–306.

Selye, H. (1982). History and the present status of the stress concept. In L. Goldberger & S. Breznitz (Eds.), *Handbook on stress: Theoretical and clinical aspects* (pp. 7–17). New York: Free Press.

Shinn, M., Rosario, M., Morch, H., & Chestnut, D. E. (1984). Coping with stress and burnout in the human services. *Journal of Personality and Social Psychology,* 40, 864–976.

Level *I*

Understanding Social Work Research

In the first section of this book, you will undertake the first level of learning in social work research. This first section is predicated upon the assumption that the reader has little, if any, prior training in research and statistics. It is organized around the four major purposes of social work research, the four major phases of the research process, and the principles of adult learning. This means that you will experience examples which take you through the entire process of research and you will be introduced to research concepts gradually. Your journey in learning will be interactive, just like the first chapter, in that you will be continually called upon to answer questions regarding what you have learned in the previous pages. Your answers to these assignments can serve as the basis for class discussion.

Chapter 2

Understanding
Descriptive Research:

Are the Clients of a Family Service Agency Satisfied with Their Services?

In this chapter, you will examine the process of social research by using an example of a client satisfaction survey. The hypothetical agency is an organization that provides marriage and family counseling services. First, you will formulate the research problem and develop the questions that are relevant to your task. Next, you will learn how to design a study to achieve your goals. Then you will consider some hypothetical data relevant to your task. Finally, you will draw conclusions about your research questions.

In this chapter, you will cover the entire research process in a simple fashion. Identifying the process of social research and the spirit of scientific inquiry that is its foundation will be emphasized.

Objectives

At the completion of this chapter, you will be able to:

1. Explain the relevance of the concepts of error, evidence, and logic to the nature of scientific inquiry;

2. Give examples of research that fits into each of the four major types of social work research: descriptive, explanatory, evaluative, and exploratory;

3. State the specific purpose of a research study in accordance with the spirit of scientific inquiry;

4. Identify the process of social research from problem formulation, to methodology, to data analysis, to conclusions, and specify tasks essential to each phase of the process;

5. Distinguish between qualitative and quantitative means of measuring variables;

6. Distinguish between a variable and a constant in a research example;

7. Distinguish between the sample and the population in a research example;

8. Articulate the relevance of sampling to the generalization of study results;

9. Distinguish between the abstract and operational definitions of study variables;

10. Interpret the meaning of common descriptive statistics as applied to an example.

The Research Process and the Spirit of Scientific Inquiry

In the first sections of this chapter, you will review some of the ideas that you encountered in the first chapter. This includes concepts related to the nature of scientific inquiry, the purposes of research, and the process of research. A few additional ideas will be presented, but much of the content will be a review of what has been covered in the previous chapter. Most of these concepts are no more relevant to descriptive research than the other purposes of scientific inquiry for social workers. As you move through the chapters in this text, you will see that re-enforcement of learning is one of the cornerstones of the approach to instruction taken here.

The scientific method uses a process of inquiry that starts with a question rather than a conclusion. Information is collected that is relevant to that question and conclusions are drawn from the analysis of that information. A rather different process is used if a researcher starts with a conclusion and then seeks information that supports the conclusion. Political parties typically seek information that supports a conclusion because they wish to prove that their party's position is superior to that of their opposition. In this process, information that is contrary to the initially stated conclusion is discarded.

The research process entails the systematic collection of data through procedures that are designed to reduce the bias that is inherent in any form of social observation. Its purpose is discovery, not justification. In other words, one does not conduct a research study for the purpose of proving a point. The study—if it is truly a research study—will be designed to discover the truth rather than to prove a point, no matter how noble the point may be.

The scientific method places emphasis on the means for discovery or the methods of investigation. It is designed to reduce *human error.* Any observation about reality has the potential for some degree of error. For example, suppose that you were a police officer investigating an automobile accident involving two cars. Would you only interview one of the two drivers and rely exclusively upon his or her story as the truth?

No? Why not? Is it because this person may have a biased view of the accident that would more likely place the blame on the other driver? Is it because this driver may be suffering psychologically from the trauma of the accident which may have distorted his or her view of reality?

What would you do if you had interviewed the other driver and gotten a very different story of how the accident happened? Would you look for witnesses who were not involved in the accident? Of course you would! And you would do this because the other person had less reason to be biased.

Would you seek the view of a second bystander? You probably would. And you would do so because you realize that everyone does not have the same powers of observation. Some people may have gotten a better view because of where they were standing. Some would have gotten a better view because they were paying more attention than others. You would be especially interested in consistencies among the observers. If three people saw things one way and one person saw things differently, you would probably be inclined to believe the view of the three people who agree.

You probably would not be content only with the reports of observers. You may also choose to examine the dents in the cars and the skid marks on the road in order to collect *evidence* to use in your determination of reality. In fact, you may use all your senses—sight, sound, etc.—in your investigation. And you would employ *logic* in your analysis. The bulk of the evidence may refute the story of one driver because his or her story could not logically be true given the other evidence.

In other words, you would employ many of the principles of the scientific method in order to gain your best view of reality. You would seek to reduce error by obtaining more than one view and being attentive to the potential of bias in observation. You would seek all forms of evidence that were available. And you would employ logic in drawing conclusions.

The Four Major Purposes of Social Work Research

In the previous chapter, you examined four types of social work research: descriptive, explanatory, evaluative, and exploratory. This typology was based on the purposes of research studies. *Descriptive research* is designed to describe a set of phenomena. If you wish to assess the needs of your clients, you would undertake a descriptive study because you would want to describe their needs. To what extent do your clients need improvement in their self-esteem as compared to their ability to express anger in constructive ways? Do they need day care more than employment training? If you wished to describe your clients in regard to their basic characteristics (e.g., age, education, gender, race, etc.), you would conduct a descriptive study. When data is analyzed in this type of research, descriptive statistics are employed. The study participants would be described, for example, in regard to the frequencies of people in each category such as male and female, or the proportions of such persons in each category. You may be interested to find that 72 percent of your clients are female. This may be a surprise because you might have had the impression that about half of your clients were male. Another descriptive statistic is the mean (average). Perhaps you would want to know the mean age of all clients.

Explanatory research attempts to explain a given phenomenon, usually by examining its relationship to other things. For example, you might want to know what explains one's level of interest in pursuing a career in social work administration. Is gender one of the things that explains it? In other words, do males and females differ in their level of interest? Perhaps having had a mentor who encouraged this interest is another explanation. If so, we would find that those with higher interest are more likely than others to have had such a mentor.

Evaluative research is designed to provide data on the question of whether a social work intervention or social program achieved a given set of objectives. Does participation in a support group enhance the self-esteem of abused wives? Does a public awareness campaign enhance the number of abused children who are identified by the protective services program? Does therapy reduce depression? These are some of the questions that would be pursued in evaluative research. A key question to ask in determining whether a given example is an evaluative study is whether there was an intervention that was given to a group of people. If not, then we do not have an example of an evaluative study.

Exploratory research provides information on topics that have not been well researched by others. A key contribution of exploratory research is the development of new theories. An example in this book deals with the experience of being placed for adoption as an older child (see Chapter 9). The author of that study had found that there was little information in the literature on what this experience was like. How do children react emotionally and behaviorally to the key events in the placement process? What factors seem to contribute to better adjustment to the adoption? These were among the questions explored in that study.

The example given in the present chapter is in the category of descriptive research, even though some may wish to classify it as evaluative. It does seek information on the outcome of a service, but it does so by collecting descriptions of client opinions about their level of satisfaction with the service they had received. Because this example does not employ specific measures of client conditions related to clearly articulated objectives, it is classified as descriptive in nature. If measures of marital harmony had been given to clients before and after treatment, it would have been classified as evaluative in nature.

The Major Phases of the Research Process

The research process begins with a research issue, a research question, or a problem that can be potentially solved through a research study. I will refer to this beginning phase of research as *problem formulation*. Researchers may be curious about a topic or have a major work task to complete that requires further study. The researchers articulate a rudimentary question that identifies the general purpose of the inquiry. They may want to know, for example, if it is really true that people are more crazy during the full moon than at other times. They may want to know why some clients fail to show up for their scheduled counseling sessions at the Family Counseling Center. They may want to know whether social support helps students cope with the stress of being in graduate school. In the example used in this chapter, you will want to know whether the clients of a hypothetical agency are satisfied with the services they have received.

After you have articulated a first draft of the research question, the next step is finding out what is already known about this issue. This is normally done through a search of the literature. It is possible that the answer to the question is already well known through the research of others and there may be little need for further research on the particular question as posed originally. Perhaps, however, there is some other aspect of the issue that has not been substantially resolved by previous research and the research question should be refocused. In this case, the existing literature cannot tell you whether clients are satisfied with the agency's services, but it may be helpful in articulating the kinds of questions to ask and the kinds of answers you might get if your clients are similar to clients of other agencies which may have conducted similar surveys.

The second major phase of the social research process is the development of the *research methodology*. When researchers develop a research methodology, they make such decisions as: (1) how they will define and measure their study variables, (2) who will be the study subjects, and (3) what method will be used to collect the data.

If you wished to examine the extent to which your clients were satisfied with the services of your agency, you would need to determine the kinds of questions to be answered by the clients to indicate their level of satisfaction. Your study subjects would be your clients, of course, but you would have the task of selecting the clients to be asked to participate. Finally, you would need to determine whether to collect the information by way of a survey questionnaire to be completed by certain clients or by way of interviews of them or by some other means.

The third major phase of the research process is the *collection and analysis of data*. If you chose to conduct a client satisfaction survey, you would send questionnaires to clients that contained questions designed to measure the study variables. You would then summarize the results by determining, for example, what proportion of your clients were satisfied with the way they were treated by the staff, what proportion felt that they had been helped with the problems that had brought them to the agency, and so forth.

The final major phase of the research process entails drawing *conclusions* about the research question. In a client satisfaction survey, you would draw conclusions about whether your results tended to indicate that your clients were satisfied with the services. You might also want to draw conclusions about which aspects of the services received the highest and lowest ratings so that you could have information to guide your efforts to improve. The limitations of your study methodology would also be addressed in this part of the research process.

ASSIGNMENT 2–A

1. Indicate whether each of the following statements are TRUE or FALSE and add your comments below each statement.

T   F   **a.** The scientific method is concerned more with the means of inquiry than in the confirmation of any particular idea as the ultimate truth.

_____

_____

T   F   **b.** The scientific method assumes that people are not capable of error in the observation of reality because, if they were, there would be no reason to study reality through human observation.

_____

_____

T   F   **c.** In a research study, you should determine the purpose of the study before you select the sample of study subjects.

_____

_____

2. Identify a limitation of each of the following approaches to determining whether clients are satisfied with agency services.

   a. The agency's executive director develops a statement summarizing his or her experiences with clients when a comment was made by a client about how satisfied they were about agency services.

_____

_____

_____

_____

b. Family counselors of the agency are asked to identify clients who would be most appropriate to include in a client satisfaction survey.

_____

_____

_____

3. Which of the following general purposes of research best fits the client satisfaction survey: descriptive, exploratory, explanatory, or evaluative?

_____

_____

_____

4. Examine the four sets of statements below. One of these statements relates to problem formulation. Another set is in the category of research methodology while a third can be classified as being in the category of data analysis. Another set is best classified as being in the fourth phase of research—conclusions. For these statements, place (1) by the problem formulation statement, (2) by the methodology statement, (3) next to data analysis, and (4) by the conclusion statement.

_____ **a.** The proportion of social work students of Midwest University who indicated that they were satisfied with their field instructors was 71 percent while only 42 percent indicated satisfaction with the field assignment. More students (83%) were satisfied with classroom instruction than with the help they had received with their problems (53%).

_____ **b.** In general, it can be concluded that the social work students are satisfied with the social work program.

_____ **c.** Social work education programs need information on the extent to which their programs are evaluated positively by students. Students tend to differ from one another on the extent to which they are satisfied with their field instructors, their field assignments, their classroom instruction, and the help they receive on the problems that they confront with their educational experiences. To what extent are the social work students of Midwest University satisfied with the social work program of that university?

_____ **d.** A survey will be conducted of all social work students of Midwest University. They will be asked to indicate the extent to which they are satisfied with (1) their field instructor, (2) their field assignment, (3) their classroom instruction, and (4) the help they received on problems that they have encountered.

Problem Formulation for the Study

The research question posed in this exercise is as follows: Are the clients of the Oakmont Family Service Association satisfied with the services they have received? The major goal (or mission) of this agency is to improve individual and family functioning by enhancing marital and family harmony, by enhancing the client's ability to cope with various forms of stress, and by reducing the problems associated with individual and family dysfunction such as separation, divorce, depression, stress, parent–child conflict, teenage pregnancy, delinquency, dissatisfaction with family relations, general discontent with life, and so forth.

This agency attempts to achieve this goal through marriage and family counseling. This entails individual counseling, couples counseling, family counseling, and group counseling. The reason for examining client satisfaction is to determine whether these services are effective in achieving the agency's goal.

Developing a Knowledge Base

One of the tasks in the problem formulation stage of research is the development of a knowledge base which can guide the research study. You are undertaking a descriptive study in that you wish to describe a particular condition—the level of satisfaction with agency services. You are not measuring client behavior directly and using statistical analysis to determine if the client's level of functioning is better after treatment than beforehand. Instead, you are measuring the client's opinions about how well the agency's services have helped.

If you wish to measure client satisfaction, you might be inclined to say that a literature review is not necessary. You are concerned about how your clients feel, not the clients of other agencies. But you can use a literature review to help you clarify the concepts that you wish to measure and to find a basis for developing expectations about what you might find out. You could, of course, take the position that a positive evaluation by a majority of your clients is good news. But what if you found that clients of family counseling agencies typically were very positive about their services and that a simple majority of favorable ratings would place your agency much below other similar agencies?

You might want to know how other surveys have been undertaken. What kinds of questions have others asked? What proportion of clients tend to respond to a mailed questionnaire? What are the categories of things you might want to ask clients? Do you want to know if certain practice principles were adhered to by the staff? Do you want to know if clients felt that they had gotten better because of the service? Do you want to know if clients would recommend the services to others? These are some of the questions that might have been examined by other agencies and reported in the literature. A brief experience with the literature is presented in Exhibit 2.1.

**EXHIBIT 2.1   A Brief Literature Review on Client Satisfaction
with Family Counseling**

While there probably have been many agencies which have conducted client satisfaction surveys, not many have been published in professional journals. For example, when the key words "satisfaction with family counseling" were entered into the social work abstracts electronic literature database (in the summer of 1994), there were only two articles that appeared and neither was especially relevant to the present study. A search of that database with the words "evaluation of family counseling" generated a few articles that were only a little more useful than the first two.

One of these articles reported on a model of divorce adjustment for Family Counseling Services of Canton, Ohio. The form of client feedback was informal and undertaken in person by the therapist. The main purpose was to improve the services. One change that was suggested by the clients was the institution of a treatment group for children with divorce adjustment reaction problems. No data were collected on the number of clients who were satisfied at one level or another (Faust, 1987).

One of the few client satisfaction surveys that was discovered in this literature was conducted by the Family and Individual Services Association of Tarrant County, Texas. This agency had instituted a special outreach project for Mexican Americans, a group that was underrepresented in its clientele. This survey took the form of personal interviews conducted by a graduate social work student. Among the questions posed were the following:

1. What kind of working relationship do you have with your counselor? In other words, do you feel that you get along with the counselor?
2. Considering all the members of your family and all the problems you discussed with the counselor, have things improved since the first session?
3. Would you consider going back to the agency if you needed help in the future?
4. Would you refer someone else to this agency?

The proportion of positive responses to these questions ranged from 75 percent to 95 percent (Watkins & Gonzales, 1982).

Somewhat related to the question of satisfaction with family counseling services was the report of satisfaction with a marriage preparation program offered by an interchurch agency in Canada. All couples served in the first ten months of 1990 were sent a questionnaire with a rather poor response rate of only 23 percent. In that survey, the mean level of overall satisfaction was 4.2 on the 5-point scale. (Russell & Lyster, 1992).

The guidance that this literature provides is rather limited. It appears typical for agencies to ask general as well as more specific questions about client satisfaction. How much the service was believed to have helped the client is one type of question that is often asked. Another is whether clients would return to the agency or recommend the agency to others.

(Continued)

EXHIBIT 2.1 *Continued*

It appears that clients of family counseling services tend to express a rather high level of satisfaction with the services they have received. Unfortunately, there were no studies reviewed which could provide concrete guidance for a family counseling agency that wishes to obtain a general picture of client satisfaction and have a basis of comparison to similar agencies.

References

Faust, Ruth G. (1987). A model of divorce adjustment for use in family service agencies. *Social Work*, 32 (1), 78–80.

Russell, Mary N., & Lyster, Rosanne F. (1992). Marriage preparation: Factors associated with consumer satisfaction. *Family Relations*, 41 (4), 446.

Watkins, Ted, & Gonzales, Richard. (1982). Outreach to Mexican Americans. *Social Work*, 27 (1), 68–73.

ASSIGNMENT 2–B

1. How would you state the purpose of the study examined in this chapter?

2. Now, restate this purpose in a way that is not in keeping with the spirit of scientific inquiry and violates the principle that research is a process of discovery rather than justification.

3. What is the general research question?

What are some of the more specific research questions that might be examined in this study?

_____

_____

_____

4. Are you in danger of making the mistake of reinventing the wheel?

_____

_____

_____

5. How positive should you expect your clients to be in response to survey questions about their level of satisfaction? What is the basis for your expectation?

_____

_____

_____

_____

The fact that the clients of other agencies have expressed satisfaction with the services they received is not proof that your agency would receive similar responses. Thus, a client satisfaction survey may be warranted.

Developing the Research Methodology for the Study

If you wished to know whether your services are effective in meeting client need, you could undertake any number of types of studies. You could secure instruments designed to measure various forms of marital and family satisfaction or various forms of individual pathology such as depression. You could employ these instruments in your study by having your clients respond to each scale before counseling begins and then again after it was over. You would check the difference in their scores on these scales at these two points in time as a measure of service effectiveness. If it were feasible, you could even compare them to a group of people who had not had counseling to see if their progress was greater than the comparison group during the same time interval.

But your resources do not allow you to undertake this type of study. Instead, you have decided to conduct a survey of clients as a means for answering the research question.

Defining and Measuring Study Variables

What Is a Variable?

A *variable* is an entity that can take on more than one value or characteristic. In other words, it can vary. There must be at least two categories into which subjects will fall on a given concept in a given study in order for it to be considered a variable. Gender would not be a variable in a study of only females. Mental illness would not be a variable in a study that included only people who were classified as being mentally ill. Patients' rights could not be a variable if, by definition, the rights of all patients in a given hospital were the same. The extent to which one exercises one's rights could be conceptualized as a variable as could the extent to which one were denied his or her rights. Likewise, knowledge of rights could vary. But the rights themselves are constants. They are the same for everyone.

In your study, you want to determine the extent to which clients of your agency are satisfied with your services. Thus, satisfaction would be a variable because it can vary from person to person. The concept of "clients" cannot vary because all your study subjects are clients. The concept of clients could be considered a variable if you were going to compare your clients to persons in the community who were not clients. If you were to include both types of people in your study, you could include the concept of clients as a variable because some of your study participants would be clients and some would not.

Two General Methods of Measuring Study Variables

Let's suppose that you have decided to construct a simple questionnaire for your survey. You are seeking a general "check-up" on how well you are achieving your goals through the eyes of your clients. You want to be able to report your results in tangible terms in which the responses of one client can be grouped with that of another client. Thus, you will conduct a *quantitative* study in which you will ask questions which have specific response categories. In this way, the form of each client's response will be the same. Thus, you will be able to group them together and report statistics on the results of your study.

In contrast, a *qualitative* type of study would utilize open-ended questions, preferably asked in direct interviews. For example, if researchers wanted to find out about a phenomenon and they didn't know what "typical" responses might be, then a qualitative study would be appropriate. The qualitative type of study is better suited for situations in which researchers are attempting to develop a theory rather than to test one or to develop a basis for predicting results rather than testing whether their predictions are accurate.

Defining the Variables for the Study

Let's suppose that you have defined the variables for your study as follows:

A. Satisfaction with the extent to which the client was treated with respect by the entire staff of the agency.

B. Satisfaction with the extent to which the client was helped to achieve his or her goals through the counseling provided by the agency.

C. A willingness to recommend the agency to others suffering from the same problems as the client.

D. The perception that the help received by the agency has aided the client in maintaining a satisfactory life since the counseling ended.

E. Descriptive information such as gender and age.

Having defined these variables, you now must develop methods of measuring each of them. The above statements are known as *abstract definitions* of variables. Your next task is to develop operational definitions of each variable.

Measuring the Variables for the Study

The *operational definition* of a study variable specifies how the variable is to be measured. The variable of gender can be measured by asking respondents to a survey to mark whether they are male or female. You can ask them to mark the category of their age or specify their exact age. You can ask your clients to respond to an instrument that measures depression. These are examples of operational definitions of study variables. However, let's not forget that if a given concept is not to be measured in any way in a particular study, it is *not* a variable in that study. It is not sufficient to know that your study subjects have a gender and that it is either male or female. If you did not ask them to identify their gender, then you cannot use this variable in your study. This is a very simple concept that is overlooked by beginning research students more than you might think.

One of the principles of questionnaire construction requires that response categories must be *mutually exclusive.* In other words, the questions given to the subjects must contain categories that do not overlap, so that respondents will not be confused as to which category to mark if they happen to fall in the space of the overlap between categories. Also, it should not be possible for a given subject to fall into two different categories in the list. Take, for example, the following question:

Check the category below that describes you.

_____   *Employed*

_____   *Looking for a job*

_____   *Not looking for a job*

You might place the above question on a survey instrument because you assume that someone who is employed is not looking for a job. But a person could be dissatisfied with their current job and be actively looking for another one. So, which category do they check? They would probably check two categories or be confused about which one to check.

Another principle is that categories should be *exhaustive.* In other words, there should be a category that fits everyone. A respondent should not be faced with the situation of looking over the list of response categories and saying, "I don't fit into any of these categories—I can't mark any of them." Consider, for example, the following question:

What is your political party affiliation?

_____   *Democrat*

_____   *Republican*

While most people would classify themselves as either Democrat or Republican, some would not fit into either category, so there is no response that fits them. A good idea when constructing instruments is to add the category "Other" to those presented. This will cover all other possibilities.

The study questions employed in this hypothetical survey of clients of your family service agency are presented in Exhibit 2.2.

EXHIBIT 2.2   Client Satisfaction Questionnaire

Directions: We are conducting a survey of clients served by our agency in the past year. We would appreciate receiving your opinions on how well we served you so that we can learn how to better serve our clients in the future. Please answer the questions below and do not place your name on this questionnaire. In this way, your identity will not be known and you can feel comfortable being completely honest in your responses.

1. To what extent were you treated with respect by the staff of our agency?

   _____   To a very little extent   _____   To a great extent

   _____   To a little extent   _____   To a very great extent

   _____   To some extent

2. To what extent did you achieve your goals through the counseling you received?

   _____   To a very little extent   _____   To a great extent

   _____   To a little extent   _____   To a very great extent

   _____   To some extent

3. To what extent has the counseling you received from our agency helped you to maintain a satisfactory life since your counseling ended?

   _____   To a very little extent   _____   To a great extent

   _____   To a little extent   _____   To a very great extent

   _____   To some extent

EXHIBIT 2.2   *Continued*

4. Would you recommend our agency to others suffering from the same kind of problem which brought you to our agency?

_____ Yes   _____ No

5. What is your age?

_____ Under30 _____ 30–39 _____ 40–49 _____ 50 & above

6. What is your gender?

_____ Male   _____ Female

ASSIGNMENT 2–C

1. Recall that one of the study variables was defined as follows: Satisfaction with the extent to which the client was treated with respect by the entire staff of the agency. Regarding this variable, what is problematic about each of the following alternatives for a survey question to be presented to clients?

   a. Don't you think that our staff treated you with respect?

   _____ Yes   _____ No

Comments:

_____

_____

   b. Do you think our staff needs to work harder at treating clients with respect?

   _____ Yes   _____ No

Comments:

_____

_____

_____

2. How is the following item superior to (a) and (b) above?

   To what extent do you feel that you were treated with respect by our entire staff?

		_____	To some extent
_____	To a very little extent	_____	To a great extent
_____	To a little extent	_____	To a very great extent

   Comments:

   _____

   _____

   _____

   _____

3. What is wrong with the following ways to measure age on your questionnaire?

   a. What is your age?

   _____ 20–29   _____ 30–39   _____ 40–49   _____ 50–59

   _____

   _____

   _____

   _____

   b. What is your age?

   _____ under 20 _____ 20–30 _____ 30–40 _____ 40 or above

   _____

   _____

   _____

   _____

4. What does the abstract definition of a variable look like?

_____

_____

_____

_____

5. How is the abstract definition of a variable different from the operational definition of it?

_____

_____

_____

_____

6. Which of the following would *not* be variables in your study? _____

a. Gender

b. Clients

c. The extent to which clients felt that they had been treated with respect

d. Race

7. Is your study an example of a quantitative study or a qualitative study?

_____ Quantitative _____ Qualitative

_____ Neither _____ Both

Choosing a Sample for the Study

You have decided to conduct a client satisfaction survey in order to determine if your services are effective in achieving the agency's goals. You must decide how to select participants for your study. You could select everyone who has ever been served by your agency going back to its beginning twenty-five years ago. But that would not be feasible because this is a really large number and because many such persons would have moved and some may have forgotten how well the experience went. Perhaps you could select everyone who has been served during the past five years. But that number comes to 1000 and you don't have the resources to conduct such a study.

This is where the idea of a study sample comes into play. A *sample* is a proportion of a larger group. The larger group is known as the *population*. Researchers normally refer to the study sample as those persons participating in the study. The study population is a larger aggregate of people for which each and every member of the sample is a member.

The nature of the sample will determine how well you can *generalize* your findings to persons not included in this study. In other words, it will help you to determine the extent to which you can conclude whether all of your clients are generally satisfied with your services even though they were not all included in the study.

Your first task is to define the population of concern. Are you interested in knowing how your present clients feel about your services, or the clients of recent months, or the last year, or what? Once you have defined your relevant population, you can determine how to define your sample. When you think of the concepts of sample and population, consider Figure 2.1.

In Figure 2.1, you can see that there are many ways that you could define your population and your sample. You could say that the clients served in the past month constitute a sample of those served in the past year, which, in turn, constitutes a sample of those served in the past five years, and so forth. It is proper to define the population of a study as any aggregate of people for whom all persons in the sample are included. This is depicted in Figure 2.1. However, any such def-

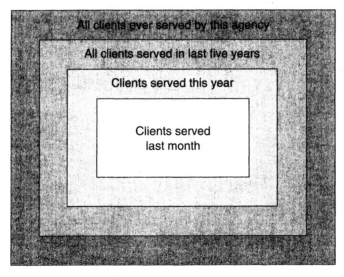

FIGURE 2.1   Defining the Sample

inition is not necessarily an optimal way to characterize the population from which your sample is drawn.

Common sense will perhaps tell you that you can be safer in generalizing your findings of a survey of clients served in the past month if you define the population as clients served in the past year than if you defined it as clients served in the past five years. It is more likely that the clients served in the past month are more like clients of the past year than clients of the past five years.

However, the way that you select your sample is the most critical question in the determination of how representative a sample is of a given population. A biased sample is one which is restricted to certain persons who are believed to represent only a portion of a given population. If you intentionally select only clients believed to be happy with agency services, you cannot say that you have a sample that is representative of all clients.

In this study, you have chosen to select a random sample of clients whose cases have been closed in the past twelve months. You will send these persons a mailed questionnaire asking them to answer a set of questions related to agency services.

A random sample is one in which all persons in the designated population have an equal chance of being in the sample of study subjects. Selecting people for the sample by rolling the dice or flipping a coin is a means that is random because the researcher does not control the outcome; thus, the researcher's biases are eliminated from the selection process.

When researchers use random sampling techniques, they can be safe in generalizing from the sample to the particular population from which the study sample was randomly selected. There is much research that demonstrates that random samples are quite similar, although not identical, to their populations. There is always a certain margin of error when researchers generalize, but that margin of error is very small when they use appropriate random samples techniques. You can, of course, speculate about the extent to which a nonrandom sample would be expected to represent a given population. But you cannot generalize with confidence about the margin of error inherent in your generalization.

ASSIGNMENT 2–D

1. Which of the following would be an improper way to define the population for your study? Keep in mind the nature of your sample discussed previously.

   a. Clients currently being served by the agency

   b. Clients whose cases have been closed

   c. Clients whose cases have been closed in the past year

   d. Females served by the agency in the past year

Comments:

_____

_____

2. Which of the following methods of generating a mailing list for the client satisfaction survey would provide the agency with the ability to generalize its findings to the population of clients served by the agency during the last year?

a. Send questionnaires to all persons served during the past two months

b. Send questionnaires to all persons currently being served

c. Send questionnaires to all current clients who volunteer for the survey

d. Send questionnaires to a random sample of 212 of the total of 424 clients served during the past year

Comments:

_____

_____

_____

Data Analysis for the Study

You have decided to conduct a survey of clients of your agency. The questionnaire mailed in this hypothetical study is presented in Exhibit 2.1. Your study is descriptive in nature because you want to describe the opinions of your clients. One might argue that it is also evaluative because you are using the opinions of your clients to determine if the agency's services have been effective. However, the methodology of evaluative research normally requires the direct measurement of clients on the behaviors associated with the goals of the program, rather than opinions. For this reason, your study is perhaps better classified as descriptive.

One of the first tasks in the presentation of the results of a study is the description of the sample of persons used to collect the data. In this regard, a key piece of information is the response rate to the questionnaire. You might, for example, have experienced the following regarding the persons who responded to your questionnaire:

> *There were 424 clients whose cases were closed during the period of the past twelve months immediately preceding the date of the study. A random sample of 212 persons from this group was mailed a questionnaire and asked to participate. A total of 129 persons returned the questionnaires for a response rate of 61 percent.*

Descriptive statistics are employed to describe a sample. What are the proportions of males and females? What is the average age? How many respondents indicated that they would recommend this agency to a friend? Each of these examples merely describes the results of a set of data.

When a study is conducted, it is usually advisable to describe the sample from which the data were collected. In your example, you should collect data on such variables as gender and age so that you can characterize your sample of respondents. This helps you to examine some of the ways by which you might find that your findings are not generalizable to populations of persons not included in your sample. For example, what if you find that only 20 percent of your respondents were males even though your service statistics indicate that 40 percent of your clients are males? This would challenge the idea that your sample is representative of your population.

When other people read the results of your study, they will want this information as well. If you had no members of minority groups who responded to your survey, your results may not be generalizable to such persons. The reader of your study who works mainly with minority groups will take such information into consideration in the examination of your data.

Perhaps the simplest way to characterize your sample is by frequencies. A *frequency* is simply the number of times a value of a variable occurs. For example, 78 of your respondents might be females and 51 males. A *proportion* is the percentage of a particular value. Using the same numbers, 60 percent of the persons in your sample are females ($78/129 = 0.60$).

Regarding a variable such as age, you might want to report the average and the range of ages. For example, you might say that your respondents ranged in age from 23 to 56 with an average age of 33.2 years.

One of the purposes of describing a sample is to check for representativeness. Is your sample of respondents representative of the population of clients typically served by your agency? If you have data on the average age of clients or the proportion of clients who are male and female, you can compare your sample to that population data.

After you have a perspective on the nature of your study sample, you will need to analyze the data regarding the questions under investigation. In this case, the task is more simple than usual. You have asked only a few questions for which you need to compute the frequencies, proportions, or means. In your hypothetical survey, the results of the answers to question (1) are provided in Table 2.1.

The first column (Frequency) contains the number of persons who gave a particular response (e.g., "To some extent") while the next column (Category Percent) presents the percentage that this frequency represents. The final column presents the proportion of persons with the given response plus the percentage of those of all previous categories of response.

For example, there were 36 respondents who marked "To a very great extent" as their response to the question. This number represents 27.9% of all respondents as indicated in the second column labeled "Category Percent." The "Cumulative Percent" reveals the proportion of persons who responded by the given category

TABLE 2.1 Extent to Which Respondents Felt Treated with Respect by the Entire Staff

	Frequency	Category Percent	Cumulative Percent
To a very great extent	36	27.9	27.9
To a great extent	44	34.1	62.0
To some extent	28	21.7	83.7
To a little extent	12	9.3	93.0
To a very little extent	9	7.0	100.0
Total	129	100.0	

plus those with a response that was higher on the scale. For example, the 34.1% of persons who answered "To a great extent" are added to the 27.9% who provided the higher answer for a cumulative proportion of 62% (27.9 + 34.1 = 62).

By organizing the data in this manner, you can easily reveal the pattern of responses. You can say, for example, that 83.7 percent of your clients felt that the staff treated them with respect to some extent or greater. It is important that the levels above "to some extent" are considered to be higher than this category. In this way, such information can be combined as presented.

Let's look at the hypothetical responses to two of the other questions in your study. These data are supplied in Tables 2.2 and 2.3.

Another question posed to these clients was as follows:

Would you recommend our agency to others suffering from the same kind of problem which brought you to our agency?

A total of 103 (80 percent) of these clients responded "Yes" to this question while the remaining 20 percent (26 persons) indicated that they would not recommend this agency to others.

TABLE 2.2 Extent to Which Respondents Were Helped to Achieve Their Goals

	Frequency	Category Percent	Cumulative Percent
To a very great extent	23	17.8	17.8
To a great extent	31	24.0	41.8
To some extent	40	31.0	72.8
To a little extent	20	15.5	88.3
To a very little extent	15	11.6	100.0
Total	129	100.0	

TABLE 2.3   **Extent to Which Counseling Aided Clients in Maintaining Satisfactory Lives Since the Counseling Ended**

	Frequency	Category Percent	Cumulative Percent
To a very great extent	10	7.8	7.8
To a great extent	28	21.7	29.5
To some extent	40	31.0	60.5
To a little extent	30	23.3	83.8
To a very little extent	21	16.2	100.0
Total	129	100.0	

ASSIGNMENT 2–E

Fill in the blanks in the statements which follow:

1. The number of respondents who indicated that they were satisfied with the extent to which they were treated with respect *to a very great extent* was _____ .

2. The number of respondents who indicated that they were satisfied with the extent to which they were helped to achieve their goals *to a very great extent* was _____ .

3. The proportion of respondents who indicated that they were satisfied with the extent to which they were treated with respect *to a great extent* or a higher level was

   _____ .

4. The proportion of respondents who indicated that they were satisfied with the extent to which they were helped to achieve their goals *to a great extent* or a higher level was

   _____ .

5. The proportion of respondents who indicated that they were satisfied with the extent to which the services they had received had helped them to maintain a satisfactory life since counseling ended *to a great extent* or a higher level was _____ .

6. Is an examination of frequencies more or less useful to this analysis than the examination of proportions? Explain.

   _____

   _____

   _____

7. What is the one finding of this survey that seems most noteworthy to you?

_____

_____

_____

Drawing Conclusions

In the final section of a research report, researchers summarize their findings and draw conclusions about what these findings mean. They also want to identify special limitations related to their study methods.

In this phase of the research process, you return to your basic research questions and provide a summary answer. Were your clients generally satisfied with the services of your agency? Were they more satisfied with certain aspects of your services than others?

You also want to help others to interpret your results for themselves. In other words, you want to help people from other agencies to determine how relevant your findings might be to their agencies. The critical question here is the generalization of your study results. To what extent do you believe you can generalize your findings to persons who did not respond to your questionnaire?

Finally, you should identify the limitations of your study results. For this question, you return to your research methodology and bring the reader's attention to ways that your results might be limited, and ways that the study could have been improved. For example, to what extent can you say that client satisfaction is an indicator of the achievement of agency goals? Is a satisfied client necessarily one whose condition has been improved?

ASSIGNMENT 2–F

The final task in the research process is the drawing of conclusions about the results of the study. In this part of a research report, the nature of the study should be restated and the results summarized. Then, you should explore the implications of these results. Let's approach this task by filling in the blanks in the appropriate spaces in the following summary of the study.

In this study, a survey was undertaken of a random sample of all clients whose cases had been closed during the past _____ by the Oakmont Family Service Association. The research question asked whether clients of this agency were satisfied with the service they had received. Specifically, they were asked to indicate the level of their satisfaction with the following:

1. the extent to which they had been treated with _____ ;

2. the extent to which they had been helped to achieve their _____ ;

3. the extent to which the help they received had aided them in maintaining a satisfactory life since the counseling ended;

4. the extent to which they would recommend the agency to others who were _____

_____

In general, it _____ (can/cannot) be concluded that the clients of this agency are satisfied with the services they received because

_____

_____

The criterion that received the highest proportion of highly favorable ratings (i.e., the top two levels) was the extent to which the client

_____

The lowest rating went to the criterion related to the extent to which their counseling had helped them maintain a satisfactory life since the counseling ended. Only _____ percent of the respondents provided a highly favorable rating (i.e., one of the top two categories on the rating scale) on this criterion. However, on a more promising note, it was learned that _____ percent of these former clients would recommend the agency to someone else who was experiencing the same problems that brought them to the agency for help.

It is safe to say that the findings of this study can be generalized to:

_____

because

_____

_____

However, to generalize these findings to

_____

would be more difficult to defend because

_____

_____

Glossary

Abstract Definition of a Study Variable. A definition of a variable which provides conceptual guidance on the boundaries that are considered fitting for the variable for the present study. It can be likened to a dictionary definition of the variable although it is not required to encompass all territory that others might want to include, but only the conceptual territory that the researcher considers proper for the given study.

Conclusions. The final major phase of the research process in which conclusions are drawn about the data which were employed in the examination of the research question.

Cumulative Proportion. The proportion of subjects in the present category plus the proportion of all subjects falling below or above the present category.

Data Analysis. The third major phase of the research process whereby data is analyzed to address the research question.

Descriptive Research. Research that describes something with precision but does not attempt to explain it.

Evaluative Research. Research that is used to evaluate whether an intervention achieved its objectives.

Explanatory Research. Research that is designed to explain something, usually by examining the relationships among a set of variables to see if one offers an explanation of another.

Exploratory Research. Research that is designed to develop knowledge about a relatively unknown phenomenon so that new theory can be developed or new insight can be acquired on the nature of it.

Exhaustive. Categories for a question on a questionnaire which include a category that fits each potential study subject.

Frequency. The occurrence of something. The number of observations falling into a specific category or value, such as the number of females in the sample.

Methodology. The second major phase of the research process whereby the study is designed in a manner that adequately addresses the research question.

Mutually Exclusive. Categories for a research instrument which are not capable of overlap such that a study subject could possibly be placed into more than one category among those presented.

Operational Definition of a Study Variable. A definition of a study variable which specifies how the variable will be measured in the present study.

Population. The larger group from which the sample was selected.

Problem Formulation. The first major phase of the research process in which the research question is developed and the research problem is analyzed.

Proportion. The percentage of something, such as the percent of the sample that was female.

Qualitative. A means of observation (or measurement) that is flexible, such as an open-ended question on a questionnaire or direct observation of behavior as it naturally occurs.

Quantitative. A means of observation (or measurement) that is fixed, such as posing a question which places people in discrete categories (e.g., male or female) or gives them a number as a value for the response to the question (e.g., age).

Sample. A portion of a larger entity. In a research study, it pertains to the study subjects from whom data were collected.

Scientific Inquiry. A systematic process of inquiry that is designed to reduce the bias inherent in human observation through the application of both logic and objective measurement of social phenomena.

Variable. Something that varies in the present study. In other words, an entity that takes on more than one value. For example, the variable of gender would be divided into the categories of male and female. A concept is not a variable in a given study unless it is measured in that study and there is some variance in responses. The concept of gender could not be a variable in a study that included only females.

$$Chapter\ \mathit{3}$$

Understanding Explanatory Research:

Does Gender Explain Social Work Salaries When Position Level Is Controlled?

In the last chapter, you examined the entire research process using an example of a client satisfaction survey. The study example in that chapter was in the category of descriptive research. In this chapter, you will look at an illustration of explanatory research. The topic is sexual discrimination in salaries among social workers. Does it exist? If so, are salary differences between men and women explained by variables other than gender, such as position level?

As before, you will first develop the research question. Then you will examine how to develop a study methodology and analyze data. Finally, you will confront the task of drawing conclusions. In the example for this chapter, you will examine some real data taken from a survey of social workers in one state.

Objectives

In the previous chapters, I identified the purposes and processes of social work research as well as the spirit of scientific inquiry. The definition and measurement of study variables were illustrated as well as the concepts of sample and population. In addition, the nature of descriptive statistics was illustrated. Many of these lessons will be reviewed in the present chapter with a new example. Thus, much of your previous learning will be reinforced with a new example. But your learning will be carried a major step further. At the completion of this chapter, you will be able to:

1. Explain the roles of theory and observation in research;
2. Explain the nature of the empirical relationship;
3. Identify the hypothesis for a given research study and explain its role in a research study;
4. Identify whether a given example of measurement would be classified as quantitative or qualitative;
5. Explain the role of probability sampling in the generalization of study results;
6. Explain the basis for the determination of statistical significance and practical significance;
7. Interpret the data in a simple table which presents information on the relationship between two nominal variables;
8. Explain the value of p in statistical significance.

The Research Process and the Nature of Scientific Inquiry

In the previous chapters, you examined the essential elements of scientific inquiry. You reviewed six basic principles of research in the first chapter. Research, for example, was portrayed as a process of discovery rather than justification. You were told not to put the cart before the horse and that two heads are better than one. Do you remember the other three principles? Perhaps you can apply these principles to the present example as you read on.

In this section of the present chapter, your knowledge about the nature of scientific inquiry will increase by examining the concepts of theory and observation.

Theory and Observation in Research

The two most fundamental building blocks of the scientific method are *observation* and *theory*. *Theory* refers to researchers' attempts to explain the world in which people live. *Observation* refers to their attempts to collect information about the world in which people live. The process of scientific inquiry can begin with observation or with theory, but both tools are utilized before the process is complete.

The interplay of theory and observation can be illustrated by looking again at the effect of the full moon on human behavior. Many people who have worked in mental hospitals or emergency rooms have overheard conversations among staff about the possibility that a sudden increase in unusual behavior is related to a full moon. In fact, some people are convinced that this is the case.

But how do they know? Was their conclusion based on theory or observation or both? Most such people have drawn their conclusions based on observations. They have noticed sudden increases in unusual behavior among their clients dur-ing times of the full moon. They have often heard others say "Wow, it must be the full moon!"

But what about theory? Theory would attempt to explain why. Most such staff members in mental hospitals have no theory on which to base their conclusions. This does not make their conclusions inaccurate; it simply means that their conclusions are based on incomplete information.

However, an astronomer might have developed a theory about the relationship between the full moon and human behavior by noting the effect of the full moon on gravity and the effect of gravity on human behavior. If the full moon affects gravity and gravity affects human behavior, it logically follows that there would be a relationship between the full moon and behavior.

The method of observation, in scientific inquiry, is designed to reduce human error. Thus, efforts are made to overcome the potential of bias or other forms of faulty observation as researchers collect information. In the example of the full moon, they would need to collect information on behavior during the full moon and compare it to information taken when the moon was not full.

For many people, however, the information in their heads is based solely on things that they remembered happening during the full moon. Their perception is that they don't normally find so many unusual behaviors when the moon is not full. But in the absence of data on behaviors during this period, their observations are subject to biased selection. It is typical that people's attention is drawn to information based on their preconceived notions about reality. If they have had their attention drawn to the full moon by others, they are more likely to remember bizarre behavior that happened during the full moon than at other times.

Theory in research is founded on *logic*. The question here is "Does it make sense?" Does it make sense that the full moon has some form of control over people's behavior? Even if researchers discovered that the emergency intake rate for a psychiatric hospital was significantly higher during the full moon than other times, they would want to know why. After all, people have no control over the full moon. But there may be drugs that will interfere with the effect of gravity on brain chemistry.

The Research Process

I have referred to the first major phase of research as *problem formulation*. In this stage, researchers articulate the question they want to address and the purpose of the study. They also find out what is already known about the question. The types of information sought in this phase include the ways that the variables have been defined and measured by others, the theories about the issue, and the results of other studies on this question. In explanatory research, the literature review is per-haps more critical than in the other types of research. This is not to say that it is unimportant in other types of studies, only that the literature review takes on special meaning in explanatory research.

Why? The main reason is that explanatory research typically attempts to explain a given phenomenon (variable) by examining its relationship with other phenomena (variables). Does agreement with a feminist perspective explain the helping person's degree of emphasis upon empowerment in one's work with the abused wife? Does exercise influence stress? Does stress lead to illness? These are some of the explanatory questions that have been illustrated in previous chapters.

When researchers attempt such an inquiry, they are in need of information to direct their attention. What information would suggest a certain theory about why things are the way they are? How have the study variables been conceptualized and measured by others? The necessity that researchers address these concerns places the literature in a critical position in the explanatory research study.

The second phase in the research process has been identified as the development of the *research methodology.* In this phase, the research question must be stated in terms amenable to measurement. For example, let's consider the question "Does the full moon make people crazy?" How can this question be stated in empirical (measurable) terms? What, for example, does "crazy" mean? Perhaps a more suitable question at this stage of research would be: Is the psychiatric emergency intake rate of Memorial Hospital higher during the day that the moon is fullest than the day the moon is least full?

The above example is easy to quantify. Thus, a *quantitative* type of measurement of variables is appropriate. But what if the research question had been "What is it like to experience the process of being placed for adoption as a child?" What if the question had been "What kinds of social support do students most rely on to cope with the stresses of being in graduate school?" What about the question "How does social support alleviate stress?" The first two questions address topics for which little information is currently available. The last question requires developing a theory to explain how support works. For each of these three questions, the *qualitative* means of measuring variables may be more appropriate than the quantitative method.

Qualitative methods of inquiry utilize means of measurement that are more natural than numerical. Such studies typically rely on interviews or direct observation of behavior rather than questionnaires to be completed or concrete data to be collected. Thus, a key initial task in the design phase of the research process is the determination of how to define and measure the variables under study. The example of the full moon given above is based upon some information on this issue. I have, for example, decided to define the full moon in relation to only two days of the moon's cycle—when it is fullest and when it is least full. I have also decided to define behavior in terms of the psychiatric emergency intake rate of a given hospital.

Another task is the definition of the study population and the study sample. What population is relevant to the study? Within that population of people, what sample of persons should be drawn for the study? Careful attention to this task is critical to the extent to which researchers can generalize their study findings to people not included in the study.

The means of collecting data is also determined in this phase of the process. For the full moon, the collecting of data from existing records is appropriate. For some studies, a mailed survey may be useful while other studies may utilize personal interviews. These are only a few of the options available.

The third phase of the research process is the *analysis of data*. In this endeavor, researchers examine the data to determine what conclusions it supports. Was the rate of emergency intakes higher during the full moon than the other selected day of the cycle? If so, how much higher was it? Was there enough difference to believe that they have discovered something of great importance? What is the likelihood that the differences could be explained by chance rather than being a phenomenon that they would likely discover if they repeated their study with other study subjects? These are the kinds of questions posed in the data analysis stage of research.

The final phase of the research process is *drawing conclusions*. You will recall the admonition in the first chapter that your study conclusions must be consistent with the data analyzed. Researchers do not draw conclusions from preconceived notions about the study subject, but from the data that they have collected and analyzed in the pursuit of the study question.

Problem Formulation for the Study

In the previous chapter, I discussed problem formulation as the first stage of the research process. In this stage, researchers consider the basic question to be pursued and the purpose of pursuing it. After they have formulated a general issue or question, they usually turn to existing knowledge about the issue for guidance. In the examination of the potential for sexual discrimination in salaries in social work, researchers would naturally turn to the literature and develop a literature review. The information given in Exhibit 3.1 will serve as a brief literature review for this study.

EXHIBIT 3.1   A Brief Literature Review on Salary Discrimination

Sexual discrimination in the workplace is well documented in the literature. Many studies have been undertaken, for example, about the presence of sex-role stereotypes in the workplace which favor the behaviors perceived as being associated more with men than with women (See, for example, York, 1988). Other studies have documented the extent to which women are underrepresented in management positions (York, Henley, & Gamble, 1987). One of the most fundamental issues is the extent to which there is sexual discrimination in salaries.

Several studies have called attention to the differences in salary between male and female social workers. In a 1972 national survey of members of the National Asso-

EXHIBIT 3.1ˈ *Continued*

ciation of Social Workers (NASW), less than 1 percent of women were found to be in the highest salary category ($25,000 or more) as compared to 6 percent of males (Fanshel, 1976). In a 1991 study of the members of this organization, 16.4 percent of males were found to be earning $40,000 per year or more as compared to only 6.6 percent of females (Gilbelman & Schervish, 1993). Studies have also documented the disparities in management positions in social work agencies between men and women. In the 1991 survey of NASW members, it was also found that 25.6 percent of males held administrative positions as compared to 12.9 percent of females. A 1983 survey conducted of NASW members in one state revealed that 33 percent of males held administrative positions as compared to 11 percent of females (York, Henley, & Gamble, 1987).

One of the questions which emerge from this literature is whether things have changed since these studies were conducted. Do female social workers receive lower salaries than male social workers? Are they less likely to be in administrative positions?

In view of the fact that men have been found in the past to be more likely to be in administrative positions than women, and persons in administrative positions receive higher salaries, an analysis of salaries by position level would contribute to the inquiry into the issue of sexual discrimination in social work. For example, how do the salaries of female administrators compare to the salaries of male administrators?

ASSIGNMENT 3–A

1. What do you think of the following statement of the purpose of our study?

   To provide evidence of the need for increased efforts to eradicate sexual discrimination in social work.

   _____

   _____

   _____

2. Do you have additional ways to state the purpose of the study? How do they differ from the above?

   _____

   _____

   _____

3. What appears to be the central research question that you should be pursuing?

_____

_____

_____

4. Why should you pursue this question? In other words, what utility would the findings of such a study have?

_____

_____

_____

5. Does the general purpose of this study place it in the category of descriptive research or evaluative research or some other category? Why?

_____

_____

_____

6. Identify the most important variables in the study.

_____

_____

_____

7. Is the concept "social worker" a variable in this study? If it is a variable, how should it be measured? If it is not a variable, why is it not a variable?

_____

_____

_____

8. Would you say that your approach to this research question begins with observation or with theory? Are you to move from observation to the development of a theory, or do you already have a theory that you wish to test through observation?

Methodology for the Study

The study methodology (study design) entails the determination of how variables will be defined and measured, and how the study subjects will be selected for inclusion in the study. Before you can know how to measure your study variables, you must first be able to define them. Before you select your study sample, you must define the population from which your sample will be drawn. Another task is determining how data will be collected. Will you examine existing records, or conduct personal interviews, or mail out a questionnaire to your study subjects, or do something else?

The Research Questions

Remember that the basic research issue is whether there is evidence that sexual discrimination exists among social workers in regard to salary. If you find that females receive lower salaries than males, you have evidence of sexual discrimination. But you also want to gain further insight into this issue by considering the variable of position level. Do females receive lower salaries, in part, because they are in lower positions in the hierarchy of human service organizations? If such is the finding, you would have a different focus for your primary concern. If you wish to reduce the inequity between men and women, your approach would focus on discrimination in organizational advancement.

In the pursuit of these interests, you would need to examine the relationship between gender and salary. You would also examine the relationship between gender and organizational position (Are women less likely than men to be employed in management positions?) Then you would want to examine the relationship between gender and salary while controlling for position level. Are female managers paid lower salaries than male managers?

If you find no significant difference in salary between male and female social workers, you will have a simple answer to the research question and you would probably find yourself moving on to another topic for your research interest. This is not to say that you would have the final word on salary discrimination, but it would provide you with information that would satisfy your interest.

Let's suppose, however, that you do find significant differences in salary between male and female social workers. Let's also suppose that you find that men are more likely than women to be employed in management positions and that those in management positions receive higher salaries. The question that would logically follow is whether position level explained the relationship between gender and salary. If female managers are found to receive essentially the same salaries as male managers, you would have evidence in support of the conclusion that position explained the relationship between gender and salary. In other words, you would conclude that women receive lower salaries because they are in lower positions.

Developing the Study Hypothesis

The study *hypothesis* is essentially a prediction of the results of the study. A simple research hypothesis is a statement of the expected relationship between two variables. The language of the research hypothesis is more precise than everyday language. It will normally identify the variables with labels that clearly link them to their operational definitions in the study. If you wanted to study whether there is a relationship between stress and social support, you might state your hypothesis as follows: There is a negative relationship between social support and stress. In this case, you are expecting that persons with more support will have less stress.

In the above hypothesis, the direction of the relationship was noted. There are situations in which the expected direction of the relationship is not clear. For example, the literature review from a study by York and Henley (1988) revealed two contrasting theories about women and satisfaction with bureaucracy, one suggesting that women were more likely to be satisfied than men while the other theory suggested the opposite. In this case, the hypothesis could have been stated as, "There is a relationship between gender and satisfaction with the level of bureaucracy in human service organizations."

The research hypothesis should be free of excess words that fail to add meaning to the purpose of the statement. For example, consider the following hypothesis: Social work students who appreciate the importance of physical health and take exercise seriously will find that their levels of stress have been reduced by this behavior. A more appropriate statement would be as follows: Social work students who engage in aerobic exercise at least three times per week will have lower stress than those who do not.

The research hypothesis should also be free of value statements. Remember the spirit of scientific inquiry. Pyrczak and Bruce (1992) warn against using the words *significant* or *prove* in the statement of the hypothesis. The word *significant* usually refers to the statistical results and is unnecessary. The word *prove* should seldom be used in any part of a research study in view of the tentative nature of research findings in the social sciences.

Finally, researchers often undertake a study in which they need to state more than one hypothesis because they are examining more than one relationship among the variables. Consider the examples regarding the relationship between social support and stress and the relationship between exercise and stress, which were stated as two hypotheses. It would be inappropriate to combine them in one hypothesis: There is a negative relationship between social support and stress and between exercise and stress. However, it is appropriate to identify more than two variables in one hypothesis if you are going to examine the relationship among three or more variables in a single statistical analysis.

Defining and Measuring Study Variables

One of the first tasks in the design of a study is the determination of whether a qualitative or a quantitative means of measurement is most appropriate. Qualitative measurement is illustrated by an open-ended question such as, "What are some of the feelings you first had about becoming a client of our agency?" This question is open in that the respondent has the option of saying any number of things in response to it, and the nature of what one person says may be quite different from what others say. Quantitative measurement, on the other hand, either places people into categories or gives them a score on a variable. The client's age, or score on an inventory of self-esteem, or the category of service received are examples.

You have identified your key variables as salary and gender. But you have also noted that position level may determine salary and may also be related to gender. Thus, in order to obtain a better picture of the influence of gender on salary, you should include position level in your study as well.

All of these variables are easy to define. You would have a more difficult task if you were studying such concepts as stress or self-concept or depression. How different people define these terms varies. But people tend to have common definitions of such concepts as gender, salary, and position level.

For example, the variable of gender is quite easy to measure. You simply ask respondents to identify their gender as either male or female. Annual salary is also easy. You can say that you are referring to one's annual salary in dollars rather than categories.

You will also have to determine the categories of work position to include in the study. You can start with direct services, meaning social workers who work directly with agency clients. Another category can be line supervisor or clinical supervisor. Another can be middle manager, referring to persons who supervise supervisors. Agency executive can be another category. In order to cover a variety of special kinds of positions in a social work agency, you will need to have a category for "other."

Identifying the Study Population and Sample

The study population is that group of persons from whom study subjects should be selected. In this case, employed social workers are the study population. But there are lots of people who call themselves social workers in the world. How can you restrict this population before selecting the sample? For this study, you are concerned with the population of employed professional social workers—i.e., social workers with professional training at either the undergraduate level (BSW degree) or the graduate level (MSW degree). Persons who work in social work positions with a degree in other fields such as history or sociology or English will not be included in the study population. In addition, social workers who are not employed on a full-time basis will not be included.

As a matter of convenience, the state of North Carolina will serve as the geographic area. Within this state you will select your study subjects from the membership list of the National Association of Social Workers, an organization of professional social workers. Thus, you will define your study population as employed professional social workers who are members of the North Carolina Chapter of the National Association of Social Workers.

The next task is to select the sample for your study. The study sample consists of those persons who participate in the study. There were approximately 2,000 members of the North Carolina Chapter of the National Association of Social Workers at the time data for this study were collected. You do not have the funds to conduct a study of all these people. But, you don't really have to do that in order to have confidence that your results represent this population. You can select a *random sample* of these persons for your study. When you do this, you can be rather confident that the sample is representative of the population. A random sample is known as a *probability sample* because all persons in the study population have an equal chance of being selected for the study.

When you select a random sample, you must use a method of selection in which each person in the defined population has an equal chance with everyone else to be selected for the study. You must determine how many people you want in the study and select this number of people on a random basis. If you want to select 200 people out of 2,000 members of NASW, you would first determine that you are selecting 10 percent of these people ($200/2{,}000 = .10 \times 100 = 10$). You could select the first person from among the first 10 persons on this list by some random means such as drawing a number from a hat, and then select every tenth person thereafter. There are other ways to select a random sample, but you will use this one because it is the most simple.

Determining How to Collect Data

There are a number of methods that can be used to collect data for a research study. If you wished to gain depth of understanding of a subject by probing the meaning of terms or experiences or feelings, a personal interview might be most appropriate. If the information you sought could be found in agency records, that would be your source of data. In this case, a mailed survey is the most efficient means of collecting information. It is inexpensive, so researchers can usually afford to collect data from a large number of persons. The personal interview, by contrast, is a rather expensive way of collecting data. When researchers use this means, they normally have to limit the number of study subjects to a small sample. Another advantage of the mailed survey is that responses can be anonymous. This condition can motivate honest response because the study subjects are guaranteed that their responses cannot be used against them.

A potential drawback to the mailed survey is that a good number of potential study subjects choose not to respond. Thus, one's response rate becomes an issue.

The key question is whether the nonparticipants would be different on the study variables than the participants. A typical response rate to a mailed survey is about 50 percent, and this is normally considered acceptable unless common sense indicates that the nonparticipants would be expected to differ from the participants.

EXHIBIT 3.2   Questionnaire Given to NASW Members in One State

1. What is your current annual salary? $ _____

2. What is your work position?

    _____   Direct practice with agency clients

    _____   Supervision

    _____   Management

    _____   Other

3. What is your gender?   _____ Male   _____ Female

ASSIGNMENT 3–B

1. What are the research questions for your study?

   _____

   _____

   _____

2. How would you state one of the possible hypotheses for this study?

   _____

   _____

3. Are you undertaking a qualitative study or a quantitative study?

   Why?

   _____

   _____

   _____

4. What are the variables in your study?

_____

_____

_____

5. What is your study population?

_____

_____

_____

6. What is your study sample?

_____

_____

_____

7. To whom can the results of your study be safely generalized?

_____

_____

_____

Analyzing Data for the Study

Describing the Study Sample

One of the tasks in the presentation of data from a study is the description of the study sample. Usually this includes the proportion of persons who are male and female, the average age, and so forth. In this way, the reader of the report can ascertain how relevant the results of the present study might be for other populations. The second major task is the presentation of data regarding the study questions.

The data presented in this chapter are drawn from a real study that was undertaken in 1986. The sample is described below.

In the spring of 1986, a questionnaire was mailed to a random sample of 25 percent of the members of the North Carolina Chapter of the National Association of Social Workers. Of the 290 persons who were mailed questionnaires, a total of 158 returned them for a response rate of 55 percent.

The ages of these respondents ranged from 22 to 65 with a mean of 40. Only 18 percent of these social workers indicated that they were in administrative positions while the other 82 percent listed either direct service, supervision, or other as their job positions. Eighty percent of these study subjects were female. Their years of social work experience ranged from 1 to 40 with a mean of 14.5.

Examining the Study Questions

The first study question asked whether females received lower salaries than males in social work. This question is best examined by a comparison of the average salaries of males and females. This can only be done, however, because salary was measured in terms of dollars rather than in categories.

These mean salaries are presented in Figure 3.1. As you can see, the mean salary for all females in the 1986 study was $23,754 while the mean for males was $32,025. This is a difference of $8,271 per year. The first issue is to determine whether this difference is noteworthy. Does this difference seem to be enough to become concerned about? With this question, you are posing the question of *practical significance*. This is a matter of judgment.

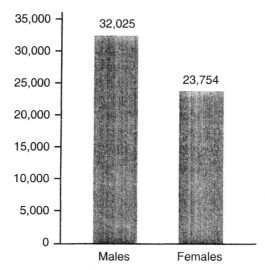

FIGURE 3.1   Mean 1986 Salaries of NASW Members in North Carolina

However, before you can make a final determination of practical significance, you must confront the issue of *statistical significance*. With this issue, you are posing the question of whether your results can be explained by chance.

Statistical significance helps with the question of whether you would be likely to obtain similar results if you repeated this study with another sample of persons. If you discovered a salary difference between males and females of only $245 annually (e.g., $28,000 versus $28,245), you might logically wonder if this small difference truly represents differences between male and female salaries or is a function of the particular sample you have drawn for this study. When you draw a sample of people, you never can be certain that your sample is completely like your population. The statistical analysis of data helps to estimate the likelihood that your sample results can be relied upon to represent the population. A difference in annual salary of $28,000 and $28,245 is less than a 1 percent difference. Surely it is easy to see how this small difference would be much more likely to be a chance discovery than a difference of $8,271.

There are a variety of *statistical tests* which are used to examine statistical significance with different types of data. These tests provide an estimate of the number of times in 100 that you would expect to find your particular results just by chance.

You have perhaps seen the notation "$p < .05$." This means that the *probability* of occurrence by chance is less than 5 times in 100. The designation of "$p < .01$" would mean that you would likely discover your particular constellation of data less than 1 time in 100 just by chance. Thus, you must change the figure after the letter p from a fraction to a full number before you can determine the number of times in 100 that your results would occur by chance. For example, "$p < .001$" means less than 1 time in 1000 while "$p = .03$" means 3 times in 100.

When you undertake a statistical analysis of data, you must determine your own standard for significance. Is it sufficient if you find your results cannot be explained by chance any more than 10 times in 100 or 5 times in 100 or do you develop a standard as high as 1 time in 100? You will notice that the lower the value of p, the better is the level of statistical significance. There is an accepted standard in social sciences of 5 times in 100. Thus, you will often see the notation "$p < .05$" as signifying the achievement of statistical significance.

Your task now is to examine statistical significance. In the example where the means of two groups are being compared, the t test for independent samples is an appropriate statistical test. When this test is applied to your data, you find that you are likely to discover results like your data less than 1 time in 1000 (i.e., $p < .001$). Thus, you have achieved a very high level of statistical significance, one that is much higher than the normal standard of .05.

The second research question was whether males were more likely than females to be found in management positions. These data are presented in Table 3.1.

As you can see from this table, only 13 percent of the females were found to be employed in management positions whereas 29 percent of males were so employed. Is this difference noteworthy? In other words, do you have practical sig-

TABLE 3.1   Gender and Position Level among
NASW Members in North Carolina

	Nonmanagement	Management	Total
Female	110 (87%)	16 (13%)	126 (100%)
Male	22 (71%)	9 (29%)	31 (100%)
Total	132	25	157

nificance? One way to examine these data is to recognize that males were twice as likely as females to be employed in management positions (13% vs. 29%).

But you must also examine statistical significance. In the absence of statistical significance, you would have difficulty making a case for practical significance because you could not be confident that you had discovered a reality that can be generalized, rather than explained by chance.

The likelihood that your results would occur by chance can be examined for these data with a statistic known as chi square. When you apply this statistic to your data you find a p value of .05, which means that your results could be explained by chance only 5 times in 100. Now that you have determined statistical significance, you can return to the issue of practical significance and examine whether these differences between men and women are noteworthy. As mentioned beforehand, this is a matter of professional opinion. Wise people can differ on such a question.

The discovery of a relationship between gender and salary and between gender and position level provides further impetus for the examination of these three variables together. You can logically assert that managers would receive higher salaries than nonmanagers; therefore, it is possible that position level helps to explain the difference in salary between males and females that was reported beforehand. In other words, it may be that males receive higher salaries primarily because they are in higher positions.

A simple way to examine this question is by comparing the salaries of male managers and female managers as well as male nonmanagers and female nonmanagers. These data are presented in Figure 3.2. As you can see, male managers reported an average annual salary of $44,044 as compared to an average salary of $25,584 for female managers. Male nonmanagers reported an average salary of $26,616 which was slightly higher than the figure for female managers. Female nonmanagers reported the lowest annual salary ($23,480).

The information in Figure 3.2 provides a rather powerful image to guide your determination of practical significance. The salaries of male managers stand out well above all other categories and are especially higher than that for female managers. Furthermore, male nonmanagers receive higher salaries than female nonmanagers.

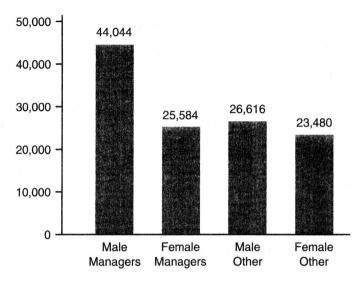

FIGURE 3.2   Mean Salaries by Gender and Position

What if you had found that male managers received roughly the same average salary as female managers and that male nonmanagers received roughly the same salaries as female nonmanagers? You might think that this couldn't be true if the overall salaries of males and females were different. But it could be true because it could be that the only reason that males receive higher salaries overall is the fact that more of them are in management positions and that persons in management positions receive higher salaries.

But this was not your discovery. You found evidence for salary discrimination at both position levels. However, you must address the question of statistical significance before you can dispense with the issue of practical significance. When comparing the average salaries of four groups of persons, you can employ a statistical test known as analysis of variance (sometimes referred to as ANOVA). This statistic helps to estimate the likelihood of discovering these salary differences by chance. When you applied this statistic to your data, you got a p value of 0.0001. In other words, your results would be expected to occur by chance only one time in 10,000. (Remember that a p value of 0.01 means 1 time in 100 and a p value of .001 means 1 time in 1,000.)

This analysis confirms that it is very unlikely to find, just by chance, a difference in mean salary of $44,044 for one group, $25,584 for another group, $26,616 for a third group, and $23,480 for a fourth group, given the particular array of salaries presented in this sample. Thus, it is very unlikely that you would find that another sample of people from your population would display a highly different set of mean salaries, such as female managers with a higher mean salary than male managers, and so forth. This means that you can take your results seriously. You don't have to worry that your results can be explained by chance.

ASSIGNMENT 3–C

1. The following statement is *not* true: This study revealed that 80 percent of all social workers in North Carolina are female.

   Explain why this statement is not true.

   _____

   _____

   _____

2. Is the following statement true or false?

   In regard to the question of salary differences between males and females in this study, it was determined that practical significance was achieved but statistical significance was not achieved.

   _____ TRUE   _____ FALSE

   Explain:

   _____

   _____

   _____

   _____

3. The mean age of subjects in this study was _____ .

4. Is the following statement true or false?

   In this study, it was found that males were more likely than females to be found in management positions.

   Explain:

   _____ TRUE   _____ FALSE

   _____

   _____

   _____

   _____

5. Is the following statement true or false?

    In this study, it was found that the primary reason males received higher salaries than females was that they were in higher positions.

    _____   TRUE   _____   FALSE

    Explain:

    _____

    _____

    _____

    _____

6. Is the following statement true or false?

    In this study, it was found that the difference in salary between male managers, female managers, male nonmanagers, and female nonmanagers was significant statistically.

    _____   TRUE   _____   FALSE

    Explain:

    _____

    _____

    _____

    _____

7. Was practical significance achieved in regard to the following hypothesis?

    Females will report lower salaries than males even when position level is taken into consideration.

    _____

    _____

    _____

    _____

Drawing Conclusions for the Study

In the conclusions phase of the research process, researchers return to the basic research question and the nature of their study. The key part of this phase is the presentation of the basic answer to your research question. What was your study question and how did you seek an answer to it in your study? Did you find differences in salary between males and females? Did you find that position level explained any differences that were observed?

Another task of the final phase of research is the identification of the limitations of a study. Some of the key issues for this analysis are the degree of accuracy in the ways that the variables were measured and the extent to which the results can be generalized to persons not in this particular study.

The number of considerations for the conclusions of a research study are vast, and vary somewhat with the type of study being undertaken. Only a few have been selected for examination in this chapter. They are presented below.

You cannot be confident in the findings of a study unless it was undertaken within the spirit of scientific inquiry.   You could have started the process with the conclusion that sexual discrimination exists in social work and it is your duty to find the evidence that supports this conclusion. This would not have been in keeping with the spirit of scientific inquiry. Instead, you must begin the research process with a question to be answered or a problem to be solved. You answer your question by reference to the information you collect.

You cannot employ only descriptive statistics if your study has the purpose of explanation rather than mere description.   If you wanted to know if males and females received different salaries, you would need to go beyond the mere description of the salary differences. You would also need to examine whether this difference could be explained by chance.

You cannot safely generalize the findings from a sample to a given population unless the sample was drawn at random from that specific population.   In the *generalization* of study results, it is important to specify the population to which the study results are relevant. It is not proper to define a study population in such a way that certain persons in the sample were not included in this definition of the population. The further removed a given definition of the study population is from the study sample, the less confident you can be that your results can be generalized. However, the only truly safe generalization is from a sample to the specific population from which it was selected on a random basis.

In an explanatory study, it should be remembered that there are typically multiple explanations for a given phenomenon; therefore, evidence for one explanation should be viewed as an incomplete explanation. Human behavior is complex. There are many potential causes of a given condition. In your study, you might be able to conclude that position level does not tend to explain the relationship between gender and salary, but this does not mean that there cannot be other things that might explain this relationship. Therefore, if you want to know the roots of sexual discrimination, you might look for other variables as explanations.

ASSIGNMENT 3–D

Fill in the blanks for the conclusions section of your study.

The purpose of the study reported in this paper was to determine whether _____ social workers received lower salaries than _____ .

Study subjects were selected _____ (randomly/nonrandomly) from the membership list of _____ .

Study subjects reported their annual salaries, their gender, and their position level within their agencies. Position level was included because

_____

_____

It _____ (was/was not) found that females received lower salaries than men among these study participants. It was also found that women _____ (were/ were not) less likely than men to be employed in management positions. Position level _____ (was/was not) found to be a variable that substantially explained the relationship between gender and salary. In other words, it _____ (was/was not) found that the primary reason that women receive lower salaries than men was that they are more likely to be in lower positions. In this analysis of gender, position, and salary, the most noteworthy discovery was _____

_____

This study _____ (did/did not) generate _____ (evidence/proof) of sexual discrimination in salary among social workers. One of the limitations of this study is related to sampling. This limitation is _____

_____

_____

_____

References

Fanshel, D. (1976). Status differentials: Men and women in social work. *Social Work*, 21, 448–454.

Gilbelman, M., & Schervish, P. H. (1993). *Who We Are*. Washington: National Association of Social Workers.

Pyrczak, F., and Bruce, R. R. (1992). *Writing Empirical Research Reports*. Los Angeles, Pyrczak Publishing.

York, Reginald O. (1988). Sex-role stereotypes and the socialization of managers. *Administration in Social Work*, 12 (1), 25–40.

York, Reginald O., & Henley, H. Carl. (1988). Women and social work bureaucracy. *Journal of Applied Social Sciences*, 12 (1), 46–61.

York, Reginald O., Henley, H. Carl, & Gamble, Dorothy N. (1987). Sexual discrimination in social work: Is it salary or advancement? *Social Work*, 32 (4), 336–340.

Glossary

Generalization. The application of knowledge about one group of study subjects to another group of persons.

Hypothesis. A statement of the expected results of a research study on a given topic based upon theory or explanations derived from existing knowledge. For example, one might hypothesize that males will report higher annual salaries than will females. This hypothesis would be based upon knowledge of sexual discrimination.

Logic. Whether something makes sense when subjected to careful analysis through the principles of good reasoning.

Observation. The measurement of something.

p. The letter p is used to designate the estimate of the probability that a set of research data would occur by chance. The designation "$p < .05$" means that the particular data would occur by chance less than 5 times in 100. The designation "$p < .01$" indicates that this likelihood is less than 1 time in 100.

Practical Significance. The extent to which a given set of study findings are noteworthy.

Probability. The likelihood of the occurrence of something that is not a certainty. Statistical tests are used to estimate probability, which is designated with the letter p.

Probability Sample. A sample that was drawn at random from the specified study population.

Random Sample. A sample in which each person in the study population had an equal chance of being selected for the sample.

Statistical Significance. The likelihood that a given set of study findings would be expected to occur by chance.

Statistical Test. A measure which is used to estimate the likelihood that a given set of study findings would be expected to occur by chance.

Theory. In the most simple terms, a theory is an attempt to explain something. Theories can be more or less formal and explicit or more or less sophisticated, but any attempt to explain is a theory, whether or not it is supported by scientific evidence.

Chapter *4*

Understanding Evaluative Research:

Is Therapy Effective in Reducing Depression?

As in the previous two chapters, you will encounter the entire research process in this chapter. Your knowledge, however, will be expanded. You will work with an example of evaluative research, and you will be introduced to some new concepts in research that are relevant to social work research of various forms. The data for the present chapter are drawn from a study conducted by a graduate social work student who was on field assignment with an inpatient psychiatric treatment unit of a general hospital. The primary question was whether this unit was effective in reducing the depression of patients who entered it with a primary diagnosis of depression. (The name of the treatment unit has been changed for this book.)

In this chapter, you will examine the same steps in the research process as before, but you will see how they are applied specifically to the evaluation of social work interventions. You will follow the process of research through its four stages: (1) problem formulation leading to the articulation of the research question; (2) the development of the research methodology; (3) the collection and analysis of data; and (4) the drawing of conclusions. In each of these phases of research, there are issues unique to evaluative research, but most of the concepts utilized in this type of research are relevant to most forms of social work research.

Objectives

As before, you will review some lessons learned in previous chapters in the present chapter. In addition, you will be able to accomplish the following at its completion:

1. Identify the major questions to be answered in each of the four phases of evaluative research;

2. When given an example from evaluative research, you will be able to address questions in problem formulation by (a) identifying the problem addressed by the intervention, (b) describing the intervention, and (c) identifying the objective of intervention;

3. When given an example from evaluative research, you will demonstrate your understanding of study methodology in evaluative research by (a) identifying the one group pretest-posttest research design, (b) identifying the dependent variable and independent variable, (c) defining the study sample and population, (d) identifying how variables are measured, and (e) identifying at least one means for testing either the reliability or validity of the means used to measure the dependent variable;

4. When given an example from evaluative research, you will be able to demonstrate your understanding of data analysis by interpreting the results of an analysis of pretest and posttest data;

5. When given an example from evaluative research, you will demonstrate your understanding of the task of drawing study conclusions by (a) identifying whether evidence was generated in support of the intervention, and (b) identifying at least one limitation of the study.

An Overview of the Evaluative Research Process

The purpose of evaluative research is to determine if an intervention was effective in achieving its objectives. In order for a study to qualify as evaluative research, there has to have been an intervention into the lives of the study subjects. Two central tasks are the identification of the intervention and the measurement of results. The intervention, however, should be justified by a knowledge base, and the measurement of results should be undertaken in a structure that maximizes the likelihood that the measured results can be attributed to the intervention rather than something else.

Phase 1: Problem Formulation

The first major phase of the research process is problem formulation leading to the development of the research question. In evaluative research, this question is more simple to develop than in most other forms of research. Researchers want to know if a treatment was effective in achieving its objectives. In this task, they must address three central questions:

1. What is the nature of the problem that the intervention addresses?
2. What is the intervention?
3. What are the treatment objectives?

The answer to the first question provides a rationale for the selection of the intervention. The second question requires that they specify the nature of the intervention with a certain amount of precision so that the reader of the evaluative report can determine just what it was that worked or didn't work. The third question provides guidance on just what should be measured in the determination of effectiveness for a given intervention.

An examination of the nature of the client problem provides a rationale for the selection of the intervention. If training is a solution to the problem, it stands to reason that ignorance of some kind must be the cause of the problem. Do people abuse drugs because of ignorance? Or, do they do it because of peer pressure, or parent–child conflict, or something else?

If the causes of child abuse lie within the pathologies of the abuser, it follows that some form of therapy for these pathologies is the solution. But if child abuse is caused by societal inadequacies, such as acceptance of violence in a culture, or poverty, a different solution would emerge.

The description of the intervention helps researchers to determine what worked or didn't work. With this information, they can better generalize the results of one study to another situation. They should describe interventions with enough detail that readers would know the same intervention if they saw it somewhere else.

What does the treatment look like? Does it entail a series of individual counseling sessions or group psychotherapy or training sessions? Does it include residential care? Is it more like talk therapy or play therapy or something else? Is case management a part of the intervention?

How much intervention is given? Is it given one hour a day once a week for six to ten weeks? If it is twenty-four-hour care, how many days are included in the typical service episode for the typical client?

The objectives of intervention provide guidance on the selection of targets for the measurement of results. Are they intended to enhance self-esteem, to reduce marital conflict, to prevent further incidents of child abuse, to restore the alcoholic to a state of long-term sobriety, to alleviate the social consequences to the family of the presence of a member with a drinking problem? These are some of the targets of intervention.

Researchers should be careful to avoid vague language in the articulation of treatment objectives. "Improving the quality of life" is rather vague. They should also avoid articulating the treatment objective in terms of the simple application of the treatment. For example, the objective "to offer crisis intervention to the victims of rape" identifies what will be done but not what will be accomplished for the client.

Phase 2: Developing the Research Methodology

In the second phase of evaluative research, researchers must do the following:

1. select a research design,
2. define the variables,

3. select a means of measuring the variables,
4. define the study population and select the study sample, and
5. select a means of collecting the data.

When these tasks are complete, they are ready to collect and analyze the data.

The Research Design.   The *research design* in evaluative research is critical to the question of *causation* in the interpretation of data. Was the clients' improvement caused by the intervention? If researchers merely ask clients after treatment if they are satisfied with the service, they are engaging in a study that best fits into the category of descriptive research, because they are only describing the clients' opinions. If they measure their condition, such as self-esteem, only after treatment, they do not have a basis for determining how much good the intervention did because they do not know the clients' level of self-esteem before treatment.

If researchers measure clients' conditions before and after treatment, they are beginning to develop a basis for gauging the effect of treatment. If clients are better off after treatment than before, the change may be attributable to the intervention. But there are other things that potentially affect a client's condition. How can a researcher know, for example, that the client would not have improved through normal growth and development during the time period of the intervention? Perhaps the typical adolescent achieves a 20 percent gain in self-esteem in the normal course of development in three months' time. If the treatment lasts for three months and there is a 20 percent gain, the investigator cannot be confident that the treatment made the difference under these circumstances.

The more you know about the normal course of development the better you will be able to judge what other variables might affect a client's condition. When researchers use the one-group pretest-posttest design, they make the assumption that there are no variables other than treatment that affect the client's target condition. For example, they assume that the clients would not improve significantly on the target behavior during the period of the treatment without the treatment that was given.

But some people do improve over time on their own. You can apply logic to determine the extent to which you should be concerned with this issue in your situation. You can logically expect a woman to be less depressed six months after her husband has died than three weeks after his death. But you would not expect a neglectful mother, who has been neglecting her children for five years, to improve on her own over a period of three months. Perhaps she would improve on her own over a longer period, such as a year or two. But if she has been neglecting her children for five years, you can reasonably expect that her behavior is not going to change in only three months without some form of intervention in her life.

A design that is superior to the one-group pretest-posttest design is the *comparison group design* (also known as the nonequivalent control group design). In this design, researchers compare the growth of clients on the target condition with that of a group of persons who did not receive the treatment. They attribute the differences in growth to the treatment. Investigators can have more confidence in this design if they have reason to believe that the two groups are similar except for the fact that one group received the treatment. However, the only way to be truly confident is if they have assigned these study subjects to their respective treatment and comparison groups on a random basis. In that case, they would be employing an *experimental design.*

Another design that is superior to the one-group pretest-posttest design is the *AB single-subject design.* This is the most common of the single-subject designs. It entails the repeated measurement of a single client's target behavior over a *baseline period* which starts before treatment and the continued measurement of this behavior during the *treatment period.* The treatment measurements are compared to the baseline measurements to see if they indicate significant improvement. This design is superior to the one-group pretest-posttest design because the baseline recordings measure the changes that might be underway in the client's behavior. If the treatment trend is superior to this trend, the difference is attributed to the treatment. In other words, it is assumed that the baseline trend would continue in the absence of treatment.

Defining the Variables.   The conditions identified in the *treatment objectives* serve as the focus of researchers' definition of variables. You should carefully define these conditions before seeking a means of measurement. What does self-esteem mean? Is it distinct from self-concept or self-efficacy or self-confidence? What constitutes an act of child abuse? Is stress a psychological condition or a condition of the environment that creates discomfort?

What are the concepts that are to be included in your broad definition? Typically, concepts that are addressed in a treatment objective can mean different things to different people. It is not essential that you define your concepts exactly as other parties have defined them, but it is essential that you specify just what you mean by the critical terms.

Measuring Study Variables.   Perhaps the most fundamental issue in measurement is whether the nature of the variable is such that a qualitative or a quantitative means is more suitable for measurement. As I pointed out in the previous chapter, a *qualitative* means of measurement is more open and flexible and is exemplified by open-ended questions given in interviews or by the direct observation of behavior. This form of measurement is most suitable when the study question is exploratory in nature, where the definitions of key study variables are not very concise, and researchers are attempting to develop new theories rather than testing existing ones. *Quantitative* measurement, on the other hand, is more suitable when they are attempting to test a theory and can find or develop an instrument that measures the variables with precision.

Evaluative research normally employs quantitative means of measurement. This is particularly true if the evaluation study attempts to measure the outcome of treatment rather than the process of treatment (e.g., What are the reasons why it did or did not work?). In evaluative research, investigators are usually testing the theory that treatment works. Research helps them to find out if it does.

In quantitative research, you should select means of measuring the variables that are congruent with your specific definitions of the variables. Existing instruments are recommended for measurement because they have been tested by others. Sometimes, however, you will have to develop your own instrument. When you examine an existing instrument, you should see if it includes the concepts in your definition.

Two critical issues in measurement are *validity* and *reliability*. *Validity* refers to the accuracy of a particular means of measurement. Does the Beck Depression Inventory accurately measure the concept of depression? Or does it more accurately measure self-esteem or some other concept? If the mental health center's clients who were being treated for depression did not score higher on the Beck Depression Inventory at intake than persons being treated for some other condition, you would have reason to question the accuracy of this instrument.

Reliability refers to the consistency of a means of measurement. If a group of social work students had scores that fluctuated wildly from day to day on a self-esteem scale, you would have reason to question the consistency of the instrument you used. An instrument must be reliable in order to be valid, but an instrument can be reliable without being valid. In other words, an instrument can be consistently inaccurate. But if it is not consistent, you don't know just what it is measuring.

Defining the Study Population and Selecting the Study Sample.   A sample is a portion of a larger entity, the larger entity being known as the population. In evaluative research, this issue is less difficult than in some other forms of research. Often, a study sample consists of all clients served by a given program at a given point in time. Thus, random sampling procedures may not be relevant. Of course, researchers do draw a sample of clients in some instances. In this case, the principles of random sampling are helpful.

The study sample, of course, consists of those persons who are your study subjects. The study population can be defined as any aggregate of people for whom each and every member of the sample is a member. However, the more remote the population from the sample, the less confidence you can have that the results of your study can be generalized to that population. Remember that a random sample is the only type of sample for which you can have a great deal of confidence that the sample is representative of the population.

The critical question posed by the notions of sample and population is whether the results can be generalized to groups of persons who were not in the study. If the mean level of self-esteem for the adolescents in a treatment program is much higher after treatment than before, would the same be true if another group of people had received this treatment? Common sense might indicate that the results are likely to be repeated with groups of people similar to the study group. The more similar, the more confidence you can have that your results are relevant to the other group.

Determining the Means of Collecting Data. Evaluative research typically employs quantitative methods of measuring variables rather than qualitative. This means that variables are measured in some discrete manner such as by a score on an instrument or a category on a scale. Such data can be collected by a survey questionnaire given to the client or by asking someone else to make certain observations about the client. For example, you might ask your clients to respond to the Self-Esteem Inventory at the beginning of treatment and at the termination of treatment. You could ask the wife of an abusive husband in treatment if the abuse has occurred during the treatment period.

When you prepare the survey instrument, you must be sure to collect all the data you will need for your analysis. This may include demographic data as well as outcome data.

Phase 3: Analyzing Data

The first approach to analysis of data in evaluative research is descriptive in nature. The question is whether the data revealed a better condition as a result of treatment. Were scores better after treatment than before? Did the treatment group have better scores than the comparison group?

The second approach is the examination of statistical significance. How likely is it that the results you obtained could be explained by chance? Is a mean gain of only 3.2 points on a 20-point scale potentially the result of chance? If so, you cannot be confident that your treatment really made a difference. You might have found that this small a gain is within the normal fluctuations on this scale and does not represent a gain that you could bet would be repeated with another sample of clients given the same treatment.

Sometimes, you might also want to analyze your data to see if certain types of clients improved more than others. You might also want to examine the scores of your clients on sub-scales of broader scales to see if improvement was achieved in one realm but not in others.

Phase 4: Drawing Conclusions

In evaluative research, several issues are relevant to the drawing of conclusions. One is the issue of practical significance. Was the gain noteworthy enough to be treated seriously? I have already addressed the issue of statistical significance in the data analysis section. You might return to this issue in the conclusions phase when you talk about practical significance. It is possible that a gain in functioning was measured that was statistically significant but was not a big enough gain to be declared to be of practical significance.

Another issue is your ability to generalize your results, a topic which was examined in the discussion of sampling above. To whom can your results be generalized? What other populations should be included in other studies in order to better answer this question?

Another task in the drawing of conclusions is the development of potential explanations of why these particular results were obtained. What might explain the successes or failures as reflected in the data?

ASSIGNMENT 4–A

Reasons

1. Which of the following is an example of evaluative research?

   a. A study of levels of stress among graduate social work students reveals that those who report that they exercise on a regular basis have lower scores on the stress scale than those who report that they do not exercise on a regular basis.

   b. A study indicates that students who participated in the Stress Reduction Program experienced a greater improvement in stress reduction than those students who did not participate in the program.

   c. A study reveals that social work students tend to have greater levels of stress during the first semester of study than in the final semester of study.

2. Determine the proper sequence of the activities of evaluative research by placing (1) next to the question below that should be addressed first, (2) by the question that should be addressed second, and so forth, until you have given a number to each of the six questions below.

   _5_   a. How is progress in the reduction of depression to be measured in your study?

   _4_   b. What is the mean score for your clients on depression at the completion of the treatment program?

   _2_   c. What might explain the results of your study?

   _1_   d. What is one of the most important causes of depression according to modern theory?

   _3_   e. What is the mean score for depression for your clients before the treatment began?

3. What part of the problem formulation phase of evaluative research is most relevant to the determination of how the treatment will be designed?

   a. Information on the importance of the problem to society

   b. Information on theories about causation of the problem

   c. The treatment objectives

4. How would you test either the reliability or validity of a scale designed to measure depression?

   Pg 95

   _____

   _____

   _____

5. Suppose that you wish to collect data on depression from all twenty-five persons admitted to the Memorial Hospital Psychiatric Ward with depression in order to examine whether the treatment received was effective in reducing depression. Which of the following would be properly labeled as the sample, and which would be properly labeled as the population? (Note: One statement does not fit as either.) Place the letter S next to the sample and the letter P next to the population.

_____   **a.** Persons admitted to Memorial Hospital for depression

_____   **b.** Females who are depressed

_____   **c.** The twenty-five persons from whom data were collected

Explain why you left out one of the above from your answers.

a & c are similar

_____

_____

_____

6. Which of the following pieces of information is the one to which your attention should be most drawn in the determination of practical significance?

a. The amount of the difference between pretest and posttest scores on depression

b. The likelihood that the differences between pretest and posttest scores on depression could be explained by chance

Analyzing the Effectiveness of the New Hope Treatment Center in the Reduction of Depression for a Group of Clients

In this chapter, you will examine the treatment of depression using an example which employs the *one-group pretest–posttest research design.* This example is drawn from the work of a graduate social work student who used her field placement for the setting of the evaluation effort. The identity of the agency has been changed for this chapter.

The New Hope Treatment Center is an inpatient psychiatric treatment program offered in a general hospital serving a county with a population of less than 100,000 in a southern state. It offers an intensive program of services along with twenty-four-hour residential care. These services include group therapy, individual therapy, activity group exercises, family counseling, and medication treatment.

The persons included in this study were the first fifteen individuals who entered this program for the treatment of depression in one month during the spring of 1992. The treatment period ranged from ten to fourteen days for these individuals. These individuals were administered the Beck Depression Inventory at the time of admission and at the time of discharge. The mean score for this group at discharge was compared to the mean score at intake to see if significant improvement had taken place.

Phase 1: Formulating the Problem for This Research Study

As identified in the previous section of this chapter, the formulation of the problem in evaluative research can be divided into three tasks: the analysis of the nature of the problem being treated; the nature of the treatment; and the objectives of treatment. The research question naturally follows from this formulation. The question is whether this particular treatment has been effective in achieving the treatment objectives.

The Nature of the Problem to Be Addressed by the Intervention

A brief literature review on the nature of the problem of depression is given in Exhibit 4.1. This review provides information on three major factors: the definition of the problem, the importance of the problem, and theories about the problem. When you finish reading this part of an evaluation research report, you should have a clear idea of just what the problem looks like, why you should give it special attention, and what explains why it exists. The theories on why it exists should help to guide the choice of the treatment to be employed.

EXHIBIT 4.1   A Brief Overview of Depression and Its Treatment

Note: The following information is drawn from the following professional paper: Dana West. (1992). An evaluation of the effectiveness of an acute inpatient unit in the treatment of depression, School of Social Work, East Carolina University. Information in quotes is directly quoted from this source while the other material is a slightly modified version of the student's paper. This information is used with the permission of Dana West.

According to information in the *Diagnostic and Statistical Manual for Mental Disorders,* 3rd ed. (DSM-III, American Psychiatric Association), the manual used for psychiatric diagnosis, it is estimated that 18 to 23 percent of all females and 8 to 11 percent of all males will suffer a major depressive episode at some point in their lives. It is estimated that approximately 5 percent of this population will require some period of hospitalization.

   "Depression is a feeling or emotion that involves sadness, feelings of worthlessness, or even guilt. This feeling is accompanied by a desire to be alone rather than with

(Continued)

EXHIBIT 4.1 *Continued*

others, and disturbances of appetite, sleep, and general activity. There are several levels of depression. One level might be characterized as normal. It is the emotional state that appears following the loss of a loved one, or the failure to achieve a strongly desired goal. This type of depression is clearly tied to an event in the environment, so we usually know why we are depressed, and we take steps to get out of it. Major depression, on the other hand, is a state in which people have given up trying. The view people have of themselves in this type of depression is uniformly negative; they feel that life is meaningless and that nothing can be done to improve the situation. This major form of depression often involves thought of suicide.

"Another level of depression that is more intense than normal depression and less severe than major depression might be referred to as the 'blues.' This type of depression can be quite unsettling; when in this state, people cannot come up with enthusiasm to begin or maintain important activities. They feel that they cannot do anything right and that they have certain negative qualities that will make it impossible for them to ever be successful."

There are several types of theories about the causes of depression. One type focuses upon physical factors such as brain chemistry. Because depression often appears to be accompanied by changes in brain chemistry, there are biological theories about its causation. One such theory is that "depression occurs when certain neurotransmitters reach too low a concentration in certain areas of the brain" (Friedman & Katz, 1974). In view of the finding that 25 to 40 percent of depressed individuals have a parent or relative with an affective disorder, it has also been suggested that certain persons may have a genetic predisposition to be depressed (Clayton, 1983).

Another type of theory focuses upon intrapersonal factors. The psychodynamic model views depression as emerging from a sense of loss early in life. Some persons become overly dependent, and if they lose the object of their dependency, they turn inward and engage in self-blame. The cognitive model of depression views this problem as a product of distorted thinking. "Emotions are consequences of thoughts, and if one is depressed it is because one is thinking in negative and unrealistic ways" (Beck, et al., 1979). In this view, depressed persons are constantly interpreting events in a negative light.

A third model in the intrapersonal category is the learned helplessness model. This model views depression as "the product of a history of faulty learnings regarding personal locus of control. This model suggests that when one is subjected to negative events perceived as outside of one's control, one becomes hopeless, passive, and depressed."

In a general sense, one might say that there are two basic strategies for treatment of depression. One entails the administration of drugs which bolster the elements that are lacking in the brain of the depressed person. However, this is not usually considered to be sufficient for long-term rehabilitation, even though it may be helpful. A second general strategy is the promotion of insight into the causes of one's depression. If people can learn that their distorted thinking has contributed to their depression, they can perhaps learn how to change their thinking patterns. Repairing relationships damaged by past behaviors and gaining support from family and friends is a necessary part of this treatment process.

EXHIBIT 4.1 *Continued*

References

American Psychiatric Association. (1980) *Diagnostic and Statistical Manual of Mental Disorders,* 3rd Ed. Washington, D.C.

Beck, A., Rush, J., Shaw, B., & Emery, G. (1979). *Cognitive Therapy of Depression.* New York: Guilford Press.

Clayton, P. (1983). The prevalence and course of the affective disorders. *The Affective Disorders.* Washington, D. C.: American Psychiatric Press.

Friedman, A. S., & Katz, S. (1974). Interaction of drug therapy with marital therapy in depressive patients. *Archives of General Psychiatry,* 32, 619–637.

ASSIGNMENT 4–B

1. What are the symptoms of depression?

   sad feeling alone, disturbances lack of participating in 'normal' activities

2. What piece of information about someone exhibiting the above symptoms would suggest that this person may not be suffering from major depression but, instead, may be suffering from a less severe form of depression or the blues?

3. Which of the following intervention approaches is *least* supported by the theories examined in Exhibit 4.1?

   a. The use of medication to reduce the symptoms of depression

   b. The use of training on the general theories of depression

   c. The use of insight therapy regarding one's specific thinking patterns as a method of reducing depression

Explain:

_____

_____

_____

_____

The Nature of the Intervention

The New Hope Treatment Center utilizes a comprehensive array of services as well as residential care. Persons admitted to this hospital unit normally stay two to three weeks for their treatment. This treatment includes medication, individual therapy, group therapy, activity therapy, and family counseling, among other things. The description of this program, as given by Dana West in her professional paper, is contained in Exhibit 4.2.

**EXHIBIT 4.2   The New Hope Treatment Center Program
for the Treatment of Depression***

"The interventions employed by the treatment program included process group, family focus, activity groups, individual therapy with their psychiatrist, specialty groups, individual therapy with their therapist, and nurse's medication group. Each subject attended one process group daily, Monday through Saturday, lasting approximately one hour. Process groups offered subjects an opportunity to share and resolve emotional difficulties and learn new ways of interacting with others. Group members shared personal feelings, ideas, problems, and developed new awareness of how their patterns of behavior affect themselves and others. The group sessions allowed subjects to experience and learn within a therapeutic context. Process groups are led by the therapists who are master level social workers (MSW degree).

"Subjects also attended family focus which was held by the therapist on Thursday evenings from 6:30 p.m. to 7:30 p.m. Family focus was offered to subjects and subjects' family members as an opportunity to educate and explore the aspects of depression. The meeting was held on a general level discussing signs of depression, coping mechanisms, and how to help the individual family member. Each subject attended two family focus meetings prior to their discharge from the unit.

"Subjects attended one activity group daily, Monday through Saturday, lasting approximately one hour. A variety of activities were offered to enhance subject's well-being. Daily activity groups included physical exercise, dance therapy, art therapy, and a selection of arts and crafts. Activity groups are led by the occupational therapist and the activity therapist who are trained and certified in their area of therapy.

EXHIBIT 4.2 *Continued*

"Subjects met individually with their psychiatrist daily, Monday through Sunday, for at least fifteen minutes to explore and discuss treatment and individual progress. Subjects also attended one-hour specialty groups three times a week. On Monday, Wednesday, and Friday, the therapist led groups on specific topics asked for by the subjects. During the time of this study, specialty groups were given on assertiveness training, relaxation training, values clarification, communication skills, problem-solving, and education on depression. Each subject met with their therapist at least three times a week for an hour each session.

"Individual therapy with a trained therapist offered the subject an opportunity to have a confidential relationship in which personal problems could be explored (clients see their individual therapist three to six times per week). And finally, subjects attended one weekly group led by a registered nurse for approximately one hour to educate and answer questions concerning medications. All subjects attended at least two of the nurse's medication groups prior to their discharge from the unit."

*Information taken from the same source as Exhibit 4.1.

The Treatment Objectives

The objective of treatment specifies the growth that is expected in the client as a result of treatment. It does not focus attention on the service to be offered. In other words, one should not develop treatment objectives such as "to offer family counseling to families in need." This statement identifies what will be done, but not what will be accomplished. Vague statements such as "to open doors for a forgotten segment of our population" or "to enhance the quality of life" are also discouraged. Instead, when you see a treatment objective, you should have clear guidance on the means that could be used to evaluate whether it had been achieved.

For those clients of the New Hope Treatment Center who were included in this study, one of the treatment objectives was to reduce the level of their depression. These clients entered this program with a level of depression that could be labeled as serious or, in the language of the trade, "clinically depressed." Not only was it intended that the level of depression for these individuals would be lowered, but it was also expected that it would be reduced to a level lower than what is considered to place a person in the category of "clinically depressed."

ASSIGNMENT 4–C

1. One of the assumptions underlying the treatment program of this agency for the treatment of depression is that depressed persons need insight into the sources of their depression. Thus, insight is addressed in various types of therapy. This is one link between an understanding of the nature of the problem being addressed and the approach taken to treatment.

Identify one additional assumption underlying this treatment program which links the treatment with the dynamics of the problem. Also identify the component of treatment that is relevant to this assumption about the nature of the problem of depression.

_____

_____

_____

2. Why do you suppose that this agency employs persons with professional training to conduct the various activities of the treatment?

_____

_____

_____

3. Approximately how many hours of professional intervention are provided by this program for the typical client?

_____

_____

_____

4. If the level of depression for clients of this program is significantly lower after treatment than before, can you assert that individual psychotherapy offered by MSW level social workers is effective in reducing depression levels of hospitalized patients?

Explain:

_____

_____

_____

5. What is the main treatment objective you are examining in this study?

_____

_____

_____

Phase 2: Developing the Research Methodology for the Study

For the previous discussion of research methodology in evaluative research, you encountered five major tasks: (1) the development of the research design; (2) the definition of the study variables; (3) the selection of the means of measuring study variables; (4) the selection of the study sample and the definition of the study population; and (5) the selection of the means of collecting the data on the study variables. In this section of the chapter, you will examine the one-group pretest–posttest evaluation design, the definition of depression, the measurement of depression using the Beck Depression Scale, the selection of fifteen subjects for study, the exploration of how the study population containing these subjects might be defined, and the use of the survey method of obtaining data.

The Research Design

The research design employed in the present study is the one-group pretest–posttest design. This means that you are studying only one group of persons and that you will measure their target behavior at two points in time—before treatment begins (*pretest*) and after treatment is over (*posttest*). An advantage of this design is that you can measure client behavior before and after treatment so that you have a basis for measuring client progress. A disadvantage of this design is that you will have no basis for controlling for a number of things, other than the treatment, that might have influenced client progress. If you had a control group of depressed persons who had received no treatment, you would have a basis for controlling for some of these other things.

The Definition of Depression

In evaluative research, the *independent variable* is the treatment. This means that something else is believed to be dependent upon treatment, and that this will be termed "the dependent variable." The *dependent variable* (the target behavior) is depression. Depression was defined in Exhibit 4.1 as a feeling or emotion that involves sadness and is often accompanied by feelings of worthlessness, guilt, and by physical symptoms such as disturbances of appetite, sleep, and general activity level. People with mild depression are not able to function at their optimal level in regard to various social, family, and work roles, even though they may be able to complete related duties in a minimally satisfactory manner. People with serious depression have major problems fulfilling these responsibilities. The most intense level of depression often leads to attempts at suicide. (For more information, refer to Exhibit 4.1.)

The Measurement of Depression

The Beck Depression Inventory was employed in this study to measure depression. This scale is designed to measure the severity of depression. It contains 21 items, each of which asks the respondent to select one of four statements that best characterizes them at the present time. One of these items is as follows:

0   *I do not feel sad.*
1   *I feel sad.*
2   *I am sad all the time and I can't snap out of it.*
3   *I am so sad or unhappy that I can't stand it.*

Another item is as follows:

0   *I have not lost interest in other people.*
1   *I am less interested in other people than I used to be.*
2   *I have lost most of my interest in other people.*
3   *I have lost all of my interest in other people.*

The themes of some of the other items on this scale are pessimism, guilt, blaming oneself, thoughts of suicide, crying, sleep, and so forth.

The number assigned to the sample items above represents the score one gets for the response. For example, a response of "I have lost most of my interest in other people" would result in a score of 2 being added to one's total score on this scale. With 21 items on the scale and the highest score for each being a 3, the total possible score would be 63 (21×3).

A score of 17 is considered to represent borderline clinical depression. This would be exemplified by someone who received a score of 1 on about four out of five of the items. For example, scores of 1 on the first four items and a score of 0 on the fifth would be represented by the following choices:

1   *I feel sad.*
1   *I feel discouraged about the future.*
1   *I feel I have failed more than the average person.*
1   *I don't enjoy things the way I used to.*
0   *I don't feel particularly guilty.*

Extreme depression is indicated by a score over forty. This would be exemplified by scores of 2 on almost all the items. Examples include the following: "I am sad all the time and I can't snap out of it; I would like to kill myself."

The Population and the Sample

The sample for this study consisted of the first fifteen persons who entered New Hope Treatment Center with a diagnosis of depression during February of 1992. The issue of how to define the population is open to discussion because any group of persons for whom these fifteen people are members would be a proper, although not necessarily an optimal, way to define the population.

The definition of the population has implications for the question of the group to whom you can generalize your findings. You can, of course, say that your data represents these fifteen persons. But who else might you generalize your findings to? Who else might have achieved the same results if you had included them in the study?

You did not employ a random sampling method. In other words, these fifteen persons do not represent a random sample of any larger group of persons; thus, you do not have what is known as a probability sample. Any generalization of your findings to groups of persons not included in this study would be speculative.

The Method of Collecting Data

The survey method of collecting data was used in this study. The survey method provides an instrument (questionnaire, scale, etc.) to which study subjects are asked to respond. The subjects' responses constitute the measurement of the variable.

There are many other methods of collecting data. One is through interviews. Another is through direct observation of the study subjects' behavior by another person. Sometimes records are used as the source of data for the measurement of variables. Two advantages of the survey method are that it is inexpensive and it obtains information directly from the study subjects.

ASSIGNMENT 4–D

1. When researchers conduct evaluative research, they are testing whether the treatment had the intended effect upon the client's target behavior. But there are other things that affect this behavior besides researchers' interventions. One of these is known as "maturation." This refers to the fact that people naturally grow over time through their own methods independently of a human service intervention. It is by no means guaranteed that depressed people will stay depressed if they are not treated. Some will get better on their own.

   Explain whether your selected research design addresses the issue of maturation as an alternative explanation of the client's behavior.

   _____

   _____

   _____

2. A dependent variable is a variable which depends upon another variable, the latter variable being known as the independent variable. In other words, the researcher has

reason to believe that the dependent variable is influenced (changed) by the independent variable.

In your study, what is the dependent variable?

a. The New Hope Treatment Center program of services for the treatment of depression;

b. Mental illness;

c. The first fifteen persons admitted to the New Hope Treatment Center in February of 1992 with a diagnosis of depression;

d. Depression;

e. Patients served by the New Hope Treatment Center in 1992.

3. Which of the above is the independent variable?

_____

4. Which of the above is the study sample?

_____

5. Which of the following concepts fits within the boundaries of the concept of depression and, therefore, might be a word that fits within a definition of this term or a theme to be included in an instrument that is designed to measure depression?

_____ marital conflict   _____   sadness   _____   career goals

_____ physical energy _____   hopelessness _____   hobbies

6. Which of the following would constitute evidence that the Beck Depression Scale is reliable?

a. A finding that scores on this scale are highly correlated with age;

b. A finding that scores on this scale administered to the same people at two points in time are highly similar;

c. A finding that scores on this scale are found to be lower after treatment than before.

Phase 3: Analyzing Data

The fifteen patients included in this study were given the Beck Depression Scale at intake (before treatment began), and were administered this same instrument at the time of discharge (after treatment had concluded). The mean score (average) of these fifteen patients for the Beck Depression Scale at the time of intake was 34.9. Recall that scores on this scale can range from 0 to 63 and that a score of 17 is considered to constitute borderline depression while a score of 40 represents extreme depression.

In evaluative research, one of the first questions about pretreatment conditions is whether the data represent a serious enough condition to warrant treatment. If social work students were found to be very satisfied with their educational program before a proposed intervention designed to improve satisfaction, there would be little evidence that an intervention was warranted and little opportunity to demonstrate that the treatment method had potential for success. If people are already rather satisfied, according to the measurement of this variable by a given instrument, there is little room for growth.

You can see from the mean pretest scores of your clients that they were typically at the brink of being severely depressed and could easily be considered as seriously depressed. They were well beyond the borderline category.

At the time of discharge, the mean score for these fifteen patients was 13.8. The mean difference between pretest and posttest scores, therefore, was 21.1. The gain in scores for these patients ranged from a low of 13 (from 33 to 20) to a high of 30 (from 41 to 11). These mean scores are graphically displayed in Figure 4.1.

These data were subjected to statistical analysis with the use of the t test for paired data. This test is appropriate when you are comparing the scores of persons before and after treatment when the variable is measured at the interval level. The results give you an estimate of the likelihood that your measured differences could be explained by chance. Technically, the way it works is that a gain score is computed for each client by subtracting the posttest score from the pretest score. The mean of gain scores is analyzed to determine if it is significantly different from a score of 0, which would represent no gain at all.

With your data, the t test value was 9.02 with an accompanying p value that was less than .001. In the report of such a finding, you might see a statement like the following: The difference between pretest and posttest scores was statistically significant ($t = 9.02$; $p < .001$). This means, of course, that you can have confidence

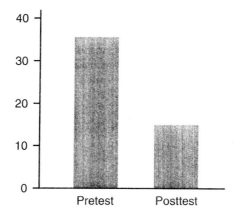

FIGURE 4.1   Mean Scores for Depression

that you have found true differences rather than chance. In other words, you can have confidence that a repeat of your test under the same circumstances would yield results similar to those you found in the differences between pretest and post-test scores.

In an attempt to determine if this treatment worked better with one gender than another, the mean gain scores for males and females were compared. The difference in mean gain scores between these two groups was not statistically significant ($t = 0.54$; $p = 0.59$). It was also found that gain scores did not correlate significantly with age. In other words, it was found that males and females did not differ on the extent to which they improved in the course of treatment, nor was it found that older patients did better than younger ones.

These patients were also asked to indicate the level of their satisfaction with each of the seven major services that comprised the total treatment program. They indicated a high level of satisfaction with each of these services. The proportion who were satisfied with each of these services ranged from a low of 86.7 percent to a high of 100 percent.

Phase 4: Drawing Conclusions

Four issues were mentioned previously in regard to the drawing of conclusions about evaluative research: statistical significance; practical significance; generalizability of findings; and, theories to explain the results. Can your results be explained by chance? Was the gain good enough? To which groups of people are your findings generalizable? What best explains your results?

Statistical significance, of course, is addressed by statistical tests. Practical significance is addressed by a review of the magnitude of the gain in functioning. This is substantially a matter of professional opinion; thus, you are the expert on this matter, once you are armed with sufficient data. Generalizability is addressed by the sampling methods employed. A probability sample is one from which you can safely generalize. Finally, theories about the results are often drawn from the clinical observations of practitioners or from published studies of the same subject with other samples of people, and are a matter of considerable conjecture. One of the issues to be addressed here are the limitations of the study. Did it utilize a good research design? Was the instrument reliable and valid? What things other than treatment might have influenced the scores on the measurement device?

ASSIGNMENT 4–E

1. The following is the hypothesis that was tested in your study: Depressed clients of the New Hope Treatment Center will receive lower scores for depression after treatment than before treatment began. Was this hypothesis supported by your findings? Explain:

_____

_____

_____

_____

2. Can you say that practical significance was achieved? Explain:

_____

_____

_____

_____

3. To whom can the results of this study be safely generalized? Explain:

_____

_____

_____

_____

4. To whom can the results of this study be generalized on a more speculative basis? Explain:

_____

_____

_____

_____

5. What is one limitation of this study?

_____

_____

_____

_____

Glossary

Causation. The explanation of the reasons that events occur. In research, the concept of causation is treated cautiously because events typically have multiple causes and the pinpointing of causation is difficult.

Comparison Group Design. A research design in which a group of treated clients are measured before and after the intervention and their gains in functioning are compared to the before and after measurements of a group that did not receive treatment. This design is also known as the non-equivalent control group design.

Dependent Variable. The variable which is believed to depend upon or is caused by another variable, the other variable being known as the "independent variable."

Independent Variable. The variable which is believed to cause the dependent variable to be the way it is.

One-Group Pretest–Posttest Research Design. A research design in which study subjects are measured on the dependent variable before an intervention and after the intervention and the differences in these two measurements of the dependent variable are analyzed.

Pretest. A measurement of study subjects on the dependent variable before treatment begins.

Posttest. A measurement of study subjects on the dependent variable after treatment has been completed.

Reliability. The consistency of a means of measurement. If a scale is reliable, persons will respond to it in a consistent fashion at different points in time.

Research Design. The protocol whereby study subjects are measured on the dependent variable and interventions are administered in evaluative research.

Single-Subject Research Design. A research design in which the study subject is treated as a single subject and data are collected on the dependent variable repeatedly for this one subject. While the single-subject design is typically used with a single client, it can also be employed with a single organization or community or group providing that each is treated as a single unit for data analysis.

Treatment Objectives. A statement of the nature of the gain in functioning that is expected for the client of a treatment program. It is a statement of a measured amount of progress toward the accomplishment of broad human goals.

Treatment Period. A period of time during which the client is subjected to the intervention.

Validity. The extent to which a measurement device truly measures the thing it is supposed to measure. In other words, it refers to the accuracy of a means of measurement.

Chapter *5*

Understanding Exploratory Research:

An Examination of Stress among Social Work Students

In this chapter, you will continue your journey in the development of competence in the use of social work research. One of the previous chapters dealt with the relationship between gender, position, and salary. Each of these variables were easily quantified, one in regard to dollars and the others in regard to categories into which study subjects fell. The purpose of that study was explanatory in nature. The question was whether gender explained salary when position level was taken into consideration.

Sometimes the research question does not identify variables that can be easily quantified, and sometimes researchers address an issue about which comparatively little is currently known from the published literature. Sometimes, they need to use research methods to enhance their understanding of the complexities of a subject so that they can develop new theories about it. In other words, sometimes researchers need to conduct an exploratory study.

This is where qualitative methods of observation can be of assistance. Because its methods of measurement are more flexible than quantitative ones, qualitative observation provides a wider lens through which one might capture the essence of a subject. Thus, there is more opportunity to recognize relationships between variables that have not been noticed beforehand.

Qualitative observation is the focus of the present chapter. You will examine how qualitative methods can be employed in the examination of stress among social work students.

Objectives

In this chapter, you will develop the ability to:

1. Distinguish between qualitative and quantitative means of measurement when given examples of research;
2. Identify several circumstances in which qualitative measurement is more appropriate than quantitative measurement;
3. Identify the parts of the process of scientific inquiry that qualitative and quantitative research share;
4. Distinguish between three basic modes of gathering information in qualitative research;
5. Identify whether quantitative or qualitative measurement is more appropriate when given examples;
6. Identify a few of the basic principles of good research interviewing;
7. Interpret a body of knowledge about stress among social work students in relation to questions which would be more suitable for a qualitative study than a quantitative one;
8. Analyze basic strengths and weaknesses in qualitative research examples taken from a study of stress among social work students.

An Overview of Qualitative Research Methods

I have discussed qualitative and quantitative methods of inquiry in previous chapters. You have seen that quantitative methods place subjects into categories or give them numbers. Qualitative methods are more flexible, and require interpretation and generalization. Examples include open-ended questions on a questionnaire, interviews, or direct observation of the behavior of study subjects. In each kind of qualitative method, the researcher must interpret the meaning of what has been said or done by the study subject.

When you have completed the *quantitative* measurement of your study subjects, you will have either a category or a number to assign to each study subject for each study variable. Such was the case of the previous study of gender and salary. Each subject was either male or female, and each had a given dollar amount for the annual salary and each was in a category for position level.

When you have completed the *qualitative* measurement of your study subjects, you will have narrative reports of what you observed and you will have generalized from those observations. You might have recognized common themes that emerged from the statements of your subjects. You might have attempted to interpret behaviors in regard to their functions in the social context in which they took place.

In *The Handbook of Qualitative Research,* Denzin and Lincoln (1994) offer the following overview:

> *The word* qualitative *implies an emphasis upon processes and meanings that are not rigorously examined, or measured (if measured at all), in terms of quantity, amount, intensity, or frequency. Qualitative researchers stress the socially constructed nature of reality, the intimate relationship between the researcher and what is studied, and the situational constraints that shape inquiry. Such researchers stress the value-laden nature of inquiry. They seek answers to questions that stress how social experience is created and given meaning. In contrast, quantitative studies emphasize the measurement and analysis of causal relationships between variables, not processes. Inquiry is purported to be within a value-free framework (p. 4).*

The choice of a qualitative or quantitative means of observation (measurement) should be guided by the nature of the research question and the existing knowledge about it. There are circumstances which can be helpful in guiding this choice. For example, a qualitative method is more appropriate than a quantitative method to the extent that the following conditions exist:

1. You are seeking to develop theories or hypotheses rather than testing existing ones;
2. You are seeking an understanding of the subjective meaning of behaviors rather than their precise description;
3. The concepts of interest are not easily quantified;
4. There is relatively little that is known about the subject (theories or precise definitions of concepts) from the existing literature, or it has some important missing links.

While the above conditions promote the qualitative over the quantitative method of inquiry, there is no clearcut guide that would give you an exact answer to the question "Which method do I use in this situation?" Instead, you have to use such guidelines as the above to help you decide which method is appropriate for a particular study.

ASSIGNMENT 5–A

1. Which of the following are examples of qualitative research? (Check each that applies.)

___NO___   a. A sample of social workers is asked to identify the category of their chosen specialization in graduate school and the category of their current employment in order to analyze the question of whether social workers tend to be employed in the fields of their graduate school specialization.

_____ **b.** Adults who were adopted as older children are interviewed in order to gather information about the experience of being adopted.

_____ **c.** A team of researchers spent many hours observing homeless people in a large city in order to gain a better understanding of the process by which one becomes and remains homeless. This led to the identification of three major phases of homelessness.

_____ **d.** A study was conducted in order to examine the extent to which social workers in rural communities differed from their urban counterparts on their emphasis upon the use of informal helping networks in their work with their clients. Rurality was measured by the population of one's work county while use of networks was measured by a question which asked workers to check the category which best represented their level of emphasis.

2. Identify the category that each of the following statements fits into using the following guide:

QUAL   This statement fits qualitative methods.

QUAN   This statement fits quantitative methods.

BOTH   This statement fits both methods.

NEITHER   This statement fits neither method.

For example, if (A) fits qualitative methods but does not apply to quantitative methods, you would place the letters QUAL next to it. However, if it fits both methods, you would write BOTH next to it.

_____ **A.** Can be helpful in our understanding of social and psychological phenomena;

_____ **B.** Is usually more useful than the other method in the testing of a theory that has been well conceptualized in the literature;

_____ **C.** Is quite superior to the other method in the generation of knowledge that is useful to social work;

_____ **D.** Is usually more useful than the other method in generating information about a relatively unknown topic;

_____ **E.** Is appropriate for the generation of information with the purpose of demonstrating that a social work intervention is effective in meeting human need.

3. Indicate which of the following situations would be more appropriate for a qualitative study than a quantitative study:

_____ **A.** A researcher wants to gain insight into the coping patterns of low-income parents who have a child who is hospitalized with a serious health condition. The researcher learns that previous research has focused on middle-income families. The researcher was not able to locate any concrete instruments for measuring coping styles or approaches and was not able to locate any useful theories about the coping process for low-income families.

_____ **B.** A researcher wants to know if the level of depression for nursing home residents is lower at the completion of a four-week group therapy program than it was before treatment.

_____ **C.** A researcher wants to know if exercise reduces stress.

What Qualitative and Quantitative Approaches Have in Common

Now that you know some of the things that distinguish qualitative from quantitative research, you will now turn your attention to the commonalities shared by these two different approaches to measurement. First, both approaches are founded upon the spirit of scientific inquiry. This means that research has the purpose of discovery rather than justification. It also means that the methods of observation are designed to reduce human error in the pursuit of understanding.

Second, both methods are grounded in a knowledge base even though the specificity of that knowledge base may be vastly different from one study to another. It is, in fact, the state of present knowledge regarding a research subject that guides the determination of whether a qualitative or a quantitative method is more appropriate.

Third, the process is fundamentally the same in that the researcher begins with problem formulation and continues with the development of the research methodology and then to the collection of information and, finally, to the drawing of conclusions. This logical process reduces the chance of fundamental error in research, such as selecting a sample that is not appropriate for the pursuit of a research question.

Fourth, conclusions are drawn from the information gathered and analyzed rather than from preconceived ideas about the nature of the subject studied. This point is connected to the first one about the spirit of scientific inquiry. When researchers tackle the task of drawing conclusions, they must be attentive to their preconceived ideas and be sure not to let these ideas form their conclusions. They must be free to let the information guide their conclusions.

Modes of Gathering Information in Qualitative Research

The literature on qualitative research lists many ways to gather information. I have referred to modes of gathering information by the terms "means of observation" and "measurement" in my previous discussions. Modes of gathering information in qualitative research can now be classified in three main categories: *interviews; direct observation; indirect observation.*

With *interviews,* researchers are posing questions to study subjects in either a structured or unstructured format. Study subjects know they are being observed and that someone wishes to know something about their opinions or ideas or experiences. With *direct observation*, researchers are observing behaviors of the study subjects rather than asking them questions about their behaviors. This requires more interpretation on the part of the researcher. With *indirect observation*, researchers are examining records or artwork or literature, or other products which represent something about the subjects of the study.

The Interview in Qualitative Research

In this book, an *interview* is defined as a personal encounter between people in which one person (or persons) is seeking information from another person (or other people). It can take place face-to-face or by way of another mode of personal interaction such as the telephone. It is distinguished from the social survey in which researchers are asking respondents to answer questions by way of a written instrument such as a questionnaire.

By its very nature, the interview is purposive interaction. It goes beyond informal conversation. It suggests that different persons play different roles in the encounter. The main purpose of the encounter is for one or more people to obtain information from another person (or persons).

Researchers categorize different types of interviews according to structure. A highly structured interview is one in which there is a precise set of questions which are to be asked in a given sequence with some preestablished categories for response. The more structured the interview, the more that the method of observation may be categorized as quantitative rather than qualitative. In this chapter, you will focus on interviews that are qualitative in nature, which means that there is a minimum of openness in the structure in which study subjects can respond in their own words to the questions.

The extent of the *interview structure* is exemplified by the number and specificity of questions posed and the existence of preconstructed categories into which respondents may fall. It is determined by the specificity of the study question and the specificity of the study subject that is apparent from the knowledge base which undergirds the research question.

Fontana and Frey (1994) provide the following guidelines for the highly structured interview:

Never get involved in long explanations of the study; use standard explanations provided by supervisor;

Never deviate from the study introduction, sequence of questions, or question wording;

Never let another person interrupt the interview; do not let another person answer for the respondent or offer his or her opinions on the question;

Never suggest an answer or agree or disagree with an answer; do not give the respondent any idea of your personal views on the topic of the question or survey.

Never interpret the meaning of a question; just repeat the question and give instructions or clarifications that are provided in training or by supervisors;

Never improvise, such as by adding answer categories, or make wording changes (p. 364).

This level of structure may not be appropriate for the typical interview for a qualitative research study in social work because of the imprecise nature of the concepts under exploration in such studies. Yet, these guidelines provide assistance with gaining an understanding of the means used in qualitative research to reduce human error in observation. In particular, it is important that the interviewer not express opinions on the topic because of the likelihood that such expressions will influence the response of the study subject.

The Semi-Structured Interview

The *semi-structured interview* is one with predetermined questions with an open-ended format that are asked of all respondents in the same manner. Examples include the following:

What does stress mean to you?

How do you experience stress?

What are the three things you are most likely to do when you are under stress?

What do you find has been the best way to cope with stress?

Each of these questions would be asked of each respondent and would be asked in the same sequence.

With the semi-structured interview, you should follow several guides. First, *be aware of your own predispositions* about the subject under study. You should, of course, avoid revealing these predispositions to the person being interviewed. It is also important that you engage mechanisms to avoid allowing these predispositions to influence your observations. Reflect upon what kinds of responses support or refute your own predispositions and force yourself to pay attention to all that is said, not just those statements that are congruent with your own views.

A second recommendation is that you *engage the interviewee in the validation of your notes.* You might repeat what you have heard to the persons being interviewed and provide them with the opportunity to correct it or place it more appropriately in their own words if you have inaccurately reworded their thoughts. When recording statements from the interviewee, you should use the interviewee's words as much as possible. You can reexamine these words later and decide upon the broader concepts that may have been expressed. You might want to say something like "Are you saying that you are more likely to use exercise to relieve stress or relaxation techniques?" By presenting options, you relieve the interviewee of the temptation to agree with you even though there may be some reservations about how you are perceiving these thoughts.

A third recommendation is to *seek disconfirming evidence of your initial impressions.* If you believe that the person being interviewed is focusing the most attention upon spirituality as a means of relieving stress, you might want to count the times that this theme was mentioned and compare it to the times that other themes were mentioned. You might want to ask the interviewee to recount the number of times that spirituality was used in the last two weeks as compared to the number of times that something else was used.

A fourth recommendation is to *engage in note-taking methods that place minimal burden on your memory.* There is a lot of information that might be provided in an interview. Long-term memories can be mistaken. You might want to take notes in stages with the first stage being the interview and the second stage taking place immediately after the interview. During the interview, you will not be able to record every word spoken by the interviewee. Instead, you will want to quote things that seem to be especially poignant and take rather sketchy notes otherwise. The sketchy notes will contain words or phrases that represent certain responses by the interviewee. However, a few days later, you may not remember what these words mean. Therefore, you should undertake the second stage right after the interview. In this stage, the unwritten words are filled in so that you will be able to return to these notes at any later date and fully understand them.

The Phases of the Interview Process

After the questions have been determined and a prospective interview subject has been identified, there are several natural phases of the interview. First, you must introduce the purpose of the interview and yourself and seek permission for the interview. In this phase, it is important that the purpose of the interview be stated, but not any conclusions that might have been drawn from the literature about any aspect of the research question. In other words, you do not want to influence the interviewee's thinking about the questions under study. You also must introduce yourself and indicate how the information from the interview will be used, including assurances that the subjects' identities will not be revealed in any report on the interview.

In this first phase of the interview process, the researcher should be sensitive to gender or cultural differences between the interviewer and the interviewee which might influence the responses of the interviewee. How open and honest will this study subject be with this particular interviewer? Sometimes women will express themselves differently to another woman than to a man. The key outcome of this first phase of the interview process is the development of trust and rapport between the interviewer and the interviewee.

The next phase is the presentation of the questions and the recording of the information. You should ask the questions in the same way to each person you interview. You should consider beforehand how to define key terms so that you can use a uniform definition with your study subjects.

The third phase is the analysis of the results. You must make sense of your notes. You do this by looking for themes that are common between persons being interviewed. You need to be attentive to the different terms that can be used to express the same thought, and you should be clear on the level of generality of your conceptions of the subject. Are you looking only for rather broad themes, or more specific themes?

In the analysis of data in qualitative research, numbers often get ignored because they are associated with quantitative research. But numbers are an essential component of the qualitative analysis of information. Researchers count such things as the number of references to a given theme or the number of study subjects who mentioned a given theme.

Researchers count in qualitative research because they need to recognize themes in responses to their questions. See, for example the following hypothetical responses of social work students to a question about their needs as students:

1. "I need more support from my advisor when I make a request for an exception to the normal policies."
2. "I need help when I am failing a course."
3. "I want more electives."
4. "I often feel all alone and wonder how I can make it."
5. "My field instructor has been so supportive—I really appreciate that."

The common theme for statements (1), (4), and (5) is support. Thus, an investigator might say that there were three references to the theme of support by this respondent. They might characterize (2) and (4) as being related to the theme of survival. In this case, there is an overlap in categories for (4). It seems to be related to a fear of failure but also to a need for support. A researcher could clarify this by further analysis or consider the statement to fit into both categories.

ASSIGNMENT 5–B

1. What is one mode of gathering information besides the interview in qualitative research?

_____

_____

_____

_____

2. In an interview study, how might interviewers assure themselves that they have interpreted the respondents' answers correctly?

_____

_____

_____

_____

3. What is one thing you would do as an interviewer that would help to keep your own biases about the subject in check (i.e., prevent it from influencing the respondent)?

_____

_____

_____

_____

4. Which of the following situations would seem to require the *most* structure in the mode of gathering information?

   a. An examination of the process whereby people become homeless and remain that way as opposed to moving out of this condition;

   b. An examination of the feelings associated with the experience of being adopted as an older child;

   c. The identification of (a) how students define stress, (b) the most common techniques for coping with stress, and (c) the extent to which students have experienced each of four symptoms of burnout.

Respond to the remaining items by circling T for True or F for False.

5. T   F   The qualitative research study differs from the quantitative study in that the qualitative study does not begin with the examination of a knowledge base about the subject under study.

6. T   F   In the structured or semi-structured interview, the interviewer should not discuss with the interviewee any theories from the literature about the study subject.

7. T   F   The qualitative research study tends to be more likely than the quantitative study to place initial emphasis upon observation rather than theory, whereas the opposite can be said for the quantitative study.

8.   T   F   The process for both qualitative and quantitative research studies follows the same fundamental path of scientific inquiry which moves from problem formulation to study methodology to data collection (observation) to conclusions.

9.   T   F   Because of the qualitative nature of the semi-structured interview, there is no counting that takes place in such a study; counting is strictly for the quantitative type of study.

10.   T   F   The interviewer should freely express his or her opinions about the study subject to the interviewee because the latter may be curious about this and such a dialogue can help to build rapport between the two.

A Study of Stress among Social Work Students

With the literature review given in Exhibit 5.1 as a guide, a class of social work students, in groups of three, undertook a study of stress among their fellow students. The researchers in this study were students in a research class in the first year of the two-year curriculum in the graduate social work program of a university.

The problem formulation phase was directed by the literature review. From this review, each group of students selected research questions to be posed in a semi-structured interview of fellow students. The goal was to generate knowledge that could be used to develop hypotheses related to stress among social work students. In view of the fact that there were already sufficient grounds from the existing literature for the development of hypotheses about several variables related to stress, students were assigned the task of identifying at least one new variable which would be incorporated into the hypothesis that they would develop.

The study methodology phase of research entailed the selection of the sample and the means for measuring variables. Each student was assigned one classmate from the research class to interview, a classmate that was not in the student's own group of first-year graduate students. Each student was also assigned the responsibility to interview one second-year student. The second-year student was selected as a matter of convenience. Because students were organized into teams of three researchers, each team had a total of six interviews to use in the development of the hypothesis. Questions for the interview were developed by each team and were used with each of the six interviews.

Students were instructed in the principles of research interviewing, a task that social workers find rather easy, especially as compared to some of the tasks of quantitative research, which are more foreign by nature to social workers. Many of the principles articulated in the earlier part of this chapter were familiar to these students either intuitively or by past training.

Because they were interviewing fellow students, these interviewers did not have the normal problems with entry into the social systems of the respondents, an issue that can require a good deal of attention in some cases. They were quite familiar with the culture being studied in view of the fact that they were part of that culture. The issue of trust and rapport were not considered to require special attention.

EXHIBIT 5.1   A Literature Review on Stress

In contrast to some fields of business and industry which have often confronted a lack of job challenge as a barrier to work motivation, the human service field has encountered the opposite—the idea that too much challenge in the presence of meager resources can hamper work performance. The term *burnout,* which has been used prominently for about two decades (see, for example, Maslach, 1976, and Patrick, 1979), has emerged as the concept of greatest concern because it is viewed as having an immediate influence on work performance. Persons who are burned out on the job experience emotional exhaustion and lack the energy to perform optimally.

   The basic idea behind this line of thinking is that human service jobs contain stressful conditions (stressors), such as work overload, which lead to psychological symptoms that have come to be called "stress." Stress can lead to health problems such as insomnia, headaches, and an increase in vulnerability to colds and the flu. In the presence of long-term stress, some persons develop burnout. Burnout hampers work performance because it causes social workers to become cynical about their clients, to lack energy for meeting the daily demands of work, and to develop a desire to leave the job.

   Intervening in the relationship of stressors and stress, however, are certain stress buffers, the most prominently mentioned one being social support (Maguire, 1991). For example, some people with high work demands do not develop the symptoms of psychological stress because they have superior support systems.

   The basic model is depicted in Figure 5.1.

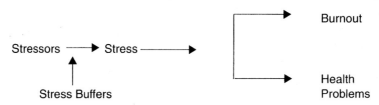

FIGURE 5.1   Stress Model

This theoretical model suggests that certain conditions (stressors) lead to certain feelings associated with psychological tension (stress). In other words, persons with a higher level of stressors in their lives will normally have a higher level of stress. But this will not always be the case. There will be exceptions to this rule, and that is why you would not expect to find a perfect empirical relationship between stressors and stress. A perfect relationship would mean that every single person with higher stressors than another will have higher stress than that other person. The more exceptions to this rule, the lower is the strength of the relationship between stressors and stress.

   Why would there be exceptions? One reason is that people are not all equal in regard to the stress buffers in their lives, such as social support. Perhaps if John has higher stressors than Jim but has lower stress, it is because John has more social support. Under these circumstances you would expect to find a negative relationship between support and stress, meaning that persons with high support would be likely to have lower stress than would those with low support. But if support serves as a

EXHIBIT 5.1   *Continued*

buffer between stressors and stress, you would probably find that the importance of support grows with increases in stressors. For example, if you studied only people with low levels of stressors, you would expect to find only a modest relationship between support and stress, because they would have little reason to have much stress. For them, support would have less influence. But for people with a high degree of stressors, you would expect to find a strong relationship between support and stress, meaning that those with high support would be much less likely to have high stress. Thus, you can see how stress buffers intervene in the relationship between stressors and stress.

This theoretical model also suggests that stress (psychological tension) leads to certain health symptoms. Health symptoms associated with stress include headaches, insomnia, and illnesses. Thus, you would expect to find that people with higher stress will be more likely than others to experience these symptoms. You also can see a line drawn between stress and burnout in Figure 5.1. This suggests that persons with high stress are more likely than others to experience burnout. You do not see a line drawn between stressors and burnout or between stressors and health symptoms. This is because it is theorized that stressors only lead to health symptoms or burnout if they lead to stress. For some persons, stress buffers will prevent the latter from happening.

Graduate school can be viewed as an environment in which students experience stressors which can lead to stress and burnout, but which can be lessened by the effects of stress buffers such as social support. While there is an extensive literature on stressors and stress and burnout for people in general, there is a rather limited body of knowledge on this topic for social work students. Perhaps this is a population for which more research is warranted. You encountered this topic in the first chapter when you had the opportunity to compare your stress score with those for a small sample of graduate social work students from one university and to examine the relationship between stress and health symptoms for this sample of students. Also included in that review were data on the relationship between exercise and stress. You are returning to this topic with further analysis. You have seen a theoretical model for the relationships among a set of variables related to stress, you will now examine some of the literature on these relationships. I will define stress in the next section. These paragraphs will be familiar to you because you encountered them in the first chapter. They are repeated here as a reminder. After this reminder, you will examine the causes and consequences of stress. This should provide you with the ability to identify the questions that are in most need of further analysis.

What Is Stress?

When researchers use the word *stress*, most people will have a general idea of what they are talking about, but definitions will vary. Most people will think of stress as an uncomfortable condition caused by demands that are made on their lives by work and family responsibilities. Feelings such as tense, up-tight, and anxious are often associated with the concept people label stress. Often, they recognize certain physical symptoms as being associated with stress, such as sleeplessness, headaches, and an increase

(Continued)

EXHIBIT 5.1   *Continued*

in minor illnesses such as colds and the flu. Some writers define stress as environmental conditions rather than psychological feelings (see, for example, Shinn, et. al., 1984).

For this study, stress is defined as a condition of psychological tension that is exemplified by such feelings and moods as apprehension, uneasiness, and nervousness and stands in opposition to such feelings and moods as cheerfulness, relaxation, and contentment. Thus, you are focusing on the psychological dimension of this concept rather than environmental conditions such as job demands, parental responsibilities, or life events such as divorce or the death of a close family member. These environmental conditions can influence stress as that term is defined here, but they are considered to be separate conceptually. You might refer to these conditions as stressors rather than stress.

Thus, stress is a condition of the individual rather than the environment. But the environment can cause stress to occur. For example, high caseloads of abused children to serve can cause social workers to be stressed. If most people with high caseloads are found to have high stress while most people with low caseloads are found to have low stress, you can say that there is a relationship between stress and caseloads. But everyone with high caseloads will not necessarily have high stress and everyone with low caseloads will not necessarily have low stress. There are other things that can potentially influence stress and can explain these exceptions to the rule.

Many studies of stress among social work students have measured stress by asking students to identify the extent to which certain conditions have led them to experience stress (see, for example, Munson, 1984). An example would be a question that asked respondents to indicate the extent to which their field supervisor caused them stress, or the extent to which their research course caused them stress. Thus, these researchers have chosen to measure stress as a perception of the individual's response to certain potential stressors. Fortune (1987), however, chose to measure stress as a psychological condition by asking students to respond to a stress scale which measured their present psychological condition. Instead of asking students to identify the things they believe caused them stress, Fortune measured stress directly as a psychological condition and then examined the relationship between this condition and certain variables thought to serve as stressors. This research is more consistent with the definition of terms used in the present literature review. It is exemplified by the instrument employed in Chapter 1 in which you were asked to indicate how often you felt tense, apprehensive, and so forth.

Researchers have to be careful to define their terms because many people define them differently, and they want others to understand what they mean when they say something like "Students who engaged in regular aerobic exercise were found to suffer from lower levels of stress than students who did not."

To What Extent Do Social Work Students Experience Stress?

In the first chapter, you examined a set of data on one group of graduate social work students, and you had the opportunity to compare yourself to that group. Table 1.1 in that chapter revealed these data. From this information, you can see that a score of 18 would be represented by a hypothetical student who consistently responded that they

EXHIBIT 5.1 *Continued*

experienced each of these stress feelings "some of the time" while a score of 36 would represent a consistent response of "often" for those terms from this list that represented the condition of stress. A response of "most of the time" to such items would result in a score of 54, the highest level of stress possible on this scale. The data in Table 1.1 from Chapter 1 revealed that about one-third of these students had stress scores at 27 or above and that students varied a good deal on their scores. Thus, while these data do not point to a profound problem for graduate social work students, it is easy to see that a good number of such students have a high enough score to cause concern.

This information is consistent with the data from studies conducted of social work students by Munson (1984) and by Kramer, Mathews, and Endias (1987). However, how one interprets the distribution of scores on such tests is subject to differences of opinion. For example, Munson found a pattern of mean scores at or slightly below the mid-point on his various scales, and he found that one-third or less of his respondents indicated physical symptoms of stress associated with various school factors. He interpreted these data as indicating that students experienced low levels of stress. While this may be a reasonable interpretation of the general pattern, one might also interpret these data as showing a cause for concern because as many as one in three students reported physical symptoms of stress.

What Causes Stress?

In the theoretical model you are using, stress is depicted as being caused by *stressors*. One of the pioneers in the study of stressors is Hans Selye (1980). Selye demonstrated the effect of stressors on health. Much of his work focused on traumatic life events such as the death of a spouse or losing a job. Selye found that stressors such as traumatic life events were associated with diminished health.

Munson (1984) found that first-year MSW students had slightly more stress than second-year students but Tait (1991) found the opposite. General demographic characteristics of students do not seem to be associated with stress. Koeske and Koeske (1989), for example, found no relationship between stress and such variables as age, marital status, and number of children. However, Tait (1991) found a nearly significant positive relationship between stress and the number of children below the age of six. Kramer, Mathews, and Endias (1987) found that part-time students had more stress than full-time ones while Koeske and Koeske (1989) found that full-time students with part-time jobs had more stress than employed part-time students.

One of the main stress complaints offered by social work students is that they face excessive demands upon their time (Kramer, Mathews & Endias, 1987). However, the demands of graduate school are rather uniform from one student to another; thus, the demands themselves do not serve as a useful variable in the study of stress. But how students combine these demands with other demands in their lives is potentially a subject of fruitful inquiry. Fortune (1987) used the students of one graduate school of social work to test the hypothesis that the number of roles occupied by students was negatively related to stress. The roles identified were marriage partner, parent, and employee. Thus, it was expected that the more roles one played, the higher one's stress. But the opposite was found. A negative correlation was found between number

(Continued)

EXHIBIT 5.1 *Continued*

of roles occupied and level of stress, meaning that those who occupied more roles had less stress. Potts (1992), however, found no relationship between number of roles occupied and psychological adjustment to the educational process, a concept somewhat different from stress as it is defined here.

Another finding from the Potts study may be quite instructive to this inquiry. This researcher found that full-time students with full-time jobs had lower psychological adjustment than others, but she failed to find any other correlates of psychological adjustment that were especially noteworthy. This finding would suggest that stress is a special problem only for those with excessive demands. Perhaps those with moderately low role demands do not differ in stress from those with very low demands or moderately high role demands. But perhaps those with very high role demands differ in stress from all those at lower levels of demand.

What Reduces Stress?

The concept of "stress buffer" refers to variables that might reduce the effects of stressors. The most prominently mentioned stress buffer is social support. Social support is often defined as comfort, assistance, and/or information one receives through formal or informal contacts with individuals or groups. When researchers talk of social support, they usually refer to sets of people with whom an individual has an enduring relationship who provide encouragement, caring, and guidance (Maguire, 1991).

Troits (1982) has identified several ways to classify social support. These are types of support, sources of support, and structures of support. Types of support include emotional support (esteem-building interactions) and instrumental support (aid with tangible tasks). Common sources of support are family, friends, and co-workers. The structure of support entails such variables as the size of the support network, the intensity of the relationships of giver and receiver, and the durability of the network, among others. With this classification, support would be measured by items which sought information on the number of close relationships one has, the intensity of those relationships, and how long they have lasted. The more relationships, the higher the score. The higher the intensity of the relationship, the higher the score. The longer the relationships have lasted, the higher the score.

Another approach to measurement of support is exemplified by the Provisions of Social Relations scale (see Corcoran and Fischer, 1987). On this scale, respondents are asked to indicate their perceptions of how much they can rely upon their family and friends when they are in need.

In the general literature, Cohen and Syme (1985) make the case that social support buffers the effects of stressors on stress and illness for the population at large. Lechner (1993) found that support reduced stress for caregivers of dependent parents.

But what about social work students? Is it logical to think that support would reduce stress for them as well? Tait (1991) failed to find a significant correlation between social support and stress for one sample of graduate social work students. But such a relationship was found between support and stress in a study of social work students by Koeske and Koeske (1989). The difference in the methodologies between these studies is quite instructive for an analysis of support as a stress buffer. Tait found that, in general, students with higher support did not have lower stress.

EXHIBIT 5.1   *Continued*

Koeske and Koeske undertook a separate analysis of the relationship between support and stress for students with higher levels of stressors. In their study, full-time students with part-time jobs were compared to part-time students with full-time jobs and with full-time students with no jobs. Among full-time students with part-time jobs, the stress score for those with high support was significantly lower than for those with low support. This relationship between support and stress, however, was not found for the other two groups of students. Thus, it appears that support makes a difference only for those with higher levels of stressors in their lives.

Another potential stress buffer is locus of control. Locus of control refers to whether people perceive actions as being determined by external forces over which they have little control, or internal forces over which they have extensive control. People with an internal locus of control perceive that personal events and their consequences depend on their own actions, while those with an external locus of control perceive that such events are dependent upon external factors such as chance or fate. In her study of graduate social work students, Fortune (1987) found that locus of control had a stronger relationship with stress than did such variables as marital status, employment, age, parenthood, years of social work experience, or total number of roles occupied. She found that students with an internal locus of control had lower stress than did those with an external locus of control.

In the first chapter, you saw data which indicated that those students who engaged in regular aerobic exercise had lower stress than those who did not. Perhaps some students alleviate stress through exercise.

One of the limitations in the study of stress buffers is that the relationships between stress and other variables tend to be rather low even when they are found to be statistically significant. Fortune (1987), for example, found that the cumulative effect of locus of control and several other variables on stress was rather modest. In her multivariate analysis, she found that the total amount of variance in student stress that was explained by locus of control and several other variables was only 24 percent, meaning that 76 percent of the variance was left unexplained. This means that one needs to look further to find a fuller explanation of what causes stress.

What Are the Consequences of Stress?

Two main consequences of stress have been identified in the model being used in this book: health problems and burnout. Burnout is a condition which results from prolonged or intense stress and is characterized by emotional exhaustion, cynicism about the clients and the nature of the work being performed, and a desire to terminate employment. These conditions logically can be considered to have a negative effect on work performance (See Maslach and Jackson, 1981).

The work of Maslach is among the most definitive of those in the field of burnout (See, for example, Maslach, 1976, and Maslach and Jackson, 1981). Among the indicators of burnout identified by Maslach and others are emotional exhaustion, cynicism, and a sense of failure. Emotional exhaustion refers to the tendency to feel overwhelmed by demands and emotionally depleted and physically exhausted from the work day. Cynicism is reflected in the depersonalization of clients. Feelings of failure

(Continued)

EXHIBIT 5.1   *Continued*

are also manifestations of burnout, according to these writers. In the human services, professionals often work with difficult clients and with minimal resources, which leads to few indicators of success in their work. Of these three dimensions of burnout, emotional exhaustion was the only one that emerged as clearly a reliable and valid dimension of burnout according to a study by Wallace and Brinkerhoff (1991). In their study of burnout, they identified several potential correlates of burnout, which, of course, would identify what others call stressors. Some of these were role conflict, role ambiguity, work autonomy, and workload.

Health problems such as insomnia, headaches, and minor illnesses have been used by some as direct measures of the concept of stress. But in this model, stress is conceived as a psychological condition rather than a physical one, even though the psychological condition may lead to physical symptoms. These symptoms are viewed as the consequence of stress rather than as a manifestation of it.

Summary

From the literature, a visual model of the relationships among the variables of stressors, stress buffers, stress, and burnout emerged. Among the potential stressors identified were traumatic life events in the recent past, multiple role demands, and place in the educational program (e.g., first-year versus second-year students). Little research appears to have been published on life events as a stressor among social work students. Some of the events found to have had the most effect upon the general population include death of a spouse, divorce, death of a close family member, loss of a job, and so forth. Do such events serve as a stressor for social work students?

The picture from the literature regarding multiple role demands is mixed. Some research suggests that more roles are better. If so, why would this be the case? Some research suggests that heavier demands lead to more stress. How can this picture be clarified?

Support has mixed reviews as a stress buffer. There is certainly a popular belief that support alleviates stress. Why has the empirical research been mixed in support of this idea? Does support only make a difference for those with the higher levels of stressors as suggested by one set of study results?

Locus of control is another candidate for the alleviation of stress. One study found that persons with an internal locus of control had less stress. Why might this be the case? Is it possible to obtain more insight into this relationship from further research?

What are other stress buffers? Surely, there are many more that have not yet been published. If we find many more, can we eventually be in a better position to more fully explain stress in the face of stressors?

References

Cohen, S., & Syme, S. L. (1985). *Social support and health.* New York: Academic Press.

Corcoran, K., and Fischer, J. (1987). *Measures for clinical practice: A sourcebook.* New York: The Free Press.

Fortune, A. E. (1987). Multiple roles, stress and well-being among MSW students. *Journal of Social Work Education, 23* (3), 81–90.

EXHIBIT 5.1 *Continued*

Koeske, R. D., and Koeske, G. F. (1989). Working and nonworking students: Roles, support, and well-being. *Journal of Social Work Education,* 25 (3), 244–256.

Kramer, H., Mathews, G., and Endias, R. (1987). Comparative stress levels in part-time and full-time social work programs. *Journal of Social Work Education,* 23 (3), 74–80.

Lechner, V. M. (1993). Support systems and stress reduction among workers caring for dependent parents. *Social Work,* 38 (4), 461–469.

Maguire, L. (1991). *Social Support Systems in Practice.* Silver Springs, MD: NASW Press.

Maslach, C. (1976). Burned out. *Human Behavior,* 5, 99–113.

Maslach, C., & Jackson, S. E. (1981). The measurement of experienced burnout. *Journal of Occupational Behavior,* 2, 99–113.

Munson, C. E. (1984). Stress among graduate social work students: An empirical study. *Journal of Education for Social Work,* 20 (3), 20–29.

Patrick, P. K. S. (1979). Burnout: Job hazard for health workers. *Hospitals,* November, 87–89.

Potts, M. K. (1992). Adjustment of graduate students to the educational process: Effects of part-time enrollment and extracurricular roles. *Journal of Social Work Education,* 28 (1), 61–76.

Selye, H. (1980). *Selye's guide to stress research.* New York: Van Nostrand Reinhold.

Shinn, M., Rosario, M., Morch, H., and Chestnut, D. E. (1984). Coping with stress and burnout in the human services. *Journal of Personality and Social Psychology,* 40, 864–976.

Tait, D. (1991). Effects of social support on stress for MSW students: An empirical examination. Professional Paper submitted in partial fulfillment of the requirements of the degree, Master of Social Work, to the faculty of East Carolina University.

Troits, P. (1982). Conceptual, methodological, and theoretical problems in studying social support as a buffer against life stress. *Journal of Health and Social Behavior,* 23, 145–159.

Wallace, J. E., and Brinkerhoff, M. B. (1991). The measurement of burnout revisited. *Journal of Social Services Research,* 14 (1/2), 85–111.

ASSIGNMENT 5–C

1. For the purposes of this study, you have defined stress as:

   a. Excessive demands of the environment upon the individual

   b. Emotional exhaustion

   c. Feelings associated with psychological tension

   d. All of the above

2. Given the above definition, identify one item for a questionnaire that would measure stress.

_____

_____

_____

3. Stressors are defined as:

_____

_____

_____

4. Indicate whether each of the following statements are true or false.

_____   **a.** Burnout causes stress.

_____   **b.** Stress buffers reduce the impact of stressors on stress.

_____   **c.** The relationship between stressors and stress has been well explained by the research reported in the literature review, so that, for example, researchers know a good deal about the things that cause social work students to experience stress.

_____   **d.** One of the potential consequences of stress is an increase in such physical symptoms as headaches and insomnia.

_____   **e.** An appropriate way to measure stress, given the definition of this concept, would be to ask students to indicate if they have had an increase in headaches or insomnia in recent weeks.

_____   **f.** According to the conceptual model, people with high stressors develop health symptoms and burnout in part because they react to stressors by acquiring stress.

_____   **g.** According to the conceptual model, one of the explanations for why two people with similar levels of stressors would have different levels of stress is that one of them may have higher social support.

_____   **h.** The literature suggests that the typical social work student suffers from high levels of stress.

_____   **i.** Among the main causes of stress for social work students are such demographic variables as age, gender, and marital status.

_____   **j.** I would expect to find that social work students with an internal locus of control would have lower stress than those with an external locus of control, and that this would be especially true for those students experiencing the higher levels of stressors in their lives.

5. For each pair of situations below, select the one that better lends itself to the qualitative method of measurement than the quantitative one.

Pair 1

   a. What are the things that social work students view as most stressful?

   b. Does being employed affect stress levels for full-time social work students?

Comments:

_____

_____

_____

Pair 2

   a. What are the ways that social work students cope with stress?

   b. To what extent do social work students experience stress?

   Comments:

   _____

   _____

   _____

Pair 3

   a. What are the stages of stress and burnout for social work students (In other words, how does it begin and how does it progress from one stage of severity to another?)

   b. Is there a relationship between social support and stress for social work students?

   Comments:

   _____

   _____

   _____

Study Results and Conclusions

The results for the present study entailed the summary of findings from the interviews while the conclusions phase identifies the hypotheses generated from these interviews. These two sections are combined for this report because there were several teams of researchers who formed different questions and identified different hypotheses, and their reports will be done separately from one another.

   Team A developed the following questions for the interviews:

   1. How do you know you are stressed?
   2. What do you think causes stress in your life?

3. How do you deal with stress?
4. What would be your definition of burnout?

The summary of the interviews for this team from one student's paper is presented in Exhibit 5.2.

Another group was Team B. A summary from one student's paper from this group is presented in Exhibit 5.3. The final assignment will ask you to reflect upon these summaries in this first major lesson in the use of qualitative research methods.

EXHIBIT 5.2   An Excerpt from One Student's Summary from Team A*

The results of our interviews led us to a better understanding of how students perceived these variables and allowed us to choose the recurring concept of social structure, which became the variable under study in the present research. Under the category of stress, the interviews revealed two main categories. The first category was somatic complaints (change in sleep habits, colds, headaches), and the second category fell under psychological tension, which dealt with relationships with others. Three of the five subjects questioned mentioned having these somatic complaints, and two subjects mentioned they recognized stress in their relationships with friends and family.

There were basically three major categories of stressors. These were school, family, and personal life. All subjects questioned spoke of how school was a stressor in their lives. Four out of the five questioned mentioned their family and personal life as possible stressors. Several common stress buffers were identified in the interviews. These included time alone, talking to friends, proper diet and exercise, music/spiritual, and alcohol. Each subject questioned mentioned at some time in the interview the importance of interacting with friends and/or family when they were experiencing stress. Burnout was identified mostly as a state way beyond the normal stress level.

From these common themes, it was decided that the relationship between the experienced psychological tension (stress), and the common stress buffer of family and friends would be explored. Since all the subjects questioned mentioned the importance of this variable, referred to as social structure in the present research, it was believed there would be a strong relationship between the variables of stress and social structure.

Social structure is defined as the frequency, duration, and proximity to friends, family, and others that are important to the individual. Stress is defined as psychological tension. It entails an emotional reaction to environmental conditions.

The hypothesis that emerged from these interviews is as follows:

Social work students with greater social structure will report significantly lower levels of psychological tension than those with less social structure.

*David Bunting, Social structure of graduate MSW students correlated with psychological tension, unpublished paper prepared as a requirement for a research course, School of Social Work, East Carolina University, 1994. Used with permission.

EXHIBIT 5.3   Excerpts from One Student's Summary from Team B*

To explore possible variables that act as either a stressor or a stress buffer, each group member conducted two interviews. The following questions were asked by the four interviewers in Team A:

1. How did entering graduate school affect you?

2. Have you found graduate school stressful?
   If Yes, go to questions 3 and 4.
   If No, go to question 5.

3. What do you think is the cause of the stress?

4. Have you alleviated the stress? If so, how?

5. What have you done to avoid stress?

6. Were there any life changes that have affected you?

7. Have you thought of dropping out of graduate school?

8. How do you define stress?

Entering graduate school affected individuals in a variety of ways. Different individuals were anxious, excited, filled with self-doubt, intimidated, and scared. One interviewee said that her "stress level cranked up high fast because I didn't know what to expect." Only one interviewee did not find graduate school stressful. She said she avoided stress by organizing her time and only taking three classes. The remaining seven interviewees all found graduate school stressful. The causes of stress as perceived by these individuals included having to complete the self-analysis papers, constantly changing roles between a student in school and a professional in the field, lack of time, children, full-time job, unknown expectations, and loss of emotional support of friends and family upon moving to [the town where the graduate school was located].

Stress was alleviated through exercise, spiritual beliefs, seeing a therapist, being active in church, doing self-hypnosis and visualization, obsessively completing assignments, sleeping, visiting family and friends, and crying. Six of the eight interviewees had life changes that affected them during the year. Three individuals lost close relatives. Another individual broke up with her boyfriend and had two family pets die. Another individual found out that her father was not her real father, and the final interviewee was in an accident and totaled her car.

All but one interviewee had thought about dropping out of school at least occasionally. Most of the individuals had only fleeting thoughts about dropping out of school while one interviewee thought about it at least once a week. The eight graduate students defined stress in various ways. Stress was defined by symptoms such as claustrophobia, irritability, inability to concentrate, headaches, negative attitude, increased body tension, heightened state of fear, increased heartbeat, and other physical symptoms.

Two of the people interviewed credited church attendance and spiritual beliefs as helping to alleviate stress, while another interviewee credited self-hypnosis as alleviating

(Continued)

EXHIBIT 5.3 *Continued*

stress. In a group discussion, the question was raised as to whether spiritual activities in general served as a stress buffer. The four members of Team A all agreed that spiritual activities had helped them relieve stress. The group sought to create a list of spiritual activities that represented both eastern and western thought. The list of spiritual activities decided upon by the group included prayer, meditation, yoga, relaxation techniques, self-hypnosis, communing with nature, and attending religious services and functions.

Little research was found in regard to the relationship between spirituality or spiritual activities and stress. Pollner (1989) found that symbolic relations with a divine other are a significant correlate of well-being. Ellis and Smith (1991) stated that religious beliefs often gave suicidal individuals meaning to life and hope for the future, therefore preventing them from committing suicide. Maton (1989) also stated that perceived spiritual support may provide individuals with hope and acceptance, thus enhancing the well-being of individuals facing stress. These same benefits may assist in lowering stress and preventing burnout in social work graduate students.

The group decided to treat the perception of the importance of spiritual activities as a single variable and not treat each activity as a separate variable because the number of respondents who participated in each individual activity may be too small to achieve practical or statistical significance. The following hypothesis will be tested:

MSW students who perceive spiritual activities as very important will receive a lower score on the Stress Scale than MSW students who do not.

The dependent variable, level of stress, is defined as a subjective experience which involves feelings associated with psychological tension such as anxiety and apprehension. Stress was measured using the Stress Scale which is a modified version of the Stress–Arousal Checklist.

The independent variable is the perceived importance of participating in spiritual activities. Spiritual activities are defined as activities pertaining to the growth and maintenance of the mind and soul as distinguished from bodily or material existence. The spiritual activities identified by the researchers include prayer, self-hypnosis, meditation, attending religious services/functions, yoga, communing with nature, and relaxation techniques.

References

Ellis, J. B., & Smith, P. C. (1991). Spiritual well-being, social desirability and reasons for living: Is there a connection? *International Journal of Social Psychiatry, 37,* 57–63.

Maton, K. I. (1989). Community settings as buffers of life stress? Highly supportive churches, mutual help groups and senior centers. *American Journal of Community Psychology, 17,* 203–232.

Pollner, N. (1989). Divine relations, social relations, and well-being. *Journal of Health and Social Behavior, 30,* 92–104.

*Jeannie H. Kerr, Perceived importance of spiritual activities: The study of the relationship of stressors, stress buffers, stress, and burnout among graduate social work students. Unpublished paper submitted as a requirement for a research course, School of Social Work, East Carolina University, 1994. Used with permission.

ASSIGNMENT 5–D

1. What do you think of the questions that Team A chose to give to the respondents? Do you have any suggestions?

2. Was the hypothesis justified by the summary of the interviews for Team A?

3. Do you believe that any other hypotheses were justified by this summary of the interviews from Team A? If so, what?

4. Was the hypothesis for Team B justified by the summary of the interviews?

5. Do you believe that another hypothesis was better supported by the summary of the interviews than the one mentioned? If so, what was it?

References

Denzin, N. K., & Lincoln, Y. S. (1994). *The handbook of qualitative research.* Thousand Oaks: Sage Publications.

Fontana, A., & Frey, J. H. (1994). Interviewing: The art of science. In Denzin, N. K., & Lincoln, Y. S., *The handbook of qualitative research.* Thousand Oaks: Sage Publications, 361–376.

Glossary

Direct observation. A means of observation in qualitative research in which the researcher is directly observing the behavior of the study subjects.

Disconfirming evidence. Evidence which is counter to a given explanation of things.

Indirect observation. A means of observation (measurement) in qualitative research in which the researcher is examining products of behavior such as records or literature as a basis for developing theories or explanations about behavior.

Predispositions. One's preconceived notions of reality. The explanations about a study subject that researchers take into their study process and which should be open to alteration by the results of their study.

Interview. A personal encounter between people in which one person is seeking information from another. It can take place face-to-face or by way of another mode of personal interaction, such as the telephone.

Interview structure. The extent to which questions for study in an interview have been narrowed or specifically focused. The more specific the focus, the more the interview is structured. The extent to which questions in an interview are open-ended. More open interview questions have less structure.

Using Social Work Research

In this section of the book, you will experience the second level of learning of social work research. You will re-visit each of the four major purposes of social work research with new examples and more advanced concepts. At the completion of Chapters 6 through 9, you will be able to critically review published articles which report social work research. You will test this competence through the review of three articles in Chapter 10. This experience should lay the groundwork for your entry into the next major level of learning in which you become a researcher yourself. A limited experience with this level will be provided in Chapter 11, but advancement into the stage of being an independent researcher will be left primarily for your next course in social work research.

Chapter 6

Using Descriptive Research:

An Examination of the Social Work Program of the Neonatal Intensive Care Unit of Memorial Hospital

Section I of this book was focused on the goal of understanding social work research. In this endeavor, you examined study examples in the categories of descriptive, explanatory, evaluative, and exploratory research. This section has the broad goal of helping you to use social work research. The format is the same as that of Section I. You will examine studies that use each of the four types of research. The difference is that each chapter will take you another step in your journey of achieving competence in the critical analysis of existing research.

This chapter focuses upon descriptive research. You will examine data taken from a neonatal intensive care unit of a hospital. The data is real, but the name of the hospital has been changed. As with the previous chapters, you will examine the four main phases of the research process. At the completion of this chapter, you should be able to review published research of a descriptive nature and make sense of it.

Objectives

Some of the specific objectives emphasized in this chapter include:

1. The uses of descriptive research, especially the description of agency clientele;
2. The special importance of the precise definition of study variables in descriptive research;
3. Levels of measurement;

4. The interpretation of descriptive statistics such as frequencies, proportions, mean, median, mode, and standard deviation;

5. Methods of presentation of descriptive data.

Special Issues in Using Descriptive Research

The research process begins with the formulation of the problem which leads to the articulation of the research question. From this analysis flows the logical methodology that should be employed in the pursuit of the research question. Data are collected and analyzed, and conclusions are reached regarding the research question. Sound familiar? It should by now, because this is the process described in previous chapters.

In this first section of the present chapter, you will examine issues that are especially important to descriptive research. You will see that a knowledge base guides descriptive research as it does other forms of scientific inquiry. This knowledge base helps researchers to better understand the nature of the thing they are describing so that they will be in a better position to describe it in meaningful terms. You will see that precision in the definition of variables is perhaps more important in descriptive research than other types of research, in view of the goal of describing a phenomenon with precision. You will practice using the statistics that are especially useful in descriptive research. And, finally, you will find out that statistical significance takes a back seat to practical significance when it comes to descriptive research.

Problem Formulation in Descriptive Research

The knowledge base for a descriptive study is concerned less with theory than with various conceptualizations of the phenomenon under study. The basic purpose of descriptive research is to describe a set of phenomena with precision. It does not seek to explain. Explanation is the purview of theory, and is more relevant to explanatory research.

If researchers are to describe something in a useful manner, they must know the dimensions that are important. For example, the study of the nature of the clientele of the neonatal intensive care unit will reveal that the concept of "gestational age" is more important than the concept of "father's occupation." Thus, you will know that it is more important to identify the former than the latter with the clients.

The knowledge base can aid in the articulation of specific questions to be answered in a descriptive study. While it may seem only to be common sense that you would articulate your questions before you determine precisely what data will be collected, you may be surprised at the extent to which professionals, when undertaking a descriptive study of their clients, start by identifying specific items to be placed on a questionnaire without a previous analysis of the information that is needed and how it will be put to use.

Because you intend to describe something with precision, you must address the task of concept definition in the knowledge base for a descriptive study. Much of what will be examined in the example presented in this chapter deals with data that is highly concrete and not subject to various definitions. But what if you wanted to describe social work students in regard to political conservatism. In that case, you would be dealing with a thorny issue from the standpoint of concept definition. What does *conservatism* mean? How is it manifested?

Definition is so critical because researchers want to be in a position to identify the proportion of such students who would logically be classified as "conservative." Given two different definitions of what this term means, they might find vastly different estimates of the phenomenon. According to one person's definition, they might find that only 10 percent of social work students are conservative. But a different definition could yield a result suggesting that a majority of such students are conservative. Thus, it is important that the researcher clearly articulate such definitions in the methodology so that the reader can make sense of the statistics that will be presented.

Research Methodology in Descriptive Research

The concept of research design was discussed in Chapter 4, in the context of evaluative research. This concept is much more relevant to evaluative research than descriptive inquiry. When researchers simply describe something, they are not introducing an intervention and trying to determine its effect. For this reason, research design will not be considered any further in this chapter.

The sampling concepts discussed previously are relevant to descriptive research, but they will not be expanded on in the present chapter. This will come later. Instead, you should be reminded that you cannot safely generalize the findings from a sample to a population unless you have a probability sample (e.g., one drawn on a random basis). In the present example of the clientele of the neonatal intensive care unit, you will only be interested in describing the population of clients currently served. In view of the fact that you have data on all such clients, you have little need to deal with the concept of sampling.

The definition and measurement of variables is especially important in descriptive studies. When researchers use agency records to describe clients, they have already completed this task. Already defined for them are such concepts as gestational age, method used to pay hospital bills, and adjustment reaction as a presenting problem for referral to social work services. This definition process took place when decisions were made about what data to collect on a regular basis. If they were conducting a mailed survey of the clients as a means of collecting data, they would have a major task on their hands.

Data Analysis in Descriptive Research

The two topics of special note in the analysis of data for descriptive studies that will be covered here are (1) levels of measurement, and (2) descriptive statistics.

Levels of Measurement.   As you determine what data to collect, you should be cognizant of three major *levels of measurement* because this phenomenon is relevant to the statistical analysis of your results. The lowest level of measurement is the *nominal* level. Nominal variables are those which only categorize responses but do not order them in any way that has numerical meaning. For example, the categories of male and female make up the variable of gender. Political party affiliation might be divided into the categories of Democrat, Republican, and other. These categories are not ordered. Democrat is neither higher nor lower than Republican. Male is neither higher nor lower than female. In each case, you are merely placing people into categories that distinguish their difference.

The second level of measurement is the *ordinal* level. At the ordinal level, variables are measured in categories that have a particular order so that you can rank them from low to high or most to least, and so forth. An example of a variable measured at the ordinal level is as follows:

Please indicate the extent to which you agree or disagree with the following statement: In the long run, people get the respect they deserve in this world.

Strongly Agree	*Agree*	*Undecided*	*Disagree*	*Strongly Disagree*

In this example, "strongly agree" is considered to be higher than "agree" which, in turn, is higher than "undecided" and so forth. However, the distance between each of these categories is not the same. For example, the distance between "strongly agree" and "agree" is not necessarily the same as the distance between "agree" and "undecided."

The issue of equality of intervals between categories on a scale is an important distinction between the ordinal level of measurement and the *interval* level. With variables measured at the interval level, the distance between categories is the same. An example would be the degrees on a thermometer. Another would be the score on the final exam for a course. A score of 78 on an exam is 1 point higher than 77 which is 1 point higher than 76; thus, the intervals are equal. The same is true for the variable of age. A person who is 25 years of age is 1 year older than someone who is 24 who, in turn, is 1 year older than someone who is 23. Interval variables typically have a much broader range of values than variables measured at the ordinal level.

The highest level of measurement is *ratio*. With ratio variables, there is what is termed a "fixed zero point." This concept is best understood if you simply remember that such a variable cannot have a negative value. There can be a negative temperature such as minus 5 degrees, but a negative height is impossible. A person cannot be minus 5 feet tall.

Distinctions between the first three levels are more important in social statistics than the distinction of the ratio level because most statistics that are suitable for ratio variables are also suitable for interval variables.

These four levels of measurement form a hierarchy, such that variables measured at a higher level can be treated as though they were measured at a lower level if necessary. Various measures of social statistics require that the variables be treated at a certain level. Thus, it is important to know just where your variables fall on this hierarchy. A ratio variable can be treated as though it is measured at any level. An internal variable can be treated as either ordinal or nominal. An ordinal variable can be treated as nominal.

However, a nominal variable cannot be treated as either ordinal or interval. Take, for example, the ridiculous idea of computing the mean political party affiliation by assigning a value of 1 to Democrat, a 2 to Republican, and 3 to Other. This would make no sense. Likewise, think of the idea of computing the mean gender of a population by assigning the value of 0 to male, 1 to female, and 2 to unknown. By this act, you would be asserting that females have twice as much gender as males and that persons whose gender is unknown have three times as much gender as males.

You normally want to measure your variables at the highest level that is feasible because the types of statistical analyses that you can do at the higher levels provide more information. Do not, for example, reduce an interval variable such as age to the ordinal level by having people respond to the age question by reference to ordered categories such as 20–29 and 30–39 and so forth. When you do this, you lose the information gained by knowing all the differences in age by year. With only categories for age, you cannot compute the mean age of a sample of study subjects.

You should measure your variables, however, at the level that is natural. For example, think of the concept of "monogamy." Can this be considered an ordinal or interval variable? No! Much like you cannot be "a little bit" pregnant, you cannot be somewhat monogamous. You are either monogamous or you are not. There are only two categories inherent in the concept.

Descriptive Statistics for Nominal Variables.   Because the nominal level of measurement is the lowest level in the hierarchy, all the statistical measures suitable for this level are suitable for higher levels as well (i.e., ordinal, interval, and ratio). Thus, all of the following statistical measures are suitable for all levels of measurement. These include the frequency, the proportion, the cumulative frequency, the cumulative proportion, and the mode.

A *frequency* is simply the incidence of something. If there are 28 cases in which the method of payment is Medicaid, you can say that the frequency of families paying by this method is 28.

A *cumulative frequency* is a frequency that includes all those in the present category plus all others that fall before it in the classification scheme. See, for example, the following data on the number of siblings of our clients:

Number of Siblings	Frequency	Cumulative Frequency
0	18	18
1	11	29
2	7	36
3	3	39
4	3	42
5	0	42
6	3	45

From these data, you can see that the cumulative frequency for 3 or fewer siblings is 39 clients.

A *proportion* is the fraction or the percentage of a total that is represented by one group. If 10 of the 45 patients in this study are found to be living in one-parent households, you would say that the proportion of patients from one-parent families is 22.2 percent (10 / 45 = 0.222 × 100 = 22.2).

A *cumulative proportion,* or cumulative percent, is the proportion that falls in the present category plus the proportion of those that fall beneath the present category in the classification scheme. If the cumulative frequency of patients with 3 or more siblings is 9 and the total in the sample is 45, you could say that the proportion of those with 3 or more siblings is 20 percent (9 / 45 = 0.20 × 100 = 20).

The *mode* is the greatest incidence of occurrence in an array of data. If there are 18 patients with no siblings, 11 with one sibling, 7 with 2 siblings, 3 with 3 siblings, 3 with 4 siblings, and 3 with 6 siblings, you would say that the mode number of siblings was 0 because more patients had 0 siblings than any other number of siblings.

Descriptive Statistics for Ordinal and Interval Variables.   In addition to the above, variables measured at the ordinal level can be analyzed with the median. The *median* is the midpoint in an array of data. To determine the median, you would line up each incidence of data and identify the figure that fell at the midpoint of that line. For example, consider the following ages for nine people: 23, 23, 24, 27, 27, 36, 44, 44, 59. The median age for this array of data is 27. The median is appropriate for variables measured at either the ordinal, interval, or ratio levels.

For variables measured at the interval level, descriptive statistics include, in addition to the above, the mean and the standard deviation. The *mean* is the arithmetic average for an array of data. The average of the array of data with the numbers 10, 20, and 30 would be 20 (10 + 20 + 30 = 60 / 3 = 20). The mean is suitable for variables measured at the interval or ratio levels.

The *standard deviation* reveals the extent to which the numbers in an array of data vary from one another, or how much *variance* the data contain. For example, there is more of a spread of ages in Example B than Example A below.

Example A	Example B
23	24
22	38
25	19
26	44
22	16

Thus, the standard deviation for Example B would be greater than the standard deviation for Example A. Knowing the standard deviation for an array of data helps researchers to understand just how similar a group of people are on a given variable. The mean can be better utilized if they also know the standard deviation.

For example, if the mean age for all persons who are having a baby is 24 and the mean age for persons who are having a premature baby is 22, you might think that you are dealing with younger parents when you deal with prematurity. But what if you found that the standard deviation for all persons having a baby was 4.5 while the standard deviation for persons having premature babies was 8.9? This new information would help you to understand that you are dealing with a much greater spread of ages for those with premature babies. Thus, to concentrate only on young parents would be a mistake. The large standard deviation would indicate that there was a good proportion of older parents with premature babies as well as rather young parents.

The *average deviation* is a rough approximation of the standard deviation, but it is not calculated the same way as the standard deviation. However, it is easier to understand, and it tells us essentially the same thing. The average deviation is the average amount that scores in a set of data deviate from the mean of that set of data. Consider, for example, the following data on ages of 6 of our clients' mothers:

Step 1: Computing the Mean

16 + 16 + 17 + 17 + 18 + 18 = 102

102 / 6 = 17 (Mean age of the 6 mothers)

Step 2: Computing the Sum of the Deviations from the Mean

Age of Each Mother		Mean Age of All Mothers		Deviation
16	−	17	=	1
16	−	17	=	1
17	−	17	=	0
17	−	17	=	0
18	−	17	=	1
18	−	17	=	1
				4 (sum of deviations)

Step 3: Computing the Average Deviation

4 (sum of deviations) / 6 (number in sample) = 0.66 (average deviation)

The average deviation is 0.66. This is calculated by subtracting each score from the mean, summing those figures, and dividing by the number in the sample.

ASSIGNMENT 6–A

Indicate whether each of the following statements is TRUE or FALSE by placing the letter T or F next to each statement.

_____ 1. In descriptive research, the precise definition of variables is somewhat more important than in some of the other types of research.

_____ 2. The process of descriptive research begins with the development of the instrument to collect the data that is relevant.

_____ 3. In a descriptive study of the clients of the Hampstead Family Service Agency, one of the most important variables would be clients.

_____ 4. If you selected twenty-five homeless people who sought the services of the Elmhurst Homeless Shelter on a given day as a group from whom data would be collected on health conditions of the homeless in the town of Elmhurst, the twenty-five persons selected would constitute your sample while your population could be defined as homeless people in the town of Elmhurst.

_____ 5. A descriptive study attempts to explain why there is a relationship between two or more variables.

_____ 6. An evaluative study examines the extent to which an intervention was successful in achieving its objectives.

_____ 7. A proper way to state the purpose of a client satisfaction survey would be as follows: The purpose of this study is to demonstrate that the agency is effective in meeting client need.

_____ 8. In descriptive research, the concept of practical significance receives more attention than the concept of statistical significance.

_____ 9. The average deviation of the scores 2, 6, 2, and 6 would be 2.

A Descriptive Study of the Clients of the Social Work Program of the Neonatal Intensive Care Unit of Memorial Hospital

When babies are born premature, they need the special services of the neonatal intensive care unit. This unit employs professionals who are specialized in the care of babies who are born with low birth weight and other inadequacies due to their premature birth. Included in this type of care is the service of the social worker who works with the parents of such babies in order to help them to adjust emotionally to their child's condition and to obtain and use special resources to meet the needs of their child.

One such program is located at Memorial Hospital. In the course of the provision of services to the clients of this hospital, the social workers of Memorial Hospital complete a client record that provides information on the nature of the problem presented, the service provided, and the disposition of the case. In addition, data are collected on the basic characteristics of the client such as age of parents, birth weight of child, and so forth. All patients of this intensive care unit are referred for social work services.

A descriptive study of the clients of this program is viewed as helpful in the determination of the types of services that might be best utilized by clients. For example, knowing the number of babies from one-parent households indicates the need for certain support services that would be more needed by single parents than dual parents. Knowing how many families are receiving medical assistance from the Medicaid Program due to financial hardships can enlighten the process of determining priorities for social work services among the types of needs that are grounded in financial circumstances and those that are not. Information on the proportion of clients who exhibit immature parental behavior, or ignorance of nutritional health, or social isolation can be used to determine the most important training needs of new social workers who are beginning to provide services to these clients.

Problem Formulation for This Descriptive Study

It has been determined that a descriptive study will be undertaken of the social work program of the Neonatal Intensive Care Unit of Memorial Hospital in the town of Elmhurst. In other words, the general purpose of this study will be to describe the services and the clients of this program with some precision. In this particular case, the purpose can be further clarified as providing a base of information that can assist key actors in making better decisions about the service options to offer clients and the training needs of social work staff who are employed in this program.

Social research is founded upon a knowledge base. Typically, this knowledge base is derived from a review of the literature. You could examine, for example, the literature on the nature of the problems associated with prematurity in birth or the nature of the role of social work services with regard to this problem. Of particular importance would be ideas from others on the most pressing needs of the parents and families of premature infants. Another important issue would be the role of the social worker vis à vis the nurse or physician in the delivery of the hospital's services to the patient and family.

While it is useful for a descriptive study to be founded on a literature review, a descriptive study of an agency program will often gain more guidance from a review of agency documents which describe the nature of the program and the information that is routinely collected. The objective of this task in the research process is to gain knowledge about the types of information that can be most useful.

In Exhibit 6.1, you will find information on the nature of the problem that confronts the clients of the neonatal intensive care unit. This should provide guidance on the kinds of information most needed in the description of the clients of this unit. In Exhibit 6.2, you will find information on the nature of the social work role in neonatal intensive care services.

EXHIBIT 6.1   The Nature of the Problem Facing Neonatal Intensive Care Services

Babies are normally born after nine months from the onset of pregnancy. The period of time from the onset of pregnancy to birth is known as gestational age. Thus, babies are typically born with a gestational age of 36 weeks ($9 \times 4 = 36$). Some babies, however, are born premature. While a few weeks of prematurity usually poses no problems for the baby, there is an increasing danger with each week of prematurity. Babies that are born three months premature (i.e., a gestational age of 26 weeks) are in serious jeopardy. Very few, in fact, survive. Babies need 32 weeks of gestation in order to develop lungs adequate to breathe without extraordinary help from medical technology.

Birth weight is another indicator of problems for the newborn. Babies born under 600 grams seldom survive. Above 600 grams, the chances of survival gradually increase, but there are no major thresholds at other gram weights.

While the cause of prematurity for some infants is genetic, for others it is environmental. Mothers who receive prenatal care are less at risk for having a premature baby. They are more likely to engage in behaviors that are healthy for the baby. Adolescent mothers are more likely than others to give birth to a premature baby.

The problem for the infant does not end with birth and the medical care received from the hospital. Premature babies require special care which some mothers are not well equipped to deliver without help. The extended stay in the hospital for the premature baby increases the danger of poor early bonding between parent and child. It has been found in research on child development that parent-child bonding begins at birth (Klaus & Dennel, 1976). Parents who do not take the infant home from the hospital until three months from delivery have an added burden when it comes to the task of developing an emotional bond with the child. Perhaps this is why premature babies have been found to be more likely to be abused by their parents (Hunter, et al., 1978)

While it is natural for new parents to focus their lives around visiting the baby in the hospital for the first few days of life, the nature of this task often changes when the baby has been in the hospital for a week or two. When this happens, the baby is at risk for insufficient emotional nurturing. To compound the problem, some parents who live in poverty do not have the resources to travel to the hospital at will.

Some parents are not emotionally mature enough to know what the child needs and how to meet those needs. The teenage parent is a good example. Teenagers often become pregnant because they are looking toward their babies as a source for meeting their own needs for love or affection, but they soon learn that babies are not equipped

EXHIBIT 6.1 *Continued*

to function in this role. Instead, they are extremely dependent. The highly immature parent may view the baby's refusal to stop crying as an insult, and may become abusive. They have difficulty understanding the helplessness of the baby's natural condition. The adolescent mother is still in the process of growing up herself and has difficulty placing her own needs in the background and focusing primary attention upon the care of the infant. To compound the problem, it has been found that adolescent mothers are more likely than older mothers to deliver a premature baby (Broman, 1981). Thus, those least likely to be able to handle this problem are more likely to be confronted with it.

The problems of prematurity are by no means restricted to conditions of poverty or adolescent parenting. Most parents of premature infants are poorly equipped to deal with the emotional reaction of giving birth to a child under less than perfect conditions. Compounding the problem of imperfection is the sight of the infant with various tubes attached to medical machinery and its small size. Some premature babies are extremely small and look quite unhealthy.

References

Broman, S. (1981). Long-term development of children born to teenagers. In K. Scott, T. Field, & E. Robertson (Eds.), *Teenage parents and their offspring* (pp. 195–225). New York: Grunne & Stratton.

Hunter, R., et al. (1978). Antecedents of child abuse and neglect in premature infants: A prospective study in a newborn intensive care unit. *Pediatrics,* 61 (April), 629–635.

Klaus, M. H., & Kennel, J. H. (1976). *Maternal–infant bonding.* St. Louis: C. V. Mosby Co.

EXHIBIT 6.2   The Nature of Social Work Services in the Neonatal Intensive Care Unit

The perinatal health care team that serves the patients on the neonatal intensive care unit includes nurses, physicians, and social workers. In addition, services are available as needed from other allied health professionals. Medical decisions, of course, are in the hands of the physicians and nurses. The primary role of the social worker is to assist the families of the patients to cope with hospital care and to provide the support needed by the patient of the hospital. This is especially important for the infant who is totally dependent upon others.

Social workers provide counseling to parents of premature infants to help them adjust to the situation emotionally. They provide information on resources available to assist with essential health care and are often called upon to serve as an advocate for the acquisition of needed resources such as transportation, parking, meals, health equipment, and so forth.

An important part of the social worker's role is to assist the parents in making critical decisions about the care of the infant. Sometimes, this decision is as profound

(Continued)

EXHIBIT 6.2 *Continued*

as whether the infant should be removed from artificial means of sustaining life so that the infant can die in peace. Often an infant is not considered to have a chance of recovering but can be kept breathing by a ventilator. A decision must be made as to whether, and when, this support should be terminated.

It is not the social workers' role to make the decision for the parent nor do they ask for a vote in the matter. Instead, they facilitate the decision process by helping the parents to understand the physician's statements about medical facts, to place that information into an emotional and intellectual framework that has personal meaning, and to resolve underlying conflicts which may be inhibiting the completion of the decision process.

Once the parents have reached a critical decision about the treatment of their child, it is often the responsibility of the social worker to serve as an advocate for the parents. If there is a conflict between parents and the physicians, the social worker should help the physician understand and appreciate the parents' viewpoint.

Social workers are often called upon to provide counseling with members of the health care team. Working with infants who die can be emotionally draining to the nurse or physician. The emotions that swell during times of crisis can also cause conflict among members of the team which the social worker is often called upon to help resolve.

ASSIGNMENT 6–B

1. A descriptive study of the clients and services of a social work program can be *least* useful in which of the following ways?

    a. To identify the social workers who most deserve a pay raise

    b. To examine the extent of the client's need for certain services

    c. To identify the types of client problems that social workers should be best prepared to address

2. The descriptive study differs from the explanatory study in which of the following ways?

    a. The descriptive study does not rely on a knowledge base whereas the explanatory study makes use of a knowledge base to support the theory that is being tested.

b. In addition to the published literature, the knowledge base for a descriptive study may draw substantially on different sources of information, such as agency documents, than an explanatory study, which often makes more extensive use of the published literature.

c. The descriptive study is designed to examine the extent to which an intervention was successful.

_____

_____

_____

_____

3. A descriptive study of the social work services of a neonatal intensive care unit of a hospital would probably make better use of which of the following pieces of data in each pair? (Place a check next to either option A or option B in each pair below. Then provide a rationale for your choice.)

A. Gestational age of the baby

B. County of residence of the family

Explain:

_____

_____

_____

_____

A. The baby's length in inches

B. The age of the mother

Explain:

_____

_____

_____

_____

A. The weight of the baby in grams

B. Whether or not the baby's grandparents are still living

Explain:

_____

_____

_____

_____

A. Whether the mother demonstrates readiness to be a parent

B. The occupation of the father

Explain:

_____

_____

_____

_____

4. List one additional piece of data that should be collected in this descriptive study.

_____

_____

_____

_____

Methodology for This Descriptive Study

This descriptive study will rely upon data that is routinely collected and recorded by social workers in the Neonatal Intensive Care Unit of Memorial Hospital. Two major tasks of the construction of this study will be discussed in this section. One is the selection of the sample for the study and the other is the measurement of variables.

The Sample

The sample upon which data were collected consisted of all premature babies served by this hospital whose cases were terminated during a six-week period in the spring of 1989. This sample did not include a few babies who were served by the neonatal intensive care unit who were full term (i.e., approximately nine months gestation) who had health problems requiring intensive care. The sample included forty-five infants.

These forty-five infants can be considered to be a sample from the population of all premature infants served by this hospital during 1989 or in recent years or some other designation. As long as these forty-five infants are all members of the larger group, you can define the population in various ways. However, your ability to generalize your findings to that other population of people will depend upon how you selected your sample and how broadly you define your population.

You might be in trouble if you defined your population as all babies born at Memorial Hospital during the spring of 1989, because premature babies are different from full-term babies; thus, you could hardly generalize your findings to that population. For example, you might find that 30 percent of the premature babies were born to teenage mothers. It would be a mistake to guess that 30 percent of all babies born at this hospital were born to teenage mothers because you know that teenage mothers have a greater than normal likelihood of having a premature baby. You would expect the proportion of full-term babies born to teenage mothers to be lower than the 30 percent of your sample.

The Measurement of Variables

The variables on which information is available from the clients' records can be grouped into three categories. There is information about the patient and the patient's family such as the gestational age and birth weight of the child, the age of the parents, the number of children in the family, and the method used by the family to pay for the hospital service. A second category is information on the nature of the problems presented by the family to the social work program. Among these problems are immature behavior exhibited by the mother, financial difficulties, and social isolation. Adjustment reaction is a problem that is listed as a problem with almost every case. The third category is the disposition of the case.

These data are recorded in *quantitative* format. In other words, each variable is recorded for each case in a form that is discretely quantifiable, such as by number (e.g., gestational age in weeks) or a category. An example of a variable that is recorded in relation to categories is the disposition of the case at termination of service. The three categories include: (1) situation worse, (2) no change, and (3) situation better.

While all variables for the present study are recorded quantitatively, some studies record information in a *qualitative* format. A qualitative measurement of a variable is one in which the information is not recorded discretely. An example would be the answer to an open-ended question such as "Describe the feelings you had when you first entered the hospital." One person may think of such words as *anxious* or *afraid* or *hopeful* while another may use such expressions as "Didn't know what to expect" or "I felt okay because I always wanted to be a nurse."

Remember that a variable must vary. A study that only included students could not include the concept of student as a variable. To measure the concept of student, you would have to include nonstudents so that students could be compared to nonstudents as the basis for the measurement of the variable. Another necessity is that you actually collect information on the concept. The hair color of the mother could potentially be a variable because hair color does vary. However, it is not a variable in the present study because no information was collected on it.

Information was collected on twenty variables for the present study. The operational definition of each of these variables and the label used to identify each variable are presented in Exhibits 6.3, 6.4, and 6.5. In Exhibit 6.3, you will find the definitions of the variables which characterize the clients and their families. For example, the variable named AGE–BABY in the data set contains the gestational age of the baby in weeks. The gestational age of a baby is the time elapsed between conception and delivery. Lower gestational ages mean greater prematurity, which is associated with greater problems. Exhibit 6.4 contains the definitions of variables which specify the presenting problem that led to the need for social work services. For example, the variables named HEALTH–P contained information on whether or not one of the presenting problems of the case was immature health behavior of the mother. In Exhibit 6.4, you will also find the definitions of variables which characterize the disposition of the case at the point of closure. For example, the variable named ADJUST–D contains information on the status of the problem of adjustment reaction at the time of case closure. The options for classification of this variable were: (a) situation worse, (b) no change, or (c) situation better.

EXHIBIT 6.3   Characteristics of the Patients

Variable Name	*Definition*
Age-Mom	The age of the baby's mother in years
Age-Dad	The age of the baby's father in years
Age-Baby	The gestational age of the baby in weeks
Parents	The number of parents living in the home
Siblings	The number of siblings of the baby
Weight	The weight of the baby at birth in grams
Pay	The method used to pay the hospital bill, classified as follows: (1) Medicaid; (2) private insurance; (3) other
Mom-Ed	The educational level of the mother, classified as follows: (1) elementary school; (2) some high school; (3) high school graduate; (4) some college; (5) college graduate; (6) unknown

EXHIBIT 6.4   Presenting Problems and Case Dispositions

Variable Name	*Description*
Immature-P	Immature behavior of the mother was or was not one of the presenting problems that led to the referral of the case to the social worker. When this is the presenting problem, it usually means that the mother has exhibited behavior that suggests that she is not generally prepared for the responsibilities of parenthood. As was the case with all the potential presenting problems that were listed on the record form, this variable was entered into the computer as 1 if immature behavior was one of the presenting problems, or it was entered as 0 if it was not a presenting problem.
Health-P	Immature health behavior of the mother was or was not one of the presenting problems. This usually means that the mother is not following medical recommendations or shows minimal concern for health conditions.
Isolate-P	Social isolation was or was not one of the presenting problems. This means that the parents do not have extended families and friends who appear to be in a position to help in times of need. The parents can rely only on each other for assistance and emotional support.
Adjust-P	Adjustment reaction was or was not one of the presenting problems. This means that the parents appeared to need help with their emotional reaction to the fact of having a handicapped baby with special needs.
Finance-P	Financial difficulties were or were not one of the presenting problems. This means that the parents need financial assistance with any of a number of needs associated with the care of the baby.
Travel-P	Transportation was or was not one of the presenting problems. Some parents do not have transportation readily available and need assistance so that they can visit the baby on a regular basis. This is especially true of parents who live in small towns located some distance from Elmhurst.
Immature-D	This is the disposition of the problem of immature parental behavior. The three categories are: (1) situation worse, (2) no change, and (3) situation better.
Health-D	This is the disposition status of the problem of immature health behavior.
Isolate-D	This is the disposition of the social isolation problem at case termination.

(Continued)

EXHIBIT 6.4 *Continued*

Variable Name	Description
Adjust-D	This is the disposition of the adjustment reaction problem.
Finance-D	This is the disposition of the financial difficulties problem.
Travel-D	This is the disposition of the transportation problem.

ASSIGNMENT 6–C

1. What is the sample for the present study?

   a. Premature babies served by Memorial Hospital

   b. Premature babies served by Memorial Hospital for a six-week period in the spring of 1989

   c. Babies who are born with low birth weight requiring extra care and attention

   d. Premature babies served by Memorial Hospital in 1989

2. What is the population for this study?

   _____

   _____

   _____

   _____

3. Classify each of the following ways to measure variables according to whether they are measured in a qualitative format or a quantitative format.

   a. What is your age? _____ years

   b. Please describe your most important need as the mother of a premature baby?

   _____

   _____

   _____

   c. Are you presently married? _____ Yes _____ No

4. Which of the following are *not* variables in the present study? (You may select more than one.)

    a. Age of the mother   **d.** Age of the grandparents

    b. Infancy   **e.** Gestational age of the patient

    c. Birth weight of the patient   **f.** Education of the mother

5. Which of the following pieces of information could be calculated from the data being collected for the present study?

    a. The percent of the patients' mothers who are single and living with a mate

    b. The percent of the mothers who are college graduates

    c. The number of clients that were referred to social work service because of immature health behavior

    d. The percent of babies in this sample who had a gestational age of thirty-two weeks or less

Analyzing Data for This Descriptive Study

The data collected for the present study are displayed in Tables 6.1, 6.2, and 6.3, as well as Figures 6.1 and 6.2. Table 6.1 presents the data regarding basic characteristics of the patients and their families. Table 6.3 presents data on presenting problems and their dispositions.

Figure 6.1 provides a graphic display of data on presenting problems. This display is known as a *bar chart* and is useful for making information more clear to the reader. The same can be said for the *pie chart* which is the graphic means used to display the method of payment for these patients, as depicted in Figure 6.2. The information in these two figures is also contained in the tables.

For each of the tables, the variable name is given in the first column. For a definition of each variable, see the previous section of this chapter. The second column displays the categories into which the variable was divided while the third column presents the frequency for that category. In the fourth column can be found the percent of the total represented by the frequency in column 3. The cumulative frequencies and the cumulative percentages are presented in columns 5 and 6. The cumulative frequency is the current frequency plus all previous frequencies. The cumulative percent is the current percent plus all previous percentages.

To illustrate, let's examine the variable named AGE–BABY in Table 6.1. This is the variable which recorded the gestational age of the patient in weeks. The first category contains the figure of 25. This line of data represents those patients who had a gestational age of 25 weeks. In the second column, you can see that there was only one such patient in your sample because the frequency was recorded as 1.

TABLE 6.1 Data on General Client Characteristics

Variables	Category	Frequency	Percent	Cumulative Frequency	Cumulative Percent
Age-Baby	25	1	2.2	1	2.2
	26	2	4.4	3	6.7
	27	4	8.9	7	15.6
	28	12	26.7	19	42.2
	29	7	15.6	26	57.8
	30	2	4.4	28	62.2
	31	4	8.9	32	71.1
	32	4	8.9	36	80.0
	33	6	13.3	42	93.3
	34	3	6.7	45	100.0
Age-Mom	16	2	4.4	2	4.4
	17	2	4.4	4	8.9
	18	2	4.4	6	13.3
	19	2	4.4	8	17.8
	20	4	8.9	12	26.7
	21	5	11.1	17	37.8
	22	2	4.4	19	42.2
	23	3	6.7	22	48.9
	24	3	6.7	25	55.6
	25	2	4.4	27	60.0
	26	5	11.1	32	71.1
	27	4	8.9	36	80.0
	28	1	2.2	37	82.2
	30	4	8.9	41	91.1
	31	1	2.2	42	93.3
	33	1	2.2	43	95.6
	43	1	2.2	44	97.8
	45	1	2.2	45	100.0
Parents	1	10	22.2	10	22.2
	2	35	77.8	45	100.0

TABLE 6.1 *Continued*

Variables	Category	Frequency	Percent	Cumulative Frequency	Cumulative Percent
Siblings	0	18	40.0	18	40.0
	1	11	24.2	29	64.4
	2	7	15.6	36	80.0
	3	3	6.7	39	86.7
	4	3	6.7	42	93.3
	6	3	6.7	45	100.0
Pay	Medicaid	28	62.2	28	62.2
	Private Insurance	11	24.4	39	86.7
	Other	6	13.3	45	100.0

This frequency of 1 represents 2.2 percent of the total of 45 patients in the sample (see column 4 labeled "Percent"). The cumulative frequency and the cumulative percent are the same as the frequency and the percent because this is the first category given in the table.

There were 2 babies with a gestational age of 26 weeks, and this frequency represents 4.4 percent of the total sample. The cumulative frequency is 3 because the 2 in the present category were combined with the 1 in the previous category. The cumulative percent is 6.7 because of the same procedure.

A little farther down this table you will see the category of 25 for AGE–MOM with the frequency of 2, and a percent of 4.4. This means that there were only 2 mothers who were age 25, and they represented 4.4 percent of the total. You will also note a cumulative frequency of 27, meaning that there were 27 mothers at or below the age of 25. The cumulative percent column tells us that these 27 mothers represented 60 percent of the total.

TABLE 6.2   **Range, Means, and Standard Deviations for Selected Variables**

Variable	N	Minimum	Maximum	Mean	Standard Deviation
Age-Baby	45	25	34	29.68	2.45
Age-Mom	45	16	45	24.40	6.05
Age-Dad	35	17	51	29.77	8.36
Weight	45	510	2150	1280.80	458.23

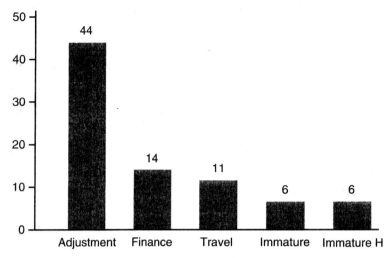

FIGURE 6.1 Number of Clients Presenting Each Problem

The range, means, and standard deviations for numerically recorded variables are displayed in Table 6.2. The first column provides the variable name while the second column presents the number of persons included in the analysis. In the case of the age of the father, you will note that the number is only 35. This is because the data on this variable were missing for 10 cases. The third column gives the minimum value for the variable while the fourth column displays the maximum value. For example, the youngest mother was 16 and the oldest was 45. The fifth column presents the mean for the variable while the final column displays the standard deviation.

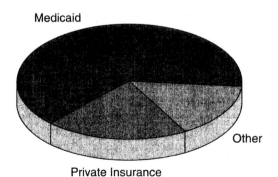

FIGURE 6.2   Means of Payment of
Medical Bills

ASSIGNMENT 6–D

Examine the data in Tables 6.1, 6.2, and 6.3, and determine whether each of the following statements is either TRUE or FALSE. Indicate either TRUE or FALSE next to each statement and explain.

1. The majority of the mothers of these premature babies does not have a high school diploma.   T _____   F _____

   Evidence:

   _____

   _____

   _____

2. Very few of the families of these babies would be considered low-income families.

   T _____   F _____

   Evidence:

   _____

   _____

   _____

3. A large proportion of these babies were born to single mothers.

   T _____   F _____

   Evidence:

   _____

   _____

   _____

4. Most of these babies were born into small families.   T _____   F _____

   Evidence:

   _____

   _____

   _____

5. The lungs of most of these babies are not sufficiently developed for them to survive without the medical care of the intensive care unit.   T _____   F _____

Evidence:

_____

_____

_____

_____

6. The fathers of these babies tend to be older than the mothers. T _____   F _____

Evidence:

_____

_____

_____

_____

7. The spread in the ages of the fathers is less than that of the mothers, meaning that the fathers tend to be more like each other in age than the mothers do. T _____   F _____

Evidence:

_____

_____

_____

_____

8. The mean number of weeks between conception and birth for these babies was 29.68.
T _____   F _____

Evidence:

_____

_____

_____

_____

In Table 6.3, you can find the data on presenting problems and the dispositions of these problems. For the presenting problems, only the number of cases with a specific presenting problem is displayed; thus, the only category listed is "Yes." For the variable IMMATURE–P, you will see the figure of 6 in the line with "Yes" as the

TABLE 6.3   Data on Presenting Problems and Case Dispositions

Variable	Category	Frequency	Percent	Cumulative Frequency	Cumulative Percent
Mom-Ed	Elem. School	5	11.4	5	11.4
	Some H. S.	23	52.3	28	63.6
	H. S. Grad.	8	18.2	36	81.8
	Some College	3	6.8	39	88.6
	College Grad.	5	11.4	44	100.0
Immature-P	Yes	6			
Immature-D	Worse	0			
	No change	6			
	Better	0			
Health-P	Yes	6			
Health-D	Worse	0			
	No change	6			
	Better	0			
Isolate-P	Yes	5			
Isolate-D	Worse	0			
	No change	4	80.0	4	80.0
	Better	1	20.0	5	100.0
Adjust-P	Yes	44			
Adjust-D	Worse	1	2.4	1	2.4
	No change	0	0	1	2.4
	Better	41	97.6	42	100.0
Finance-P	Yes	14			
Finance-D	Worse	1	7.1	1	7.1
	No change	2	14.3	3	21.4
	Better	11	78.6	14	100.0
Travel-P	Yes	11			
Travel-D	Worse	0			
	No change	3	27.3	3	27.3
	Better	8	72.7	11	100.0

category. This means that 6 persons out of the total had this problem and 39 persons did not (6 + 39 = 45). The variable labeled as IMMATURE–D displays the disposition of each of these six cases.

ASSIGNMENT 6–E

1. What was the most frequent presenting problem? Explain:

_____

_____

_____

_____

2. What were the least frequent presenting problems? Explain:

_____

_____

_____

_____

3. What was the problem with which it would appear the social work program had the most success?

_____

_____

_____

_____

4. What were the two problems with which the social work program appeared to have had the least success?

_____

_____

_____

_____

Drawing Conclusions for This Descriptive Study

In descriptive research, as in many types of research, the conclusions (or discussion) section of the report should include at least the following: (1) a summary of the most important findings; (2) a discussion of the limitations of the data analyzed; and (3) recommendations for the future in regard to practice and research. The summary should be brief. It should not repeat essentially everything already said. It should only highlight the most important findings. The limitations can be found in the generalizability of the findings and the research methods employed. Recommendations can focus upon either practice or research. What are the implications of these findings for the improvement of practice? What future directions for research are suggested by these results?

So, what about this study? How should it be summarized? First, let's examine what the summary should *not* look like. You have a myriad of data in your tables. It would be laborious to repeat these pieces of data one by one. For example, you could (but should not) begin the summary as follows:

> *It was found that the mean gestational age of these babies ranged from a low of 25 to a high of 34 with a mean of 29.68 and a standard deviation of 2.45. The mothers ranged in age from 16 to 45 with a mean of 24.4 and a standard deviation of 6.05 while the fathers' mean age was 29.77 with a range of 17 to 51 and a standard deviation of 8.36. These babies weighed an average of 1280.8 grams with a range from 510 to 2150 and a standard deviation of 458.23.*

As you read the above, you may have become a bit bored with the repetition of numbers. Just think how you would have felt if this had gone on and on. Not only is it not advised to be so monotonous in the presentation of the summary, it is also ill-advised to do so in the body of the results section. Such a string of data is best presented in tables with narrative description of only samples of the data in the tables.

In the summary, you want to focus upon the highlights. What are they for this study? One, perhaps, is the fact that the most frequent presenting problem was adjustment reaction. And this problem stood out among the others as the most frequent by far. Almost all the clients (44 out of 45) had this as one of the presenting problems while the second most common one was financial difficulties with only 14 families referred for help with this problem. To highlight this fact, a bar chart was presented with data on presenting problems. What are the other important findings? You will address this challenge in the next exercise.

The second issue to address in the conclusions section is the limitations of the study. First, you may want to say something about the generalizability of the findings. If you do not have a probability sample, you cannot safely generalize from your study sample to other populations. Without a probability sample, you can only speculate. And your speculation becomes weaker the farther you move beyond the sample to broader and broader definitions of people.

Another area of limitation lies within the strength of the methods of observation employed in the study. How well were the variables defined and measured?

Did you leave out important variables? Was the source of data valid? In this case, you should consider whether client records generally contain valid information. Unfortunately, you have no concrete information on this issue for your study, so you are left only to speculate on the extent to which such records are normally valid.

The recommendations part of the conclusions section is perhaps the most important. This requires some creativity. Recommendations do not normally leap out of the data to be articulated. They require some knowledge of the nature of the problem being addressed, and in this case, the nature of the service being offered.

You examined three kinds of data: the characteristics of the families being served; the kinds of problems that led to the need for social work services; and the dispositions of these problems at case closure. Knowing such things as the proportion of single mothers and the proportion of families who are low in income can be of assistance in considering the kinds of need to be given priority. Social workers can ask themselves if they are giving priority according to these indicators of need.

Knowing what presenting problems are most common should help social workers to determine if they should shift their priorities regarding the kinds of interventions employed. Adjustment reaction as a problem suggests some form of counseling or supportive interaction as an intervention. Financial problems may require a very different kind of intervention.

You also have information on case disposition. How well are social workers doing with different kinds of problems? Does this suggest something in the form of a change in their priorities?

These are some of the kinds of issues to be addressed in the conclusions section of a descriptive study. You will notice that some of these topics were peculiar to the data you collected. Other topics will emerge in different descriptive studies depending on the kinds of information analyzed.

ASSIGNMENT 6–F

On a separate page, prepare a brief summary of the present study. This summary should briefly remind the reader of the place and time of this study as well as its general purpose. It should present a concise overview of the most essential information generated by this study. It should not repeat a myriad of details already presented in the previous pages and tables of the text.

After you have completed this task, review the summary in Exhibit 6.5 and compare it to your own. Did you leave out anything that should have been included? Does the summary leave out anything that you believe should have been included?

EXHIBIT 6.5   A Suggested Summary of the Descriptive Study of the Clients of the Neonatal Intensive Care Unit of Memorial Hospital

This report presented descriptive data on all of the cases referred to the social work department of the Intensive Care Unit of Memorial Hospital during a six-week period in the spring of 1989 (N = 45). Data on client characteristics, reasons for referral, and case disposition were presented. The purpose of this study was to assist the social work department in the assessment of client need and the examination of the present array of services rendered.

A majority of the babies served by this program were from low-income households as indicated by the fact that many of them (62 percent) paid their hospital bills through the Medicaid Program. Most of these patients had both parents living in the home (78 percent) and had one or no siblings (64 percent). Only about one in five of the mothers of these babies had at least a high school diploma. The average gestational age of these babies (29.68 weeks) indicated that most were very vulnerable to respiratory distress due to underdeveloped lungs and required specialized care to survive.

The families of these babies were referred to the social work department for a variety of reasons, the most prominent one being a problem with adjustment to the fact of having a premature baby (44 of these 45 families presented this problem). The second highest reason for referral was financial problems ($n = 14$) while the third was problems with transportation ($n = 11$). The vast majority of the clients referred for adjustment reaction ($n = 41$) was classified by the social worker as better on this condition at the point of case closure. The same was true for clients referred for financial problems (11 improved out of 14 referred) and for transportation problems (8 better out of 11 referred). The same was not true for those referred for the problems of immature behavior, immature health behavior, and social isolation. Most of the clients achieved no gain on these three problems as a result of social work services.

Glossary

Average Deviation. The average of all deviations from the mean in an array of data. For example, the ages of 24, 26, 28, and 30 would have a mean of 27 (24 + 26 + 28 + 30 = 108 / 4 = 27) and an average deviation of 2 (3 + 1 + 1 + 3 = 8 / 4 = 2).

Bar Chart. A chart which depicts the frequencies for the various categories for a variable.

Cumulative Frequency. A frequency that includes all those in the present category (reference category) plus the frequency for all categories which come before the present one in the classification scheme.

Cumulative Proportion. A proportion that includes all those in the present category (reference category) plus the proportion for all categories which come before the present one in the classification scheme.

Frequency. The incidence of something, such as the number of females and males in a study sample. There could be, for example, a frequency of 24 females and 21 males in a given sample.

Interval. A level of measurement in which subjects are given scores on a scale in which the interval between each level is equal to the interval between each of the other levels. For example, the temperature of 32 is 1 degree lower than the temperature of 33 which is 1 degree lower than the temperature of 34. This scale is measured in reference to degrees on the scale in which each interval between degrees is equal to each of the other intervals between degrees.

Levels of Measurement. The hierarchy of measurement for study variables, each level of which provides a different level of sophistication in measurement, and is suitable for different statistical tests. The levels are nominal, ordinal, interval, and ratio, in that order from lowest to highest. A variable measured at a higher level can be treated as though it is measured at a lower level for statistical analysis purposes if necessary. For example, a variable measured at the interval level can be treated as though it is measured at the ordinal level. However, researchers lose information when they do this, so it is not optimal.

Mean. The average. The mean is calculated by summing the frequencies in a sample of data and dividing the sum by the number of people in the sample.

Median. The midpoint in an array of data laid out in numerical order. For example, let's examine the following numbers: 12, 15, 16, 19, 27, 28, 31. The median for this array of data is 19.

Mode. The greatest incidence of occurrence in a set of data. A set of data with the ages of 10, 14, 15, 15, and 16 would have a mode of 15 for age because there were more persons with this age than any other age.

Nominal. The lowest level of measurement. At the nominal level, the attributes of a variable are in categories which have no particular order (such as low, medium, and high). Examples include gender, political party affiliation, and favorite color.

Ordinal. The next level of measurement beyond nominal. Ordinal variables place subjects into categories that are ordered from low to high or most to least, and so forth. The response categories of "agree," "undecided," and "disagree" place respondents into categories of agreement that are ordered from most to least.

Pie Chart. A chart that is pie-shaped and which depicts the proportions of subjects (or entities) in each category for a variable.

Proportion. The percentage of something. For example, if there are 25 females and 25 males, the proportion of females is 50 percent.

Ratio. The highest level of measurement. Variables measured at the ratio level have all the characteristics of variables measured at the interval level, with the addition that all scores on the scale are based upon a fixed zero point. A practical way to remember this characteristic is to realize that variables measured at the ratio level cannot have negative values, because 0 is the lowest possible value. For example, a person cannot have negative weight, or height, or age.

Standard Deviation. A measure of variance for a distribution. It measures how much the subjects in a particular sample are similar or different from one another.

Variance. The extent to which numbers in a set of data are different from one another. The greater the difference from one number to another, the greater the variance. (The term *variance* in statistics has a special meaning. It is the square of the standard deviation.)

$$C\ h\ a\ p\ t\ e\ r\ \ 7$$

Using Explanatory Research:

Is Rural and Urban Social
Work Practice Different?

In this chapter, you will work with another example of social work research, a study in the category of explanatory research. As before, you will explore the entire research process and will be given the opportunity to answer questions about it. The present study deals with a comparison of rural and urban social work practices. The fundamental question is whether type of locality (rural versus urban) explains the practice of the social worker. You will begin with the introduction to the study.

At the completion of this chapter, you should be able to make use of explanatory research from the literature. While there will always be additional lessons to be learned, your level of competence should be such that you will not shrink from the task of reading an explanatory research study. You will not, of course, fully understand every statistical measure used in such studies, but you will be able, in most studies, to focus on the essential information that will enable you to interpret the findings.

Objectives

The present chapter will build on the previous ones, and you will find some review of previous concepts in addition to the expansion of your knowledge in regard to those concepts. The learning objectives of the present chapter include the enhancement of your ability to:

1. Develop a relevant research question when given a literature review;
2. Articulate the reasons why a given study uses a quantitative method of measuring variables rather than a qualitative method;

3. Articulate the hypothesis for a study, including the identification of the independent and dependent variables;
4. Describe several of the most common sampling techniques;
5. Describe how to employ the systematic random sampling technique;
6. Identify several of the means used to assess the reliability and validity of measurement devices;
7. Identify the two main factors that influence statistical significance.

A Review of Some Issues in Explanatory Research

The problem formulation stage is the first in the research process. As you have seen, it entails the examination of the existing knowledge about an issue of concern. This examination reveals unanswered questions from which you can make a choice for your own study. The research question leads logically to the development of a research methodology which provides details on the way you will undertake your study. Data are collected and analyzed and conclusions are reached about the research question.

Among the issues to be addressed in the literature review are the following:

1. What is the subject of concern and why is it important?
2. How are the central concepts defined in the literature? Do these definitions suggest quantitative or qualitative means of measurement?
3. What do you know, from theories and previous research, about this subject?
4. What are the questions that have been left substantially unanswered by the existing literature?
5. Do the unanswered questions suggest the development of new theory or the testing of existing theories?

The nature of problem formulation has critical relevance for the development of your research methodology. Problem formulation will suggest the following:

1. The type of study to be undertaken (descriptive, explanatory, evaluative, or exploratory);
2. The population to be studied;
3. How you should define your study variables;
4. Whether you should measure the variables in a qualitative or quantitative format; and
5. How you should articulate the study hypothesis.

The study hypothesis is appropriate to the explanatory study as well as the evaluative study, which can be conceived as a type of explanatory study in view of the fact that its focus is on, for example, whether or not treatment explains client improvement. But it is not relevant to the descriptive study, which has the purpose of simply describing what is. In exploratory studies, the purpose often is the development of hypotheses. In this case, there is usually not an existing hypothesis to be tested, but, instead, a need for the development of new ones.

The explanatory study attempts to test a hypothesis. Data are examined in order to determine if the hypothesis was supported. In explanatory research, researchers do not speak of proof or disproof, but of support or nonsupport. Statistical analysis helps them to deal with one type of alternative explanation for their data—that of chance. For example, in the study of salary and gender, you used statistics to help estimate the probability that the observed differences in salary between men and women could be explained by chance. In the study of the effectiveness of the New Hope Treatment Center, you used statistics to help estimate the likelihood that the differences between pretest and posttest scores on depression would occur by chance.

But there are other reasons why your clients may have received higher scores at the completion of treatment than before. It could be that something else happened to them to cause them to improve. It could be that they felt that they *should* improve in functioning because of all this attention, and this condition could have caused them to offer inflated responses at the posttest time. Thus, when researchers speak of the results of the testing of a hypothesis, they talk about support rather than proof.

When researchers draw conclusions, they address the issue of practical significance. It is possible, of course, that they might have found statistical significance but not practical significance. If the treatment objective is to reduce the client's depression to a level at which they can manage their lives, they might find that a reduction of depression scores from 68 to 60 is not enough to achieve this objective. Yet, it is possible that such a change is statistically significant.

Problem Formulation for a Study of Rural and Urban Social Work Practice

The Introduction

The introduction to an explanatory research study should accomplish several objectives. For one thing, it should clearly identify the research question or issue. This clarification should be presented rather early in the report. The reader should not be kept wondering for many paragraphs just what this study is all about. The introduction should also explain why the issue or research question is especially important. Does the study subject deal with a subject that has been growing in recent decades, or does it deal with an issue that has been substantially ignored, or is it a subject that is relevant to social work practice? How might the findings of a study on this subject be put to use?

The introduction to the study should also identify the key study variables. In a previous chapter, you examined a study of salaries among social workers. The key variables were gender, salary, and position level. The purpose of the study should be stated in the introduction and it should be stated in the spirit of scientific inquiry. Remember that the overall purpose of social work research is discovery rather than justification. Finally, the uses of the results of the study should be identified in the introduction.

In Exhibit 7.1 you will find an introduction to a study of rural and urban social work practice. Examine this introduction with the above thoughts in mind and then respond to the questions in the assignment that follows.

EXHIBIT 7.1   An Introduction to a Study of Rural and Urban Social Work Practice

For decades, sociologists and social workers have described the rural community as different from the urban community (see, for example, Glenn & Hill, 1977; Denton, York, & Moran, 1988). Rural people, for example, have been found to be more likely than urban dwellers to rely upon informal support networks and to embrace traditional values. Such distinctions have prompted scholars to advocate for a form of social work practice that is focused on the rural community. If the rural community is different, the logical assertion is that social work practice for the rural community should be different from that in an urban location.

The literature on rural social work specifies that rural social workers should emphasize different professional roles, should be generalists rather than specialists, and should rely more on the use of informal networks than should their urban counterparts. However, little empirical evidence is available which supports the notion of actual differences in practice between social workers in rural and urban areas. In fact, one study suggests that there is little difference in the way rural and urban social workers practice (Whitaker, 1986). This one study, however, was rather limited in the range of rural and urban populations from which the sample of social workers was selected.

If rural and urban social workers are found to be similar rather than different, one might ask why. Is it because social workers are unaware of the differences in the communities in which they work? If rural and urban social workers do not perceive that their communities differ on the extent of the importance of informal helping networks, it would seem logical that they would not practice differently in regard to this variable. If they do perceive differences but do not practice differently, what are the implications of this finding? In the analysis of differences in perceptions, the question of how rurality should be conceptualized will inevitably arise. Some suggest that it should be viewed as a continuum; yet, researchers often seem to conceptualize this variable as dichotomous.

The purpose of the present study is to determine whether social workers in rural communities differ from their urban counterparts in relation to perceptions of their communities and in regard to their practice in those communities. The results of such a study should be of assistance to leaders of the social work profession as they evaluate the relevance of social work practice to the social context in which it exists. If social workers in rural and urban communities do *not* differ, perhaps we should reexamine

(Continued)

EXHIBIT 7.1 *Continued*

the educational preparation of social workers, or perhaps we should reexamine whether differences in community dynamics *should* make practice different.

References

Denton, R. T., York, R. O., and Moran, J. R. (1988). The social worker's view of the rural community: An empirical examination. *Human Services in the Rural Environment,* 11 (3), 14–21.
Glenn, N., & Hill, L. (1977). Rural-urban differences in attitudes and behaviors in the United States. *Annals of the American Academy of Political and Social Science,* 123, 36–50.
Whitaker, W. (1986). A survey of perceptions of social work practice in rural and urban areas. *Human Services in the Rural Environment,* 9 (3), 12–19.

ASSIGNMENT 7–A

1. The introduction to a research study should do several things. Circle either the word YES or NO for each of the following items.

   YES   NO   Clearly identifies the research question or issue

   YES   NO   Explains why the issue or question is important

   YES   NO   Identifies the study variables

   YES   NO   Clearly states the purpose of the study and does so in a manner that is consistent with the spirit of scientific inquiry

   YES   NO   Explains how the results of the study could be used

   Notes:

   _____

   _____

   _____

2. What are the key variables in this study?

   _____

   _____

   _____

3. What is the purpose of this study?

_____

_____

_____

_____

The Literature Review

The literature review should provide a guide for the development of the research study. It should help you to refine your research question, to determine what type of study is most appropriate, to develop a theory about what you are likely to find from a study of an issue, and to determine ways to define your variables.

A literature review should be well organized. Division of the material into sections is helpful in the illustration of the organization of the material. There should be transition paragraphs or sentences that help the reader to move from one section to another without being lost or confused.

A clear understanding of the nature of the variables in the research question should emanate from the literature review. In other words, the literature review should guide your determination of how to define the variables for your study.

From the literature review you should be able to develop a basic theory about the issue under study. A theory, in its most rudimentary form, is simply an explanation of a relationship between two or more variables. For example, you might theorize that males earn higher salaries than females because various studies have demonstrated this reality. You might also theorize that one of the reasons that males earn higher salaries is that they are more likely to be found at higher positions in the organizational hierarchy. You could theorize that clients will be better off after counseling than before counseling. You could further theorize that clients with high motivation for treatment will achieve a greater gain in functioning than clients with low motivation for treatment. And so forth.

A literature review about rural and urban social work practice is presented in Exhibit 7.2. It is drawn from two published works which addressed the issues in the study for the present chapter:

> Denton, Roy T., York, R. O., and Moran, J. R. (1988). *The social worker's view of the rural community: An empirical examination.* Human Services in the Rural Environment, 11 (3), 14–21.

> York, Reginald O., Denton, Roy T., and Moran, James R. (1989). *Rural and urban social work practice: Is there a difference?* Social Casework, 70 (4), 201–209.

The data from those studies have been reexamined to some extent in their presentation in this chapter.

EXHIBIT 7.2   A Literature Review on Rural and Urban Social Work Practice

The theory and practice of social work in rural areas, after a hiatus during the 1940s and the 1950s, have reemerged as relevant concerns for the profession. Part of the stimulus for this renewed concern is the perception that social work practice principles derived from urban settings may not be relevant to rural problems (Martinez-Brawley, 1980). If the rural context is different in terms of its needs, culture, and value systems, then the logical assumption would be that social work must be practiced differently if it is to be appropriate to its context.

The literature on rural social work specifies that rural social workers emphasize different professional roles, are generalists rather than specialists, and rely more on the use of informal networks than do their urban counterparts (Mermelstein and Sundet, 1982; Ginsberg, 1976; Johnson, 1983). However, little empirical evidence suggests that social workers in rural areas actually differ from their urban counterparts in relation to these practice issues. In fact, one study suggests that they are generally not different at all (Whitaker, 1986).

Defining Rurality

Several approaches have been used to define rurality. In rural sociology, most definitions fall into three categories: occupational, sociocultural, or ecological. Occupational definitions focus on types of work that dominate the social landscape. Agriculture, fishing, and mining have been found to be more prevalent in what has been viewed as the rural community, contrasted with industry, which is more prevalent in urban areas. Sociocultural definitions focus on social values and mores as distinguishing the people of different communities. Rural communities, for example, have been viewed as placing more emphasis upon relationships than upon specialized roles in the decision-making process, whereas the opposite is the view of the urban community.

Most of the social work literature has relied on an ecological definition, that is, reference to the distribution of people in space. Therefore, many professionals measure rurality in terms of population size and population density.

Although some definitions of rurality propose a dichotomy between rural and urban, many researchers and theoreticians have long recognized that rural–urban differences are best represented along a continuum. In an overview of research on rural–urban differences in attitudes and behavior, Norvail Glenn and Lester Hill (1977) examined support for the idea of a continuum. They pointed out that the largest communities usually differ from the medium-sized communities about as much as the medium-sized communities differ from the smallest communities, and that the direction of these differences is consistent from one size to the next. This pattern of variation suggests that it is useful to conceive of rurality as a continuum.

Redfield (1953) and Toennies (1963), recognized the interpenetration of rural and urban settings with each other. Duford (cited in Farley et al., 1982), has hypothesized a rural–urban continuum ranging from isolated farm to metropolitan area based on population and proximity to urban areas.

One of the more elaborate efforts to conceptualize rural–urban differences by population is illustrated by the work of Whitaker (1986). Using both a ten-category classification of counties developed by the United State Department of Agriculture

EXHIBIT 7.2 *Continued*

and a rural–urban typology employed by the Maine State Planning Office, Whitaker developed a complex rating typology by which respondents could classify both their work and home communities. This typology essentially represented a continuum.

Differences Between Rural and Urban Communities

Part of the stimulus for focusing upon rural practice is the perception that social work practice principles derived from urban settings may not be relevant to rural problems (Martinez-Brawley, 1980; Davenport and Davenport, 1984). In social work and other disciplines, numerous writers have attempted to delineate the differences between rural and urban needs, cultures, perceptions, and value systems. If the context is different, the logical assumption would be that practice must be different to be appropriate to its context.

There is substantial evidence of differences between rural and urban communities in attitudes, values, lifestyles, and belief systems. For example, Willets, et al. (1982, p. 72) assert that evidence continues to indicate that rural people in comparison to urban are more traditional in their moral orientation, less accepting of minority rights, more ideologically religious and conservative in their practices, more likely to oppose federal government, and, though evaluating their community facilities less favorably, are more satisfied with their lifestyle. Furthermore, rural governance operates with different internal organization and style, i.e., decision-making is based more on consensus and maintenance of the status quo. After an extensive review of the literature, Larson (1978) concluded that, while many changes have occurred over time, there continue to be value and lifestyle differences between rural and urban people with farm persons demonstrating the most extreme of the rural values.

A question that arises, however, is whether social workers in rural and urban communities view their communities differently. If not, there would be little reason to expect social workers in rural areas to operate differently from their urban counterparts. If rural and urban social workers do perceive differences between their communities, another question that arises is whether these perceptions of the community have any influence on their practice.

From the literature on rural and urban differences, several generalizations have appeared. Suggestions have been made that rural communities are more likely than urban communities to exhibit the following traits:

1. Employing informal, rather than formal, decision-making processes regarding the governance of the community;
2. A slow, rather than fast, pace of life.;
3. A stable, rather than changing, lifestyle, which exhibits a strong sense of history and a concern for the preservation of present or past values and morals;
4. A traditional, rather than cosmopolitan, value system which seems to tolerate a narrow, rather than broad, spectrum of values, behaviors, and beliefs;
5. The use of informal, rather than formal, support systems in which the individual depends for assistance on being known in the community, and on family and friends;

(Continued)

EXHIBIT 7.2 *Continued*

6. An orientation toward being more concerned with acceptance in the community than with the expression of individuality;
7. Rather little emphasis on educational credentials as a necessity for achievement.

Rural Social Work Practice

The conception of the rural practitioner as a generalist, originally proposed by Ginsberg (1976), has been a central principle in the development of literature around rural practice. While this conceptualization has had some critics (see, for example, Webster and Campbell, 1977; Farley, et. al., 1982; Couch, 1977), a recurring theme has been the definition of *generalist* in terms of roles, which proposes that rural social workers must engage in activities that span several roles and are not in a good position to specialize.

Considerable debate has been devoted to which roles should be preeminent or whether certain practice roles are even appropriate for rural areas. Webster and Campbell (1977), for example, have advocated for a rural worker oriented toward program development and have questioned the appropriateness of certain roles such as mediator, therapist, and advocate. Mermelstein and Sundet (1982) have suggested five roles which they think are most advantageous to the rural worker while Farley et al. (1982) have stipulated thirteen roles for the rural worker. The most comprehensive work on practice roles was undertaken by the Southern Regional Education Board (Ginsberg, 1976). This typology included the roles of outreach worker, broker, advocate, evaluator, teacher, behavior changer, mobilizer, consultant, community planner, caregiver, data manager, and administrator.

In light of the scarcity of resources in rural communities, there has been a focus on the use of informal networks (Johnson, 1983). The assumption is made that rural social workers utilize and help develop these networks in the absence of formal service systems. Furthermore, the heavy reliance on informal systems in the rural community suggests that this may be a fruitful resource for the social work practitioner.

In summary, the literature suggests that rural social work practice should be different from urban practice in regard to roles, specialization, and the use of informal helping networks. Yet, several studies have failed to reveal a difference between the rural and urban social worker. One potential explanation for similarity between rural and urban practice is the possibility that rural and urban communities are not perceived as different by social workers.

One of the limitations of previous surveys of social workers on this issue is that these studies have been conducted with somewhat limited samples. It is suggested that a survey be conducted of social workers from a broad spectrum of practice settings in a state that has a rather diverse population in regard to the rural–urban continuum.

The first question to be pursued in new research is whether rural social workers differ from their urban counterparts in regard to their perceptions of their communities. The second question is whether differences between social workers in differing levels of population are gradual, suggesting a continuum, or abrupt, suggesting a dichotomy. In other words, should locality (rural and urban) be conceptualized as a dichotomy or as a continuum? The third question is whether rural and urban social workers are different in their practice.

EXHIBIT 7.2   *Continued*

References

Couch, B., Dutton, E., & Gurass, A. (1977). A specialist–generalist model of social work practice for contemporary rural America. In R. K. Green and S. A. Webster (Eds.), *Social work in rural areas: Preparation and practice* (pp. 95–107). Knoxville: University of Tennessee School of Social Work.

Davenport, J., & Davenport. J. A. (1984). Theoretical perspectives of rural/urban differences. *Human Services in the Rural Environment*, 9 (1), 4–9.

Farley, O. W., Griffiths, K. A., Skidmore, R. A., & Thackeray, M. G. (1982). *Rural social work practice*. New York: Free Press.

Ginsberg, L. H. (Ed.) (1976). *Social work in rural communities: A book of readings*. New York: Council on Social Work Education.

Glenn, N., & Hill, L. (1977). Rural–urban differences in attitudes and behaviors in the United States. *Annals of the American Academy of Political Science*, 123, 36–50.

Johnson, L. C. (1983). Networking: A means of maximizing resources. *Human Services in the Rural Environment*, 8 (2), 27–31.

Larson, O. (1978). Values and beliefs of rural people. In T. Ford (Ed.), *Rural U.S. A.: Persistence and change* (pp. 91–112). Ames, Ia.: Iowa State University.

Martinez-Brawley, E. E. (Ed.) (1980). *Pioneer efforts in rural social work: First hand views since 1908.* University Park: Pennsylvania State University Press.

Mermelstein, J., & Sundet, P. (1982). Worker acceptance and credibility in the rural environment. In H. W. Johnson (Ed.), *Rural human service: A book of readings*. Itasca, Ill.: F. E. Peacock.

O'Neil, J. F., & Horner, W. C. (1982). Two surveys of social service practice in the northwest: Comparing rural and urban practitioners. In M. Jacobsen (Ed.), *Nourishing people and communities through the lean years*. Iowa City: University of Iowa School of Social Work.

Redfield, R. (1953). *The primitive world and its transformation*. Ithaca, N. Y.: Cornell University Press.

Toennies, F. (1963). *Community and society*. Translated and edited by C. P. Lommis. New York: Harper and Row.

Webster, S. A., and Campbell, P. M. (1977). The 1970s and changing dimensions in rural life—Is a new practice model needed? In R. K. Green and S. A. Webster (Eds.), *Social work in rural areas: Preparation and practice* (pp. 75–93). Knoxville: University of Tennessee School of Social Work.

Whitaker, W. H. (1986). A survey of perceptions of social work practice in rural and urban areas. *Human Services in the Rural Environment*, 9 (3), 12–19.

Willits, F. K., Bealer, R. C., and Crider, D. M. (1982). Persistence of rural/urban differences. In D. Dillman and D. Hobbs (Eds.), *Rural society in the U.S.: Issues for the 1980s* (pp. 69–76). Boulder, Colo: Westview Press.

ASSIGNMENT 7–B

1. Which of the following research questions is *least* supported by the previous literature review?

   a. Does rural and urban social work practice differ?

   b. Do male and female social workers differ in their practice in rural and urban localities?

c. Do rural and urban social workers differ in their perceptions of the communities in which they work?

d. Should locality (rural and urban) be conceptualized as a continuum or as a dichotomy?

Comments:

_____

_____

_____

_____

2. What is one way that the variable of locality (rural and urban) might be defined and measured?

_____

_____

_____

_____

3. What is one way that the variable of social work practice might be defined and measured?

_____

_____

_____

_____

4. Examine the research questions identified in (1) above. Identify the variables for each of these questions.

a. The variable(s) for question A is/are:

_____

_____

_____

b. The variable(s) for question B is/are:

_____

_____

_____

c. The variable(s) for question C is/are:

_____

_____

_____

b. The variable(s) for question D is/are:

_____

_____

_____

Developing the Study Methodology

The study methodology in explanatory research contains information on the definition and measurement of the study variables, the study sample, the means of collecting information, the study hypothesis to be tested, and the statistical measure that will be employed in this endeavor. But before you undertake these tasks, you should remind yourself of the three study questions which identify the variables you must measure.

1. Do rural and urban social workers perceive their communities differently?
2. Should locality be conceptualized as a dichotomy or as a continuum?
3. Is the practice of rural and urban social workers different?

One of your first tasks is to define your variables in abstract terms so that you will know precisely what you are going to measure. The question of whether a quantitative or qualitative method of observation is more appropriate for this situation is one of the next issues to be addressed. In explanatory research, quantitative measurement is more typical because it lends itself to more precise interpretation.

One of the next tasks is the determination of the means to be used to collect information. The *social survey* is probably the best method of observation in explanatory research because it provides the most efficient means for collecting information on large samples. Another task in the research methodology is the determination of the instrumentation used to measure the study variables. It is desirable to measure study variables through existing instruments because they have normally been subjected to tests of reliability and validity. However, it is not uncommon for the researcher to have to develop a tailored measurement device because a suitable tool cannot be found in the existing literature.

The development of the hypothesis is a task that can be articulated with precision when the measurement devices have been determined. A general hypothesis, however, can be developed earlier in the research process. The study hypothesis is a statement which predicts what the outcome of the study will be if present theory is supported. If the specific tool for measurement is incorporated in the statement of the hypothesis, it will be possible to use this statement to determine the statistical measure to be employed in the testing of the hypothesis.

Sampling is another task in the development of the research methodology. You must define your study population and determine the method to be used to select a study sample from that population. Your sampling methods will determine the extent to which you can generalize your findings to persons not included in the study.

Defining and Measuring the Study Variables

Remember that a variable is something that can take on more than one value—i.e., a variable must vary! In this study, you are going to conduct a survey of social workers in which you are going to ask questions that enable you to measure social work practice and rurality by examining the relationship between these two things. Before you undertake the task of determining how to measure your variables, you should first define them in abstract terms.

An *abstract* definition of a variable provides a conceptual map of the variable. It directs the reader's attention to how a concept is being defined for the purposes of a study. An abstract definition of social work practice, for example, might describe that practice in terms of social work roles rather than on the basis of some other concept such as agency setting, attitudes, or effectiveness in meeting client need. An abstract definition of a variable differs from its *operational* definition in that the latter specifies how the variable will be measured in a given study. For example, an operational definition of social work practice might provide the specific question that will be asked of social workers in order for the variable to be measured.

One of our variables is *community perception*. You want to know if rural and urban social workers perceive their communities to be different along the lines that have been identified in the literature. An abstract definition of this variable would specify the dimensions of community perception, identified in the literature review. In particular, it was mentioned that rural and urban communities differ in regard to the following:

1. The employment of informal or formal decision-making processes;
2. A slow or fast pace of life;
3. A stable lifestyle which exhibits a strong sense of history and a concern for the preservation of present or past morals or values, or a changing lifestyle which does not place emphasis in this way;
4. A traditional value system which seems to tolerate a narrow spectrum of values, behaviors, and beliefs, or a more cosmopolitan value system which tolerates more diversity;
5. The use of informal or formal support systems;
6. More concern with being accepted in the community or the expression of individuality;
7. The extent of the emphasis upon educational credentials as a necessity for achievement.

In your definition of *social work practice,* you could choose to focus on the purposes of social work or the values that social workers are supposed to possess or the things that social workers do or the extent to which they meet client needs or something else. The focus, of course, should emanate from the purpose. Do you want to know if social workers in rural and urban areas feel differently or do things differently? If you are studying whether practice differs, you normally are talking about what things social workers do, rather than the way they feel.

When researchers think of the differences between rural and urban communities, they often focus on differences in lifestyle and availability of service. With regard to differences in lifestyle, the use of informal networks is often mentioned in the literature. If people in rural areas are more likely to rely upon informal networks, shouldn't social workers make more use of them in their work with their clients? Another issue is availability of service, which affects the roles that social workers play. Perhaps they should place more emphasis on being a broker than a therapist, or being a generalist rather than a specialist.

Another variable that you must define is *locality* (sometimes referred to as "rurality"). By locality, researchers are referring to rural–urban differences. Your first task is to determine what this concept means. The following quote from the literature review may be useful:

> *Several approaches have been used to define rurality. In rural sociology, most definitions fall into three categories: occupational, sociocultural, or ecological. Most of the social work literature has relied on an ecological definition, that is, reference to the distribution of people in space. Therefore, many professionals measure rurality in terms of population size and population density.*

Another major task of the abstract definition of this variable is the determination of whether you should define the variable as a dichotomy or as a continuum. With regard to this issue, the following quote may be helpful:

> *Although some definitions of rurality propose a dichotomy between rural and urban, many researchers and theoreticians have long recognized that rural–urban*

differences are best represented along a continuum. In an overview of research on rural–urban differences in attitudes and behavior, Norvail Glenn and Lester Hill (1977) examined support for the idea of a continuum. They pointed out that the largest communities usually differ from the medium-sized communities about as much as the medium-sized communities differ from the smallest communities, and that the direction of these differences is consistent from one size to the next. This pattern of variation suggests that it is useful to conceive of rurality as a continuum.

Determining Whether to Use Qualitative or Quantitative Means of Measurement

In general, there are two means for measuring variables—qualitative and quantitative. In qualitative measurement, researchers use open-ended questions in which people can express their answers in their own words. In quantitative measurement, they provide categories for people's responses or ask them to express their responses in a specific quantitative dimension such as years of age or weight in pounds and so forth. In this way, they can readily compare one person's answer to another's when they use quantitative means of measuring variables.

Quantitative measurement is more appropriate when investigators have precise ways to measure their variables. If the variables can readily be translated into discrete categories, they should measure the variables this way. Quantitative measurement is also more appropriate when they are attempting to test a hypothesis or theory rather than developing a theory where there is none.

The state of knowledge about the subject of research is a prime determinant of the approach researchers should take to measurement. If little is known, they may need to use a qualitative approach because they do not know the dimensions of the subject. An example is an interview study of adults who had been adopted as older children many years earlier and were in a position to reflect upon what the experience had been like. There being little literature about the experience of being adopted as an older child, the researcher did not have convenient categories into which to place people's answers; as a result, open-ended questions were used in an interview format. No theory was being tested because there was a dearth of theory about this phenomenon. What was needed was the creation of knowledge that could lead to a theory to be tested by others.

ASSIGNMENT 7–C

1. In your definition of social work practice, what should you focus your attention on?

   a. How social workers feel

   b. What social workers think

   c. What social workers do

   d. Where social workers do the things they do

Explain:

_____

_____

_____

_____

2. Based on the above answer, what might be the specific focus of your definition of social work practice?

   a. The roles social workers play such as advocate, broker, therapist, case manager, and so forth

   b. The extent to which social workers embrace a humanitarian value set

   c. The settings in which social workers are employed, such as health, mental health, family and child, etc.

   Explain:

   _____

   _____

   _____

   _____

3. What approach should you take to the definition of rurality—ecological, sociocultural, or occupational?

   _____

   _____

   _____

   _____

4. Should you measure your variables in a qualitative manner, as the following examples of items for a questionnaire would?

   a. How would you characterize the community in which you work?

   b. Please describe what you do as a social worker.

Or, should you use quantitative means of measuring your variables?

a. What is the population of the county in which you are employed?

b. To what extent do you make use of informal helping networks in your work with your clients?

_____	Not at all	_____	To some extent
_____	To a very little extent	_____	To a great extent
_____	To a little extent	_____	To a very great extent

Determining How to Collect Data

There are several alternative methods you could employ in the collection of data. You could conduct personal interviews with social workers. You could employ a mailed survey. You might even be able to obtain some of the data for your study by examining agency records or other agency documents such as organizational charts and so forth.

The mailed survey has several advantages for this study. Perhaps the most important one is that you can obtain information from a larger number of people with a limited amount of resources through a mailed survey. In other words, this method of data collection is more efficient than the personal interview, which takes much more time. In this case, it is very important that you obtain a large sample. Another advantage of the mailed survey is that the participant can record information anonymously. This advantage is not very important in the present study because you are not dealing with a sensitive issue, such as sexual practices or illegal behavior.

A disadvantage of the social survey is that you will miss the more subtle nuances of the topic. With the survey, especially the one which employs quantitative means of measurement, you are bound by the limits of the particular definitions of the variables and the particular way you have chosen to measure them. It may be, for example, that you choose to measure social work practice in relation to specialization among roles and the use of informal helping networks. But what if the reality is that rural and urban social workers do not differ on these variables but do differ on some other aspect of practice? Your survey would miss this new information, whereas a more flexible approach to observation would have the potential to pick up such information.

Instrumentation

Survey instruments should conform to many standards of good research practice. For one thing, items on the instrument should be clear. You should not, for example, use terms that are not well understood by the subjects of the study. You should not use double-barreled questions that pose two questions in one. For example, consider the question, "Have you ever beaten your child so severely that the child required medical attention or witnessed someone else doing so?" If a person answers *yes,* what does this mean? Are they child abusers or simply witnesses to the event?

Questions should not show a bias or provide a cue to the socially desirable response. Some respondents will answer the way they think you want them to answer rather than revealing their true thoughts.

Questions that present categories for the subject's response should contain categories that are *mutually exclusive* and *exhaustive.* Categories are mutually exclusive if they do not overlap. If categories overlap, a given subject may fit into more than one of the categories. Categories are exhaustive if they contain a category that will fit everyone. In many situations, it is necessary to add the category of "other" so that people who do not fit into any one of the established categories have a place for their responses.

For this study, you must decide how you are going to measure the variables of

1. community perception,
2. locality (rural and urban), and
3. social work practice.

In the previous discussion, locality was defined in terms of population. The greater the population or population density, the more urban is the community.

One of the ways that population can be measured is in terms of population density or the number of persons per square mile of land. A large city, of course, has a great number of people per square mile whereas an isolated rural county would have few persons per square mile. Population density is one way of measuring rurality. In the present study, respondents were asked to identify the county of their employment and the county's population and population density were secured from statewide statistical manuals.

To measure perception according to a specific set of dimensions, a survey instrument should be used which asks respondents to identify the extent to which each of these dimensions of community life is present in their work communities. The items used to measure perception of community are presented in Exhibit 7.3. Each item provides higher scores for the more urban orientation. The respondents' answers to these questions were summed for a total score,

Social work practice is the other major variable in this study. There are many ways that you could measure social work practice. The literature review suggested that roles would be one way to characterize social work practice. Another way would be with reference to the use of informal helping networks. In this study, you will describe social work practice in terms of the roles social workers perform. The items used to measure social work practice are presented in Exhibit 7.4. These items describe different roles. The label for each role is given at the end.

EXHIBIT 7.3   Items on the Community Life Scale That Were Asked of Respondents to the Survey

Listed below are seven descriptive dimensions of community life, each of which is followed by a seven-point continuum. The extreme points of the continuum are delineated by terms describing opposite features. Please circle the number along the continuum for each dimension which appears to best describe the community in which you work.

Decision-making: the process by which decisions concerning the governance of the community appear to be made. 1 = Informal—decisions are made on the basis of relationship networks and being "known" to the decision-makers; 7 = Formal—decisions are made on the basis of position (elected or appointed), merit, or legislated procedure.

1   2   3   4   5   6   7

Informal   Formal

Pace of Life: the speed with which life is lived, change is incorporated into community life, or innovations are accepted by the majority of individuals within the community. 1 = Slow;   7 = Fast.

1   2   3   4   5   6   7

Slow   Fast

Lifestyle: the orientation of the community toward continuing past ways of doing things or toward accepting new ways of living. 1 = Stable—the community exhibits a strong sense of history and a concern for the preservation of present or past values and morals; 7 = Changing—the community moves rapidly to adapt to a diverse population; decisions are based on expediency and contractual relations.

1   2   3   4   5   6   7

Stable   Changing

Values: those internalized beliefs which people use to guide their choices and behaviors. 1 = traditional—the community seems to approve of a narrow spectrum of values, behaviors, and beliefs; 7 = Cosmopolitan—the community seems to tolerate a broad spectrum of values, behaviors, and beliefs.

1   2   3   4   5   6   7

Traditional   Cosmopolitan

Support Systems: the networks of relationships on which individuals rely when they experience life difficulties. 1 = Informal—the individual primarily depends for assistance on being known in the community, on family, or on friendship networks; 7 =

EXHIBIT 7.3   *Continued*

Formal—individuals depend on formalized, legislated, or contractual services through public or private institutions.

1   2   3   4   5   6   7

Informal   Formal

Internal–External Focus: the orientation of the community toward being concerned with acceptance in the community or toward expression of individuality. 1 = Community —community members govern their behavior to a great extent by its acceptability in the community and a concern for how others will view their behavior; 7 = Individualism—community members appear to be concerned with expressing their individuality with little external orientation.

1   2   3   4   5   6   7

Community   Individualism

Educational Emphasis: the degree to which the community seems to emphasize education as a necessity for achievement. 1 = None; 7 = Great emphasis.

1   2   3   4   5   6   7

None   Great emphasis

EXHIBIT 7.4   Questionnaire Items Designed to Measure Social Work Practice

Listed below are nine activities which describe some of the ways in which social workers intervene with client systems. Using a typical two-week period of your work as a baseline, rate these activities according to the emphasis you typically place on each one. Following the activity description is a seven-point continuum ranging from "1," which represents "not at all," to "7," which represents "to a very great extent." Please circle the number which appears to best approximate the emphasis you place on each activity.

1. Guiding client systems toward existing services, helping them negotiate the service system, and/or linking components of the service system with one another.

1   2   3   4   5   6   7

Not at all   To a very great extent

(Continued)

EXHIBIT 7.4   *Continued*

2. Working with groups or communities to create resources that relate to existing problems.

     1   2   3   4   5   6   7
Not at all   To a very great extent

3. Working with groups or individuals to resolve conflicts by mediating the interaction in an impartial manner.

     1   2   3   4   5   6   7
Not at all   To a very great extent

4. Attempting to obtain services or rights for an individual or a group by fighting for those services or rights in order to overcome obstacles.

     1   2   3   4   5   6   7
Not at all   To a very great extent

5. Working with individuals, families, or small groups to bring about specific changes in their behavior patterns, symptoms, or perceptions, including the imparting of information in order to develop various skills.

     1   2   3   4   5   6   7
Not at all   To a very great extent

6. Collecting, classifying, and analyzing data generated within the social welfare environment in order to aid in the development of action plans.

     1   2   3   4   5   6   7
Not at all   To a very great extent

7. Managing a program, organization, or service unit.

     1   2   3   4   5   6   7
Not at all   To a very great extent

8. Working with large groups, organizations, or communities to help them increase their skills in solving social welfare problems.

     1   2   3   4   5   6   7
Not at all   To a very great extent

9. Informal helping networks are sets of enduring relationships of a nonprofessional nature which provide emotional support, advice, mutual self-help, and, in some cases, even concrete assistance with life problems. Examples include networks of extended family members, self-help groups, friends and neighbors, church members, and so forth.

EXHIBIT 7.4   *Continued*

In your work with your clients, to what extent do you make use of informal helping networks?

	1	2	3	4	5	6	7
Not at all							To a very great extent

Roles   1 = Broker   2 = Mobilizer   3 = Mediator

4 = Advocate   5 = Clinical   6 = Data Manager

7 = Manager   8 = Community Organizer

9 = Informal helping networks

ASSIGNMENT 7–D

1. Give one reason that a social survey will be used in this study of the relationship between locality and social work practice.

_____

_____

_____

2. Give one disadvantage of this means of observation (i.e., the social survey).

_____

_____

_____

3. How does item (1) in Exhibit 7.4 compare with the following way of measuring one of the variables related to social work practice?

To what extent do you employ the broker role in your work?

_____   Very much   _____   Quite a lot   _____   Some   _____   Little

4. How does item (9) in Exhibit 7.4 compare with the following way of measuring one of the study variables?

How much do you agree with the idea that social workers in rural areas should make use of informal helping networks?

_____ Strongly   _____ Agree _____ Disagree   _____ Strongly
       Agree   Disagree

5. How does the following compare with item (9) from Exhibit 7.4?

The literature on rural and urban social work practice suggests that social workers in rural areas should make use of informal helping networks in their work with clients.

Do you work in a rural area? _____ Yes   _____ No

Do you make use of informal helping networks? _____ Yes   _____ No

_____

_____

_____

6. The variable of locality (rurality) could be measured by asking respondents to identify the county in which they work and by looking up the population density of that county (i.e., the number of persons per square mile). What do you think of that means for measuring rurality compared with the following item?

Do you live or work in a rural area? _____ Yes   _____ No

_____

_____

_____

Assessing the Reliability and Validity of the Measurement Devices

When researchers seek to measure a variable, they need to know if their devices for measurement are credible or trustworthy. How do they know they can really depend on these instruments to truly measure what they are trying to measure? In the pursuit of the answer to this question, they can utilize the concepts of reliability and validity.

Validity refers to the accuracy of the measurement device. Does it measure what researchers intend for it to measure? If one researcher defines the concept of self-esteem in the same way as another and undertakes a study of the correlation of scores on one instrument with that of the other researcher, there should be a high correlation. For example, if John is higher than Tom on one scale, he is likely to be higher than Tom on the other scale. If this does not turn out to be the pattern of responses, then researchers have reason to believe that one or both of the instruments are not valid—i.e., are not truly measuring the concept of self-esteem. While it is possible that the first researcher's instrument is valid and the other instrument is not, there is no way to know from this one correlation which instrument is inaccurate, or if both instruments are inaccurate. Thus, researchers cannot have confidence in an instrument unless they have other information that supports the validity of their measurement tool.

Another way to examine validity is to see if an instrument operates the way it should logically. For example, if researchers have conceptualized an *environmental role set* as containing the roles of broker, advocate, and mobilizer, and conceptualized a *relationship role set* as containing the roles of clinician and mediator, they have said that these roles are found in different sets. In other words, there is something common about the roles in each set that sets it apart from the roles in the other set. Thus, they would expect that certain social work jobs that emphasized one role in a set to emphasize the other roles in that set more so than the roles in the other set. Otherwise, they have not really found distinctions between the role sets. In other words they have not found meaningful distinctions among role behaviors that would support their conceptualizations. Some other conceptualizations would perhaps be more meaningful.

If an item on a questionnaire has wording that is confusing, it will be of little use in the analysis of a research question because researchers will not know how to interpret the response of the participant. One study subject may interpret the question one way and another subject may interpret it another way. As a result, their responses (e.g., yes or no) cannot be treated in the same manner.

Take, for example, question (6) from Exercise 7–C:

Do you live or work in a rural area? _____ *Yes* _____ *No*

Some respondents may interpret "rural" to mean a town with a population below 50,000 and will classify themselves as working in a rural area because the town has a population of 35,000, while other respondents living in the same town of 35,000 may interpret "rural" to mean a population of less than 10,000 and will answer that they do *not* work in a rural area. Thus, this means of measurement would not be accurate.

Does the Beck Depression Scale truly measure what most clinicians know as depression? One way to check this out is to have a group of clients take the Beck Depression Scale and have these same clients rated by their clinicians in relation to the level of their depression. Do scores on the Beck Depression Scale tend to vary in the anticipated pattern with regard to ratings by clinicians? In other words, do clients with high levels of depression as indicated by the Scale tend to be more likely to be rated with high levels of depression by clinicians? If not, researchers can say that they failed to find evidence of the validity of the Scale.

Reliability refers to the consistency of a measurement device. A measurement tool is reliable if the same person responds to it in a consistent fashion at two points in time, or if scores on one-half of the tool measuring a concept are consistent with the scores on the other half. If the instrument is worded in a confusing manner, inconsistency in responses would occur because respondents would not know what they were answering. Scores at two points in time would not be related; responses to questions on one half of the instrument would not be congruent with responses on the other half.

Researchers could check reliability of a measurement tool by having the same person respond to an instrument at two points in time to see if their responses were consistent between the time periods. Would people tend to classify themselves as rural one day and as urban a few weeks later? If so, their responses are not consistent and researchers don't really know what they are measuring with the instrument.

Developing the Study Hypothesis

One of the steps in the research process is the prediction of the results of the study. This prediction emanates from the literature review and any other information that constitutes the knowledge base for the study. In research terms, this prediction is the *hypothesis.* The hypothesis is a statement of a predicted relationship between the dependent and independent variables. It is much like a theory except that it is stated with greater precision.

The *dependent variable* is the variable that depends upon another variable for its status, the other variable being the *independent variable.* To put it another way, the dependent variable is caused by the independent variable. The independent variable is the cause and the dependent variable is the effect. If social workers are treating clients, they would refer to the treatment as the independent variable and the clients' condition as the dependent variable because they believe that treatment causes clients to get better. (However, researchers should employ the word *cause* with much caution when they are dealing with social research. In social research, there are several strict conditions that must be met in order for a statement of causality to be justified.)

On what does the grade on the final exam for a research course depend? Does it depend on how much the student studied? Does it depend on how much previous knowledge the student had about research? Does it depend on how smart the student is? You would probably answer yes to each of these questions. If so, you are identifying each of these as independent variables and the grade as the dependent variable. You are saying that, generally speaking, students who put more time into studying for the final exam will receive a higher grade on it. But you are also recognizing that study time is not the only variable that can predict the exam grade.

The hypothesis has a critical role in the research process. It helps to guide the analysis of the results and an understanding of the nature of the statistical findings. It links the results with the work of others. It helps researchers to avoid thinking that they have found something profound when, in fact, they may have discovered only a random fluctuation in the world.

To illustrate, let's suppose that you want to know what predicts the clients' level of satisfaction with agency services. You give a set of questions that are measured on ordinal scales in which they rate the level of their satisfaction and you combine these responses into a general scale of satisfaction. What variables predict the clients' scores on satisfaction? In order to find out, you ask questions about twenty-five different variables such as gender, age, type of problem, whether they are left-handed or right-handed, their nationality, the color of their hair, their level of depression, whether they had a parent who was an alcoholic, and so forth.

Notice that several of these variables make little sense as predictors of satisfaction. What would make you believe that being right-handed or left-handed would determine a client's level of satisfaction? Let's suppose that this variable is the only one of twenty-five variables that proves to be a statistically significant predictor of satisfaction score. Do you have a noteworthy finding?

The answer is No! Why? Because one variable in twenty-five could appear as significant only by chance. The next time you conduct the same study, you might, by chance, find that another variable is statistically significant but that left-handedness is not. Thus, the construction of a hypothesis based on a knowledge base helps to avoid "fishing with a net" as a basis of discovery. If you throw out a large enough net, you will likely catch some fish but this does not prove that you are in good fishing waters.

The hypothesis is presented in the form of a statement, not a question. It identifies both the dependent variable and the independent variable and should be presented with as much clarity as possible. Examples include the following:

1. Males will report higher annual salaries than will females.
2. Clients will receive lower scores on depression after treatment than before treatment.
3. Older clients will report higher levels of satisfaction with agency services than will younger clients.
4. The school dropout rate of Ashley High School will be lower in the six months following the completion of the Dropout Prevention Program than it was in the six months preceding the initiation of the Dropout Prevention Program.

ASSIGNMENT 7–E

1. Because of the tendency of rural areas to be lacking in resources that are more typical of urban communities, it would be expected that rural social workers would be more likely to emphasize the role of mobilizer. One way to state this expectation as a hypothesis is as follows:

   Among social workers, there will be a negative relationship between population of work county and emphasis on the role of mobilizer.

Why was this hypothesis stated as a negative relationship between the study variables rather than a positive one?

_____

_____

_____

_____

2. What kind of relationship would you expect to find between the use of informal helping networks and population of work county? State this as a hypothesis.

_____

_____

_____

_____

3. In your hypothesis given in problem (2), what is the dependent variable?

_____

_____

_____

_____

4. What is the independent variable in this hypothesis?

_____

_____

_____

_____

5. If you gave item (3) in Exhibit 7.4 to a group of social workers at two different points in time, what would you expect to find in the way of a correlation between their answers at time 1 and time 2?

_____ No   _____ Positive   _____ Negative
        correlation   correlation   correlation

Explain:

_____

_____

_____

_____

6. In the example given above, would this be an example of the testing of the validity of your measurement device or the reliability of it?

_____

_____

_____

_____

7. How might you test the other thing that contributes to the credibility of your measuring tool (i.e., either reliability or validity)?

_____

_____

_____

_____

Sampling

The state of North Carolina is a good population from which to draw a sample because it is quite diverse regarding the issue of rurality. In other words, it has many rural areas and many urban areas and other areas that fall along the rural–urban continuum. You would not be able to address your question very well if you only asked questions of people in rural areas because you would not have people in urban areas to which the rural participants could be compared.

For example, suppose that you collected data only from social workers working in communities with less than 10,000 population and defined these communities as rural. What if you found that 53 percent of these workers indicated that they made use of informal helping networks. So what! It might be that **65 percent** of social workers in urban areas do the same thing; thus, urban workers are *more* likely than rural ones to engage in this practice behavior. If such were the case, you would have ignored the most important piece of information by including only rural social workers in the sample.

You need to collect data from a broad spectrum of practice settings. The membership list of the North Carolina Chapter of the National Association of Social Workers probably would be the best resource, so your population is the membership of this organization. This membership constitutes a sample of all social workers in the state of North Carolina but it does *not* constitute a *probability* sample of all the social workers in this state.

Why? Remember the statement from the previous lesson. A probability sample is one in which all persons from the population have an equal chance of being included in the study. In this case, people not in NASW cannot be included in the study if you use this membership list from which to draw your sample. But, if you use a random basis for making choices from this list, you can say that you have a *probability* sample of people from the *membership of NASW in this state*.

You have decided that you cannot afford to send questionnaires to every member of NASW in North Carolina because there are about 1,600 members. So you have decided to select a probability sample from this organization. You have also decided that you can afford to include two hundred people in your survey. Two popular ways for employing the random sampling method are the simple random sample and the systematic random sampling procedure. In the former, you consult a book containing a table of random numbers and select two hundred persons from the list using these numbers.

The Systematic Random Sampling Procedure.   The systematic random sampling procedure includes the following steps:

1. The total in the population is divided by the number of people to be included in the sample to derive a *sampling interval*.

   (Example: 1600 / 200 = 8)

2. If the sampling interval is 8, then the first 8 people on the membership list constitute the first sampling interval. The first person to be included in the study is selected at random from among these 8 people. (Example: Place eight pieces of paper with numbers 1 through 8 in a hat and draw one out. This is the number of the first person to be selected.) If you select number 3, then the first person selected for the sample would be person number 3 on the list.

3. The person who falls exactly one sampling interval beyond the first person will be the second person selected. Suppose that the first person is number 3 on the list. You would then select person number 11 (3 + 8) as the second person in your sample. You would then select person number 19 as the third person (11 + 8), and so on.

ASSIGNMENT 7–F

1. What if you went down the membership list alphabetically, starting with A, until you had secured 200 names. For example, you might select everyone named Adams and then everyone named Baker and the one person named Bennett and so forth, ending perhaps with someone named Davis. Would you have selected a *probability* sample? Explain.

_____

_____

_____

_____

_____

2. If you define your population as NASW members in the United States, can you say that you have selected a *probability* sample? _____ Yes _____No

3. If you define your population as social workers in the state of North Carolina, can you say that you have a *probability* sample? _____Yes _____No

4. Can you define the population as social workers who work in rural areas?

_____

_____

_____

_____

_____

5. Suppose that you wished to employ the systematic random sampling procedure to obtain a sample of social work students in your school. You have two hundred social work students and you want to draw a sample of fifty. You have randomly selected student number 3 on your list. Which student is the next one to be selected for this sample?

   a. Student number 5   c. Student number 7

   b. Student number 6   d. Student number 13

Analyzing the Study Results

After the questionnaires have been collected, you are ready to analyze the data. There are three types of information that explanatory studies typically provide:

1. the description of the sample
2. the presentation of descriptive data regarding the key study variables
3. the presentation of data regarding the testing of the hypotheses

The sample description gives the reader the opportunity to speculate on the applicability of the study findings to populations not included in the sample. If a group of readers are working with a population that is very different from the study sample in regard to variables such as gender or race, they would exercise caution in estimating whether the study's findings would likely be relevant to their population.

The descriptive data portrays the patterns of variation regarding study variables which helps in the interpretation of the results. Perhaps a relationship between two variables was not found in part because there was very little variation in the subjects' responses. For example, I conducted a study of the relationship between social support and stress among social work students, and found that few social work students were lacking in a strong support system. The pattern of variation was low. The vast majority had either moderately high or very high levels of social support. A proper interpretation of these results would be "Students with high social support were not found to have lower levels of stress than students with moderately high social support." In other words, moving from moderately high social support to high social support does not seem to make any difference in one's level of stress. This may not be surprising to the reader. Small increments in one variable are not likely to influence another variable. However, the danger in this situation would be the temptation for the researcher to conclude that social support does not seem to influence stress. It may well be that there would be differences in stress levels between people with low social support and those with high social support, but people in the former category were not included in these particular data.

The heart of the data analysis, of course, is the testing of the hypotheses. Each hypothesis should be presented and analyzed with appropriate statistical tests. Both the strength of the relationship found between study variables and the statistical significance of the results should be examined. The former will aid in the determination of practical significance and the latter will guide the determination of statistical significance.

Sample Description

One way to describe the sample for the present study follows.

The respondents ranged in age from 22 to 65 with a mean of 39.7. There were more females (81%) than males and more Caucasians (93%) than members of minority groups. A majority (70%) of the respondents listed their job positions as direct ser-

vice while only 6 percent indicated supervisory positions and 18 percent, administration. Six percent listed their positions as "other."

Respondents came from 40 of the 100 counties in the state of North Carolina. The following table presents the proportion of respondents by size of work county.

County Population	Percent of Respondents
Less than 30,000	5 percent
30,000–49,999	10 percent
50,000–99,999	17 percent
100,000–249,000	39 percent
250,000–420,000	29 percent

The latter variable is especially relevant to the present study because of the pattern of variation of study subjects with regard to the key variable of locality. Some of the previous studies of rural and urban social work practice have been rather limited in the extent to which subjects represented a range of rural and urban areas. However, there are no really large cities (i.e., in excess of one million population) in the state of North Carolina. Thus, one might challenge the relevance of the present study results to states with such large population centers.

You will now begin testing the study hypotheses. In this endeavor, you will present each study question and deal with descriptive data regarding study variables and the testing of the hypothesis in the same sections.

Examining the Reliability of the Community Life Scale

Because the Community Life Scale was developed especially for the present study, the issues of reliability and validity must be addressed. One means for addressing reliability is the examination of *internal consistency.* An instrument is internally consistent if people respond to the various items on the scale in a consistent fashion. For example, if John has a higher score than Mary for item one on the Beck Depression inventory, he should also have a higher score than Mary for item two on this scale, and for item three, and so forth. Such results would indicate strong correlations between items on the scale and this would constitute evidence in support of the reliability of the scale.

Respondents to the survey in the present study answered each of seven questions in order that perception of community could be measured. The respondent's score for this variable was composed of the sum of scores for each of these questions. Did the respondents answer these seven questions in a consistent fashion?

It is possible that communities with a fast pace of life are *not* more likely to have a changing lifestyle, or an emphasis on formal support systems. Perhaps communities with great emphasis upon education are *not* more likely to emphasize individualism over community. Yet, our development of the Community Life Scale is based on these kinds of assumptions. We have proposed, based on the literature, that a given pattern exists in communities, and that this pattern distinguishes the rural from the urban community. If we find that this is not true, we do not have reason to combine the scores of the subjects on these seven questions into a scale that represents rural and urban differences.

You can examine the *internal consistency* of this scale in several ways. The simplest way is to split these questions into two halves and compute the correlation of each half. If the scale is internally consistent, there should be a positive correlation. A positive correlation between the two halves of the scale would mean that if John has a higher score on Half Number 1 than Mary, he is likely to have a higher score than Mary on Half Number 2.

A formula known as "alpha" provides a more comprehensive test. This formula considers the correlation of each item on a scale with each of the other items on the scale and computes a coefficient that represents the level of internal consistency of the scale. It is generally considered acceptable if the formula results in a coefficient of 0.70 or higher. When we applied this formula to our data, we found the alpha coefficient to be 0.74.

ASSIGNMENT 7–G

1. The examination of the frequencies or means or variance of responses to the study variables can best be used to:

   a. Determine whether the study results can be generalized to populations of people not included in the present study;

   b. Determine if statistical significance has been achieved;

   c. Assist with the interpretation of the meaning of the data results and to determine whether the data provided an optimal test of the study hypothesis.

2. Is there any evidence of the reliability of our means of measuring perception of community? If so, briefly explain. If not, what could we do to assess reliability?

   _____

   _____

   _____

   _____

3. Is there any evidence of the validity of our means of measuring perception of community? If so, briefly explain. If not, what could we do to assess validity?

4. Suppose that you have found that Susan has given a higher rating to the question about lifestyle than did Barbara. Should you expect that Susan will give a higher rating for her community on pace of life than Barbara will?

Examining Empirical Relationships

You will be examining several *empirical relationships* in this analysis. One is the relationship between locality and community dynamics as measured by the Community Life Scale. The question here is whether social workers in rural areas perceive their communities differently than those in urban communities. Another empirical relationship to be analyzed is the one between locality and social work practice. Do social workers in rural and urban communities practice differently?

There are many statistical measures for examining the relationship between two variables. The choice of a particular statistic depends upon several considerations, one of which is the level of measurement for the variables. When there are two variables measured at the interval level, the *Pearson correlation coefficient* is appropriate. For two variables measured at the ordinal level, the *Spearman rank order correlation coefficient* is one of the statistics that could be used. For two variables measured at the nominal level, the *phi coefficient* is one statistical measure that may apply. For each of these measures, correlation *coefficients* are depicted in numbers that range from 0, which represents no relationship at all, to 1.0, which represents a perfect relationship between the variables. The latter will almost never happen because of the complexity of social variables and the variety of influences of one upon the other. It is more typical to obtain correlations of .23 or .35 or .61 and so forth. The higher the value of the coefficient, the stronger is the relationship between the variables. For example, a coefficient of .55 is much higher than one of .17.

A critical issue, of course, is whether the coefficient represents a statistically significant relationship. If not, there is no reason to think that your coefficient value can be relied on to depict the truth of the nature of the relationship between the variables. If you have determined that statistical significance exists, you can consider the issue of practical significance. This is where the value of the coefficient is quite useful. How high must the coefficient be in order to have practical significance? This is a question that is open to much debate, and will always be a matter of professional judgment. To aid in your deliberations on this issue, you can examine different forms of data that represent different values of the phi coefficient. For information on this issue, see Exhibit 7.5. Then review the following discussion on the different types of empirical relationships.

EXHIBIT 7.5   Explaining the Value of the Phi Coefficient

To determine the meaning of the value of a coefficient that measures the strength of the relationship between two variables, you can examine the case of the comparison of a treated group of clients with a nontreated group. Consider the following data:

	Treatment Group	Comparison Group	Total
Recovered	40 (80%)	40 (40%)	80
Not Recovered	10 (20%)	60 (60%)	70
Total	50 (100%)	100 (100%)	150

In this illustration, 40 of the 50 people in the treatment group recovered from their problem while 40 of the 100 persons in the comparison group recovered. Thus, the treatment group had an 80 percent recovery rate compared to the recovery rate of 40 percent for the comparison group. The difference between these two percentages, when converted to a fraction, represents a good estimate of the value of the phi coefficient (The actual value of the phi coefficient, however, is not calculated this way and you can expect small differences between these estimates and the actual value of phi.) In the above case, you would estimate the value of phi coefficient to be 0.40.

When you consider the interpretation of this value, bear in mind the fact that the comparison group should represent the effect of maturation upon the clients' condition. If 40 percent of the comparison group recovered without treatment, you would expect about 40 percent of the treatment group to have done the same in the absence of treatment. Consequently, the difference between the two groups represents the difference that treatment made in the lives of clients. In this example, treatment seems to have made a difference for about 40 percent of the clients even though the rate of recovery was 80 percent. In other words, 4 clients out of 10 (or 40 percent) recovered because of treatment rather than something else. Converting this to a fraction gives the value of 0.40, which is the estimate of the phi coefficient.

Another means of making the value of the correlation coefficient meaningful is to confront the fact that if you square the value of the coefficient, you will have a figure that represents the amount of variance in one variable that is explained by the other variable. For example, a correlation of 0.50 when squared would be 0.25, meaning that 25 percent of the variance in the dependent variable is explained by the independent variable. When you examine a relationship between two variables such as gender and salary, you are saying that you expect to find that gender is one of the things that might influence the salary one receives. But it would be naive to say that gender is the *only* thing that matters. There will be several other things that influence salary. If you find that gender explains 25 percent of the variance in salary, you are saying that 75 percent of the variance is left unexplained. This finding would be considered to be meaningful in spite of the fact that gender is not the only explanation for salary. If it explains any of the variance in salary, you would probably consider this to be meaningful information to know. But the lower the explained variance, the less you will be inclined to pay a great deal of attention to this particular relationship between variables.

Types of Empirical Relationships. There are three patterns of empirical relationships. The first is no relationship. In this case, the values on one variable do not vary in a consistent fashion with the values on the other variable. For example, it may be that there is no relationship between life satisfaction as measured by a life satisfaction scale and the population of one's home town. Such a finding is illustrated by the following hypothetical data:

Population of Home Town

Life Satisfaction	High	Low	Total
High	20 (50%)	10 (50%)	30
Low	20 (50%)	10 (50%)	30
Total	40 (100%)	20 (100%)	60

If you compare the proportion of highly satisfied people from large home towns with the proportion of highly satisfied people from small home towns, you can see that they are the same. Fifty percent of people with large home towns are high for life satisfaction, which is the same as the percentage of highly satisfied people from small home towns. This indicates that there is no relationship between life satisfaction and the size of one's home town. Thus, if you want to know about life satisfaction, the size of one's home town would not be a good variable for study. It would appear that size of home town does not influence life satisfaction.

The second pattern is a *positive* relationship. A positive relationship means that subjects who are high on one variable tend to be high on the other variable. For example, people who have high self-esteem may tend to have higher school performance than do persons who have low self-esteem. Take, for example, the following data:

Self-Esteem

School Grades	High	Low	Total
High	70 (70%)	10 (20%)	50
Low	30 (30%)	40 (80%)	100
Total	100 (100%)	50 (100%)	150

As you can see from these data, 70 percent of those high for self-esteem were found to be high for school grades, whereas only 20 percent of those low for self-esteem were found to be high for school grades. This suggests that one is more likely to be high for school grades if one is high for self-esteem. Thus, perhaps self-esteem influences school grades, and it does so in a positive direction.

The third pattern is a *negative* relationship which means that subjects high on one variable tend to be low on the other variable. For example, it may be that people higher on depression have lower school performance. Review the following data.

Depression

School Grades	High	Low	Total
High	40 (40%)	40 (80%)	80
Low	60 (60%)	10 (20%)	70
Total	100 (100%)	50 (100%)	150

As you can see from these data, people who are *lower* on depression tend to be *higher* for school grades. Only 40 percent of those high on depression had high grades as compared to 80 percent of those who were low on depression.

Positive and negative relationships, however, are possible only in cases in which the variables are measured at the ordinal or interval level. The values of a nominal variable (i.e., the categories into which the subjects fit, such as gender or race) have no numerical meaning. Thus, it makes no sense to talk of a positive or negative relationship between gender and salary because neither of the categories of gender is higher or lower than the other. You can say that there is a relationship between gender and salary if males and females differ significantly on salary, but you cannot say that this relationship is either positive or negative.

Do Rural and Urban Social Workers Perceive Their Communities Differently?

Before examining whether social workers in rural and urban areas were different in their practice, you have decided to examine the question of whether they perceive their communities differently. If they do not, perhaps a low level of difference in practice, if such were found, could be explained, in part, by a lack of perception of differences between rural and urban localities. The first hypothesis may be presented as follows:

> *Social workers in more rural localities will be more likely than their urban counterparts to perceive their communities as exhibiting the characteristics of rural communities as measured by the Community Life Scale.*

There are two key variables in this hypothesis: locality and perception of community. Locality will be measured by both population and population density. Perception of the community is measured by the Community Life Scale.

The population of the work county is one means of measuring the variable of locality. Another is population density, or the number of people per square mile. Each of these variables is measured at the interval level. One's score on the Community Life Scale is also measured at the interval level. Thus, you have two ways of measuring locality and one way of measuring perception of community. You will have two analyses to perform: the relationship between population and community perception and the relationship between population density and community perception.

An appropriate statistic for examining the relationship between two variables measured at the interval level is Pearson's correlation coefficient, which is designated with the small letter r. The value of r for the correlation coefficient can range from 0 to 1.0, the latter representing a perfect relationship. Correlations can be either positive or negative. Positive correlations are designated with the letter r (e.g., r = 0.36) while negative relationships are designated with the minus before the coefficient (e. g., r = −0.41). A correlation of 0 would mean that there was no relationship at all between the two variables.

There is no clearcut guide for interpreting the values of the correlation coefficients in regard to magnitude. One can easily see, of course, that a correlation of 0.45 is stronger than a correlation of 0.31. But is a correlation of 0.45 considered to be strong or moderate or what? This is a question that is not easy to answer. Some textbooks have ventured into this territory with suggestions that, for example, a correlation of 0.50 is moderate while a correlation of 0.70 is strong, and so forth. But such statements have little practical meaning. You will often find published studies with correlations of 0.30 to 0.50, which are interpreted as meaningful, even though many textbooks on research would suggest that such correlations are weak. The previous discussion on empirical relationships should be helpful in your examination of the values of various coefficients of relationships.

Perception of community was measured by the Community Life Scale, which is displayed in Exhibit 7.3. The higher that people scored on this scale, the more they tended to describe their communities in terms consistent with the urban perception. The results of the analysis regarding the relationship between locality and population of work county for the sample of social workers can be summarized as follows:

The correlation between population of work county and score on the Community Life Scale was found to be 0.46 (p < .001). This indicated a substantial relationship between the two variables that was highly significant statistically. The fact that the correlation was positive rather than negative meant that people working in larger communities had higher scores on the Community Life Scale, a scale that gave higher scores for a more urban orientation. Social workers who were working in smaller counties were found to perceive their communities as possessing the traits thought to characterize the rural community. The correlation between population density and scores on the Community Life Scale was 0.40 (p < .001).

Should Rurality Be Conceptualized as a Continuum?

Now that it is established that the social workers in this study hold community perceptions different from their urban counterparts, you can see if these community characteristics tend to be patterned as a dichotomy or as a continuum. If scores on the Community Life Scale were similar for very small communities and small communities and moderate-sized communities, but were different for large communities, and large communities did not differ from very large communities, you would find a natural dividing point between moderate-sized communities and large communities. But if there is a gradual increase of CLS scores along the continuum of population, that would be evidence that would support the notion of rurality (i.e., locality) as being viewed as a continuum. The results of this analysis are summarized in the following paragraph.

The mean CLS scores were computed for six levels of county population: (1) up to 50,000; (2) 50,000–99,999; (3) 100,000–149,999; (4) 150,000–199,999; (5) 200,000–249,999; and (6) 250,000 and over. These mean scores, rounded off, are graphically depicted in Figure 7.1. As you can see, these scores gradually went up, even though the pattern was not perfect. For the smallest population category, the mean CLS score was 22.0 while the next category received a mean of 25.45. The next had a mean of 23.66 while the next mean was 27.87. The next-to-largest size county received a mean CLS score of 26.84 while the largest had a mean of 30.6. These scores are depicted in Figure 7.1.

You can see the pattern of mean scores in Figure 7.1. But you cannot tell from this display whether these differences in mean score between categories of population are statistically significant. There is some chance that this configuration of data can be a rather random occurrence in life and does not represent a picture that truly represents reality. If this is true, it is possible that another sample of similar people might not produce the same results, so there would be no way of knowing if the data from this study are meaningful.

The statistic known as analysis of variance (ANOVA) can help with this determination. It can be used to estimate the likelihood that mean scores between groups can be explained by chance. When this statistic was applied to this data, a p value of 0.0001 was calculated.

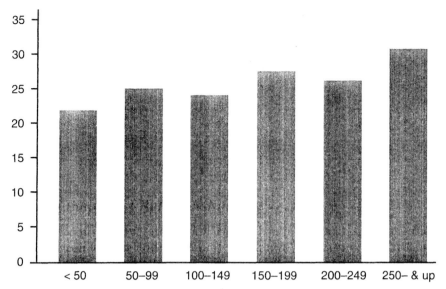

FIGURE 7.1   **Mean CLS Scores by Size of County** *(Population given in thousands)*

ASSIGNMENT 7–H

1. In the examination of the relationship between population of work county and score on the Community Life Scale, what kind of relationship were we expecting to find?

   a. A positive relationship   **c.** No relationship

   b. A negative relationship

2. What kind of relationship did we find?

   a. A positive relationship   **c.** No relationship

   b. A negative relationship

3. Was this relationship found to be statistically significant?

_____

_____

_____

_____

4. What kind of relationship did we find between population density and community perception?

    a. A positive relationship   **c.** No relationship

    b. A negative relationship

5. Was it statistically significant?

    _____

    _____

    _____

    _____

6. What is your basic conclusion (in one sentence) about the relationship between locality and perception of community?

    _____

    _____

    _____

    _____

7. Do we have evidence that the concept of rurality (or locality) should be conceptualized as a continuum or as a dichotomy? Explain.

    _____

    _____

    _____

    _____

Is the Practice of Rural and Urban Social Workers Different?

You have decided to measure social work practice in relation to eight social work roles and the use of informal helping networks. Each of these nine variables were measured on seven-point ordinal scales with the number 1 representing "not at all" and the number 7 representing "to a very great extent." The mean level of empha-sis on each of the eight roles is presented as follows:

Clinical Role = 5.74

Broker Role = 4.71

Manager Role = 3.81

Mediator Role = 3.81

Advocate Role = 3.33

Mobilizer Role = 2.99

Data Manager Role = 2.63

Community Organizer Role = 2.19

For each role, respondents gave answers that ranged from the minimum of 1 to the maximum of 7. The standard deviation for these responses ranged from a minimum of 1.66 to a maximum of 2.54, meaning that there was a good deal of variance in responses to these questions.

In view of the fact that the variables measuring emphasis on roles and the use of informal helping networks were each measured at the ordinal level, the Spear-man rank order coefficient of correlation was employed in the examination of the relationships of each of these nine practice variables with the two variables repre-senting locality (population and population density). Thus, you have the task of examining eighteen different correlations. One of these correlations is the one between the social worker's emphasis on the broker role and the population of the work county. Another is the relationship between emphasis on the broker role and the population density of the work county. Each of the other measures of social work practice (clinical role, community organizer role, use of networks, etc.) must also be correlated with both population and population density.

Remember that correlations between ordinal or interval variables can be either negative or positive and can range from 0 to 1.0. A minus sign in front of the cor-relation coefficient means that the relationship is negative. If there is no sign (either plus or minus) in front of the correlation coefficient, you can interpret the relation-ship as positive. Correlations that are close to 0 (e.g., 0.06, 0.12, 0.15, etc.) indicate that the relationship is very weak and probably not noteworthy.

If you found a correlation between self-esteem score and depression score that was −1.0, for example, this would tell you that there was a perfect negative rela-tionship between these two variables. With this information, you would know with *certainty* that if Bob is higher than Jim on self-esteem, then he will be lower than Jim on depression. But typically, there is not a perfect relationship between variables. A correlation of −0.50 between these two variables would mean that if Bob is higher than Jim on one of these variables, he is *probably* going to be lower than Jim on the other variable. But Jim and Bob may be exceptions to the rule for the study sample, so you would not be able to predict their scores on one of these variables if you knew their scores on the other variable with complete certainty.

Each exception to this rule in the comparison of scores of various study subjects will reduce the value of the correlation coefficient from a perfect 1.0 to something lower. If there are many, many exceptions, you would have little confidence in your ability to predict whether Bob is higher or lower than Jim on one of these variables by knowing their scores on the other variable. And, in this case, you would have a rather weak correlation coefficient between the two variables.

The Spearman rank order coefficient of correlation, represented by the letters "Rho", is a measure of the relationship between two variables measured at the ordinal level. Like other measures of correlation, it can range from 0 to 1.0, and be either negative or positive. In this case, there is one set of variables that are ordinal (practice emphasis) and one set of variables that are interval (population and population density). You can treat an interval variable as ordinal for statistical analysis because it is measured at a higher level than ordinal, but you should not treat an ordinal variable as interval. In other words, you can come down the ladder of measurement in the selection of a statistic but you cannot go up. Nominal measurement is the lowest level, so it can only be treated as nominal in statistical analysis. However, both ordinal and interval variables can be treated as nominal if you need to do so.

The statistical analysis of data also includes an estimate of the likelihood that a given correlation coefficient would occur by chance. I am speaking here of "statistical significance." Normally, researchers determine that a given correlation is statistically significant if it cannot be explained by chance any more than 5 times in 100. This result is typically given the designation of "$p < .05$". The information below summarizes the data on rural and urban social work practice.

The following correlations were found between population of work county and each of the measures of social work practice:

Broker Role	*0.07*
Mobilizer Role	*0.06*
Mediator Role	*0.06*
Advocate Role	*0.05*
Clinical Role	*0.12*
Data Manager Role	*0.04*
Community Organizer Role	*−0.01*
Use of Networks	*0.18**
*p< .05	

The asterisk next to the Use of Networks means that it was significant at the .05 level. In other words, this relationship was found to be statistically significant, but none of the others were. Remember that the absence of a negative sign before the value of the coefficient means that the relationship between the variables is positive.

ASSIGNMENT 7–I

1. What are your observations about the data regarding the relative emphasis on the different roles? What does this say about the way that most social workers practice?

_____

_____

_____

_____

2. Did the data tend to reveal that there was a relationship between locality and social work practice?

_____

_____

_____

_____

3. What about the relationship between population of work county and the use of informal helping networks? Was it found that people in more rural areas were making more use of these networks than persons in more urban areas? Was it statistically significant? Was it of practical significance?

_____

_____

_____

_____

The pattern of relationships between social work practice and locality was somewhat the same when population density was substituted for population. In other words, the pattern of very weak correlations that were nonsignificant (statistically) was repeated even though the specific values of the correlations were slightly different. There was, however, one minor deviation from this pattern: the correlation between the broker role and population density was found to be 0.17

(p < .05). Thus, the relationship was weak, as was the case of the other correlations, but it did achieve statistical significance. This would hardly be considered noteworthy, however, because of the weak relationship indicated by this low correlation.

Perhaps the single most important correlation is between the measures of locality and the use of informal helping networks, because this is one of the most important distinctions between rural and urban communities. You have seen that the relationship between these two variables was very weak, and the slight differences indicated that it was the *urban* social worker who was more likely to use such networks.

You have found that these rural social workers perceived that their communities placed more emphasis on informal helping networks than did their urban counterparts. And, yet, these rural social workers do not place more emphasis on these networks in their work with their clients. You might ask why?

Perhaps some further light can be shed on this issue through an examination of the relationship between the use of networks and the perception that the community places more emphasis on networks. The data in Table 7.2 depicts this relationship. For this analysis, the study subjects were divided into the categories of high and low for perceived community emphasis on networks and into the categories of high and low for use of networks in practice. The division of these study subjects was at the point of 4 on the 7-point scale which they used for their responses. Those who answered as 4 or more were placed into the high category while the others were placed into the low category. The question is whether those who perceive a high emphasis on networks in their communities are more likely to use them.

These data tell us that 76 percent of those who viewed their communities as high on informal networks reported that they placed high emphasis on networks in their practice compared to 67 percent of those who viewed their communities as low on emphasis on networks. Both groups tended to place emphasis upon networks and the difference between them was rather small. When these data were subjected to statistical analysis, the phi coefficient value was 0.09 and the p value associated with it was 0.24. In other words, this relationship was not statistically significant. This would suggest that these social workers' perception of their com-

TABLE 7.1   **The Relationship between Use of Networks and Community Emphasis on Networks**

Use of Networks in Practice	Perceived Community Emphasis Upon Networks		Total
	Low	High	Total
Low	28 (33%)	20 (24%)	48
High	58 (67%)	62 (76%)	120
Total	86 (100%)	82 (100%)	148

munity's emphasis on informal helping networks had little influence on their tendency to use these networks in their practice.

Drawing Conclusions

The conclusions section of the research report for an explanatory research study should provide a summary of the findings and a discussion of several issues. Included among these topics is the issue of practical significance, the limitations of the study, the utility of the results for social work, and the directions for future research.

The summary paragraph might start by reminding the reader of the nature of the sample and the general theme of the study. For example, you might begin the summary paragraph of the previously discussed study of gender and salary in the following way.

> *The major question examined in the present study was whether females received lower salaries than males in social work when position level was taken into consideration. The study subjects were drawn randomly from the membership list of the North Carolina Chapter of the National Association of Social Workers.*

This is a succinct statement that covers the two points mentioned. Remember that you are writing a *summary* here, not a repeat of most of what has already been said. The summary paragraph should also present the basic findings of the study. But the researcher is cautioned against reporting differences between study groups that were *not* found to be statistically significant. If the differences were not significant, this finding is treated as a failure to discover a difference.

Another issue is the practical significance of the findings. Just how noteworthy was your discovery, if you did find a statistically significant relationship between variables? In this endeavor, the researcher is directed to the question of the strength of the relationship between the dependent and independent variables, or the size of the differences in mean scores between groups. Is this difference enough to suggest that there should be some reordering of priorities in the social work profession with regard to the theme of the study?

The limitations of the study should also be addressed in the conclusions section of the report. The key place to look for limitations is in the study methodology. Specifically, you want to address the generalizability of the findings and any potential limitations with regard to the reliability and validity of the methods used to measure variables.

The utility of the study results for the social work profession is another issue to be addressed. How can social workers make use of this information? By social workers, you mean the entire profession, not just clinicians. Are there implications for social work educators or social work administrators, as well as clinicians?

Directions for future research is a topic in the conclusion section of the paper, if it is truly a comprehensive report. Should this study be replicated with different populations? Should study variables be measured differently in future research? Are new research questions suggested from the present findings?

ASSIGNMENT 7–J

Prepare a portion of the conclusions section for the present study by addressing the following topics:

1. the summary of the findings

2. the practical significance of the results

3. *one* of the following:

   a. limitations of the study

   b. utility for social work

   c. directions for future research

Glossary

Coefficient. A figure that represents the strength of the empirical relationship between variables. There are various statistical tests which employ the term "coefficient." For example, there is the phi coefficient, the contingency coefficient, the Pearson correlation coefficient, the Spearman rank correlation coefficient, and so forth. The values of such coefficients typically can range from 0 to 1.0.

Empirical Relationship. A relationship between variables which can be depicted through concrete measurement devices. An example would be the relationship between gender and salary.

Instrumentation. The means used in a study to measure variables.

Internal Consistency. The tendency of items forming a common scale to operate the same way. For example, a self-esteem scale would have internal consistency to the extent that the items on the scale, when treated as separate variables, could be correlated with one another when given to a sample of study subjects. Thus, if John has a higher score than Tom on item 1 on this scale, he would probably have a higher score than Tom on item 2 on this scale as well. If this were *not* the general pattern for items on this scale, then it would *not* be considered to have internal consistency. This situation would suggest that the items on this scale are not measuring the same thing.

Negative Relationship. A relationship between study variables in which *high* values on one variable tend to be associated with *low* values on the other variables (with low values on one being associated with high values on the other.) For example, you would expect to find a negative relationship between self-esteem and depression, meaning that people with higher self-esteem scores would tend to have lower scores for depression. As a result, if Paul has a higher score for self-esteem than Jim does, he is likely to have a lower score on depression than Jim.

Pearson's Correlation Coefficient. A measure of the degree of relationship between two variables measured at the interval level. It is designated in research literature with the small letter r (e.g., r = .46). The value of this coefficient can range from a low of 0 to a high of 1.0, and it can be either negative or positive. In other words, possible values include -1.0, 0, and 1.0 and all possible values in between, such as $-.21$, $-.58$, $-.94$, .12, .33, .78, and so forth. Values close to 0 mean that there is little, if any, relationship between the variables.

Phi Coefficient. A measure of the strength of the relationship between two variables measured at the nominal level. It can range from 0 to 1.0, but cannot be negative, because relationships between nominal variables can be neither negative nor positive, because nominal variables have no order to the categories of the variables such as low, medium, and high. For example, you would not speak of a negative relationship between gender and political party affiliation. To do so would suggest that the categories of these variables are ordered such that male is higher or lower than female.

Positive Relationship. A relationship between study variables in which high values on one variable tend to be associated with high values on the other variables (with low values on one being associated with low values on the other). For example, you would expect to find a positive relationship between IQ scores and college grades, meaning that persons with higher IQ scores would tend to have the higher grades, while persons with low IQ scores would tend to have the low grades. Thus, if Mary has a higher IQ than Bob, she is likely to have higher college grades than Bob.

Social Survey. A means of collecting information from people through questionnaires or interviews in which the information to be collected is specified ahead of time and the questionnaire items for obtaining this information have been developed.

Spearman Rank Order Correlation Coefficient. A measure of the strength of the relationship between variables measured at the ordinal level. The value of this coefficient can range from 0 to 1.0 and be either negative or positive.

Chapter *8*

Using Evaluative Research:
Is the SOAR Program Effective in Rehabilitating Sexual Offenders?

In this chapter, you will learn how to use evaluative research through another example of human service research. You will examine the effectiveness of the SOAR Program in the rehabilitation of incarcerated sexual offenders. The data for this chapter are taken from the professional paper of Shari Lisa Turner, a graduate social work student at East Carolina University, who conducted her study in the spring of 1993.

As before, you will take your knowledge of social work research a step further while continuing to focus on the entire process of research and the purpose of the study. At the completion of this chapter, you will be able to make critical use of published research articles that evaluate social work interventions.

Objectives

At the completion of this chapter, you will be able to:

1. Describe the process of evaluative research;
2. Explain the role of the literature review in the identification of targets of intervention and the justification of the treatment model in evaluative research;
3. Explain the role of the research design in clarifying the extent to which measured change in client behavior can be attributed to the intervention rather than something else;
4. Identify whether each of four group research designs and each of five single-subject research designs addresses each of three important threats to internal validity;

5. Identify the basis for determining whether practical significance has been achieved with a given level of change in client behavior in evaluative research;
6. Write the hypothesis for an evaluative research study;
7. Prepare the conclusions section of an evaluative research study.

In this chapter, you will reexamine some of the topics covered in the previous chapter on evaluative research. For example, you will see how interventions are described and justified, how problems addressed by interventions are analyzed, how variables are measured and research designs are developed, and how data is examined. The ways that reliability and validity are assessed has been discussed in previous chapters and will receive additional attention here. You will encounter the AB single-subject design for the first time and obtain a basic understanding of how it works and how one analyzes data for this type of research. This should provide you with the necessary knowledge to develop a simple application of this design yourself and to evaluate reports in which this design has been employed.

An Overview of Evaluative Research

You have encountered the four major phases of the research process several times in previous chapters. By now, you know that these phases entail problem formulation, study methodology, data analysis, and conclusions. In evaluative research, these phases take some slightly different turns than in the other types of research. In this section, you will review some of these differences and add a few additional wrinkles to your pursuit of knowledge.

In the problem formulation phase of evaluative research, you should find a clear definition of the problem that constitutes the client's target behavior for treatment. The importance of this problem can be addressed by information on its incidence and whether it is growing and, thereby, giving people cause for alarm in the future. The consequences of this problem for human functioning should also be addressed in the quest for information on the problem's importance.

The client's problem should also be analyzed in such a manner that the practitioner can be guided in the development of the intervention. Information on the effectiveness of different treatment approaches to this problem can also aid in this choice. Also included in this phase is a clear description of the intervention to be tested and the treatment objectives that are going to be the focus of the evaluation. (For some, however, the description of the intervention may more properly fit in the research methodology section in view of the fact that it constitutes the independent variable for the study.)

The study methodology provides information on the research design, the means of measuring variables, the method of observation, and how the study sample was selected. With knowledge of the research design, social workers can better determine how much comfort they should have in attributing measured changes in the client's behavior to the treatment itself rather than something else.

The treatment objectives should serve as a guide for the determination of what variables will be measured in the assessment of treatment effectiveness. Knowledge of the way the dependent variables were defined and measured provides an understanding of the limitations of the data analyzed as a means of evaluating program performance. Perhaps there were four treatment objectives, but only two were subjected to measurement in the present study. In this case, you must consider your evaluation to be only a partial evaluation of the effectiveness of the treatment. There are further limitations imposed by your choice of measurement devices. Perhaps there are ten ways to define and measure the behavior addressed by a treatment objective, but you select only one. You don't know what would have been the results if you had used some other measurement tool rather than the one you selected.

There are several approaches to the observation of behavior. In evaluative research, researchers typically administer an instrument designed to measure the client's target behavior as illustrated in Chapter 4 when you examined the Beck Depression Inventory. But they could also examine agency records for the data, or have someone make direct observations of the client's behavior as the means of observation.

In evaluative research, the topic of sampling is usually a bit more simple than in some of the other types of research. Researchers typically select current clients as their study sample, and are left with the task of speculating on the extent to which their current clients represent some larger population. When they do not have a probability sample, they cannot safely generalize their results to persons not included in the study.

Data analysis is the third major phase of research. As in other types of research, social workers are concerned with statistical significance in the analysis of data. What is the likelihood that their data can be explained by chance rather than being a set of results that they could depend upon to represent the truth?

The final major phase of research is the drawing of conclusions about the findings. A major issue in this phase is practical significance. Of particular importance in evaluative research is an understanding of differences in scores on measurement devices. What does a difference in mean scores of 21.3 and 24.5 truly represent from a practical point of view? Does a difference in scores for a client of 21 and 24 mean that the client answered "true" rather than "false" to three more statements out of fifty presented? If so, just how noteworthy is this?

A question sometimes examined in evaluative research is whether the treatment had a better rate of success with certain kinds of clients than others. Knowledge of the answer to this question can assist in screening clients or in the redesign of the approach of the intervention.

Phase 1: Problem Formulation

The SOAR treatment program is designed to alter the behavior of convicted sexual offenders. The basic goal of treatment is to reduce the chance that these individuals will repeat their sexual offenses. The program is offered while the clients are in prison. The specific objectives of treatment address behaviors that are thought to be related to the propensity of a person to commit sexual crimes.

A brief literature review on the nature of this problem is presented in Exhibit 8.1. The SOAR program for the treatment of sexual offenders is described in Exhibit 8.2.

EXHIBIT 8.1   A Brief Literature Review on Sexual Crimes and the Treatment of Offenders*

The growth in the commitment of sexual crimes in recent decades has led to the reevaluation of treatment programs for the perpetrators of these crimes (Kratcoski, 1989). Particularly troubling is the fact that the population of incarcerated sexual offenders is growing much more rapidly than the resources for treating these individuals (Szymanowski & McKee, 1988). In 1986, for example, there were only eighteen formal state-run intensive treatment programs for sexual offenders in this country (Freeman–Longo and Wall, 1986).

There are two main categories of sexual crimes: rape and child sexual abuse. Rape involves forcible sex while child sexual abuse entails any sexual contact with a minor. The causes of sexual crimes are multiple. It has been found, for example, that most sexual offenders have themselves been the victims of sexual crimes as a child (Kruttschnitt, 1989) and that sexual offenders have low social skills when dealing with the opposite sex (Overholser & Beck, 1986). One author on this subject described sexual offenders as having experienced parental rejection and peculiar upbringing, meaning that these individuals did not have upbringings that we would characterized as normal in a general sense (Kruttschnitt, 1989).

There are some candidates for causation, however, that differ by the offense. For example, rapists have been found to have a higher than normal level of hostility and anger but this is not true for child molesters (Hall & Nagayama, 1989). Overholser and Beck (1986) describe rape as a sexual means of expressing anger and power. It apparently originates, in part, from displaced anger toward the perpetrator of their own childhood incidences of sexual abuse.

Child molesters, on the other hand, have been found to be socially inept, withdrawn, unassertive, and socially isolated. They tend to have a high fear of negative evaluation, which may be the reason that the child, a less threatening source of affection, is sought for sexual gratification (Curtis, 1986).

The clinical picture of the sexual offender is that of a person with tendencies toward low empathy toward victims, a reluctance to accept responsibility for the consequences of the sexual offense, and efforts to rationalize the acts as justified in some limited way. It is believed that these characteristics contribute to the propensity of an individual to commit sexual offenses. Consequently, these behaviors have become the target of many treatment programs.

Empathy means putting yourself in someone else's shoes. It is a vicarious emotional response to another person (Hoffman, 1979). It means being able to feel another person's pain or joy. Most people can do this, but they do it better with certain persons than others. Sexual offenders seem to have little ability to do this for their victims. In a sense, this may seem to be functional for the criminal because it means that they do

(Continued)

EXHIBIT 8.1 *Continued*

not have to experience this pain. One of the consequences of being the victim of child sexual abuse is the tendency to stop feeling because the pain is too great. This reduces the ability to feel another person's pain.

The PEER program is a highly structured, ten-week program designed to enhance empathy among sexual offenders. An evaluation of this program in the Kansas State Penitentiary showed that treated clients improved in empathy as compared to a control group (Leak, 1980). Some of the elements of this program are included in the SOAR program being evaluated in the present study.

A cognitive distortion is any thought that denies responsibility for action. An example is the thought, "My problem is not sexual; it is just that I really love children." One of the therapeutic techniques designed to address this condition is covert sensitization, a method of gradually sensitizing the individual to how sexually aggressive behaviors affect others. Because of the discomfort this increased awareness brings, such treatment needs to be offered in a nonjudgmental and supportive therapeutic environment. (Freeman–Longo & Wall, 1986).

Justification is another part of the clinical portrait of the sexual offender. Acts of pain inflicted on others must be justified if the offender is to maintain a basic emotional balance. An example is the thought, "My sexual offense occurred as a result of my wife's lack of understanding of me and my needs." This pattern of explanation needs to be confronted with contrary information; thus, treatment strategies with an educational or cognitive orientation are warranted. Education and rational emotive therapy are viewed as strategies for addressing this condition.

References

Curtis, John M. (1986). Factors in sexual abuse of children. *Psychological Report, 58* 591–597.

Freeman-Longo, Robert E., & Wall, Ronald V. (1986). Changing a lifetime of sexual crime. *Psychology Today, 20*, 58–64.

Hall, Gordon, & Nagayama, C. (1989). Self-reported hostility as a function of offense characteristics and response style in a sexual offender population. *Journal of Consulting and Clinical Psychology, 37* (2), 306–308.

Hoffman, Martin L. (1979). Development of moral thought, feeling, and behavior. *American Psychologist, 34* (10), 958–966.

Kratcoski, Peter C. (1989). *Correctional counseling and treatment.* Illinois: Waveland Press.

Kruttschnitt, Candace (1989). A sociological, offender-based study of rape. *The Sociological Quarterly, 30* (2), 305–329.

Leak, Gary K. (1980). Effects of highly structured versus nondirective group counseling approaches on personality and behavioral measures of adjustment in incarcerated felons. *Journal of Counseling Psychology, 27* (5), 520–523.

Overholser, James C., & Beck, Steven (1986). Multimethod assessment of rapists, child molesters, and three control groups on behavioral and psychological measures. *Journal of Consulting and Clinical Psychology, 54* (5), 682–687.

Szymanowski, David, & McKee, Geoffrey R. (1988). Computer profiles guide sex offender therapy. *Corrections Today, 50*, 150–159.

*This literature review is a slightly revised version of portions of the following professional paper: Turner, S. L. (1993). Evaluation of the SOAR Sex Offender Program at Harnett Correctional Institution. School of Social Work, East Carolina University. Used with permission of Shari Lisa Turner.

EXHIBIT 8.2   A Description of the SOAR Program for the Treatment of Sexual Offenders*

The Sexual Offender Accountability and Responsibility (SOAR) Treatment Program is offered to sexual offenders by the Division of Prisons of the North Carolina Department of Corrections. This program's main focus is on the education of the sex offender so that cognitive distortions and justifications can be confronted. The program emphasizes the philosophy that sexual behavior is learned; thus, dysfunctional sexual behavior has to be replaced by new learned behaviors that are more appropriate. To accomplish this effect, the program utilizes discussions, lectures, and role-play exercises. The role-playing exercises are also directed toward the enhancement of empathy for the victims of sexual crimes.

The program is intensive. It covers a ten-week period of time in which the client is engaged in therapeutic activities for several hours each day for five days per week during this ten-week period. It takes place while the client is incarcerated; thus, the issue of motivation for treatment is of special concern. A total of eighteen inmates are allowed to enter the program for each ten-week episode of service. It takes place in a men's prison.

The basic goal of the program is to reduce the likelihood that the offender will repeat his sexual crimes after he is released. Four specific treatment objectives served as the focus of the present study:

1. to reduce the clients' cognitive distortions about their crimes;
2. to reduce the clients' justifications for their crimes;
3. to enhance the clients' empathy for the victims of their crimes; and
4. to improve the clients' motivation for treatment.

*This information was taken from the following professional paper: Turner, S. L. (1993). Evaluation of the SOAR Sex Offender Program at Harnett Correctional Instituion. School of Social Work, East Carolina University. Used with permission of Shari Lisa Turner.

ASSIGNMENT 8–A

1. What is probably the most important cause of sex crimes? In other words, why do some people commit these offenses?

_____

_____

_____

_____

_____

2. What are two of the traits of sexual offenders that should be addressed in a treatment program?

_____

_____

_____

3. Which of the following treatment approaches is *not* supported by the literature review?

   a. the use of cognitive therapy for the offender

   b. the use of medication

   c. the use of an educational strategy

4. How many different days is the client engaged in treatment activities by the SOAR program?

_____

_____

_____

5. What is one suggestion you would make for the treatment of sexual offenders that is not mentioned in this book? What is your justification?

_____

_____

_____

_____

Phase 2: Developing the Study Methodology

As I have previously discussed, the study methodology contains information on the research design employed, the definition and measurement of variables, the method of observation, and the study sample. The better the research design, the more confidence social workers can have that their treatment was the cause of the observed changes in the client's behavior. The more clear the definition of variables, the more they know about what kinds of effects their treatment had, and they are in a better position to know what was *not* tested, as well as what was tested. The more information researchers have on the reliability and validity of their measurement devices, the more confidence they can have that they truly measured what they intended. The better their sampling procedures, the better they are able to generalize their findings to people not included in a study.

Research Designs

The research design employed in the present study is the pretest–posttest one-group design. In this design, the clients are measured on the dependent variable before treatment and again after treatment. The difference in these two scores is taken as evidence of the effect of the treatment. The data for this analysis was taken from the professional paper of Shari Lisa Turner, a graduate social work student at East Carolina University. This student employed data from a program in her field placement for her study. In addition, you will examine hypothetical data for three clients as a method of examining the single-subject research design for the evaluation of social work interventions.

There are two basic types of research designs for the evaluation of social work practice. One is the group design and the other is the single-subject design. The group design employs measurements of a group of clients being served by a common program while the single-subject design employs measurements of a single client being given a tailored intervention.

Threats to Internal Validity

For all types of designs for evaluative research, there are certain indicators of strengths and weaknesses which have been labeled "threats to internal validity" in the research literature. When researchers measure client behavior, they make the assumption that observed changes are due to the intervention rather than something else. But other factors may be the cause of these changes rather than the treatment itself. The various *threats to internal validity* deal with a number of these alternative explanations for the observed behavior of the client.

One of these threats, or alternative explanations, is known as *history*. This refers to the fact that changes in the environment, independent of the treatment, may have caused changes in the client's behavior. If an unemployed client has gotten a job during the treatment period, there may be good reason to believe that the job has increased his or her self-esteem rather than the treatment. In order to take history into consideration, your research design must have a comparison group or control group that did not get the treatment and whose lives are believed to be consistent with people in the treatment group with regard to potential environmental influences. In this way, the effect of history is believed to be the same for the two groups; thus, any differences between the groups cannot be attributed to history. For example, it would be estimated that the new factory that opened in town provided as many new jobs for people in the comparison group as the treatment group; thus, differences in outcome between the two groups cannot be attributed to the new factory.

Another threat is that of *maturation*. This refers to the fact that people naturally grow over time and find ways to solve their problems on their own without the help of treatment. You can expect, for example, that the level of depression of a recently separated marriage partner will naturally shrink with the passage of time for most people. If social workers employ treatment during this period and measure depression before and after treatment, how can they be confident that the treatment was the cause of the reduction in the measured level of depression? There are two basic ways to deal with maturation as an alternative explanation. One is to obtain information on trends in the client's behavior before the treatment began and to project this trend into the treatment period and to compare the treatment measurements to this trend. Another way to address maturation is to have a comparison group that did not receive the treatment. The effect of maturation is believed to be consistent between the two groups; thus, any differences in growth between the treatment and comparison groups cannot be attributed to maturation.

A third threat to internal validity that you will consider here is known as *testing*. This alternative explanation refers to the fact that people are sometimes affected by the testing process itself. For example, people learn to take tests of knowledge better by the experience of taking a test, so that researchers can expect slightly higher scores on knowledge at posttest even if there is not an intervention. If they employ an instrument for a client once a week for several weeks, the client is likely to be aware of how he or she responded the last time and may be influenced by this fact. Perhaps the client wants to be consistent, or wants to believe that he or she is growing. In these cases, the scores would be influenced by a factor other than the treatment.

To take testing into consideration, researchers must have a design that either compares the clients with a nontreated group (comparison group) or have a baseline of measurements on the dependent variable before treatment. If there is a comparison group, the effect of testing would be assumed to be consistent between the two groups. Thus, any difference between the two groups could not be attributed to testing. If researchers have baseline data, the effect of testing would be apparent from the baseline trend. Thus, superiority of recordings of client behavior during the treatment period could not be attributed to testing.

There are several additional threats to internal validity which I will not discuss here. For more information, consult a standard text on research methods.

Group Research Designs

I will discuss four group designs for evaluative research in this section: the pretest–posttest one-group design; the alternative treatment design; the comparison group design; and the basic experimental design. These designs vary in the extent to which they address the various threats to internal validity.

We have already discussed the *one-group pretest–posttest* design. It is a better approach to evaluation than the procedure of taking only one reading of the client's behavior after treatment and then speculating on how much credit the treatment should take. But it is inferior to the third and fourth designs discussed here because it does not address any of the three threats to internal validity that were discussed above.

Researchers should be more or less concerned about these threats in accordance with the extent to which they know of information that would logically cause concern about these alternative explanations. For example, just how much would you expect a person to grow naturally on a given condition over a given period of time? If you measure the client's depression and find a serious level of it and then learn that the client has acted very depressed for the past six months, you would not expect this depression to significantly change without treatment in a short period of time, such as, for example, two months.

The shorter the period of treatment, the less researchers need to be concerned about either maturation or history as alternative explanations for client change. In the case of history, of course, they must be attentive to changes in the environment that they know about. If there are such changes, they must be concerned. The longer the treatment period, the greater is the likelihood that there have been changes in the environment that they do not know about.

With the *alternative treatment design,* researchers are comparing two treatments to see if there is a difference. It is an extension of the previous design in that pretest and posttest measures of the dependent variable are compared to see if there was a significant gain. What is different is that the gain in functioning for the two groups is compared. This helps them to know what treatment is more effective than another, but they do not have a comparison group which represents no treatment, so they do not know how much change would have occurred in the absence of treatment.

The third group design I will discuss is the *comparison group design,* also known as the nonequivalent control group design. With this design, you have a treated group and a comparison group that did not receive the treatment. They are measured on the dependent variable before and after the treatment period and their relative gain scores are compared to see if they are significantly different. In other words, you would measure both the treatment group and the comparison group before and after the treatment period. For each study subject, a gain score would be computed which reflects the difference between the pretest and posttest measures of the dependent variable. The mean gain score for the treatment group would be compared to the mean gain score for the comparison group to see if there was a significant difference that favored the treatment group. (This illustration, of course, is only relevant if the dependent variable is measured at the interval level and the computation of mean scores is warranted.)

It is assumed that the two groups are comparable in regard to potential effects of changes in the environment (history) and the effects of normal growth (maturation) and the effects of testing. In other words, whatever is happening with regard to these factors will be evenly distributed between these two groups and, thus, any differences between the two groups cannot be attributed to these factors. This enhances researchers' ability to attribute changes to the treatment.

A variation of the comparison group design is the one in which only a posttest recording of behavior is taken. The two groups are assumed to be equivalent at the pretest time; thus, any differences in measurements are assumed to be attributed to the treatment. This assumption is subject to question in many situations. It is clearly superior to take a pretest measurement of the dependent variable. In the absence of this opportunity, it is important to logically rule out reasons why the two groups may have been different at the pretest time.

The *basic experimental research design* is the final design for evaluative research discussed here. This design is similar to the comparison group design except that the two groups are assigned to their status as either treatment group or control group on a random basis. The great advantage is that the random assignment of people to the two groups takes care of a host of threats to internal validity. It is assumed that various nontreatment factors which might effect changes in clients' behaviors are evenly distributed between the two groups; as a result, any observed differences in gain between the two groups can be attributed to the intervention.

There is a major difference between the comparison group design and the basic experimental design. What if a researcher wanted to use people on the waiting list as the comparison group. Those people cannot be considered to be a true control group for the experimental design unless they were assigned to the waiting list on a random basis. If they were placed on this list because they had a less serious problem, there is a clear difference between the two groups (treatment and comparison) that may influence changes in behavior. If they are on the waiting list on a first-come-first-served basis, a researcher would have less concern about differences, but there still could be important differences between the two groups. For example, the researcher might know that a certain percentage of clients drop off the waiting list before they are called for treatment. The treated group does not have this segment of potential clients in it, and, thus, is different.

There are a number of variations of experimental research designs. I have mentioned only one here and have labelled it the "basic experimental design" because it is the one most familiar to the beginning research student. All experimental designs employ the random assignment technique for controlling for threats to interval validity. The basic experimental design may seem to have much in common with the comparison group design, but there are major advantages for the basic experimental design. The random assignment of subjects to treatment groups and control groups covers a host of threats to internal validity and does so in a superior fashion to the methods of control offered by the comparison group design. If people are not in the nontreatment group on a random basis, there are potential differences between these people and those in the treatment group that may account for differences in behavioral outcome. But random assignment should make groups similar on a host of variables that might influence outcome other than treatment itself.

Single-Subject Designs

I will discuss four single-subject designs in this section: the AB design, the ABC design, the BC design, and the BA design. The designation of the letters for these designs has a pattern. The letter A always represents a baseline period during which the client's behavior is measured repeatedly but no treatment is given. The other letters refer to treatment periods during which the client's behavior is repeatedly measured. The letter B refers to the first (or only) treatment given while the letter C refers to a second treatment (or a change in the treatment approach). For example, the AB design refers to the situation in which the client's behavior is measured several times before treatment begins and several times while treatment is being given. The BC design is one in which there is no measurement of the client's behavior before treatment. Instead, the client's behavior is measured several times during the initial treatment period and the treatment is changed. Measurement continues during the second treatment period.

With all single-subject designs, the client's target behavior (the dependent variable) is measured many times during each phase (A, B, C). This array of measurements is used for the statistical analysis of the data to estimate the likelihood that differences can be explained by chance. Statistical analysis depends on an array of data (i.e., many pieces of data) rather than one or two measurements. With group research designs, you have a group of people who are measured; thus, you have an array of measurements for statistical analysis. When you have only one study subject, you must measure the behavior many times in order to obtain the necessary array of data for statistical analysis.

The *AB design* is the basic single-subject design. It has an advantage over certain other designs in that it addresses the issue of maturation as a threat to internal validity. The baseline period is considered to be a reflection of the pattern of behavior present before treatment. If maturation is occurring, it will be reflected in the pattern of measurements during this baseline period. If the treatment period recordings of the client's behavior are significantly better than the projection from the baseline trend, then researchers would tend to attribute this change to the intervention. In other words, they assume that the trend in behavior demonstrated by the baseline measurements is a reflection of what would continue in the absence of treatment. If the trend shows a gradual improvement, they would extend this trend of gradual improvement into the treatment period and compare the actual treatment recordings to this trend to see if it is better.

The *ABC design* is an extension of the AB design. It simply adds a second intervention (the C phase) to see if it is more effective than the first. The C time period can be compared to both the B period and the baseline (the A period) to see if it is better.

The *BC design* is one that can be used if there is no opportunity to take a baseline set of measurements. It entails the recording of client behaviors during the implementation of the first treatment strategy (the B period) followed by a change in the treatment approach and the continued recording of client behaviors during this second treatment period (the C period). With this design, you are not taking maturation into consideration because you have no baseline of data for estimating the effect of spontaneous development. What you can see from this set of data is whether the two treatments are different in their effects.

The *BA design* is a little unusual because it does not take a baseline before treatment begins. Instead, the baseline is taken after treatment has been completed.

This baseline is compared to the treatment recordings to see if the target behavior has gotten worse. If so, it is assumed that the treatment produced the superior behavior, and, thus, was effective. However, if treatment had an enduring effect, you would expect the baseline recordings to illustrate the maintenance of the effects of the treatment. But this maintenance of behaviors could mean that this was the pattern before treatment, and the treatment made no difference. Thus, the data from this design is not easy to interpret.

The *ABAB design* is considered by some investigators to qualify as an experimental design. With this design, there are two baseline periods and two treatment periods. The first two phases (AB) are similar to the AB design. The difference is that a second baseline follows the withdrawal of treatment, and a second treatment period follows this second baseline period. If the client's behavior is significantly higher in each of the two treatment periods than in either of the two baseline periods, there is good reason to have confidence that the treatment was to be credited with the gains. Consider, for example, the internal validity threat that has been labeled "history." The AB design does not address this threat because it is reasonable to argue that a change in the client's environment during the treatment phase was the cause of the client's gain in functioning rather than the treatment. However, it would be highly unlikely that history is to be credited with client gain if treatment is withdrawn and reintroduced later. How likely is it that changes in the environment would take place only in the two treatment phases of the ABAB design and not influence behavior during the two baseline periods? If there have been changes in the client's environment during the first treatment phase, this change would likely continue to influence the client's behavior during the second baseline as well as the second treatment period. If the client's behavior regresses during the second baseline and improves during the second treatment period, it could be easily argued that the treatment had the desired effect on client functioning.

ASSIGNMENT 8–B

1. Given the research design employed in the present study (the one-group pretest–posttest design), which of the following alternative explanations (threats to internal validity) might you need to be concerned about?

   a. Any improvement in the target behavior during the treatment period might be attributed to the subjects' normal growth and development with regard to their problem;

   b. Any improvement in the target behavior during the treatment period might be caused by changes in the subjects' environment;

   c. Any improvement in the target behavior during the treatment period might be caused by the effects of being measured on the dependent variable at the beginning of treatment.

    d. All of the above

    e. None of the above

2. The kind of research design researchers employ helps them to determine:

    a. whether their measurement devices are valid

    b. whether their measurement devices are reliable

    c. whether their measured results can be attributed to the intervention

    d. whether they have addressed an important problem

    e. all of the above

    f. none of the above

3. What are the advantages of the AB single-subject design over the pretest–posttest one-group design?

4. Which of the designs does the best job overall of addressing threats to internal validity?

Defining and Measuring the Dependent Variables for the Study

The four treatment objectives enumerated in Exhibit 8.2 served as the guide for selecting the dependent variables to be defined and measured. These dependent variables are (1) cognitive distortions, (2) justification, (3) motivation for treatment, and (4) empathy.

A *cognitive distortion* is defined as an inappropriate way of thinking about sex with regard to the acceptance of personal responsibility for one's actions. It was measured by the cognitive distortion subscale of the Multiphasic Sex Inventory (Nichols and Molinder, 1984). This instrument presents a set of statements that describe cognitive distortions about sex, including "My problem is not sexual, it is that I really love children," and "I feel like a victim as a result of the accusations made against me." The clients marked each statement as being either true or false for themselves. For this subscale, there were 21 items. The respondent received 1 point for each statement marked as true; thus, the worst possible score would be 21 and the best possible score would be 0.

A *justification* is defined as an excuse made by the offender for the sexual crimes he has committed. It was measured by a subscale of the Multiphasic Sex Inventory which contains statements such as "My sexual offense occurred as a result of my wife's lack of understanding of me and my needs." This subscale presented 24 such statements of excuses in the true–false format; the worst possible score would be 24 and the best possible score would be 0.

Motivation for treatment is defined as a recognition of a need for help and a desire to receive such help. It was measured by a subscale of the Multiphasic Sex Inventory which presents 8 statements in a true–false format, such as "I need help because I cannot control my sex thoughts." The best possible score on this subscale is 8 while the worst possible score would be 0.

Empathy is defined as a vicarious emotional response to another person. It is the ability to feel someone else's pain. Sexual offenders tend not to be able to do this for the victims of their crimes. For the present study, empathy was measured by a subscale of the Interpersonal Reactivity Index. This subscale contains 7 items, an example being "Sometimes I don't feel very sorry for other people when they are having problems." Each statement is responded to on the following scale:

A	B	C	D	E
Does not describe me very well				Describes me very well

The client marked A if the statement did not describe him very well or E if the statement did describe him very well. The client also had the option of marking B, C, or D, depending on how well he felt the statement described him. Responses were given scores from 0 to 4 depending upon how positive the response was. If the respondent indicated that a negative statement described him very well, he received a score of 0. If it did not describe him very well he received a score of 4. Scores of 1, 2, or 3 were given for the middle positions on the scale. Scores could range from a low of 0 (the most negative score) to a high of 28.

Assessing the Validity and Reliability of Measurement Tools.   Validity   refers to the accuracy of a measurement device, whereas reliability refers to its consistency. A measurement tool can be consistent without being accurate. In other words, it can be consistently inaccurate. But it cannot be accurate without being consistent.

When behavioral scales are developed and published, they are normally subjected to a set of tests of reliability and validity. Reliability is normally tested by means which determine whether it operates in a consistent fashion. One such means is the *test–retest* method. With this method, study subjects are given the instrument at two points in time and these responses are analyzed to determine if persons had similar responses at the two points in time. Similarity would indicate consistency.

The time difference should normally be short to reduce the possibility that the phenomenon being measured has actually changed for the study subjects. Obviously, researchers would not want to use a test–retest method for assessing the reliability of a depression scale for clients undergoing treatment for depression because they would expect their levels of depression to change during this time period. Instead, they would want to examine people who would not be expected to change on the variable being measured. If their responses are not consistent under these circumstances, there is reason to wonder what is wrong with the instrument. Is it confusing so that people don't really know what they are saying in their responses?

Another way of addressing reliability is to examine the *internal consistency* of the responses to a common scale. If there are 20 items on a depression scale that are to be summed for a depression score, the scores on one-half of these items should be correlated with the scores on the other half of these items. In other words, if John's score is higher than Mary's score for the first half of the items, it would be expected to be higher than Mary's for the second half of these items. If not, maybe these items aren't all measuring the same thing. If not, there's no way to interpret the scores.

The simplest form of validity is known as *face validity*: does the instrument seem to be measuring what it was intended to measure? This can be tested by asking informed persons to give their opinions about the instrument. This method does not have a great deal of scientific credibility.

A better method is known as *criterion validity*, which compares the present instrument to another way of measuring the same variable. This could be done by correlating scores on the present instrument with another instrument designed to measure the same variable. Another way would be to compare scores on the present instruments with the observations of clinicians regarding the subjects who took the instrument. Do clients labeled as depressed by clinicians tend to score higher on the depression scale than clients not labeled as depressed?

At the time of the study, information on the reliability or validity of the Multiphasic Sex Inventory and the Interpersonal Reactivity Index was not available. It was undergoing tests of this nature at the time, but the results had not been published. These instruments had been selected by the staff of the correctional institution in which the SOAR program was being implemented, and at least had face validity to these people.

The Study Sample

The sample for the present study consists of fifty-two sex offenders, both rapists and child molesters. These persons had undergone the SOAR treatment program in three different groups on consecutive ten-week time periods in 1992. There were 17 persons in groups 1 and 2 and 18 persons in group 3. Information was not provided on the way that people were selected for participation, but I am assuming that participation was voluntary and highly valued because it may improve the inmates' chances of parole. Without such information, the issue of motivation for treatment and honesty in response must be addressed in the interpretation of the outcome of treatment.

ASSIGNMENT 8–C

1. If it is to be concluded that the SOAR program was effective, the posttest scores for four dependent variables on instruments must differ from the pretest scores. Indicate whether the difference should be lower or higher for each of the variables.

   a. _____ (Lower/higher) for cognitive distortions

   b. _____ (Lower/higher) for justification

   c. _____ (Lower/higher) for motivation for treatment

   d. _____ (Lower/higher) for empathy

2. Which of the scales used in the present study would include the following item? When I see someone being treated unfairly, I sometimes don't feel very much pity for them.

   _____

   _____

   _____

   _____

3. Which of the following findings would tend to support the reliability of the scale used to measure cognitive distortion? (You may select more than one.)

   a. a finding that posttest scores on this scale were *lower* than pretest scores

   b. a finding that posttest scores on this scale were *higher* than pretest scores

   c. a finding that scores for one-half of this scale had a *positive* correlation with scores for the other half of the scale

d. a finding that scores for one-half of the scale had a *negative* correlation with scores for the other half

e. a finding that scores on this scale had a positive correlation with scores for motivation for treatment

4. Describe how you would test the validity of any of these scales. Don't just give a label; describe how you would go about this task.

_____

_____

_____

5. From a practical point of view, how would you describe a difference of three points on the instrument used in this study to measure cognitive distortions? Would a gain of three points on this scale be a noteworthy gain? What is the basis for your conclusion, given the range of possible scores and your interpretation of what a one-point gain means for this particular scale?

_____

_____

_____

6. From a practical point of view, how would you describe differences in scores of two points for the instrument used in this study to measure empathy?

_____

_____

_____

7. To whom can the results of this study be safely generalized? I am not speaking here of speculative generalization, but safe generalization based upon the sampling method employed.

_____

_____

_____

Phase 3: Analyzing Data for the Study

The fifty-two clients included in the present study were given a pretest and post-test measurement of each of the four dependent variables. The mean pretest score for *cognitive distortions* was 6.31 while the mean posttest score was 4.6. The mean gain was analyzed with a statistic known as the *t test* for paired data. The result indicated that the mean gain on this variable was statistically significant (t = 3.25; p < .01). The mean pretest score indicated that the typical respondent answered "false" to about 15 of the 21 negative statements on the scale. The mean posttest indicated a typical gain of about 2 points, indicating that two additional statements were answered as false at the posttest time by a client whose responses reflected the mean.

The mean pretest score for *justification* was 4.62 while the mean posttest score was 6.0 (t = 2.66; p < .05). Remember that the scale used to measure justification had 24 statements that persons could use to justify their sexual offense. They got one point for each response of "true," which would indicate a tendency to justify their behavior. The highest possible score was 24 and the lowest was 0. The mean pretest score of 4.62 indicates that the average respondent gave a justifying response to only about 4 or 5 of these 24 statements, reflecting a low tendency to justify their behavior.

The mean pretest score for *motivation for treatment* was 3.25 while the mean posttest score was 5.02 (t = 3.90; p < .01). This difference indicates that the typical client responded with "true" to about 3 of the 8 positive items on this scale and "false" to the other 5 at the pretest time. At posttest, the responses had risen on the average to about 5 statements responded to as "true."

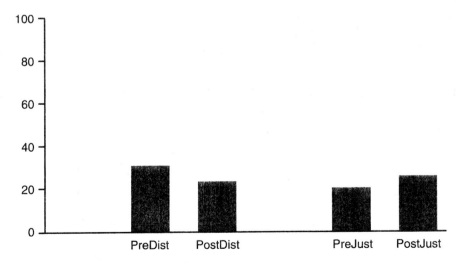

FIGURE 8.1   Scores for Justification and Distortion *(Presented as a percentage of the maximum possible score)*

The mean pretest score for *empathy* was 18.78 while the mean posttest score was 20.06 (t = 1.65; p = .10). There were seven items on this scale, each with possible scores of 0 to 4; the worst possible overall score for this scale was 0 while the best possible score was 28 (7 × 4).

These scores are graphically depicted in Figure 8.1 and Figure 8.2 as percentages of the maximum possible score on the scale. For example, a score of 10 on a scale with a maximum possible score of 20 would be presented as 50 because 10 is 50 percent of 20. This is not the normal way that results are displayed. It is presented here as an alternative, in view of the difficulty of comparing mean scores which are derived from scales with very different ranges. For example, a score of 10 on a 20 point scale is not comparable to a score of 10 on a 50 point scale.

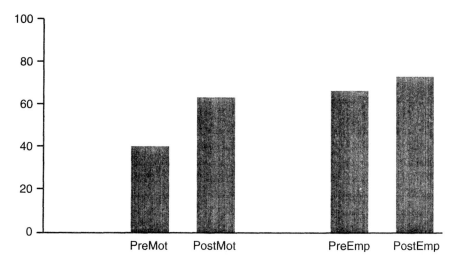

FIGURE 8.2 **Scores for Motivation and Empathy** *(Presented as a perentage of maximum possible score)*

ASSIGNMENT 8–D

1. One of the study hypotheses being tested was: Clients of the SOAR Program will have lower scores for cognitive distortion after treatment than before treatment. Was this hypothesis supported by the data from this study? Explain with reference to the test of statistical significance.

Would you say that practical significance was achieved? Explain the basis for your response.

_____

_____

_____

2. Write the hypothesis dealing with the variable of *justification.*

_____

_____

_____

_____

Did the data from this study support this hypothesis? Explain.

_____

_____

_____

Would you say that practical significance was achieved? Explain.

_____

_____

_____

3. Write the hypothesis for the variable of *motivation for treatment.*

_____

_____

_____

_____

Did the data support this hypothesis? Explain.

Would you say that practical significance was achieved?

4. Write the hypothesis dealing with the variable of *empathy*.

Was this hypothesis supported by the data? Explain.

Would you say that practical significance was achieved? Explain.

Phase 4: Drawing Conclusions for the Study

The conclusions section of an evaluative research report should contain several things. There should be a summary of the nature of the study that was undertaken. The findings regarding support for each study hypothesis should be presented briefly. (Remember that a hypothesis is supported only if the data achieve statistical significance.) Results which come close to achieving statistical significance might be reported as such, although some researchers would not do this. A critical thing to remember is that if the results are not close to statistical significance, what you are saying is that chance cannot be reasonably ruled out as the reason for the gain in scores on the dependent variable. Thus, you cannot be confident that your scores represent a true gain that might be attributed to the treatment.

An examination of practical significance is perhaps the heart of the conclusions section. Just how noteworthy were the findings? Was the commitment of resources by this intervention justified? Remember what statistical significance means when you are dealing with practical significance.

The limitations of the study should be mentioned. One place to look for the limitations of an evaluative study is the design of the study. The particular research design employed will provide information on the extent to which you can have confidence that the clients' gain in functioning can be attributed to the intervention rather than something else. You can refer to other things that might have caused the clients' change as alternative explanations or *threats to internal validity*. You know, for example, that some people have a tendency to grow (or recover) on their own without treatment. Does your research design take this fact into account? In other words, does your research design address *maturation* as a threat to internal validity? Another key place to examine limitations is in the sampling procedures employed. A nonprobability sample cannot be safely generalized to larger populations.

Finally, there may be some recommendations for practice that emanate from the study. Should the intervention be recommended for other agencies in its present form? Should the program be modified? What further research is suggested by the results of this study?

ASSIGNMENT 8–E

Try your hand at the development of a conclusions section for this study. Fill in the blanks for the following:

The present study examines the effectiveness of the SOAR program for the treatment of incarcerated sex offenders. This program utilized an educational strategy for intervention. Treatment was provided on a daily basis for five days per week for a period of _____ weeks.

The _____ research design was employed. Dependent variables included the following: (1) a tendency to engage in cognitive distortions of one's sex crimes; (2) a tendency to justify one's sex crimes; (3) _____

and (4) _____ .

The following is a summary of the statistical results:

1. Clients _____ (did/did not) improve on the extent to which they used cognitive distortions to avoid responsibility for their crimes;

2. A significant gain _____ (was/was not) observed in regard to the client's tendency to find excuses to justify their crimes;

3. _____

   _____

   _____

4. _____

   _____

   _____

In general, it _____ (can/cannot) be concluded that this program achieved practical significance because: _____

_____

_____

_____

One of the limitations of these findings can be found in the research design employed. This design has certain weaknesses such as _____

_____

_____

_____

It ___ (is/is not) feasible to safely generalize these findings to people not included in the present study because _____

_____

_____

_____

One recommendation that emerges from the present study is _____

_____

_____

_____

Using the Single-Subject Research Design

In this section of the chapter, you will examine some hypothetical data on a few cases that might have been clients of the SOAR program. This will give you the opportunity to explore the single-subject research design in further depth than was accomplished in the previous chapter on evaluative research. In particular, you will learn how to analyze single-subject research data statistically.

First, let's review the phases of evaluative research. You have already examined the problem of sexual crime and the nature of the SOAR program for the treatment of incarcerated sexual offenders. In this section of the chapter, you will employ what has already been written for the first major phase of evaluative research: problem formulation.

The second major phase is the research methodology. In the present section of this chapter, you will use the same definition and measurements of variables as those employed in the previous section except that you will use only one of the dependent variables—cognitive distortion. In other words, you will examine the progress of several hypothetical clients on the level of their tendencies to engage in cognitive distortions of their crimes.

There are two major differences in the research methodology between the present and the previous sections of this chapter: You will be using the single-subject research design, and you will have samples of one in each case rather than a group of clients analyzed *as* a group. The final two major phases of research will be different for the present section because these phases deal with data analysis and the drawing of conclusions. You will examine new data and will, of course, draw conclusions that may be different.

You will use the AB single-subject research design for your hypothetical clients. This design, as you should recall, entails the recording of data from clients repeatedly during a baseline period before treatment begins. The repeated measurement of client behavior continues during the period of treatment and the data is analyzed to see if the client's behavior suggests a trend that is significantly better than the projection from the baseline.

Analyzing the Baseline Trend That Is Level

The first task in the statistical analysis of data for the AB single-subject design is the examination of the baseline trend. It provides the data which will be projected into the treatment period. There are a number of basic types of trends. One is the level trend in which there seems to be a pattern that indicates that the target behavior is neither improving nor getting worse. When you have such a trend, you can employ the *standard deviation method of statistical analysis.* This method requires that you compute both the mean and the standard deviation of baseline recordings. Statistical significance is illustrated by measurements of the client's behavior during the treatment period that are better than the figure that represents the mean of baseline recordings plus two standard deviations. Figure 8.3 illustrates a level trend during the baseline period.

In Figure 8.3, the client's score on the target behavior (dependent variable) is 18 on the first baseline recording and 17 on the second, followed by recordings of 18 and 17 for time periods 3 and 4. If you were to visually project this trend into the treatment period, you would naturally draw a straight line that is level with the horizontal axis of the chart. You might note that the mean score for these baseline recordings is 17.5 and you would decide to draw the line at this point. If you did so, you would have completed the first step in the statistical analysis of the data—the drawing of a line representing the mean of the baseline recordings. This line is drawn into the treatment period and those recordings are compared to this line.

But having a treatment trend that is better than the baseline mean is not enough to have statistical significance. You must do better than this. And you determine just how much better the treatment recordings must be to demonstrate statistical significance by calculating the standard deviation of the baseline recordings and drawing a line that represents a score that reflects the baseline mean plus or minus two standard deviations. Whether you draw the line above the mean (plus two standard deviations) or below the mean (minus two standard deviations) depends upon whether your treatment is supposed to raise the scores or lower them. In this case, you are using an example in which lower scores are better. For example, the standard deviation for the baseline scores presented above is 0.5. A figure that represents the mean minus two standard deviations would be 16.5 $(17.5 - 0.5 = 17.0 - 0.5 = 16.5)$. If your mean for treatment recordings is better than this figure, you can declare statistical significance at the .05 level.

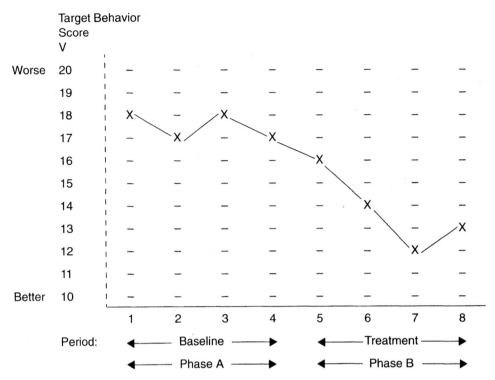

FIGURE 8.3 **Analyzing a Trend Line That Is Level During the Baseline Period**

In this example, the mean of the treatment recordings is 13.75 (16 + 14 + 12 + 13 = 55 / 4 = 13.75), so you can say that this client's recordings during the treatment period reflected behavior that was significantly better than the baseline trend.

Analyzing Data When the Trend Is Going Up or Down

If you have a trend that is either going up or down, you use a different approach to statistical analysis, known as the *celeration line method.* With this approach, you draw a line into the treatment period that is a good fitting line for representing the baseline trend. You do this by calculating the mean of each half of the baseline period and placing a dot on the chart representing these figures and drawing a line that connects these dots and extends into the treatment period. Treatment recordings that are not better than this trend are considered to be ones that do not represent statistical significance. You determine the statistical significance of the pattern of treatment recordings by consulting a statistical table.

The example given in Figure 8.4 makes the examination of data rather easy because the baseline figures represent a straight line. This is seldom the case, but is useful for the illustration of how data are analyzed with the celeration method.

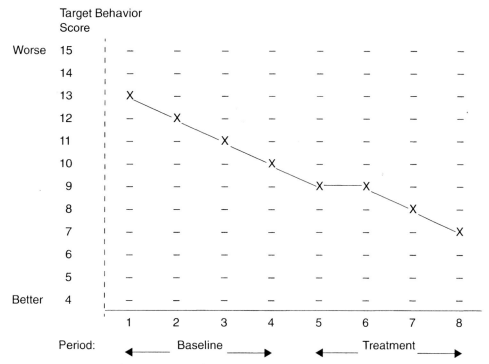

FIGURE 8.4   Analyzing a Trend Line That Is Going Up or Down During the Baseline Period

In this example, you would simply draw a line connecting the four baseline scores by placing a ruler on the page, and extend this line into the treatment period. Return to the last illustration and do this for that set of data. In other words, place a ruler on the four baseline recordings, which conveniently form a straight line, and draw a line that extends throughout the treatment period.

As you can see, the recordings of client behavior during the treatment period are better than those during the baseline period, *but they are not better than the trend that was projected into the treatment period.* In other words, they were not better than the trend that was already underway with the client. If you can assume that this trend would continue in the absence of treatment, you cannot say that the treatment made any difference.

Normally, a trend in the baseline period does not form a perfectly straight line. This requires that you develop a best fitting line for your data. A simple method for doing this is to place a dot on the page at the midpoint of the first half of the baseline recordings, which represents the mean of those recordings, and to do the same for the second half of the baseline recordings. In the example given in Figure 8.5, the @ symbol will represent the dot to be drawn at the midpoint of the first half of the baseline recordings and then again at the midpoint of the second half of these baseline recordings. Place a ruler that connects these two symbols (@) and draw a

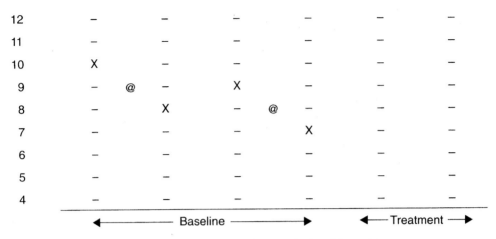

FIGURE 8.5   **Drawing the Trend Line That Is Going Up or Down**

line into the treatment period. This trend line represents what would be expected of the client's behavior in the absence of treatment.

The first four time periods constitute the baseline period; the first two recordings make up the first half of the baseline, while periods three and four comprise the second half. In Figure 8.5, the mean of 10 and 8 is 9, so a dot (in this case, the @ symbol) is placed at the point of the score of 9 at the midway point of the first half of the baseline. For the second half of the baseline, calculate the mean of 9 and 7, which is 8, and place a mark at the point of 8 at the midway point of the second half of the baseline. Then draw a line with a ruler that extends this line into the treatment period. All treatment recordings that fall on the line are recordings that are predicted by the baseline trend and are assumed to represent the client's progress in the absence of treatment. Recordings that are worse than the line represent behavior that is worse than the baseline prediction without treatment. You must have recordings of target behavior that are better than this predicted trend in order to have confidence that your treatment is effective. However, having only a few such recordings is not sufficient to give you confidence that your trend is not easily explained by chance.

To find out about statistical significance, you must consult a statistical table. This table is dependent upon the proportion of baseline recordings that were better than the trend line and the number of treatment recordings and the number of treatment recordings that were better than the trend line. Armed with this information for your data, you can consult a table and determine if your results are statistically significant.

You will not consult such a table in the present chapter. Instead, there are a few things to keep in mind if you do not have such a table available. First, the more treatment recordings you have, the better your likelihood of discovering statistical significance. It is advised that you have a minimum of six such recordings. In this case it is very likely that you will achieve statistical significance at the .05 level (i.e., $p < .05$) if all of the treatment recordings are better than the trend line. The only exception to this possibility would be a baseline trend with a high proportion of recordings that are better than the trend line (i.e., 70 percent). Furthermore, you will have statistical significance at this level even if one of the treatment recordings fails to be better than the trend line unless one-half or more of the baseline recordings are better than the trend line.

From the above discussion, perhaps the second point has become clear: the higher the proportion of baseline recordings that are superior to the trend, the less likely that you will achieve statistical significance. If this proportion is greater than 50 percent, it is likely that you will need a good number of superior treatment recordings to achieve statistical significance. This factor becomes less problematic if you have a good number of treatment recordings (e.g., eight or more).

If all of your treatment recordings are superior to the trend line, your treatment has obviously done all it can to achieve statistical significance. If your table says that your data has failed to achieve statistical significance, perhaps you should look upon this situation as one in which statistical analysis is not suitable. This option is discussed in more detail below.

Trends That Are Not Suitable for Statistical Analysis

There are two basic trends that are not suitable for statistical analysis of single-subject research. One is the example in which the baseline does not demonstrate a clear trend, and the other is the situation in which the projected trend would be impossible (or nearly impossible) to achieve during the treatment period. In the first case, I am talking about a highly erratic trend. Suppose, for example, that you had cognitive distortion scores of 19 for the first baseline recording followed by a score of 11 for the second, 17 for the third, and 10 for the fourth. There is a wild trend fluctuating from rather low to rather high from one recording to another. This trend is difficult to interpret and poses serious problems for statistical analysis.

Another problematic trend would be one which depicts a serious level of client progress during the baseline. If the client is making a lot of progress on his or her own, you have to wonder whether the client needs treatment. From the standpoint of data analysis, a problem will arise if the projected trend reaches the maximum score (or near the maximum score) before the treatment period is over. In this case, there is no chance to have data that would show that the treatment is effective.

ASSIGNMENT 8–F

1. Examine the following steps in the use of the AB single-subject design and determine the proper sequence of these steps. Place (1) by the first step, (2) by the second step, and so forth, until you have given a number to each step.

_____ Collect data on client behavior during the baseline period

_____ Analyze the data and determine whether statistical significance has been achieved

_____ Determine the treatment objectives .

_____ Select a means of measuring client behavior

_____ Determine whether practical significance has been achieved

_____ Collect data during the treatment period

_____ Select the study sample

_____ Define and analyze the client's problem

2. There is one major step missing from the above list. What is it?

_____

_____

_____

_____

3. What is one advantage of the AB single-subject research design over the one-group pre-test–posttest design?

_____

_____

_____

_____

4. Which of the following situations would not be suitable for statistical analysis for the determination of statistical significance? (You may select more than one.)

_____ Using the AB single-subject design, you discover baseline measurements of 11, 12, 11, and 10.

_____ You measure a single client one time before treatment and one time after treatment has been completed.

_____   You measure twenty clients one time before treatment and one time after treatment has been completed.

_____   With the AB single-subject design, you discover measurements during the baseline of 36, 12, 19, 29, and 9, in that order.

Explain your above choices.

_____

_____

_____

_____

5. Suppose that you have employed the AB single-subject design for a client and have found a level trend in baseline recordings, a baseline mean of 6.25, a baseline standard deviation of 1.0, and a treatment mean of 8.72. The dependent variable is self-esteem and your treatment objective is to raise self-esteem. You are employing an instrument that provides higher scores for higher self-esteem. Have you achieved statistical significance? Explain.

_____

_____

_____

_____

Data on Hypothetical Clients

In Figures 8.6, 8.7, 8.8, and 8.9, you will examine data on hypothetical clients A, B, C, and D. Each figure represents a special case in statistical analysis. For each figure, the baseline represents four weekly recordings for cognitive distortions as measured by the scale described in the previous section of this chapter. These recordings took place before the client entered the treatment program. Week 4, the last of the baseline recordings, was the time immediately before the first treatment session. Week 5 was one week later, the first recording in which the effect of treatment could be felt. The treatment recordings occurred once per week for weeks 5 through 13, a total of nine measurements during the treatment period.

Examine these figures and respond to the questions of the assignment that follows them.

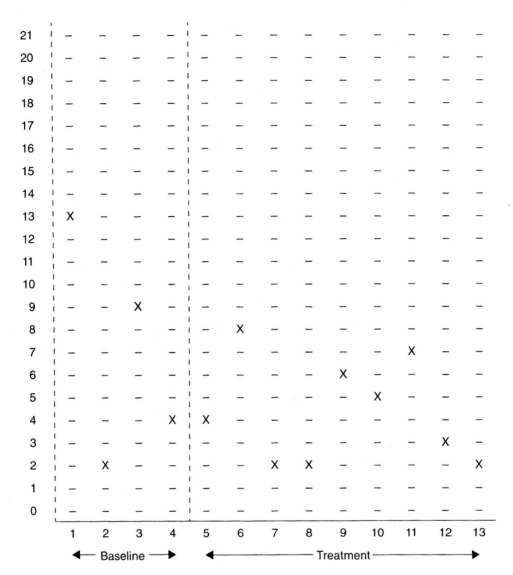

FIGURE 8.6   Cognitive Distortion Scores for Client A

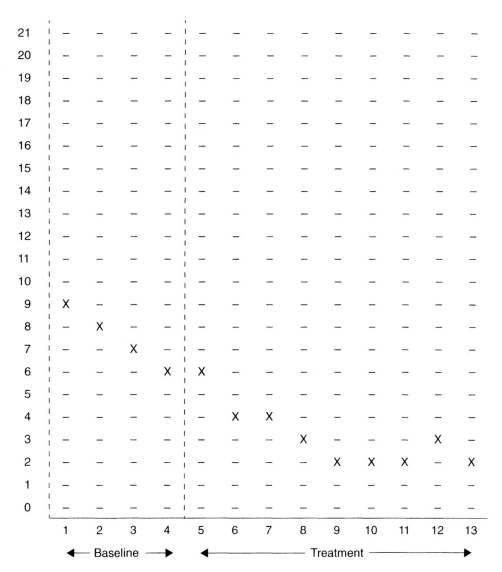

FIGURE 8.7   Cognitive Distortion Scores for Client B

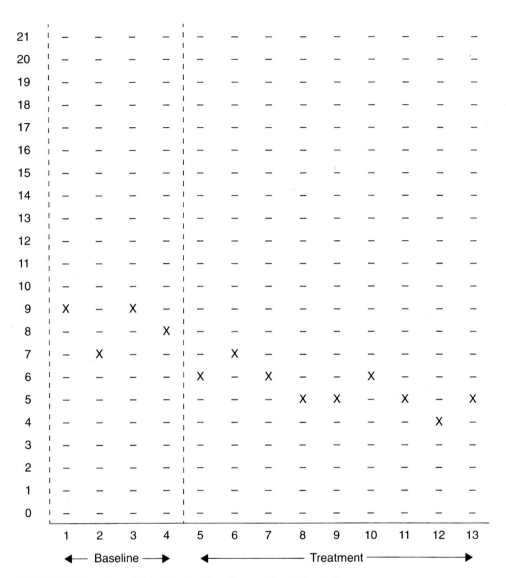

FIGURE 8.8   Cognitive Distortion Scores for Client C

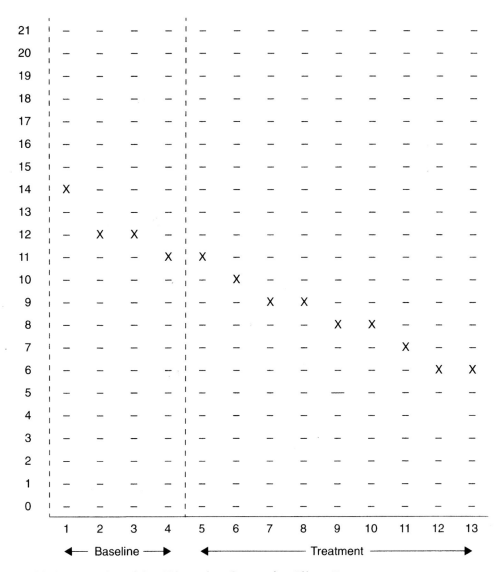

FIGURE 8.9   Cognitive Distortion Scores for Client D

ASSIGNMENT 8–G

1. What is your interpretation of the scores for Client A with regard to both statistical significance and practical significance?

_____

_____

_____

_____

2. What is your interpretation of the scores for Client B with regard to both statistical significance and practical significance?

_____

_____

_____

_____

3. What is your interpretation of the scores for Client C with regard to both statistical significance and practical significance?

_____

_____

_____

_____

4. What is your interpretation of the scores for Client D with regard to both statistical significance and practical significance?

_____

_____

_____

_____

Reference

Nichols, H. R., and Molinder, I. (1984). Multiphasic Sex Inventory. Tacoma, WA: Nichols & Molinder.

Glossary

AB Single-Subject Research Design. A research design in which a single subject (client, group, organization, community) is measured on the dependent variable several times during a baseline period before treatment begins and is repeatedly measured on the dependent variable during the treatment period.

ABAB Single-Subject Research Design. A research design in which a single subject is measured repeatedly during a baseline period (period A), is given a specific treatment and repeatedly measured during the treatment period (period B), is measured repeatedly during a second baseline period (the second A period), and a second treatment period when the same treatment is administered (the second period B).

ABC Single-Subject Research Design. A research design in which a single subject is measured repeatedly during a baseline period (period A), is given a certain treatment and is repeatedly measured during this treatment period (period B), and the treatment is changed, with the client continually measured on the dependent variable during this second treatment period (period C).

Baseline Period. A period of time during which the client is not receiving treatment.

Basic Experimental Research Design. The basic experimental design entails the assignment of people to two groups on a random basis, one group being given the intervention (known as the experimental group) and the other group being excluded from treatment (known as the control group). Both groups of people are measured on the dependent variable before treatment and again after treatment has been completed. The gain in functioning for the two groups is compared to see if the experimental group had a significantly greater gain than the control group.

The BA Single-Subject Research Design. A research design in which a single subject is measured repeatedly on the dependent variable during the treatment period and during a baseline period which follows treatment.

The BC Single-Subject Research Design. A research design in which a single subject is measured repeatedly on the dependent variable during a treatment period (period B) and the treatment is changed and the subject is measured repeatedly during the second treatment period (period C).

Celeration Line Method of Statistical Analysis (for single-subject research). A method of statistical analysis for single-subject research in which the baseline trend is not level, i.e., is either ascending or descending. The proportion of recordings of the dependent variable during the treatment period that fall on the favorable side of the trend line is compared to the same for the baseline period to see if the former is significantly greater than the latter. In most circumstances, if you have as many as six treatment recordings and all the treatment recordings are superior to the trend line, you will achieve statistical significance; however, you should consult a statistical test to be sure.

Criterion Validity. A measurement device has criterion validity to the extent to which it corresponds to (correlates with) other criteria for observing the concept under study. For example, scholastic aptitude test scores should correlate with college grades if this test has criterion validity. A marital satisfaction scale should be able to predict divorce. One person's self-esteem scale should correlate with another person's self-esteem scale.

Face Validity. A measurement device has face validity if it appears to knowledgeable people to be an accurate means of measuring the particular concept it is supposed to measure. This is the least objective of the various methods of assessing validity, but is often the only reasonable alternative for self-developed instruments.

History (as a threat to internal validity): When a client improves during the treatment period, it may be because of the treatment, or it may be because of a change in the client's environment, such as obtaining a job or getting a promotion. History as a threat to internal validity refers to changes in the client's environment which may be the cause of improvement. The comparison group design addresses history as a threat to internal validity because it is assumed that the two groups will be equivalent on history; thus, the superiority of the gain for the treatment group over the gain for the comparison group would be better attributed to the treatment than to history. The AB single-subject design, however, does not address this threat.

Maturation. Sometimes people overcome their problems on their own through time and the normal process of growth. This is referred to as maturation, and is one of the most important threats to internal validity. The comparison group design addresses maturation because it compares a treated group with an untreated group, the assumption being that the effects of maturation would probably be equal for the two groups; thus, the superiority of the treated group's improvement in functioning over the comparison is normally better attributed to the treatment rather than to maturation. The AB single-subject design also addresses maturation because the baseline trend is assumed to be an indicator of the progression of maturation; thus, if the client's functioning during the treatment period is significantly better than the projected baseline trend, the client's growth can be better attributed to the treatment than to maturation.

One-Group Pretest–Posttest Research Design. A research design in which a group of clients are tested on the dependent variable before treatment and again after treatment has been completed. The gain in functioning evidenced by these two tests serves as a measure of the effects of treatment.

Standard Deviation Method of Statistical Analysis for Single-Subject Research. A means of statistical analysis of single-subject research data when the trend during the baseline period is relatively level. Statistical significance is achieved if the mean for treatment recordings of the dependent variable is two standard deviations better than the mean for the baseline recordings.

t Test. A means of determining the statistical significance of data measured at the interval level for either of two groups of subjects (t test for independent samples) or a single group of subjects measured at two points in time (t test for paired data). The formula for these two situations is not the same. When testing a directional hypothesis, a t value of 2.0 or greater is significant at the .05 (i.e., $p < .05$) level if the sample size is greater than five. Slightly lower t values are significant (at the .05 level) with larger samples. Consult a statistical text with a table of t values for further information.

Testing (as a threat to internal validity): As a threat to internal validity, testing refers to the effect of being tested. One may develop a sensitivity to the administration of a pretest which may affect the posttest score. This is of special concern if the pretest and posttest deal with knowledge, because one may remember items on the pretest when taking the posttest and may have been especially sensitive to this specific piece of information. Thus, it may be this sensitivity rather than the intervention that mostly effected the gain illustrated by the posttest. The comparison group and AB single-subject designs both address this threat. It is assumed that the comparison group would have the same reaction to the testing situation as the treatment group, so that any differences in growth between the two groups can be better attributed to the treatment than to the effects of testing. For the AB single-subject design, the baseline period establishes a trend that illustrates the effects of testing, if there are any. Thus, the superiority of client functioning during the treatment period is better attributed to the intervention than to testing.

Test–Retest Reliability. To assess reliability using this method, a group of subjects are measured on the scale at two points in time and the two scores for this same group of people are correlated. High positive correlations indicate reliability, or consistency.

Threats to Internal Validity. In evaluative research, a threat to internal validity is something other than the intervention that may be the reason for the client's change in behavior. For example, a change in the client's work situation may be the reason that he is no longer depressed, and the treatment may not have caused the improvement in functioning. There are a variety of threats to internal validity, also known as alternative explanations. Among these threats are maturation, history, and testing, which are defined in this glossary. Some research designs do a better job of dealing with certain threats to internal validity than other research designs do. In general, experimental designs which use random assignment of subjects to treatment and control (comparison) groups do a superior job of addressing the various threats to internal validity.

Chapter 9

Using Exploratory Research:
Examining the Experience of Adoption as an Older Child

You have previously examined exploratory research in regard to the topic of stress among social work students. Exploratory research was the category of inquiry because the purpose of that study was to identify new aspects of stress beyond those identified in the literature. The outcome was to be the development of new hypotheses to be tested by additional research. For this reason, qualitative methods of measurement were viewed as more appropriate than quantitative ones. If the purpose had been to test a hypothesis about stress that was well documented in the existing literature, quantitative methods might have been more appropriate, and the category of the study would have been labeled as explanatory.

In the present chapter, you will continue your examination of exploratory research and qualitative research methods with an example related to the experience of being adopted. With limited work having been done on this experience, John Powell (1984) turned to qualitative methods to gain a better understanding of this experience, especially as it related to older children. You will examine his study in the present chapter.

Objectives

Special attention will be given in this chapter to:

1. How the concepts of theory and observation serve as the building blocks of social research;
2. The distinctions between deductive and inductive processes of inquiry;
3. Methodologies of qualitative inquiry;
4. How analytic induction works as one method of qualitative research.

Qualitative Research Methods

Qualitative research methods employ a flexible means of observation. Instead of placing study subjects into categories or giving them numbers, qualitative measurement records their behaviors or ideas in a format that is somewhat unique from one subject to another. This provides for potentially more breadth of understanding of the phenomenon being studied, but makes generalization more difficult because of the more open format for measurement.

Qualitative methods have been described in a previous chapter as being more suited to the development of a theory than the testing of one, the latter being more suitable to the quantitative format for measurement. Qualitative measurement is also more suitable if the purpose of the study is the description of the subjective meaning of human processes or events as opposed to the precise description of them. If you want to enhance your understanding of what it is like to be a client of your agency, from the initial intake interview to the termination of service, you would likely conclude that qualitative methods of measurement would be appropriate. But if you wanted to describe your clients in terms of gender, age, type of problem, and so forth, a quantitative format would be more suitable.

Researchers can distinguish between qualitative and quantitative measurement in regard to three topics: the purpose of inquiry, the process of inquiry, and the role of the observer (researcher). You have already covered the first topic. Qualitative measurement is more suitable to the development of theory and the subjective description of social phenomena while quantitative methods of measurement are more suited to the testing of theory or the precise description of things.

Description

I have previously used the category of descriptive research to indicate the precise description of social phenomena. Thus, descriptive research has been exemplified by quantitative methods of measurement. However, this was not intended to suggest that qualitative methods are not suitable to description. Indeed, they are. But in this classification scheme, I have arbitrarily employed the term "descriptive research" to refer to the precise description of things and the term "exploratory research" to refer to the description of things in more subjective ways.

One form of qualitative inquiry is known as *ethnography*. This refers to the study of cultures in their natural settings. One might observe the culture of homeless people by living in a homeless shelter for several days. This experience would afford one the opportunity to observe much more behavior than would be possible by conducting a survey of homeless people.

In the study of Mexican and Vietnamese newcomers to the United States, Goodson–Lawes (1994) identified common errors in quantitative research that suggest that qualitative methods are more appropriate. Mistrust and fear of outsiders was one of the realities of people in this culture. Thus, such people need an opportunity to become comfortable with the researcher. Another observation was the tendency of such people to answer questions in formal inquiry according to what they believed was expected of them rather than their most meaningful thoughts on the subject. The latter would only be revealed by situations in which they were naturally interacting with others rather than being questioned by a person in a position of authority. Several additional errors were mentioned in this analysis.

To overcome some of these errors, Goodson–Lawes made the following observations:

> *Fieldworkers must take several steps to gain legitimacy in the eyes of the group of people who have no real reason to trust an outsider. They must learn to speak the language; they must gain at least nominal social status to be taken seriously; they must develop sufficient social skills to be accepted, if not as a native, at least at an admissible level. The "normality" of the ethnographer's presence in a community is heightened by complete participation in daily life and constant observation of others' interactions and actions . . . Because the intent of ethnography is to comprehend, without judgment, alien ideology, ritual, behavior, and social structure, one of the most important aspects of such fieldwork is that the investigator's attitude not be "loaded" before entering the field. Ethnography seeks to understand the meaning of actions, events, and physical objects for the people who are teaching us, rather than what they mean to us directly. (Goodson–Lawes, 1994, p. 26)*

Theory Development

A theory is an attempt to explain a phenomenon. Do abused wives remain with their husbands because they are socialized to be helpless and psychologically dependent or because they are economically dependent upon their husbands? These are two potential explanations of the behavior of abused wives subsequent to the experience of abuse. One focuses on psychological dependence while another focuses on economic dependence. Perhaps there are other potential explanations of this phenomenon, and, thus, other theories about it.

There is a specific methodology in qualitative inquiry known as *grounded theory,* which is specifically designed to develop theory. The basic idea behind this approach is that theory is derived from observations. Thus, the researcher should enter the field with an open mind, whether or not a literature review has been undertaken. Too much attention to present research is believed to potentially restrict the openness of inquiry and close the door on the recognition of important social phenomena.

In an article in a book on qualitative methods for social work, Jane Gilgun indicated that some grounded theory researchers do a thorough literature review but some do not. Those who use the literature review do so in order to obtain guidance on what is known about the subject while those who avoid this procedure do so because they do not want to be restricted by what others have chosen to observe about the subject.

> *Whether or not researchers do prior reviews, they enter the field with minds as open as possible, attempting to be aware of their own biases and preconceptions. As the research proceeds, they begin to define concepts, see relationships among*

concepts, and discover patterns. They continually pit their emerging empirical findings against new data. They modify their findings to fit the data. They are therefore continually defining and redefining concepts and relationships among concepts. (Gilgun, 1994, p. 116)

While it is generally argued that quantitative methods are better suited to the testing of a theory or hypothesis, there are qualitative methods that are designed to test hypotheses. In fact, you will examine such a method in this chapter, noting that when qualitative methods are used to test hypotheses that have been formulated from the literature, their purpose may be better characterized as the refinement of hypotheses than the testing of them. In this chapter, for example, you will see how hypotheses were first articulated and then modified by the methodology known as analytic induction.

Deductive and Inductive Processes of Inquiry

Qualitative and quantitative means of measurement are different with respect to the process of inquiry as well as its purpose. When researchers use quantitative measurement in explanatory research, they tend to move from theory to observation. In other words, they develop a theory (or hypothesis) from what is already known about a subject and seek to test this theory or hypothesis through observation (measurement). When they move from theory to observation, they are engaging in what is known as a *deductive* process of inquiry. When they employ qualitative measurement in exploratory research, they tend to move from observation to theory. In the latter case, there is not a sufficient basis for developing a theory or hypothesis from what is known from the existing literature, so investigators use observations of study subjects to develop theories. When they move from observation to theory, they are employing an *inductive* process of inquiry.

The grounded theory approach is inductive. The beginning emphasis is on observation. In fact, it can be quite inductive if one avoids the literature before beginning observations because the literature will contain some theoretical guidance even if it is a little vague. When the literature is employed by grounded theory researchers, it is for the purpose of gaining conceptual clarity rather than the formulation of concrete theories before their observation begins.

The Role of the Observer

Qualitative research places emphasis on the context in which behavior is observed. Many writers in this field believe that observation cannot be separated from the observer. Quantitative research tends to assume that objective observation is possible; thus, if researchers employ objective means of measurement, they will be prepared to test theories about reality. But some would argue that the choice of what to measure is guided by a subjective thought process and highly restricts the nature of the reality that could be observed.

This topic brings you to the third basis of difference between quantitative and qualitative methods: the role of the observer. With quantitative methods, the observer is believed to be completely objective. Reality is believed to exist independently of observation. For the qualitative researcher, becoming a participant is often needed. For some researchers, their own experiences with the phenomenon being investigated are thought to produce a rich array of information for analysis.

There are several roles for the observer in qualitative research. In some studies, the observer does not interact with those being observed. This procedure maintains more objectivity but reduces the richness of the information to which the researcher is exposed. In some studies, the role of the researcher is that of *participant observer*. In this case, those being observed are clear about the role of the researcher. He or she is not a full member of the group, but is an observer of what is happening. In some cases, the researcher is a complete participant in the group. This requires complete entry into the dynamics of the group. For example, a person might join various civic organizations in order to observe certain behaviors. Such people would be full members of the organization and would not reveal that their purpose was to study their fellow organization members.

ASSIGNMENT 9–A

1. Which one of the following purposes for social research seems to be the least suitable for the qualitative method of inquiry?

    a. Description   **b.** Exploration   **c.** Evaluation

2. Which method of inquiry is better suited to the development of theory?

    a. Quantitative   **b.** Qualitative

3. Which purpose seems to be the one that would best lend itself to either qualitative or quantitative methods of inquiry? In other words, which purpose could use both means of inquiry given a slightly different focus?

    a. Description

    b. Evaluation

    c. Explanation

4. Suppose that you have two people who are curious about whether the full moon makes people act strange. Person A has discovered from research that the full moon is related to the tides and that the tides are related to atmospheric conditions that might affect the brain's chemistry. From this knowledge, Person A suspects that there would be a relationship between the presence of the full moon and strange behavior. He will study this question by comparing the rate of disturbances of psychiatric patients during the days of the full moon with the same rate for days in which the moon is not full. Person B, on the other hand, has no such knowledge of the tides and atmospheric conditions but has noticed that her patients in the psychiatric ward seem more troubled and difficult during the full moon. She asserts, therefore, to her colleagues that it appears that there is something about the full moon that makes people act strange.

Which of these persons appears to be operating from a deductive process?

_____

Which of these persons appears to be operating from an inductive process?

_____

5. Ethnographic methods seem better suited for which purpose?

   a. Description

   b. Explanation

   c. Evaluation

A Study of the Experience of Being Adopted

John Powell (1984) undertook a study of people placed for adoption as older children. His purpose was to gain a better understanding of this experience so that ideas could be generated for improving the process. He was also interested in the special circumstances of the child who is placed for adoption as an older child because of the potential of special problems with this situation. Because there was little that had been published on this issue, he employed qualitative methods of inquiry. Some of the literature that guided his work is presented in Exhibit 9.1. This review is a summary drawn from John Powell's dissertation. It was reorganized and rewritten, in part, specifically for this exercise.

**EXHIBIT 9.1   A Brief Summary of the Literature Review
(based on the work of John Powell)**

Introduction

According to John Powell (1984), the decade of the 1970s saw a major increase in the movement to place older and emotionally troubled children in adoptive homes. Such children had previously been considered unadoptable and were typically left in foster family care or institutions until they reached adulthood, an alternative that was increasingly viewed as inadequate for the long-term health of children.

> *Yet with the national emphasis on placing all available children in adoptive homes, little evaluation has been done to determine what long-term benefits are derived from such adoptions, and this is due partly to the recency of acceptance of such adoptive*

(Continued)

EXHIBIT 9.1   *Continued*

practices. Even if attachments are formed between the older adoptee and the adoptive parents, do the bonds of attachment reach to the extended family as well, and do such attachments endure throughout the life of the adoptee? (Powell, 1984, p. 1)

Some of the limited research on adoptive placements suggests that children placed for adoption have a slightly higher incidence of trouble later in life than do children raised by biological parents. Furthermore, it is believed that children placed at an older age have more difficulty than those placed as infants. Yet, the recent pressure from advocacy groups for agencies to speed up the process of adoption has resulted in the lessening of the historic role of professionals in the adoptive process.

What can we expect from this movement? Can these children achieve success in adoptive placements? What is the quality of family life for such children? Is it different from that of children raised by their biological parents or children placed for adoption at an early age? What is the experience of being adopted like? What hypotheses about the nature of the adoptive process are suggested from the experiences of people who have gone through it?

These were the questions examined in an interview study of 17 adults who had been placed for adoption as older children. Extensive interviews were conducted with these individuals. These interviews were examined with the use of the analytic induction method of qualitative research and several hypotheses were developed and examined.

Adoption Services

"In the past 50 years, adoption services have focused primarily on the placement of healthy white infants born to unmarried mothers.... These children were placed with young, white, middle-class couples who were unable to conceive.... Adoptive practice consisted of evaluating the couple's motivation to adopt and their ability to parent a child, and then providing minimal postplacement services prior to finalization of the adoption.

"In the 1960s social changes began to have a major effect upon adoption services. These changes included the widespread use of birth control, the changing mores allowing an unmarried mother to keep her child, and the liberalization of abortion laws in some states.... The result was a decrease in the number of white infants available for adoption.... At the same time, as part of the impact of the civil rights movement, large numbers of black infants and older children lost in the maze of foster care came to the attention of adoption agencies and were placed with adoptive families...As the supply of healthy white infants continued to diminish, children who in the past were considered unadoptable were placed with families.... A similar reexamination of adoptive parenthood led to the acceptance of many adults who formerly would have been classified as unsuitable (Powell, 1984, pp. 9–10).

Review of Research on Adoptions

Several studies have been conducted which compare the proportion of adopted persons with nonadopted persons in relation to their prevalence among the clients of

EXHIBIT 9.1   *Continued*

mental health agencies. While the percentage of the total population who have been placed for adoption is about 2 percent, the percent of the clientele of mental health agencies has been found in various studies to range from 2.4 percent to 13 percent (Powell, 1984, p. 12).

Many have criticized such studies because it is believed that persons who have adopted children are more agency-oriented and more likely to turn to mental health services than are people in the general population. To correct for this possibility, Wolkind (1979) examined three studies of random samples of the populations of two European countries. He found that adopted boys, but not adopted girls, had a slightly higher rate of disturbance than the general population, but that this incidence was less than that for one-parent families. Thus, the question of whether adopted persons fare worse is not entirely clear. If they do, it appears that their higher incidence of difficulty is rather small.

One theory regarding the adoption experience is known as the theory of shared fate (Kirk, 1964, 1981). This theory contends that adoptive parents suffer from role handicap and a lack of role support because this society has insufficiently developed expectations about the role of the adoptive parent as distinct from the natural parent. Ambiguities regarding this role will tempt some to avoid a healthy confrontation of this reality. Adoptive parents who openly acknowledge their uniqueness will achieve a better bond with the adopted child who also must confront their differentness (Powell, 1984, p. 16).

Adoption of Older Children

Information about older adoptions was found to be more sparse when John Powell examined the literature. But he did find some limited guidance. For example, Smith and Sherwin (1983) assert that bonding for older adoptees is more complex than for the younger ones. They concluded from their research that adoptive families should take into consideration the child's life history because it is more developed than for the young adoptee. Thus, the bonding process will take longer (Powell, 1984, p. 15).

Newson and Newson (1976) theorized that an unnoticed function of parents is to act as a memory store for the child by which the child can compare present experiences. Children placed at a later age have less history with the parents on which this function can be realized; thus, one of the foundations of bonding is less strong (as cited in Powell, 1984, p. 18).

No published research could be found by Powell that examined how adults who were placed in adoption as older children feel about such matters as family identification or parental bonding. (Powell, 1983, p. 16). However, Powell engaged in personal communication with D. H. Kirk, author of *Shared Fate* (1964), who offered a hypothesis about the issue of arbitrariness. "Kirk (personal communication, May 6, 1983) suggested that adults adopted as older children often struggle with a feeling of arbitrariness in the selection of their adoptive family. Whereas one might perceive the acquisition of a family by birth as divinely inspired, an older adopted child can remember the arbitrary selection of his family by a social worker, physician, lawyer, or other professional" (Powell, 1984, p. 18).

(Continued)

EXHIBIT 9.1 *Continued*

Rationale for the Study

"Young children whose parents seem unlikely ever to be able to look after them adequately are believed to fare better with an early decision for adoption or long-term foster care. Child psychoanalytic theory contends that lack of consistent parenting or loss of parent figures leads to feelings of helplessness and profound deprivation. The earlier in a child's life a decision is made for permanent parents, the greater the chance of healthy development (Goldstein, Freud, & Solnit, 1973) (as cited in Powell, 1984, p. 19).

"Anticipation during the months of pregnancy and bonding at a child's birth and early in life usually cement a permanent attachment between a child and caring, nurturing parents (Fraiberg, 1980; Smith & Sherwin, 1983). Many children, however, are not privileged to enjoy such a fate. For one reason or another they may be placed in a series of foster homes. Can she be expected to find a way to develop a healthy attachment to a permanent family without dealing with the past? Can an adoptive family be expected to assimilate her without deliberate assessment of its own needs, its expectations of the child and the new family?" (Powell, 1984, pp. 19–20)

Thus, one would expect that older children placed for adoption would undergo a different experience from younger adoptees and would be more vulnerable to difficulties in their adjustment to this experience. In view of the dearth of research on this experience, a new inquiry into this subject is warranted.

"More knowledge and understanding of the perceptions, feelings, and decisions of older children as they move through the process of adoption is needed to guide the people involved" (Powell, 1984, p. 22). The identification of a model of this process can enable those in the helping professions to understand how to make the process healthier.

Research Questions

The present study was developed to investigate adult adoptees who were placed in their adoptive homes with memory traces to their biologic families. The following questions inspired this study:

1. What are the memories of birth families, former foster parents, or institutions that adoptees have?

2. Did the adoptees feel pressure from social workers to move quickly into adoptive homes?

3. What knowledge do adoptees have of other attempts to place them in adoptive homes?

4. How has the arbitrariness of the selection process of adoptive parents been perceived by adoptees who were placed as older children?

5. What rights do children have to keep various options open without being forced to align with biologic parents or adoptive parents?

6. What is the quality and quantity of family life that is afforded older adopted children?

EXHIBIT 9.1 *Continued*

7. Are these family attachments durable beyond childhood?

8. How do adoptees feel about biologic siblings?

9. How does one deal with having two families in one's memory?

10. How has the experience of being adopted as an older child affected the childhood and adulthood of adoptees?

References

Fraiberg, S. (1980). *Clinical studies in infant mental health: The first year of life.* New York: Basic Books.

Gilgun, J. F. (1994). Hand into glove: The grounded theory approach and social work practice, in *Qualitative research in social work,* E. Sherman and W. J. Reid, (Eds.) New York: Columbia University Press.

Goldstein, J., Freud, A., & Solnit, A. (1973). *Beyond the best interests of the child.* New York: Free Press.

Kirk, D. H. (1964). *Shared fate.* New York: The Free Press.

Kirk, D. H. (1981). *Adoptive kinship: A modern institution in need of reform.* Toronto: Butterworth.

Newson, J., & Newson, E. (1976). *Seven year old in the home environment.* New York: John Wiley and Sons.

Powell, J. Y. (1984). *Adults who were adopted as older children.* PhD dissertation, University of North Carolina at Greensboro.

Smith, D. W., & Sherwin, L. N. (1983). *Mothers and their adopted children: The bonding process.* New York: Tiresias Press.

Wolkind, S. (1979). Psychological development of the adopted child. In S. Wolkind & M. Klaus (Eds). *Medical aspects of adoption and foster care.* Philadelphia: J. P. Lippincott Co.

ASSIGNMENT 9–B

1. Why should social workers be especially concerned about studying the adoption of older children?

   a. There has been an increase in the number of such adoption placements, resulting in the placement of some people who would not have previously been considered suitable to adoption.

   b. The older child placed for adoption has a past family history that must be reconciled with the new family.

   c. There is little research on how this experience is different from that of the younger child placed for adoption, leaving social workers to generalize from what they know about the younger adoption to the older adoption, when this may not be appropriate.

   d. All of the above

   e. None of the above

2. Are adopted persons (of all ages) a great deal more vulnerable to mental health problems than the general population of persons raised with biological parents?

_____

_____

_____

3. Which of the following would be *least* appropriate as a topic for the development of a hypothesis about the adoption of older children?

   a. Bonding between adoptive parents and adopted child

   b. Adoptees' reconciliation of life history before and after the adoption

   c. Anger and a tendency toward violence among adoptees

   d. Adoptees' feelings of powerlessness due to the arbitrariness of the adoptive placement

   e. Adjustment of adoptees to life in general

4. Develop one interview question for a study on the adoption experience for the older child. Identify the rationale for this question given the literature examined on this topic.

_____

_____

_____

_____

Study Methodology

Analytic induction is a means of qualitative inquiry that is designed to test, or refine, hypotheses. Viewing it as a means of testing hypotheses, it is a deviation from the rule that quantitative research is better suited to testing theory than is qualitative research. Looking at it as a means of refining hypotheses, its ultimate purpose is the development of theory. In any event, it was this methodology that John Powell used in his study of adoption.

Powell identified the steps of analytic induction as follows:

1. A rough definition of the phenomenon to be explained is given.
2. A hypothetical explanation of that phenomenon is formulated.
3. One case is studied in light of the hypothesis with the object of determining whether the hypothesis fits the facts in that case.
4. If the hypothesis does not fit the facts, either the hypothesis is reformulated or the phenomenon to be explained is redefined, so that the case is excluded.

5. Practical certainty may be attained after a small number of cases has been examined, but the discovery by the investigator of a single negative case disproves the explanation and requires a reformulation.
6. This procedure of examining cases and then redefining the phenomenon or reformulating the hypothesis is continued until a universal relationship is established, each negative case calling for a redefinition or a reformulation.
7. For the purposes of proof, cases outside the area circumscribed by the definition are examined to determine whether or not the final hypothesis applies to them. (Powell, 1984, p. 25)

The first two steps given above precede the collection of information from study subjects. The following information on the definition of the phenomenon to be explained and the hypothetical explanation of the phenomenon are drawn from Powell's work.

Definition of the Phenomenon to Be Explained

The phenomenon being studied is the experience of being adopted as an older child. Of particular concern is the ability of such adoptees to reconcile (to restore to harmony) their family histories given their experiences with a change from birth family to adoptive family at an age when they had acquired a significant family history before the transition. Another focus of concern was how this reconciliation had influenced their lives.

Hypothetical Explanation of the Phenomenon

The theory of shared fate was the hypothetical guide. According to this theory, the *acceptance of difference* in adoption and birth status on the part of parents and children facilitates understanding and closeness, whereas the rejection of difference tends to cause misunderstanding and detachment.

Another variable is *arbitrariness*. The biological child has a link to the parents which forms the basis for a natural bond. With the adoptive child, there is the opportunity for a choice of the parent. To what extent does the child participate in this process? The greater the child is prepared for the adoption and the more the child is allowed to participate in the process of selection and placement, the better the child's adjustment to the experience will be.

Another variable is *identification*. The older adoptive child has the special problem of changing identification from one family to another, and identification with the adoptive family must follow some form of reconciliation of the past identity. People who are better able to achieve this transition in identity will be better reconciled with the past.

Powell brought the above considerations together in his hypothetical statement:

> When the adoptee's path is through greater acceptance of differentness, less arbitrariness by others, and more identification with the adoptive kin, then there will

be greater reconciliation with the past and thus better adaptation to life for older adoptees. (Powell, 1984, p. 28)

ASSIGNMENT 9–C

1. Two of the variables identified by Powell in his hypothetical statement were (1) acceptance of differentness, and (2) arbitrariness. Identify the other three variables that Powell identified in his statement.

   1.

   2.

   3.

2. For each of the above variables, identify which ones are dependent variables and which are independent variables. Place either the word *dependent* or *independent* next to each number below, using the variables you identified as (1), (2), and (3) above.

   1.

   2.

   3.

3. Qualitative methods of observation (or measurement) such as personal interviews have been suggested as more appropriate than quantitative methods when there is limited knowledge that can guide *either* the development of hypotheses *or* the measurement of variables in a quantitative manner. Concepts such as self-esteem and depression have been extensively defined in the present literature and tools for their quantitative measurement are readily available to researchers. If they wished to know whether there is a relationship between these two variables, a quantitative method of measurement would be suggested.

   Take one of the variables listed above and identify whether you believe it should be measured by a qualitative method or a quantitative method and explain why you believe this.

Sample

The sample for this study was drawn from the experience of a single children's agency located in the south. This was a children's institution which had engaged in the placement of some children for adoption at a later age. From approximately 50 records available, 22 known addresses were secured and 17 of these persons agreed to participate in the study. The reasons for refusal were varied, some for convenience and others because of painful memories.

Procedures

An interview guide was developed for the interviews. Among the 23 items on the interview guide were the following: background information; adoption memories such as events leading to the adoption, meeting with the adoptive parents, etc.; childhood experiences in the adoptive home with siblings, parents, and extended family; adult relationships with adoptive families; and effect of adoption experience on present life.

Pilot interviews were conducted with two adoptees prior to the beginning of the study with the sample of 17 persons. Problems with identification, fearfulness, and loss of control were issues that were identified in these pilot interviews.

All interviews were tape-recorded with verbatim transcriptions made from each tape. After approximately three interviews were completed and studied, tentative hypotheses were developed and tested case by case.

The following guidelines were adopted by Powell:

An attempt was made to be flexible and tolerant to allow for richness of information and to avoid bias.

An effort was made to elicit from the subject what he considered to be important points, a description of his situation, and a determination of what is happening or has happened to him.

Various concerns or puzzlements were noted from the interviews, as well as from the professional literature. Each area was noted on a separate list in order to generate future research areas as well as to help explain raw data.

An attempt was made to observe indicators or prompts that helped to elicit more information. Such indicators were used in subsequent cases. (Powell, 1984, p. 37)

Most interviews were conducted in the homes of the study subjects. In some cases, spouses or children would listen in and even participate at times. The identities of the subjects were not given in the report. Nevertheless, opportunities were given to each subject after the interview to indicate any information that they did not want to be revealed.

Study Results

The Analysis of Patterns of Adaptation

Each of the interviews was described by Powell in the order in which they took place. Following each summarized case, the pattern of the process and its modifications were given. If a case seemed out of the general boundaries of the pattern, the phenomenon was redefined.

Case #1

Mary A. (age 21; adopted at age 6)—Living in a university town, Mary and her husband rent an apartment in a newly developed suburb. They were recently married, and their home is sparsely furnished. Although few pictures and accessories are out, the apartment has a sense of style and grace. Both husband and wife are college graduates. She is a commercial artist, and he works as a pharmaceutical salesman.

She experienced early childhood trauma, abuse, and deprivation, while her husband's early life was stable. She and her younger siblings were orphaned. As a preschooler, Mary became "an instant little mother" after her birth mother's death, changing diapers, cooking, and taking care of her siblings and her ailing father. She describes the birth family as extremely poor, but she has renewed contacts with them along with continuing relationships with her adopted parents.

She was adopted at age 6. Her adoptive father is a high school principal, and her adoptive mother works as a dental hygienist. She visited her birth father in a chronic disease hospital periodically after being placed for adoption. He died several years after her placement. Mary expresses strong desires for beautiful surroundings, such as a Mercedes and a well-designed and constructed home and furnishings, but interestingly she does not seek a country club lifestyle as it conflicts with the Protestant religious values she acquired from her adoptive family.

Mary is easy to admire; she has a will to survive and to excel. Self-reliant and at the same time sensitive, Mary recalls biting her adoptive father's arm in the transfer meeting and fighting to get out of the car in route to her new home. She describes rebelliousness and resentments during her adolescent years in the adoptive family, but she also acknowledges that her lifestyle and values were shaped by her adoptive family, their close friends, and their extended family. She believes maturity will help, and that it takes "years for wounds to heal." (Powell, 1984, p. 41)

The tentative pattern was that early trauma prior to adoption had left Mary feeling abandoned. She felt helpless and unprepared for adoption. Somehow she developed a will to survive, a self-protective phenomenon. Could adoption as an older child make one more aware and perhaps stronger, more self-reliant?

Tentative pattern:

A. Early trauma (felt abandoned)
B. Adoption (unprepared—felt helpless)
C. Self-protection (developed self-reliance; will to survive; sensitivity). (Powell, 1984, p. 42)

The *second interview* was of Amy (age 28, adopted at age 9), who has been married for 6 years and has a three-year-old daughter who is a very high priority in her life. Powell summarized this interview as follows: "Amy suffered preadoption trauma. She shared with Mary (Case #1) a unique sense of awareness both now and in childhood memories. She seemed to have adopted her family along with their adoption of her. The feeling continued to be that adoption as an older child somehow requires adaptation skills that make people different. Doubts arose as to whether the process of adoption added to the trauma. However, at this time, the tentative pattern was continued" (Powell, 1984, p. 43).

The *third interview*, however, did not confirm this pattern because it was with a person who had been adopted before the age of 6 (at age 3) and had limited memory of the experience. The age of his adoption apparently made it easier for him to identify with the adoptive parents and maintain a lasting bond with them. As a result, this case was considered to be an exception. This exception led to the redefinition of the phenomenon to include only those persons placed for adoption at the age of 6 or older. As the interviews proceeded, the model was either expanded, confirmed, or was an exceptional case of someone adopted before the age of 6.

At the completion of the interview process, the following pattern had emerged:

A. Early trauma
B. Loss of family and environment
C. Self-protection
D. Intervention (adoption)
E. Trusting vs. mistrusting

This pattern was graphically depicted by Powell in the chart provided in Exhibit 9.2. This chart uses the example of Maynard S., case #14, age 20, who was adopted at age 7. There are five stages which represent the process identified by the completion of the interviews. Quotes are given from this study subject to illustrate each stage in the process.

**EXHIBIT 9.2   A Model of Analytic Induction
for the Adoption Experience**

Stage in the Process

Example from One Study Subject

Early Trauma

Deprivaton, abuse, neglect, death of a parent, etc.

"I was six and my mother was killed in a car accident and then my father went kind of crazy."

Loss of family and environment

Taken from known environment; sense of helplessness and fear; old enough to remember events.

"I didn't understand anything.... I was taken away from my father. It's like you take a little animal from its mama and taking it somewhere else, and it doesn't know what to do. It's just wondering where its mama is and not knowing."

(Continued)

EXHIBIT 9.2   *Continued*

Stage in the Process   *Example from One Study Subject*

Self-protection:

Developed ability of surveillance of   "I look at things different from other
environment; who can be trusted?   people. A lot different. I can sense
who is to be feared?   almost instantly if someone is mean
or if they are nice. Most people can't
until they actually meet them and
stay with them a lot. Like, I could
look at somebody, and I can say,
well, they're going to treat me bad or
they're going to treat me good.

Intervention

Intervention by adoption made at   "After I was adopted, I felt like I was
age six or older; in some cases it was   part of the family. I think I know
successful and in others only par-   what love means more so than some
tially helpful; tends to give one   people do cause I feel it in a different
memory of bad and good; attempts   way, and I know there are some
to replace lost love objects.   good people around here."

Trusting vs. Mistrusting

Generally adults tend to choose   "I've seen both sides of life, I've seen
trusting side of memory; they tend   the good, and I've seen the bad; and
to be sensitive, caring, and to have   I don't like the bad. I am going to
warm, trusting relationships; but   treat people the way I want them to
also they tend to be wary of being   treat me. If somebody treats me bad,
hurt again.   I just withdraw from them and stay
away. If somebody treats me good,
I'll try to do good for them."

Special Themes Regarding the Adoption Experience

An analysis of the cases revealed several recurring themes which characterize the older adoptee: significance of the extended adoptive family; appreciation of adoption; contact with birth family, and adult life satisfaction. The method used to determine the categorized headings was threefold: (a) the typed, verbatim transcripts were read through several times and headings were identified; (b) A diary was kept during the field-gathering phase of the study that was used to suggest possible headings; (c) key phrases were written down and considered in the selecting of the final headings to be analyzed. "Once headings were established, the verbatim transcripts were scrutinized to determine the frequency and the quality of statements that referred to each subject heading" (Powell, 1984, p. 67).

Significance of the Extended Adoptive Family

"The participants unanimously reported that the extended adoptive family treated them as part of the family. It appears that these relatives helped many of the adoptees to make the transition into their new families." Even one person who had experienced a good deal of tension with the adoptive parents had positive things to say about the extended family such as, "I went and spent some summers with some of the folks in the family. They're a great family, really. They're a really nice family." Another person who had experienced tension with the adoptive parents spoke glowingly of the adoptive grandparents: "They loved us to pieces. They treated us like we were one of them." (Powell, 1984, p. 67)

Appreciation of Adoption

"There was a trend toward appreciation of their adoptions by many of the participants in this sample. They perceived improvements in educational and economic attainment resulting from their adoptions . . . There was a sense of appreciation even when there appeared to be little closeness between adoptee and adoptive parents." One person interviewed offered the following observations: "I feel like that if I wasn't put through the adoptive home, that there's no telling where I'd be. I know I wouldn't have gone to college, and I probably wouldn't have finished high school. I'm just appreciative of what I do have." (Powell, 1984, p. 69)

Contact with Birth Family

"The data revealed that 16 out of the 17 participants have reunited with their birth families. However, the tendency seems to be that the participants contact, and are more actively involved with, biologic siblings than with birth parents . . . Of the 16 subjects who had reunited with their birth family, none seems to have a close, intimate relationship with their biologic parents as adults. Some of the comments related to this theme are as follows:

"In speaking about a birth father, one person had said to him, 'If God can forgive you, and I know you've had to live through hell all these years not knowing where all five kids were—I forgive you if God forgives you. And I don't hold any grudges against him whatsoever. But there is not a feeling of love whatsoever there. The feeling I have is pity.'

"After years of separation, one person recalled the reunion with his birth mother. 'She took me in her arms and she loved me and I think she still does today even though we don't associate quite that much.'" (Powell, 1984 p. 72)

Adult Life Satisfaction

These study subjects tended to respond to the question of life satisfaction in vocational terms. Life satisfaction was a specific item listed on the interviewer's guide. Here are some of the comments from these individuals:

Oh yes! . . . Yeah, if I can find a job. If I can feel more useful than this housewife business, then things will be better.

It could be better. When I get out of the Coast Guard, it will be better. Get married, get out, get me a job in the field of electronics which I have always been interested in and then it will be better.

We want to move out to the country so we can have things we want. Living in town, you can't have a dog or that type of thing.

I really love being married, I can tell you that . . . I really love sports and I've always wanted to coach.

I am very proud (of his life's accomplishments). Most people that had the life that I had would be on dope or out drinking all the time and wouldn't have any goals. And wouldn't even care about getting married. And if they did, it wouldn't last . . . I always wanted to have my own family. (Powell, 1984, pp. 75–77)

A Model of Older Adoption

A model of older adoptions was developed and tested through an examination of the key variables in the model. This model predicted that as more choice, more preparation, and more participation were given an adopted child there would be a greater tendency for closeness with the adoptive family. This in turn would lead to greater reconciliation with the past as manifested in less uneasiness and a greater sense of well-being (Powell, 1984, p. 91).

The hypothesized positive relationship between a positive adoption placement process (as evidenced by choice, preparation, and participation) and a sense of well-being was tested by classifying these study subjects into three categories for positive adoption placement process, and the number of statements of well-being were counted. Each person's interview was scrutinized for evidence for the extent of choice, preparation, and participation, and each person was placed into either the category of high, moderate, or low for this variable. The interviews were also examined for statements of well-being.

Choice, Preparation, and Participation. The definition of the terms that constitute the more positive placement process were given by Powell as follows:

More choice in adoption—To be consulted and given a sense of choice of their new family; less arbitrariness in selection process

More preparation in adoption—To be told in advance about adoptive plans; given an opportunity to visit and move in at adoptee's pace; having follow-up support from agency social workers after placement

More participation in adoption—To be respected and listened to; to be given an opportunity to discuss adoption with adoptive parents; to be allowed to visit appropriate birth family members; to be able to keep in contact with biologic siblings (Powell, 1984, p. 95)

A Sense of Well-Being.   Such words as love, feeling wanted, feeling comfortable, a sense of belonging, and so forth were subsumed under the general heading of "a sense of well-being". The number of such expressions ranged from a low of 2 for one subject to a high of 15 for the most positive study subject. As you can see from Table 9.1, the mean number of expressions of well-being for persons with high choice, preparation, and participation was 13.5 as compared to a mean of 8.0 for those in the moderate category, and a mean of 7.5 for those in the low category for choice, preparation, and participation.

A Sense of Uneasiness.   It was also hypothesized that there would be a relationship between the positive placement process (choice, preparation, and participation) and a sense of uneasiness. This hypothesized relationship, of course, was negative. In other words, it was expected that those with more choice, preparation, and participation would have a lower incidence of expressions of uneasiness as compared to their peers. Expressions that evidenced a loss of control, helplessness, a fear of the unknown, and anxiety about changing caretakers were subsumed under the heading of "a sense of uneasiness." This hypothesis was tested in a similar fashion to the former one. As you can see from Table 9.1, the mean number of expressions of uneasiness for those in the high category for choice, preparation, and participation was only 2.75 as compared to a mean of 13.0 for those in the moderate category, and a mean of 20.5 for those in the lowest category for choice, preparation, and participation.

TABLE 9.1   **Mean Expressions of Well-Being and Uneasiness by Category of Choice, Preparation, and Participation**

Level of Choice, Preparation, and Participation	Mean Number of Reports of Well-Being	Mean Number of Reports of Uneasiness
High	13.5	2.75
Moderate	8.0	13.0
Low	7.5	20.5

ASSIGNMENT 9–D

1. Indicate whether each of the following statements are TRUE or FALSE as revealed in the results of this study of older adoptions.

   T   F   **a.** These people were generally appreciative of having had the opportunity to be adopted.

   T   F   **b.** These individuals tended to be suffering from serious mental problems due to the trauma of adoption and the life they had experienced previously.

T   F   c. These individuals tended to have little interest in maintaining contact with their biological siblings.

T   F   d. These people tended to have positive feelings about the extended families of the adoptive parents. Even the subjects who had experienced rebellion and difficulty with the adoptive parents tended to have positive things to say about the extended family members.

T   F   e. These individuals tended to have very positive adult relationships with their biological parents and felt well bonded to them in spite of the fact that they had been adopted by someone else.

2. Given the experiences of these individuals adopted as older children, which of the following would you believe would be the *least* difficult for such people?

   a. Maintaining a sense of happiness as an adult

   b. Trusting people they do not know well

   c. Situations in which they have reason to feel powerless

   Explain:

   _____

   _____

   _____

3. What is one lesson you have learned from this study that you would put into practice as a social worker in adoptions of older children?

   _____

   _____

   _____

   _____

4. Did the data from this study convince you that older children should be given choice, preparation, and participation in the adoption experience? Explain.

   _____

   _____

   _____

   _____

5. Should researchers study this issue further? If so, how?

_____

_____

_____

_____

_____

Glossary

Analytic Induction. A method of qualitative inquiry that is designed to test, or refine, a hypothesis. The process begins with a tentative hypothesis and cases are studied in light of that hypothesis, with each case either confirming the hypothesis or suggesting a modification of it.

Deductive. A process of inquiry that begins with theory and moves to observation for the purpose of testing theory.

Ethnography. The study of cultures in their natural settings through qualitative research methods.

Grounded Theory. A qualitative research methodology that is designed to develop theory through a highly inductive, but systematic, process of discovery. A major focus is on the observation of similarities and differences in social behavior across social situations.

Inductive. A process of inquiry that begins with observations from which theory or generalizations are derived.

Participant Observer. A role in research in which an individual is both a participant in a social process and a researcher of that process.

Chapter 10

The Critical Review of Research Articles

In this chapter, you will examine how to analyze published research. You have developed the foundation for this task by your examination of research processes and concepts in relation to four major types of social work research. You have learned, for example, that research studies are founded on a knowledge base, and that you should not pursue research questions that are not supported by (or relevant to) the knowledge that you have assembled. You have learned better and worse ways to state the specific purpose of a research study in regard to the spirit of scientific inquiry. You have also been encouraged to exercise much caution in generalizing your study findings to a given population unless you selected your sample from that population on a random basis. And you have learned many, many more tips that you can employ in the analysis of published research.

The purpose of this chapter is to review some of these points and to provide a synopsis of the kinds of questions to pursue. These questions will be applied to a few published articles which you will look up in the library and review for yourself as you apply these questions.

Problem Formulation

The primary issue in the examination of the problem formulation phase of a research report is whether there is a logical connection between the problem statement and the study methodology. For example, a descriptive study should not be undertaken if the purpose of the research was evaluative. Researchers don't learn whether the objectives of an intervention were achieved if they simply count the number of clients who received the service or simply characterize them in terms of demographics.

The literature review provides the foundation upon which the methodology is constructed. It clearly identifies the study issue and the reasons that it should be further studied. It sets forth the definition of key terms around which variables will be defined and measured. Some of the specific questions to address in the examination of the problem formulation statements for a research report are provided below.

1. Was the problem or issue addressed by the study clearly identified and analyzed in the article?

   The problem or issue addressed by the study should be clear to the reader. Clarity on the problem (or issue or question) should be provided early in the article. Some of the most important things that are known and unknown from the existing literature should be revealed in the literature review. This information will provide a foundation upon which the purpose of the study rests.

2. Was the importance of the problem or issue clearly articulated?

   Social work research is not done for the purpose of satisfying idle curiosity. In view of the fact that social work is a profession rather than an academic discipline like sociology, it is important that social work research be relevant to concerns of the social work profession. Researchers might ask if a problem should be addressed in a new study because it is increasing in scope or because there are new developments that have not been researched or that previous research has left some important unanswered questions. The literature review should help the reader to distinguish between those issues related to the general study subject that are and are not going to be addressed in the study.

3. Did the literature review provide adequate guidance on how relevant concepts should be defined and measured?

   There are many ways that a given concept can be defined and measured. The task of doing so for a research study lies with the methodology section of the report. However, the existing literature on the study subject should provide guidance on this task. Readers normally should not quarrel with how the researcher chooses to define concepts in published research, but only with the clarity of the definitions. If terms are clearly defined, readers can better interpret the results of the study, whether or not they would have chosen to define these concepts in the same way. Guidance on how concepts should be measured is another necessary part of the literature review. On the completion of the literature review, the reader should have an idea as to whether the nature of what is known and unknown suggests a qualitative or a quantitative means of measurement.

When the reader has completed the literature review, he or she should be able to identify the following:

1. the research issue or problem
2. how key concepts are defined
3. some of the important things that are known and unknown about this topic
4. the general research question or task which emerges from the analysis

How well each of these tasks are completed in the research article can also be addressed by the reader. It is not unusual to find articles in which the author assumes that the reader knows the definition of key concepts and defines them the same way. While some concepts such as salary or gender do not require definition, because one can reasonably assume that others share a common definition of such terms, psychological constructs such as self-esteem and depression should be defined because researchers cannot assume shared definitions of complicated concepts such as these. While it is rather unusual, it is possible to find that the author of a research report has strayed into questionable territory in the specification of the study's purpose. Readers should be wary of such terms as "to demonstrate that" or "to challenge the idea that" when they review the stated purpose of the research study. Such statements suggest that the researcher's purpose was to prove a point rather than to discover the truth.

Study Methodology

The study methodology provides information on how a study was conducted. On completion of this section of the research article, readers should have some idea of how much confidence they can have in the study results, because all methodologies are not created equal. You will find that means of measuring variables can range on a continuum from weak to very strong. You will find that research designs vary on the extent to which they address some of the common threats to internal validity. And you can easily see that certain samples will provide a better means than others for generalizing the findings of a study.

The review of the study methodology will take different paths in the examination of qualitative and quantitative studies. In both cases, however, the reader should learn how the researcher went about the process of collecting information regarding the question or issue under study. In both cases, the reader should be able to identify the sample that was studied and how that sample was selected from a larger population of people that it should represent in some way.

Qualitative studies often have an exploratory purpose. This may entail the development of theory (or hypotheses) about the study subject. Sometimes qualitative studies have a descriptive purpose, such as the identification of the process whereby people become and/or continue to be homeless.

Some of the questions to pose in the examination of the research methodology section of the article are given below.

1. What are the general and specific purposes of the research study?

The reader should be able to identify the general purpose of a study as being either descriptive in nature or explanatory or evaluative or exploratory. The specific purpose should also be clear (e.g., to determine if gender explains salary when position level is taken into consideration). And this specific purpose should be stated in terms that are consistent with the spirit of scientific inquiry.

2. What is the research question (and study hypotheses, if applicable)?

For some articles, the research question may be clearly identified in the literature review section. This is fine. The important thing is that it is clearly articulated. Some types of studies will have a study hypothesis while others will not. Descriptive and exploratory studies typically do not have hypotheses to be tested while explanatory and evaluative studies do have such statements.

3. How are variables defined in abstract terms?

The definition of key terms will vary in their specificity and importance from one study to another. Some qualitative studies may have the purpose of determining how people define certain terms; thus, it would be inappropriate for the researcher to determine ahead of time just what these definitions should be.

In quantitative studies, the importance of abstract definitions will vary with the type of concepts being examined. Such concepts as "gender" and "age" require no abstract definition. Such terms as "self-esteem" or "job satisfaction" should be defined in the research report, even though it will not be unusual to find articles which do not go to the trouble to do so.

4. How are variables measured?

Qualitative studies may not have specific variables identified in the methodology section of the report. But there will be a description of how observations were made. Perhaps the question "What are the means by which observations were made?" would be more appropriate for such studies.

For the quantitative study, there should be a clear identification of how variables were measured. Researchers refer to this as the operational definition *of study variables (as distinct from the abstract definition of them). The operational definition of each variable should be consistent with its abstract definition. The identification of the measurement devices should be adequately clear that the reader can identify the level of measurement of each variable. Information should also be given on the extent to which the instruments have been found to be reliable and valid.*

5. What is the study design (in the case of evaluative studies)?

If the concept "study design" is understood broadly, it would be necessary to consider a broad array of ways to classify research. To keep this issue simple, you will only deal with research designs for evaluative research studies. The research design will help you to determine the extent to which you can attribute the results to the influence of the intervention rather than something else. If a group of clients gained significantly in their functioning during the treatment period, can you be confident that it was because of the treatment rather than because of their own normal patterns of growth over time, or because of some change in their environment? The one-group pretest–posttest design does not address maturation as a threat to internal validity (i.e., alternative explanations for the results) whereas the AB single-subject design does (as do several other designs). If you know that the one-group pretest–posttest design was employed, you know that, among other things, the issue of maturation was not addressed.

5. What is the study sample and population?

The study sample is the group of subjects from whom data were collected. The study population is the larger group from which study subjects were selected. The method used to select the sample should be identified so that the reader can understand whether study results can be safely generalized to the population.

Results

The presentation of results will vary with the type of research undertaken. Explanatory and evaluative studies will have hypotheses to be tested and will typically employ statistical tests. Descriptive studies will present frequencies, means, and other descriptive data. Exploratory studies will present general themes and processes identified and may present hypotheses that were suggested by the study experience.

The study results section of quantitative research articles will provide information on the data that were collected. Descriptive data should be presented in a format that is easy to understand. Bar charts and graphs are often useful for this purpose. One type of descriptive information that should always be presented is the description of the sample. The reader should learn things such as the proportion of subjects who were male and female, the mean age, the racial composition, and so forth.

Descriptive results of study variables should also be presented in addition to the analysis which tests the research questions or hypotheses. Descriptive information will assist in the interpretation of the results. For example, suppose that you gave a tool to social workers to measure their level of social support and found that the vast majority of them had either high or very high support and that practically no one had low levels of support. Then you compute a correlation between support and stress and find that there is not a significant correlation between them. Does this mean that support should no longer be viewed as something that can alleviate stress? Perhaps a better interpretation would be that people with very high support are not likely to experience less stress than persons with high support. In other words, the jump between high and very high support does not seem to make any difference in the level of stress. But the question of whether people with high support have less stress than those with low support remains to be examined by other studies which have a better range of scores for social support.

For explanatory and evaluative studies, data will be presented on the study questions or hypotheses that were developed. There should be adequate information presented to guide the reader in the determination of both practical significance and statistical significance. For statistical significance, you should turn your attention to the p value that is reported. Guidance for practical significance can be found in the magnitude of the relationships discovered. For information on this topic, you should examine such things as the size of the correlation between the dependent and independent variables or the difference in mean scores between the study groups. More will be said about practical significance in the next section.

In short, the results section of a quantitative study should provide the following information:

1. The nature of the study sample employed (gender, age, etc.)
2. The distribution of responses on the key study variables. This would include such things as the pretest and posttest scores of clients and the means or frequencies for key study variables.
3. The results of the testing of the study hypotheses (if appropriate). This could include the value of the correlation between study variables, the mean pretest and posttest scores of clients, etc.
4. The statistical significance of data which tests study hypotheses, if appropriate

Conclusions

A good research report will include a conclusion or discussion section which summarizes the findings and places these findings into perspective. Such a report will summarize the nature of the study and the study questions and will summarize the key findings. The *key findings* should be emphasized in this section of the research report. The author should not repeat all the findings which have just been presented. Such would be redundant. But the reader should be informed of the author's opinion of the key findings.

The issue of *practical significance* is a critical component of this section of the report. Practical significance refers to the extent to which the findings are noteworthy and useful. For an evaluative study, the question is whether the clients' gain in functioning is enough gain to justify the resources expended to achieve it. For an explanatory study, the question might be whether the differences between study groups were big enough to be noteworthy or whether the magnitude of the correlations were such as to suggest that the study makes a notable contribution to understanding the relationships among the variables.

A correlation of 0.23 is rather low, while correlations higher than 0.50 are normally considered to be quite noteworthy. However, the nature of the study will determine just what kind of correlation is to be considered noteworthy. Whether the primary concern is the dependent variable or the independent variable can assist with this determination. If researchers wish to do a good job of explaining the dependent variable, they will have a higher expectation for the size of the correlation. For example, if they want to explain salaries for social workers, they would be seeking variables that were highly correlated with how much money those people earn. When the square of the correlation is computed, the result is a figure that indicates the amount of the variance in the dependent variable that is explained by the independent variable. A correlation of 0.50 means that 25 percent of the variance in the dependent variable is explained. This means that 75 percent of the variance in the dependent variable is left unexplained. Thus, a researcher may not have reason to jump for joy on the discovery of such a correlation. But what if the focus was on the independent variable rather than the dependent variable? In other words, suppose that the purpose was not to explain salary fully but to find out whether gender was a significant predictor of salary. In this case, any size correlation that is statistically significant may be considered to be noteworthy. The higher the correlation, the more noteworthy the finding.

Perhaps inherent in the examination of practical significance is the question of the utility of the findings. How can these results be put to use in the design of social work interventions or in the development of social policy or social action? Often the reader will need assistance in seeing this practical utility.

The *limitations* of the study should be identified in the conclusions (or discussion) section of the research article. The research methodology provides a good deal of information on the limitations of the study results. Two key places to look for these limitations are the research design (especially for evaluative studies) and the nature of the sample. For the evaluative study, the research design will provide information on how well the study addressed threats to internal validity. This helps readers to identify potential alternative explanations for the findings (other than the intervention). The sampling method employed will provide information on the extent to which the results can be generalized to people not included in the present study.

The direction for *further research* is another topic that is addressed in the good research report. The study should be based upon insufficiently answered questions in the existing literature. When the study is complete, there will be other questions that are not well answered. Perhaps the present study will only have addressed a portion of the key research question, suggesting that it is left to others to examine other aspects of it.

ASSIGNMENT 10–A

The questions in this exercise are based on the following article:

> Thompson, M. S., & Peebles–Wilkins, W. (1992). The impact of formal, informal, and societal support networks on the psychological well-being of black adolescent mothers. *Social Work*, 37 (4), 322–327.

You must read this article in order to answer the questions in this exercise.

1. Identify which of the following is the research question (RQ) and which is the statement of the purpose of this study (P).

   _____ **a.** To demonstrate that social support is related to the psychological well-being of black adolescent mothers.

   _____ **b.** Is social support related to general distress, depression, and self-esteem among black adolescent mothers?

   _____ **c.** To broaden our understanding of the relative importance of different support systems on the general distress, depression, and self-esteem of black adolescent mothers.

   _____ **d.** Is general distress, depression, and self-esteem a predictor of social support among black adolescent mothers?

   _____ **e.** To encourage generalist social work practice to recognize the linkage of informal, formal, and societal resource systems as a means of meeting human needs.

   _____ **f.** Is psychological well-being influenced by support, gender, and race?

2. Which is the best way to characterize the rationale for conducting this study?

   a. The importance of the male partner to adolescent mothers has not been sufficiently addressed in previous research

   b. The importance of caseworker support has not been sufficiently addressed in previous research on adolescent parenting

   c. Both (a) and (b) above

   d. Little attention has been previously given to the theoretical and empirical aspects of the impact of collective helping efforts on the psychological health of black adolescent mothers.

3. Why did these researchers select *adolescent* mothers for a study of psychological well-being rather than older mothers?

   _____

   _____

   _____

   _____

4. Why did these researchers decide to study support as a potential influence on psychological well-being among black adolescent mothers?

   _____

   _____

_____

_____

5. Examine the literature review and indicate whether it suggests that the following statement is true or false and explain your answer.

> *The psychological risks of teenage childbearing diminish as mothers become more experienced in their role.*

The above statement is _____ true _____ false. Explain.

_____

_____

_____

6. Do the authors provide an abstract definition of the concept of support? If so, what is it? If not, how do they seem to be defining it?

_____

_____

_____

_____

7. Has the previous research on social support shown that support is always helpful? Explain.

_____

_____

_____

_____

8. What does the above suggest in the way that the concept of support should be defined? What does it mean to you? How do the authors seem to be defining it in abstract terms?

_____

_____

_____

_____

9. How is this study best classified with reference to its purpose?

a. descriptive   **b.** exploratory   **c.** explanatory   **d.** evaluative

Why?

_____

_____

_____

_____

10. With reference to the way that variables were measured, how should this study be classified?

a. quantitative   **b.** qualitative

Why?

_____

_____

_____

_____

11. No hypotheses were officially stated in this study but there are several hypotheses that could have been stated. Construct one such hypothesis.

_____

_____

_____

_____

12. In this study, identify the abstract definitions (AD) of key variables and the operational definitions (OD) of these variables by reference to the statements below:

_____   **a.** General psychological distress is nonspecific psychological distress in life functioning that produces problems of daily living that are not linked to any particular psychiatric disorder.

_____   **b.** Psychological well-being is defined as one's state of general distress, depression, and self-esteem.

_____ c. General psychological distress was measured by Langner's 22-item Symptom Index.

_____ d. Depression was measured by the Wakefield Self-Assessment Depression Scale.

_____ e. Self-esteem refers to a positive attitude about oneself with particular reference to self-acceptance.

13. Provide an operational definition of self-esteem as employed in this study.

_____

_____

_____

_____

14. What method was used to collect data in this study?

a. Interview   **b.** Survey   **c.** Direct observation

_____

_____

_____

_____

15. What evidence was presented of either the reliability or validity of the means employed in this study to measure the concept of self-esteem?

_____

_____

_____

_____

What about depression?

_____

_____

_____

_____

16. The research design employed in this study was:

   a. The AB single-subject design

   b. The one-group pretest–posttest design

   c. The experimental design

   d. None of the above

17. What is/are the dependent variable(s) in this study?

_____

_____

_____

_____

18. Select one of these dependent variables and provide the following information:

   a. The name of the variable

_____

_____

_____

   b. The abstract definition of the variable

_____

_____

_____

   c. The operational definition of it

_____

_____

_____

19. What is/are the independent variable(s) in this study?

_____

_____

_____

_____

20. What constitutes the study sample for this study? How was the study sample selected?

    a. 407 mothers who delivered their first child in a large urban hospital during the twelve-month period between September 1978 and August 1979 and were under age 21.

    b. The 296 persons from the above group who signed the consent form agreeing to participate in the study

    c. Both of the above

    d. Other

Specify:

_____

_____

_____

21. Which one of the following would be classified as an *improper* definition of the population for this study?

    a. Black adolescent mothers

    b. Black adolescent mothers who have male partners

    c. All black women who delivered their first child during a twelve-month period between September 1978 and August 1979 from a certain large urban hospital who were under the age of 21 at the time of the birth

22. To whom could the results of this study be generalized safely?

_____

_____

_____

_____

23. Which variables were found to be negatively related to distress?

_____

_____

_____

_____

What does a negative relationship between these variables mean?

_____

_____

_____

Were there any variables that had a positive relationship with distress?

_____

_____

_____

What does a positive relationship between these variables mean?

_____

_____

_____

24. Which variables were found to be negatively related to depression?

_____

_____

_____

_____

Were there any variables that had a positive relationship to depression?

_____

_____

_____

_____

25. Which variables were found to have a positive relationship with self-esteem?

_____

_____

_____

_____

Were there any variables that had a negative relationship with self-esteem?

_____

_____

_____

_____

26. Examine the following quotes from the article. One is questionable, given the results of this study. Which one is it?

    a. "support from a male partner has beneficial effects on psychological well-being."

    b. "A supportive relationship with a caseworker reduced symptoms of both general psychological distress and depression."

    c. "Informal assistance from friends or peers tended to increase distress among this group of adolescent mothers."

    d. "A professional service plan that effectively incorporates maternal grandmothers, male partners, and self-help groups in a complementary manner appears to offer the best possibilities for reducing or alleviating the distress of black teenage mothers."

ASSIGNMENT 10–B

This exercise is based on the following article:

Edleson, J. L., & Syers, M. (1991). The effects of group treatment for men who batter: An 18-month follow-up study. *Research on Social Work Practice,* 1 (3), 227–243.

You must read this article before you can answer these questions.

1. The social problem addressed by the intervention in this study is:

   a. The absence of follow-up studies

   b. Wife/mate abuse

   c. The educational and self-help models

2. Was the cause of the social problem addressed by this study's intervention adequately discussed in this article? Explain.

   _____

   _____

   _____

   _____

3. What is the objective of treatment in this study?

   _____

   _____

4. Describe the sample and the population(s) from which the sample was drawn by thinking of several concentric circles with the sample in the middle circle (labeled S) and various definitions of the population being placed in varying distances from the sample. The first definition of the population should be labeled P1 and should be that aggregate of people from which the sample was immediately drawn. Then label the next larger group from which the P1 group was drawn as P2, and so forth.

5. The *content* of an intervention refers to the model of treatment or the subjects of training. Describe the content of the intervention for this study.

_____

_____

_____

_____

6. The *structure* of an intervention refers to the form that treatment takes, such as a therapeutic interview, a group session, classroom instruction, behavior modeling, residential care, and so forth. It also refers to the amount of such treatment, such as once a week for one hour each session for a total of six weeks. From this description, one should be able to calculate the total hours or days of treatment given as a part of the intervention plan. These hours may vary from client to client, in which case one would be expected to describe the typical amount of service given and/or the range of time from the most intensive to the least intensive treatment plan.

Describe the structure of the service evaluated in this study.

_____

_____

_____

_____

7. There should be a *rationale* for a particular intervention for a particular social problem. The question is: Why would one expect for a given intervention to solve a given problem? If, for example, the investigators believe that drug abuse is caused by ignorance of the consequences of drug abuse, they would logically provide training on the consequences of drug abuse for people with this type of problem. If they believe that rapists lack empathy for women, they would conceptualize a treatment strategy for convicted rapists aimed at the promotion of empathy for women.

Did this article do an adequate job of providing a rationale that justified the interventions employed? Explain.

_____

_____

_____

_____

_____

_____

8. What research design was employed in this evaluation?

   a. The one-group pretest–posttest design in which a group of clients is measured on the dependent variable before treatment and again after treatment to determine if the average gain was significant.

   b. The alternative treatment design in which different treatments are compared to one another on their relative effectiveness.

   c. The comparison group design in which a treated group is compared to a nontreated group to see if the treated group achieved a greater gain in functioning on the dependent variable.

   d. The single-subject design in which a single subject is measured on the dependent variable during a baseline period and this trend in functioning is projected into the future and the treatment recordings of functioning are compared to this trend to see if the client fared better under treatment than would have been predicted by the baseline trend.

   e. The experimental design in which people are assigned to a treated group and a control group on a random basis and the gain in functioning of the two groups is compared after the treatment period to see if the treated (experimental) group achieved a greater gain.

9. Does this design address the issue of maturation as a threat to internal validity?

   _____

   _____

   _____

   _____

10. What data about the general characteristics of these men stood out as most noteworthy to you?

   _____

   _____

   _____

   _____

11. Identify whether each of the following is an example of a dependent variable (D) or an independent variable (I).

_____   Terroristic threats of violence (threw or smashed objects, physically harmed pets, etc.)

_____   The self-help model versus the educational model versus the combined model

_____   12 sessions of treatment versus 32 sessions of treatment

_____   Threats of violence (screamed or insulted partner, restricted physical movement, etc.)

_____   Physical violence (hit, burned, or shoved partner, physically forced partner to have sex, etc.)

12. Were the operational definitions of the dependent variables at the 18-month period clearly given? Explain.

_____

_____

_____

_____

13. Examine the data in the five tables and determine whether each of the following statements is true or false. Explain your response.

T   F   **a.** The 12 sessions of treatment appear to be just as effective as the 32 sessions of treatment in the prevention of further acts of violence.

T   F   **b.** The self-help model was clearly superior to the educational model and the combined model in the prevention of further acts of violence.

T   F   **c.** Those men who had received prior mental health treatment were found to be less likely than others to have been violent during the follow-up period.

T   F   **d.** Those men who had been involved with the courts prior to treatment were found to be less likely than others to have been violent during the follow-up period.

T   F   **e.** The 32-session intensity of treatment was found to be superior to the 12-session intensity of treatment in the reduction of terroristic threats.

T   F   **f.** There was no difference in the effectiveness of the three treatment models in the reduction of nonthreatening violence.

T   F   **g.** Approximately two-thirds or more of the men in this study were found to be physically nonviolent during the follow-up period.

14. Reflect on the concepts of practical significance and statistical significance, especially with regard to the question of whether a study can have one without the other and examine the following quote from this article:

> *The rates of men reported nonviolent in the self-help groups are substantially higher than either what was reported for men in the other two groups or what we found for completers of this program at 6 months posttreatment. One explanation of this result may be that the effect of self-help groups requires a longer time period to take hold. Although this may be true, the same trend does not appear in the data concerning terroristic threats. Men completing the education and combined groups were reported to be considerably less threatening during this and the prior follow-up than were those completing the self-help program.*

Do you find anything problematic about this statement? Explain.

_____

_____

_____

_____

ASSIGNMENT 10–C

This assignment is based upon the following article:

Gutierrez, L., GlenMaye, L., and DeLois, D. (1995). The organizational context of empowerment practice: Implications for social work administration. *Social Work*, 40 (2), 249–258.

You must read this article in order to answer the following questions.

1. How would you characterize the purpose of the study reported in this article?

_____

_____

_____

_____

2. How is the concept of empowerment defined in this article?

_____

_____

_____

_____

3. Is this definition of empowerment clear to you? If so, can you illustrate it? If not, can you improve upon it?

_____

_____

_____

_____

4. Let's suppose that you were attempting to observe empowerment in practice by sitting in on a series of interactions between social workers and the persons they serve. Let's suppose that someone has developed a tool for aiding your observations and classifying the extent to which a given social worker engaged in empowerment practice. The social worker is given a number of pairs of words to contrast empowerment practice from non-empowerment practice. The following are these paris of concepts. For each of these pairs of concepts, select the one that better illustrates empowerment practice. In other words, select the one that, if more emphasized in practice than the other, would represent an empowerment approach to practice. Explain your responses.

Concepts   *Comments*

Pair 1
(a) strengths
(b) problems

Pair 2
(a) treatment
(b) education

Pair 3
(a) diagnosis
(b) self-awareness

Pair 4
(a) self determination
(b) agency objectives

5. Why is the study of empowerment practice important?

_____

_____

_____

_____

6. What is/are the key research question(s) in this study?

_____

_____

_____

_____

7. Does this study employ a qualitative or quantitative method of measurement?

_____

_____

_____

_____

8. Explain the rationale for the above choice.

_____

_____

_____

_____

9. Can you think of a research question regarding empowerment practice that would be better suited to the other type of measurement (i.e., the type that was not selected for this study)?

_____

_____

_____

_____

10. Which research design was employed in this study?

    a. The one-group pretest-posttest design.

    b. The pretest-posttest control group design.

    c. The AB single-subject design.

    d. None of the above.

11. How would you describe the study sample?

    _____

    _____

    _____

    _____

12. How would you describe the study population?

    _____

    _____

    _____

    _____

13. The method used to select a study sample has major implications for the extent to which a study's findings can be generalized to persons (agencies, communities, etc.) that were not included in the present study. Would you say that a study that was attempting to identify barriers to empowerment practice would be more or less in need of attention to the generalization of study results than a study that was attempting to determine if emphasis upon empowerment was positively associated with client satisfaction? Explain.

    _____

    _____

    _____

    _____

14. What are the implications of your above answer for the issue of generalization of study results for the present study?

_____

_____

_____

_____

15. Would you say that the research methods employed in this study were more characteristic of the structured interview format, or the semi-structured interview format, or the unstructured interview format?

_____

_____

_____

_____

16. Were there any procedures that addressed the concepts of reliability and validity in research measurement in this study? If so, describe them. If not, describe how this could have been done.

_____

_____

_____

_____

17. Based upon the findings of this study, which of the following statements are true and which are false?

   T   F   **a.** Most study participants indicated that the empowerment approach was less time-consuming than using traditional approaches.

   T   F   **b.** The empowerment approach often conflicts with the priorities of funding agencies which typically are more interested in concrete client outcomes than empowerment.

T   F   **c.** Having an administrator who is an advocate for consumers and staff was viewed as a critical support for maintaining an atmosphere of empowerment.

T   F   **d.** When agencies emphasize empowerment for social workers, this has the effect of encouraging the empowerment of clients by social workers.

T   F   **e.** Social workers who emphasize empowerment usually have to struggle with letting go of emphasis upon the achievement of tangible client outcomes.

18. What are two study results that you found most important? Explain.

_____

_____

_____

_____

19. How would you summarize this study?

_____

_____

_____

_____

Level *III*

════════════════════════════

Conducting Social Work Research

Chapter 11
Conducting Research That Illustrates the Nature of Science:
Is the Theory of Numerology Valid?

In this final section of the book, you will experience research through a study of the theory of numerology. This is designed as your first experience as a researcher. The topic, knowledge base, and methodology have been selected for you, but you will critically examine these tasks before you complete the research process by collecting and analyzing original data, and drawing conclusions accordingly.

Developing skill as an independent researcher will await your next course in social work research. However, you will find that the three appendices will serve you in this endeavor. The first deals with the development of a literature review, the second, with the use of standardized instruments for measuring study variables, and the third, with the preparation of the research hypothesis.

Conducting Research That Illustrates the Nature of Science:
Is the Theory of Numerology Valid?

In this chapter, you will undertake a test of the theory of numerology. Numerology is a theory that attempts to describe people's personalities or natural tendencies. You will engage in a test of this theory along with your classmates by responding to an instrument in which you will rank order a number of statements according to how much you believe they describe you. You will then examine the personality profile that is supposed to describe your essence according to numerology. You will combine your results with those of your classmates in order to determine if the theory had a significant tendency to be congruent with the self-perceptions of class members.

A supplementary exercise will follow in which all class members will examine the reliability of their self-perceptions that were used as a test of the theory. Then, you will return to the study and reexamine your data in light of the new information on the reliability of your self-perceptions.

At the completion of this experience, you will have gained a greater appreciation of the spirit of scientific inquiry and you should be more inclined to approach theories about life with scientific skepticism. In addition, you should be better prepared to assist in the design of a research study and the analysis of data from it.

A Special Note to You as a Study Participant Regarding Research Ethics

In this chapter, you are being asked to engage in the research process as both participant and researcher. When you become researchers, you must address the issue of ethics in scientific inquiry. For example, the researcher should avoid posing a harm to the study subjects or violating their rights to privacy and voluntary participation. The Code of Ethics of the National Association of Social Workers spells out six basic guiding principles:

1. The social worker engaged in research should consider carefully its possible consequences for human beings.
2. The social worker engaged in research should ascertain that the consent of participants in the research is voluntary and informed, without any implied deprivation or penalty for refusal to participate, and with due regard for participants' privacy and dignity.
3. The social worker engaged in research should protect participants from unwarranted physical or mental discomfort, distress, harm, danger, or deprivation.
4. The social worker who engages in the evaluation of services or cases should discuss them only for professional purposes and only with persons directly and professionally concerned with them.
5. Information obtained about participants in research should be treated as confidential.
6. The social worker should take credit only for work actually done in connection with scholarly and research endeavors and credit contributions made by others. (National Association of Social Workers. (1980). *Code of ethics.* Silver Spring, MD.)

The first issue is harm. Harm can come to research subjects who are placed under hypnosis or are given a shocking situation to confront where they could be harmed psychologically, such as being told the building is on fire so that panic behavior can be observed, or being told their spouse has just died so that grief reactions could be examined. Of course, being exposed to experimental drugs would fall into this category. In the present study, no such elements exist. The designer of the study included in this chapter has no reason to believe that any harm will come to participants. In fact, this exercise in research has been conducted by the author many times without any incidents of harm in any way.

Confidentiality of responses is another consideration. People who are called on to answer research questions are normally informed that their responses will be treated confidentially, meaning that their identities will not be revealed in the report that emanates from the research. It is even better if their responses can be anonymous, because privacy is assured in this way and research subjects do not have to worry about whether confidentiality will be violated. In this study, your identity will not be displayed on your responses; thus, your responses will be anonymous.

Another issue is voluntary participation. It is important that each study subject's participation be voluntary. In the present study, your participation is voluntary. If you wish not to participate in this study, you can simply refrain from giving your information when the time comes.

An issue that is not a part of this discussion of ethics is that information be collected in a way that minimizes the potential that one's biases will determine responses to the instrument, or that subjects will respond according to the conventions of social desirability (i.e., giving responses believed to be socially desirable rather than the way one really feels or thinks). To deal with this issue, you are instructed to respond to the questions on the instruments that follow strictly according to the instructions given and in the sequence given. In other words, you should not read ahead. *To do so will violate the research methodology and will render your responses invalid for use in this research study.* Your next step is to respond to the instruments on the following two pages. You should do this as the next step. You should not continue beyond the next page until you have completed that part of the study.

EXHIBIT 11.1 Choosing Your Self-Description

Directions: Examine the list of ten descriptions given below and rank order them from 1 to 10 by assigning a rank of 1 to the statement that is most like you, a rank of 2 to the next best description of you, a rank of 3 to the next, and so on until you have assigned a rank to each of the ten statements, with the rank of 10 being given to the statement that is the least like you. Be sure to respond to each statement. (Note: There is no statement numbered 10.)

_____ 1. Wants to lead and direct. Prefers to work alone or to be the boss. Is proud of abilities and desires praise. Wants to create and originate. Is not very emotional. Is capable of great accomplishment, a loyal friend. May be boastful, critical, impatient.

_____ 2. Wants and needs love, companionship. Prefers to work with or for others. Wants harmony and peace. Wants ease and comfort (not necessarily wealth and luxury). Is kind and thoughtful. Attracts friends. Is sensitive and emotional. Falls in love easily. Devoted, easygoing.

_____ 3. Wants to give out joy and happiness. Wants popularity and friends. Wants beauty. Never mopes over mistakes—tries again. Artistic, expressive, entertaining, playful. Doesn't worry or get depressed. Wants to scatter love, energies, talents.

_____ 4. Wants respectability and solidity. Wants to be a rock of dependability. A great disciplinarian. Loves home and family. Is not fond of innovation. Loves order and regularity. Is thorough and methodical. Needs and wants love, but often repels it.

_____ 5. Wants personal freedom in every direction. Wants change, variety, and constant new opportunity. Wide open to life's experiences. Loves pleasure, travel, strange and new people. Injects new life into all that s/he touches. Will not be hampered by convention. Is progressive, intellectual, emotional, spiritual.

(Continued)

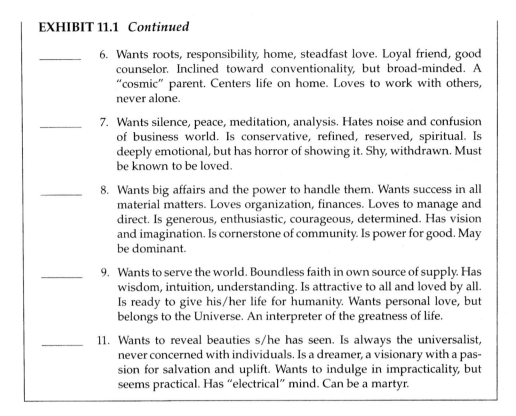

EXHIBIT 11.1 *Continued*

_____ 6. Wants roots, responsibility, home, steadfast love. Loyal friend, good counselor. Inclined toward conventionality, but broad-minded. A "cosmic" parent. Centers life on home. Loves to work with others, never alone.

_____ 7. Wants silence, peace, meditation, analysis. Hates noise and confusion of business world. Is conservative, refined, reserved, spiritual. Is deeply emotional, but has horror of showing it. Shy, withdrawn. Must be known to be loved.

_____ 8. Wants big affairs and the power to handle them. Wants success in all material matters. Loves organization, finances. Loves to manage and direct. Is generous, enthusiastic, courageous, determined. Has vision and imagination. Is cornerstone of community. Is power for good. May be dominant.

_____ 9. Wants to serve the world. Boundless faith in own source of supply. Has wisdom, intuition, understanding. Is attractive to all and loved by all. Is ready to give his/her life for humanity. Wants personal love, but belongs to the Universe. An interpreter of the greatness of life.

_____ 11. Wants to reveal beauties s/he has seen. Is always the universalist, never concerned with individuals. Is a dreamer, a visionary with a passion for salvation and uplift. Wants to indulge in impracticality, but seems practical. Has "electrical" mind. Can be a martyr.

Review of a Few Basic Principles of Scientific Research

In the first chapter of this text, you were introduced to several basic principles which guide the scientific research process. These principles will be restated here in brief terms. One of these principles was stated as **Social research is a process of discovery rather than justification.** You engage in research in order to find out the truth rather than to support a given position about reality that has been derived beforehand. In other words, good research is objective and relatively free of human bias. Another statement in regard to these basic principles was **Don't reinvent the wheel.** You should focus your attention on matters for which new knowledge is needed. If a topic has been thoroughly researched, you should focus your attention on topics for which your efforts can make a contribution to the advancement of knowledge. In the first chapter, you were told about the results of numerous studies about the effect of the full moon on human behavior. The results were very consistent—there was no difference in behavior during the full moon than at other times. Why do additional research on this issue, unless, of course, you can develop a rather new approach to this topic.

The third principle, **Don't put the cart before the horse,** suggests that the research process is systematic and flows naturally in a given order. That process will be reviewed in the next section of this chapter. A fourth principle was stated as **Two heads are better than one.** In scientific research, researchers do not assume that the truth is easy to find. They realize that they have limited ability to observe social phenomena directly. Instead, they develop representations of those phenomena. For example, does anyone know for sure what happiness is? How do people know that someone is happy? You could ask them, but they may answer incorrectly because their definition of happiness may differ from yours. Thus, researchers tend to develop means of measurement of variables in a chosen topic that are tested by comparing one means of observation with another. If two people develop instruments to measure depression, you would expect to find a positive correlation of the scores of a set of people on both instruments. For example, if John is higher on depression than Bill on one instrument, he should also be higher than Bill on the other instrument. If not, then one or both of these instruments is a weak means of measuring the phenomenon known as depression. They cannot both be measuring it well if their scores do not correlate because this result would tell us that these two instruments are not measuring the same thing. Another means of testing a means of measurement is to ask more than one person to observe the same thing and examine whether there is congruence between the two observers. If not, the researcher cannot have confidence in the observations of either person. One of them may be exactly correct, but which one? If they are not consistent in their observations, there is potentially something wrong with the chosen means of measurement. If they are consistent, the investigator can have more confidence in the chosen measurement device.

Another of these basic principles was presented as follows: **Some things happen just by chance.** Suppose that you arrive at the airport to find that the flight has been canceled. You realize that this is the second flight that you have had canceled by this same airline in the last three years and that you have only scheduled four flights with this particular airline during this period of time. You suddenly say that you will never voluntarily schedule a flight on this airline again because they are always canceling their flights. What is wrong with this thinking pattern? Perhaps this airline has a good record of takeoffs but you have just been very unlucky. You might have the foresight to ask others you know about their experiences with this airline. Now, you would have a larger sample for your analysis. If their experiences have been similar to your own, you can be more confident in your conclusion. An even better approach would be to check the public records about the rate of flight cancellations for each airline in your area and compare this airline to others. Now you have a very large sample of data for your analysis.

A final principle was stated as: **When you wear the research hat, you must be very cautious in your conclusions.** There are any number of ways to measure the phenomena that researchers seek to better understand. There are many different samples of people that could serve as study subjects. Either of these two facts can render your own findings of limited utility in the search for the ultimate truth. Each study contributes to your understanding as you move closer and closer to what you are confident is the reality that you seek to find. But one study's results can be rather different from another study's results. These differences provoke scientific analysis which leads to better studies and better understanding of research topics.

The Research Process

The research process begins with a problem or a topic about which you wish to know more. The theory of numerology attempts to identify the essence of people's personalities, but is not based upon the principles of scientific inquiry. Yet, many people believe in this theory. In fact, it is not uncommon to see full-page ads in newspaper magazines offering to provide people with their own personality profile based on this theory.

The question which emerged for me was whether this theory would stand up to a test undertaken according to the principles of scientific inquiry. These principles are designed to reduce human error in observation. It is believed that inquiry which reduces human error is more likely to approximate the truth, even though no one can ever be sure that they have found ultimate truth, given the complex nature of human reality and people's limitations in its observation.

The first major phase in the process of research is *problem formulation.* In this phase, researchers identify and analyze the nature of a problem. This analysis provides them with the ability to focus their research questions and define their critical concepts. This is the phase of research in which they normally undertake a literature review.

In this study, you will examine a brief literature review about the theory of numerology. This will provide a conceptual framework for the study. You can examine for yourself whether this theory makes sense. But whether it does or does not make sense, you are obligated, by the principles of the scientific method, to give this theory a fair test. Consequently, structures will be used which will reduce the opportunity for your biases to influence the outcome of the study.

The second major phase of research is the development of a *research methodology.* In this phase, researchers articulate the research question, develop means of measuring the variables, select a study sample, develop a research hypothesis (if appropriate), and determine how data will be collected.

In this study, the research question is whether numerology is a valid theory. You will pursue an answer to this question by comparing the self-perceptions of a sample of social work students with the personality profiles given by a formula developed by the theory. The procedures call for the study subjects to determine their personality profiles before they learn about the theory and learn what their personality profiles are supposed to be. These procedures call for a group of study subjects to pool their results in order to test the research question. And these results will be subjected to statistical analysis in order to determine the likelihood that the results could occur by chance.

The *analysis of the data* is the third major phase in the research process. In this phase, you organize your data in accordance with your research question (or hypothesis) and subject it to statistical analysis when appropriate.

As a study subject, you were given ten statements of personality (or "soul urge" in the terminology of the theory) and you were asked to rank-order these statements from 1 to 10 according to how well they described you. The theory of numerology has a means of determining exactly what your personality is supposed to be like. You will get a number from 1 to 10 from that procedure and this will be what the theory says you are like. Ideally, the theory of numerology would be able to select your first choice of a personality profile. If you ranked statement (3) as the one most like you, this should be the one selected by the method employed by the theory to find the essence of your personality. But you might think this procedure was too severe a test of the theory because you might have struggled between statement (3) and statement (5) in determining which one was most like you. Perhaps on a different day, you would have selected (5) instead of (3). A less severe test would be to consider the theory to be congruent with your self-perception if it selects either of your first two choices. This would be doing rather well in view of the fact that there were ten statements from which to choose. This would seem better than just flipping a coin or rolling a pair of dice, activities that would represent chance. The theory must do better than chance if it is to be supported by your results.

To simplify the analysis, all study subjects will be asked to divide these ten statements into two categories—those that were ranked from 1 to 5 by the study subject and those that were ranked from 6 to 10. In this way, each of the ten statements will be in one of two categories: (1) high ranking from the study subject (rank of 1–5), or (2) low ranking from the study subject (rank of 6–10). Because you have placed these ten statements into two categories (high and low), a match between the choice given by the theory and your high category (ranks of 1–5) could occur by chance 50 percent of the time. If there were twenty students in class, ten would have a match with the theory just by chance. Thus, the theory must do better than this. How much better? This is a question for statistical analysis. You will use a statistical test known as the binomial test to help with this question.

The final phase of research deals with *conclusions.* What does the data suggest in regard to the research question? What are some of the limitations of the study in regard to the testing of the research question or hypothesis? What are the implications of the results for practice? What is the next step in further research on this topic? These are among the questions to be addressed in the conclusions phase of the research process.

Problem Formulation

In the problem formulation phase of research, researchers seek a conceptual understanding of the topic of their study and develop a research question from this endeavor. In this case, the development of a research question has been undertaken by me. This question emerged from a desire to subject theories with nonscientific origins to scientific analysis. Perhaps there is wisdom in these theories even though there is, as yet, no scientific basis for them. If they stand the test of scientific inquiry, they should be taken more seriously. If they do not, this information should be known for those who care about the scientific method as a basis for understanding.

You have previously studied theory and observation as the building blocks of scientific research. A theory is an attempt to explain something. The theory of numerology does nothing less than attempt to explain people's basic personalities. It suggests that the essence of personality derives from the vibrations from the vowel sounds of birth names.

When you examine theory, you should subject it to some form of logical analysis. For example, let's examine the question "Does the full moon make people act strange?" You might have heard the opinion offered by people working in mental hospitals or crisis hotlines that there is a different kind of activity that takes place during the full moon. You can, of course, examine this question with data, as you saw in the first chapter of this text. Researchers say, for example, that the number of incidents of certain kinds of behavior was not found to be different in the times of the full moon as at other times. But that is the observation part of scientific inquiry. What about the theory? Why would someone expect that the full moon would influence behavior? Is the moon full when the tides are different? Do the tides regulate atmospheric conditions? Do these atmospheric conditions potentially change body chemistry? Do changes of this kind in body chemistry affect behavior? If the answer to all these questions is "yes," there would be a theoretical basis for hypothesizing that certain behaviors will be different during the full moon than at other times. Incidentally, I am not aware of the answers to these questions from research. This example is used hypothetically.

When you examine the theory of numerology, you must ask yourself if it makes sense from a theoretical standpoint and does it have empirical support. The purpose of the study in this chapter is to subject this theory to empirical testing. This means that you will seek to measure something that can serve to test the theory. A literature review on this theory is given in Exhibit 11.2.

EXHIBIT 11.2 A Brief Literature Review on the Theory of Numerology

Numerology presents a theory about life. It proposes that the vibrations from people's birth names and the constellation of the universe in relation to their birth dates will explain life. It will explain much about us, what we are like, how we can be in a better state of harmony with nature, and what our destiny is. But how did this knowledge come about?

Among the published books on numerology are ones by Vincent Lopez, entitled *Numerology* (New York: The Citadel Press, 1961), and by Florence Campbell, entitled *Your Days are Numbered* (Ferndale, Penn.: The Gateway, 1931). The latter one is generally recognized as one of the most important works on the subject. According to both books, the origins of numerology go back to an ancient philosopher and mathematician, Pythagoras, who developed the theory in the sixth century.

Neither book provides evidence that the knowledge base upon which this theory is built was derived from anything other than the shared thoughts of people through

EXHIBIT 11.2 *Continued*

the centuries. In other words, it was first conceived in the mind of one person who handed it down to others but who, himself, was influenced by earlier works on the so-called "Science of Number." Over the centuries people have interpreted this theory in their own ways and have handed it down to others. For advocates of this theory, the wisdom of it seems to be self-evident and requires no systematic investigation of a scientific nature.

To understand how such theories originate, the ideas of Vincent Lopez (1961) will be helpful:

> Numbers are truly awe-inspiring. There is something sublime about their sequence as it continues on and on into Infinity. Suddenly, when you study them arduously, there is revealed to your mortal mind the humming rhythm of the galaxies, the ebb and flow of Time, and the Law of Periodicity which operates throughout the Universe (p.125).

Lopez (1961) explains that numerology is founded on the metaphysical plane of thinking:

> All schools of metaphysical thought have made this point clear: there is an "outer" vibration or esoteric side and an "inner" vibration or esoteric angle to all forms of occult learning, and numerology is no exception. You may use the practical numerical values for your daily living and material problems. But there is also a spiritual expression to each number... Through meditation and a constant research into the esoteric philosophy of numbers you will soon recognize your own pattern of transmutation (p. 150).

While the word "research" is used above, there is no suggestion that one employ the scientific method to test the validity of numerology. The scientific method requires objective methods of measuring phenomena and attempts to control for biases and other sources of human error in the pursuit of knowledge about reality.

People are expected to believe numerology because it makes sense to them. Campbell (1931) explains by analogy the importance of being in harmony with the world we live in:

> In trying to relate ourselves to life as we find it, we must discover how to play harmonies instead of discords. The piano, for example, stands in the living room, capable of many varieties of sounds and noises. If we do not understand how to play it, perhaps it will remain silent until someone comes along who does; if we make the attempt without any understanding, the attempt is likely to be disastrous to ears and nerves.
>
> Why not learn what will produce the harmonies?
>
> We are all equally capable of harmonies and discords but, unlike other manufactured instruments, we may not remain mute and inexpressive. We must take our place in the Cosmic Orchestra...
>
> The clue to this we find in the world around us, for if we pause long enough to sense and feel it we discover: Vibration (p. 1).

(Continued)

EXHIBIT 11.2 *Continued*

Campbell further explains:

> We are all affected by the vibrations that govern the Universe for we are all part of it. As a part of the whole we are affected by every change in the Universal rate of vibration—and the rate changes every time there appears a different number in year, month, or day... Finding your own number gives you the chance to take your place in the world and keep it (p. 2).

One of the critical elements in the theory of numerology is that of the *Soul Urge*. Each person has a soul urge which is determined by the numbers associated with the vowels in their name given at birth. Campbell (1931) explains the soul urge as follows:

> The *Soul Urge*, or Identity, is the number of your heart's desire—that which you would like best to do (or that your best self would like to have you do). It is the *motive* that lies behind your acts; the feeling and inclination you put into the day's work; your attitude toward things and people; your judgment, your principles and point of view. This is the great HOW that answers every move you make and every thought you have (p. 3).

Lopez offers the following keywords to help us to understand the nature of each personality type. The number by each statement corresponds with the number which is derived from the formula offered by numerology.

Keywords for each Soul Urge (from Lopez, pp. 98–105):

1. Initiative, leadership, originality, creativity, self-started drive, inspirational, spontaneity, organization and self-sufficiency.

2. Tact, diplomacy, coordination, negotiation, collector, and appraiser.

3. Charm, culture, form-perfection, attraction powers, affability, artistic leaning, literary talents.

4. Facts, logic, practicability, sobriety, partial harvests, perfection of form.

5. Magnetism, nervous tension, inspirational ideas, restlessness, curiosity, inventiveness, salesmanship.

6. Association, partnership, domesticity, personal adjustments, marriage and divorce, a permanent home.

7. Receptivity, passiveness, secretiveness, diplomacy, and silence.

8. Honor, prestige, conservatism, wealth, business acumen, financial genius.

9. Universalism, fame, artistic achievement, idealism, global consciousness.

11. Analysis, inspiration, moral courage, discrimination, inventiveness, revelation.

EXHIBIT 11.2 *Continued*

Theories such as numerology are taken seriously by many people today who are attracted to metaphysical explanations of reality. One such group publishes a newsletter called *In Harmony* from Charlotte, N.C. In the January, 1988 issue of this newsletter is an article on numerology. It is from this article that the instrument for the present test was derived.

Little, if any, research has been published in the social work literature on this theory. A search of the Social Work Abstracts Database in July of 1995 revealed that there were no articles, among the 26,000 in this database, that referred to numerology. Perhaps the time has come for this theory to be subjected to empirical evaluation.

ASSIGNMENT 11–A

1. According to the theory of numerology, what is the dependent variable and what is the independent variable?

_____

_____

_____

_____

2. Does the theory of numerology make sense to you? Explain.

_____

_____

_____

_____

3. Is there any empirical support for this theory?

_____

_____

_____

_____

4. What is the justification for conducting a study on this theory?

_____

_____

_____

_____

5. Which of the following are statements of the purpose of this study that are consistent with the spirit of scientific inquiry?

   a. To prove that the theory of numerology is valid

   b. To prove that the theory of numerology is not valid

   c. To challenge the metaphysical basis for learning

   d. None of the above

_____

6. What do you suppose will be your interpretation of each of the following potential results of this study?

   a. You find that the personality profile selected by the theory of numerology matches the one you selected as your first choice, but this is not true for anyone else in the class.

_____

_____

   b. You find that the personality profile selected by the theory of numerology matches with one of the top five selections of almost everyone in class, but it does not match for you.

_____

_____

   c. You find that the personality profile selected by the theory of numerology matches with one of the top five choices by students for less than half the people in the class.

_____

_____

Study Methodology

Your research question is whether the theory of numerology is valid. On a specific level, you are posing the question, "Does the soul urge description given by the formula offered by the theory of numerology correspond to the study subjects' self-descriptions?" If the theory's choice does correspond with the self-descriptions, the theory would be supported. If not, it would not be supported by the data in the study.

The methodology of a research study includes the methods of measuring variables, the sample, the hypothesis (if appropriate), and the method used to collect data. You will collect data on your research question from students in this research course. Your data analysis will be guided by the following procedures:

1. Students will be asked to rank-order a set of ten statements of soul urges.
2. These students will determine their soul urge, as predicted by the theory of numerology, by using a formula for doing so.
3. These students will first compare their first ranked statement with the choice given by the theory to see if it is a match. The total number of students with such a match will be calculated. With ten statements, the likelihood of a chance match is 1 in 10 or 10 percent. If less than 10 percent of the students have such a match, the theory will not be supported by this analysis. If there is at least 10 percent of the students with a match for their first choice of a self-description, the question becomes how much more than 10 percent must there be to achieve statistical significance at the .10 level. A second analysis will be undertaken that will help you to answer this question. It is presented in the next statement.
4. These students' first five ranked statements will be placed in Category A while the other five statements will be placed in Category B. With each student having divided their ten statements into only two categories, there is a 50 percent likelihood that there would be a match with the choice given by the theory just by chance. Thus, a 50 percent match would not support the theory beyond the explanation of chance. It must be higher. But just how much higher? That will be determined in the next step.
5. These students will determine whether they have a match with the theory of numerology by considering themselves as a match if the soul urge statement given by the theory is the same as any one of the students' first five statements. The number of matches with this procedure will be calculated for the entire class. If the proportion of students with a match is 50 percent or less, the theory will not be supported by these data. If the proportion of matches is greater than 50 percent, you will apply the binomial test to determine if this proportion of matches is *significantly* greater than 50 percent.

Assignment 11–B follows. After this assignment, you will be given the opportunity to determine your personality profile number (soul urge) as calculated by the theory of numerology. Then you will confront the task of data analysis.

ASSIGNMENT 11–B

1. What is the sample for this study?

2. What is the study population?

3. Is this sample a probability sample?

4. To whom can the results of this study be safely generalized?

5. To whom can the results of this study be generalized on a more speculative basis? What is the rationale for this speculative generalization?

---

6. Which of the following is the best way to state the study hypothesis?

   a. There is a relationship between numerology and self-perception.

   b. Numerology will be demonstrated to be valid.

   c. The number of study subjects whose personality profile, selected by the method used by the theory of numerology, will match with one of their top choices from their self-description will be *greater* than the number of students without such a match.

   d. The number of study subjects whose personality profile, selected by the method used by the theory of numerology, will match with one of their top choices from their self-description will be *less* than the number of students without such a match.

7. One method of measurement used in this study is the ranking of the ten statements by the study subjects. How might the issue of reliability be addressed with this means of measurement?

   ---

8. How might the issue of validity be addressed?

   ---

9. What type of study is being undertaken?

   a. Descriptive   b. Explanatory   c. Exploratory   d. Evaluative

Data Analysis

Does Your Self-Description Match Your Soul Urge as Determined by Numerology?

In Exhibit 11.3, you will find the method for determining what your soul urge is supposed to be according to the theory of numerology. The numbers assigned to the self-descriptions in Exhibit 11.1 correspond to the soul urge. In other words, if your soul urge is four, then numerology says that you are supposed to be like the description given for the number four in Exhibit 11.1 The person with a soul urge of four, according to numerology, "wants respectability and solidity; wants to be a rock of dependability...," and so forth. You should return to Exhibit 11.1 and find the statement that is beside the number that you obtained by the procedures in Exhibit 11.3. This is what you are supposed to be like according to the theory. If you selected statement number three in Exhibit 11.1 as the one most like you and found

---

EXHIBIT 11.3 Determining Your Personality (Soul Urge) as Determined by the Theory

To determine your soul urge as determined by the theory of numerology, follow these procedures:

1. Print out your full name as given at birth.

   Example: AMELIA CLARE BRONN

2. Circle each vowel in your full name. Vowels are a, e, i, o, u, and sometimes y. It is y when it is pronounced like a letter that is a vowel, such as when it is pronounced the same as though it were the letter e.

3. Using the numbering scheme below, place the appropriate number above each vowel in your name.

A = 1	E = 5	I = 9	M = 4	Q = 8	U = 3	Y = 7
B = 2	F = 6	J = 1	N = 5	R = 9	V = 4	Z = 8
C = 3	G = 7	K = 2	O = 6	S = 1	W = 5	
D = 4	H = 8	L = 3	P = 7	T = 2	X = 6	

   ```
              1    5   9  1         1    5        6
   Example:   A  M E L I  A    C L A R E    B R O N N
   ```

4. Add up these numbers for each name and reduce this number to its final number by adding the two figures together if they number more than 9. For example, the name AMELIA has the numbers 1, 5, 9, and 1. When you add these together the result is 16. But 16 is greater than 9. Therefore, you add together these two numbers to determine the value given by the name AMELIA. That number is 7 (1 + 6).

EXHIBIT 11.3 *Continued*

Example

Amelia = 7 $(1 + 5 + 9 + 1 = 16)$

                    $(1 + 6 = 7)$

Clare = 6 $(1 + 5 = 6)$

Bronn = 6

5. Add these numbers together.   Example: $7 + 6 + 6 = 19$

6. Reduce this number to its final number by adding the two numbers together if the figure is greater than 9 as was done in step 4.

    Example: $1 + 9 = 10.$

                          $1 + 0 = 1$ This person's soul urge is 1.

An exception is the case of the numbers 11 and 22 which are not to be reduced to their final numbers but which remain as they are. Unfortunately, if your final number is 22, you cannot be included in the present study.

Adding Up the Vowels in Your Three Names:

First Name =   _____   Reduced to _____

Second =   _____   Reduced to _____

Third =   _____   Reduced to _____

Total = _____ Reduced to _____ (This is your soul urge)

*Instructions taken from In Harmony (January, 1988).

that the procedures in Exhibit 11.3 led to the number three, you would be a perfect match with the theory.

Did your first choice match with numerology? If it did, what does this mean? Let's examine this question. There were ten items on the list and one to be selected as the best description of yourself. You could flip a coin and match your first choice one time in ten. Thus, numerology has one chance in ten of "hitting the nail on the head" just by chance.

You might say that you have found evidence of the validity of numerology at the 10 percent level. But this would be a limited view of the situation! Why? Because you have rather limited data on which to draw conclusions. Statistical tests of data such as these generally take a more conservative position. They require more information. In other words, more trials are needed. Perhaps you are the only person in your class that matched perfectly with numerology; thus, numerology was just lucky when it predicted the essence of your character. One piece of data is never enough to prove or disprove a theory.

Testing the Theory of Numerology with Data from the Class

How can you give a fair test to the theory? You must combine the results of a group of people. In this case, you will combine the results of all class members.

Deciding how to do this will take a little innovative thinking because the situation is organized a little differently than most. For example, if you wanted to know if males earned higher salaries than females, you would examine whether the proportion of males with high salaries was significantly greater than the proportion of females with high salaries. If you wanted to know whether there was a relationship between depression and income, you would examine whether people with high income tended to be more or less depressed than those with low income.

In this study, you want to know whether the match between numerology and personality is significant. In other words, did the theory predict your self-description at a level much better than chance? The data are in the form of a set of rankings of self-descriptions done by you and your classmates along with the choice from the theory of numerology. As stated before, there will be a match by chance one time in ten. If you divide your chosen self-descriptions into the groups of high (ranks of 1 through 5) and low (ranks of 6 through 11), you will have reduced the data on self-descriptions to two groups. This will make the analysis simpler.

In such a case, you have a 50 percent chance of the self-descriptions being matched with numerology regardless of whether there is any wisdom to the theory. In other words, you could flip a coin with heads being classified as high and tails being low and expect to hit on the high category 50 percent of the time, just as numerology could match with it 50 percent of the time by chance.

What if numerology matches with one of the top five choices more than 50 percent of the time? How much more than 50 percent must it match in order to be considered to have predicted the self-descriptions at a *statistically significant* level? This is a task for the field of statistics.

In this case, there are two groups of people—those who do match with numerology on one of the top five choices, and those who do not match with numerology on one of the top five choices. The question is whether the proportion of those who did match is significantly greater than the proportion of those who did not match.

The next step in this statistical analysis is to collect information on each student's choices of self-descriptions and the choice derived from numerology. Place a check in the proper columns in Exhibit 11.4 for each student in your class. For example, if student number 1 did match with numerology on one of the first five ranks of self-descriptions, you would check the column labeled YES for student number 1. If this person did not have a match, the column labeled NO would be checked. Then add the totals for all who did match and all who did not match.

The proper statistical test for this data is the *binomial test.* It can be used to determine whether the proportions of people in two groups are significantly dif-

EXHIBIT 11.4   Tally of Matches for the Class

STUDENT NUMBER	MATCH Yes	No	STUDENT NUMBER	MATCH Yes	No
1	____	____	16	____	____
2	____	____	17	____	____
3	____	____	18	____	____
4	____	____	19	____	____
5	____	____	20	____	____
6	____	____	21	____	____
7	____	____	22	____	____
8	____	____	23	____	____
9	____	____	24	____	____
10	____	____	25	____	____
11	____	____	26	____	____
12	____	____	27	____	____
13	____	____	28	____	____
14	____	____	29	____	____
15	____	____	30	____	____

Total Students = _____   Number with match = _____

ferent from a 50–50 split. The normal standard for statistical significance is the 5 percent level (i.e., $p < .05$). In other words, if the statistical test says that your data can be explained by chance less than 5 times in 100, you will accept these data as reflections of reality rather than chance. But this standard is arbitrary. There is no particular scientific basis for it. Instead, it is a standard that has been widely accepted as safe and conservative. The higher the standard, of course, the more confidence that you can have in your results. Higher standards are warranted in situations in which serious matters are at stake such as the effect of a drug on health. For less serious matters, a lower standard may be argued. In this case, let's be generous with the theory of numerology and establish the .10 level rather than the .05 level as the standard. This means that you will consider the data to support the theory if the number of students with a match is greater than those without such a match and that this difference would not occur by chance any more than 10 times out of 100.

You can either consult a table of the binomial test or obtain the answer by a formula. The following information was derived from Table D in the Appendix to the text, *Nonparametric Statistics for the Behavioral Sciences,* by Sidney Siegel (New York: McGraw–Hill, 1956).

In this paragraph, a few of the numbers from the table of the binomial test from Siegel's book will be presented in order to give you a general idea of how it works. If there are fewer than 10 students in class, you should consult a table of the binomial test. If you have nine or ten or eleven students in class, you can have two students without a match between numerology and self-perception and still declare your data to be statistically significant. In other words, with nine students, you need eight matches; with ten students, you need nine matches; with eleven students, you need ten matches. With twelve or thirteen students you will achieve significance with three nonmatches, while classes of fourteen or fifteen require no more than four nonmatches for significance. With sixteen or seventeen students, you need no more than five nonmatches. As you can see, the proportion of matches needed for statistical significance goes down as the number in the sample goes up. Two additional figures will be presented. With twenty students in class, significance at the .10 level is achieved with no more than six nonmatches, while there can be as many as eight nonmatches with a class of twenty-five (and still achieve significance).

ASSIGNMENT 11–C

1. What was the number of students in this class?

_____

_____

_____

_____

2. How many of the students had a match with the theory of numerology?

_____

_____

_____

_____

3. How many matches were required to achieve the .10 level of significance?

_____

_____

_____

_____

4. Did the results support the theory?

_____

_____

_____

_____

Conclusions

Did your results tend to support the theory of numerology? This is the critical question to be addressed in the conclusions phase of your research study. The limitations of your study as a test of this theory should also be addressed in this phase. Keep in mind that your study is one test of this theory. Whatever the results, you should be cautious in your conclusions. The more confidence you have in your methods of testing this theory, the more confidence you can have in the results of your study.

What are some of the limitations of your study? The two critical places to look for an answer to this question are in the sample and the study methodology. Can you generalize your findings to others? If you find support for the theory, can you generalize this finding to others? What if you fail to find support for it? Is there anything about this theory that would suggest that it should apply differently to different kinds of people? If so, perhaps social work students are not the types of people to use to test this theory. If not, why would you expect to have a different outcome if you applied your test with a different sample? You would, of course, have more and more confidence in your results if you repeated this study with other samples of people and had similar results.

But you must also address the issue of your study methodology. Was it a fair test of the theory? You chose, for example, to employ the study subjects' self-perceptions as a basis for your test of numerology. Is this a fair way to test this theory? What if these subjects really don't know their true nature?

In the conclusions part of your study, you confront the issue of practical significance. Practical significance refers to the practical utility of your findings. If you had conducted an evaluative study and found the mean pretest score of your clients on depression was 32.4 and the mean posttest score was 29.2, you might declare that these differences were not of practical significance even if these differences had achieved statistical significance. In other words, you might say that the treatment did not achieve success even though the gain was statistically significant, because you believed that this much gain is not very noteworthy and does not justify a particular expenditure of resources.

Practical significance is substantially a matter of judgment. When you address this issue, you are determining whether you are satisfied that your results truly gave you an answer to your research question that is worthwhile. If the theory of numerology was not supported by your data, was the lack of support convincing? If it was supported, you could ask the same question.

ASSIGNMENT 11–D

1. What are your basic conclusions about the theory of numerology?

_____

_____

_____

_____

2. What limitations do you see in the sampling methods employed in this study?

_____

_____

_____

3. How might these limitations be overcome?

_____

_____

_____

4. What limitations do you see in the methods of measurement?

_____

_____

_____

5. How might these limitations be overcome?

_____

_____

_____

6. If your class found support for this theory, does this constitute proof of its validity?

_____

_____

_____

If you failed to find support for this theory, does this constitute proof that it is not valid?

_____

_____

_____

A Test of Numerology, Part II

In the previous study methods, there were no means employed to assess either the reliability or validity of our chosen means of measurement. This study of numerology employed the self-perceptions of students as a method by which the theory was tested. Can you always be confident that you know yourself? Perhaps the theory is better able to characterize you than you can characterize yourself? But who is a better judge about who you are than you?

While many researchers would be perfectly comfortable with the previous methodology, which assumed that each student was self-aware, there are methods of testing the validity or reliability of this procedure. You can ask others to assess you and you can compare your answers to their answers to see if these perceptions are consistent. If your best friend describes you in a rather different manner than you described yourself using the tool in Exhibit 11.1, you would have reason to question the reliability of using your answers to this instrument as a measure of your personality (or soul urge).

In this part of the chapter, you will test the reliability of your self-perceptions by asking two people who know you well to rank order the statements in Exhibit 11.1 according to the extent to which each one of these statements describes you. You will employ a statistical test to determine whether there is significant consistency in the three rankings of you (you and the two other people). Each member of your class will do the same and you will return to the previous data which tested the theory and consider the implications of the results of this test of the reliability of the chosen means of measurement. Class members without consistent rankings can be eliminated from the study so that the methodology can be enhanced in this test of numerology.

Step 1: Obtaining Rankings of Your Behavior by People Who Know You Well

Your next step is to select two people who know you well and ask them to offer you their perceptions of your personality by responding to the same instrument that you used in the first part of this experience. You should *not*, of course, tell these people which of these statements you ranked as high or low, because this practice might influence their judgments.

It is also preferable that you give them the opportunity to respond anonymously, even though this may not be easy to do. One way to insure anonymity is to have each of them place their responses in a sealed envelope which you agree to open in a situation in which you will not know which person's response was in

---

EXHIBIT 11.5 Ranking of Statements by Person Number 1

The following is a description of _____

Directions: Examine the list of ten descriptions given below and rank order them from 1 to 10 by assigning a rank of 1 to the statement that is most like the person named above. Then give a rank of 2 to the next best description of that person, a rank of 3 to the next, and so on until you have assigned a rank to each of the ten statements, with the rank of 10 being given to the statement that is least like this person. Be sure to respond to each statement.

_____ 1 Wants to lead and direct. Prefers to work alone or to be the boss. Is proud of abilities and desires praise. Wants to create and originate. Is not very emotional. Is capable of great accomplishment, a loyal friend. May be boastful, critical, impatient.

EXHIBIT 11.5 *Continued*

_____   2. Wants and needs love, companionship. Prefers to work with or for others. Wants harmony and peace. Wants ease and comfort (not necessarily wealth and luxury). Is kind and thoughtful. Attracts friends. Is sensitive and emotional. Falls in love easily. Devoted, easygoing.

_____   3. Wants to give out joy and happiness. Wants popularity and friends. Wants beauty. Never mopes over mistakes—tries again. Artistic, expressive, entertaining, playful. Doesn't worry or get depressed. Wants to scatter love, energies, talents.

_____   4. Wants respectability and solidity. Wants to be a rock of dependability. A great disciplinarian. Loves home and family. Is not fond of innovation. Loves order and regularity. Is thorough and methodical. Needs and wants love, but often repels it.

_____   5. Wants personal freedom in every direction. Wants change, variety, and constant new opportunity. Wide open to life's experiences. Loves pleasure, travel, strange and new people. Injects new life into all that s/he touches. Will not be hampered by convention. Is progressive, intellectual, emotional, spiritual.

_____   6. Wants roots, responsibility, home, steadfast love. Loyal friend, good counselor. Inclined toward conventionality, but broad-minded. A "cosmic" parent. Centers life on home. Loves to work with others, never alone.

_____   7. Wants silence, peace, meditation, analysis. Hates noise and confusion of business world. Is conservative, refined, reserved, spiritual. Is deeply emotional, but has horror of showing it. Shy, withdrawn. Must be known to be loved.

_____   8. Wants big affairs and the power to handle them. Wants success in all material matters. Loves organization, finances. Loves to manage and direct. Is generous, enthusiastic, courageous, determined. Has vision and imagination. Is cornerstone of community. Is power for good. May be dominant.

_____   9. Wants to serve the world. Boundless faith in own source of supply. Has wisdom, intuition, understanding. Is attractive to all and loved by all. Is ready to give his/her life for humanity. Wants personal love, but belongs to the Universe. An interpreter of the greatness of life.

_____   11. Wants to reveal beauties s/he has seen. Is always the universalist, never concerned with individuals. Is a dreamer, a visionary with a passion for salvation and uplift. Wants to indulge in impracticality, but seems practical. Has "electrical" mind. Can be a martyr.

Note: There is no statement numbered 10.

EXHIBIT 11.6 Ranking of Statements by Person Number 2

The following is a description of _____

Directions: Examine the list of ten descriptions given below and rank order them from 1 to 10 by assigning a rank of 1 to the statement that is most like the person named above. Then give a rank of 2 to the next best description of that person, a rank of 3 to the next, and so on until you have assigned a rank to each of the ten statements, with the rank of 10 being given to the statement that is the least like this person. Be sure to respond to each statement.

_____ 1. Wants to lead and direct. Prefers to work alone or to be the boss. Is proud of abilities and desires praise. Wants to create and originate. Is not very emotional. Is capable of great accomplishment, a loyal friend. May be boastful, critical, impatient.

_____ 2. Wants and needs love, companionship. Prefers to work with or for others. Wants harmony and peace. Wants ease and comfort (not necessarily wealth and luxury). Is kind and thoughtful. Attracts friends. Is sensitive and emotional. Falls in love easily. Devoted, easygoing.

_____ 3. Wants to give out joy and happiness. Wants popularity and friends. Wants beauty. Never mopes over mistakes—tries again. Artistic, expressive, entertaining, playful. Doesn't worry or get depressed. Wants to scatter love, energies, talents.

_____ 4. Wants respectability and solidity. Wants to be a rock of dependability. A great disciplinarian. Loves home and family. Is not fond of innovation. Loves order and regularity. Is thorough and methodical. Needs and wants love, but often repels it.

_____ 5. Wants personal freedom in every direction. Wants change, variety, and constant new opportunity. Wide open to life's experiences. Loves pleasure, travel, strange and new people. Injects new life into all that s/he touches. Will not be hampered by convention. Is progressive, intellectual, emotional, spiritual.

_____ 6. Wants roots, responsibility, home, steadfast love. Loyal friend, good counselor. Inclined toward conventionality, but broad-minded. A "cosmic" parent. Centers life on home. Loves to work with others, never alone.

_____ 7. Wants silence, peace, meditation, analysis. Hates noise and confusion of business world. Is conservative, refined, reserved, spiritual. Is deeply emotional, but has horror of showing it. Shy, withdrawn. Must be known to be loved.

_____ 8. Wants big affairs and the power to handle them. Wants success in all material matters. Loves organization, finances. Loves to manage and direct. Is generous, enthusiastic, courageous, determined. Has vision and imagination. Is cornerstone of community. Is power for good. May be dominant.

EXHIBIT 11.6

_____ 9. Wants to serve the world. Boundless faith in own source of supply. Has wisdom, intuition, understanding. Is attractive to all and loved by all. Is ready to give his/her life for humanity. Wants personal love, but belongs to the Universe. An interpreter of the greatness of life.

_____ 11. Wants to reveal beauties s/he has seen. Is always the universalist, never concerned with individuals. Is a dreamer, a visionary with a passion for salvation and uplift. Wants to indulge in impracticality, but seems practical. Has "electrical" mind. Can be a martyr.

Note: There is no statement numbered 10.

each envelope. If you do this, you should communicate this information to each of the other two persons.

After you complete the procedure that follows, you will be given the opportunity to statistically analyze the extent of agreement between yourself and these two friends regarding the essence of your personality.

Step Two: Statistical Analysis of Congruence among the Rankings

After you and your two friends have rank ordered the ten statements according to how well each statement describes you, you can examine whether the three of you have a statistically significant degree of agreement on these ranks by employing the Kendall Coefficient of Concordance.

The Kendall Coefficient of Concordance is a statistical measure which can be employed to determine if several judges agree on the ranking of a set of objects. In this case, there are three judges—you and your two friends—and ten objects (the ten self-descriptions). For situations in which there are seven or more entities being ranked, there is a formula for converting the data into a chi square value. Chi square can be used to determine statistical significance (i.e., the probability that the results could occur by chance).

In order to establish that your self-description is reliable, you must have data that reveals that the other two judges agreed with you to a significant degree. You will use the following formula in the determination of reliability.

$$\text{Chi Square} = \frac{s}{1/12\ (k)(N)(N+1)}$$

where

s = *The sum of squared deviations from the mean rank as illustrated below*

k = *Number of judges doing the ranking (in your case $k = 3$)*

N = *Number of items being ranked (in your case $N = 10$)*

Thus, you will compute a chi square value and use that value to determine statistical significance. But first, you must compute the value of **s** as indicated in the formula above. This is done by adding the values of the ranks of each object by each judge and by computing a mean for those ranks. Then each sum of ranks is subtracted from this mean and squared and these squared values are added to comprise the value of **s.**

There is a worksheet in Exhibit 11.8 which can be used in the computation of **s** for your data. An illustration of how to compute it is given in Exhibit 11.7. In case you have forgotten some of your math, you should note that a negative score is converted to a positive score any time that it is squared. You can see an illustration of this in the final column in which you will see no negative signs.

Examining Statistical Significance

In determining whether chi square is statistically significant, it is necessary to know the *degrees of freedom*. In your case the degrees of freedom is computed by

---

EXHIBIT 11.7 An Illustration of the Use of the Kendall Coefficient of Concordance

State-ment	Rank from You	Rank from First Friend	Rank from Second Friend	Sum	–	Mean	=	Deviation	Deviation Squared
1	3	4	4	11	–	16.5	=	–5.5	30.25
2	5	2	5	12	–	16.5	=	–4.5	20.25
3	7	7	6	20	–	16.5	=	3.5	12.25
4	2	3	3	8	–	16.5	=	–8.5	72.25
5	1	1	2	4	–	16.5	=	–12.5	156.25
6	4	5	1	10	–	16.5	=	–6.5	42.25
7	9	8	9	26	–	16.5	=	9.5	90.25
8	6	6	7	19	–	16.5	=	2.5	6.25
9	8	9	8	25	–	16.5	=	8.5	72.25
11	10	10	10	30	–	16.5	=	13.5	182.25

Sum of Ranks = 165 / 10 = 16.5 (Mean)   648.50
                                                (This is **s**)

$$\text{Chi Square} = \frac{648.5}{1/12\,(3)\,(10)\,(10+1)} = \frac{648.5}{0.0833 \times 3 \times 10 \times 11} = \frac{648.5}{27.499} = 23.58$$

EXHIBIT 11.8 Worksheet for Using the Kendall Coefficient of Concordance

Step 1: Calculating the Sum of Ranks and the Mean of Ranks

In the chart below, enter the rank for each statement that you gave yourself and place this figure in the column labeled "Yourself." Then list the rank given for each statement by Friend #1 and Friend #2 in the next two columns. The sum of ranks for each statement is the sum of these three figures for the statement. The sum of all ranks is the sum of all ten of these figures. The mean of ranks is the sum of all ranks divided by ten (the total number of statements)

		Ranks of Statements as Given By			
Statement	*Yourself*		*Friend #1*	*Friend #2*	*Sum of Ranks*
1	_____	+	_____ +	_____ =	_____
2	_____	+	_____ +	_____ =	_____
3	_____	+	_____ +	_____ =	_____
4	_____	+	_____ +	_____ =	_____
5	_____	+	_____ +	_____ =	_____
6	_____	+	_____ +	_____ =	_____
7	_____	+	_____ +	_____ =	_____
8	_____	+	_____ +	_____ =	_____
9	_____	+	_____ +	_____ =	_____
11	_____	+	_____ +	_____ =	_____

Sum of All Ranks = _____ / 10 = _____
(Mean)

Step 2: Determining the Sum of Squared Deviations from the Mean of Ranks

Transfer the sum of ranks for each of the 10 statements from the previous step into the first column on the worksheet which follows in the continuation of Exhibit 11.8. Then transfer the mean of ranks into the second column. (You will place the same figure into this column for each statement—there is only one mean of ranks.) Your next step is to subtract the mean of ranks from the sum of ranks for each statement and place this figure in the third column labeled "Deviation." The next step is to square this figure for each statement and place that figure in the last column below. Your final task in this step is to sum these squared deviations and place that figure at the bottom. This is the sum of squared deviations, which is **s** in the formula for determining the value of chi square.

(Continued)

EXHIBIT 11.8 *Continued*

Statement	Sum of Ranks	(minus)	Mean of Ranks	(equals)	Deviation	Deviation Squared
1	_____	-	_____	=	_____	_____
2	_____	-	_____	=	_____	_____
3	_____	-	_____	=	_____	_____
4	_____	-	_____	=	_____	_____
5	_____	-	_____	=	_____	_____
6	_____	-	_____	=	_____	_____
7	_____	-	_____	=	_____	_____
8	_____	-	_____	=	_____	_____
9	_____	-	_____	=	_____	_____
11	_____	-	_____	=	_____	_____

Sum of Squared Deviations (**s**) = _____

Step 3: Determining the Value of Chi Square

You want to know whether there is a significant amount of agreement between you and the other two people who ranked the statements about your personality. Your next step is to use the value of **s** that you have calculated in order to determine a value for chi square, which will lead you to the determination of statistical significance. In order to determine chi square, you must divide **s** (in this case) by 27.499 as previously described.

s   =   _____   /   27.499   =   _____ (chi square)

In this situation, a chi square value of 14.68 is significant at the 0.10 level, a chi square of 16.92 is significant at the 0.05 level, and a chi square of 21.67 is significant at the 0.01 level.

subtracting 1 from 10 (your N). In other words, the degrees of freedom in this case is 9. Then you will need to consult a statistical table for chi square and determine if your chi square value is statistically significant.

The normal standard for statistical significance that is generally accepted in the social sciences is the 5 percent level (also referred to as 0.05). The 5 percent level means that a result would be expected to occur by chance no more than 5 times in 100. If you can say that your result could occur by chance no more than 5 times in 100, you can say that you have achieved *statistical significance*. In research studies, you will see the five percent level presented as .05. You have probably seen a statement that the relationship between variables was significant with the notation "p < .05" in parentheses. This means that the results could occur by chance less than 5 times in 100.

However, you should keep in mind that the 5 percent level is an arbitrary decision. There is nothing magical about it. There is no scientific reason that you cannot set your standard at another level. In this case, let's set the standard a little lower. Let's say that you will consider your degree of agreement among judges to be significant if you achieve the 10 percent level (i.e., 10 chances in 100 or 1 chance in 10).

When you consult a statistical table for chi square, you can learn that, with 9 degrees of freedom, a chi square value of 14.68 is significant at the 0.10 level, a chi square of 16.92 is significant at the 0.05 level, and a chi square of 21.67 is significant at the 0.01 level. Thus, if your chi square value is 14.68 or greater, you will consider your self-description (i.e., the one that you selected) to be reliable.

You can now revisit the test of the theory of numerology employing only those students who achieved statistical significance for their self-descriptions. Return to the pages that were used to record the number of students in the study and the number with a match with the theory of numerology.

ASSIGNMENT 11–E

1. Did your data reveal that you and your two friends had a significant level of congruence in your ranking of the ten statements about yourself? If not, what is your explanation?

_____

_____

_____

_____

2. What proportion of students in class achieved statistical significance?

_____

_____

_____

_____

3. What is your interpretation of this fact? If the proportion was rather low, should this be of concern?

_____

_____

_____

_____

4. After you have reexamined the data with only the students with significant congruence, what is your interpretation of the results?

_____

_____

_____

_____

Glossary

ABAB Single-subject Research Design. A research design in which a single subject is measured repeatedly during a baseline period (period A), is given a specific treatment and repeatedly measured during the treatment period (period B), is measured repeatedly during a second baseline period (the second A period), and a second treatment period when the same treatment is administered (the second period B).

ABC single-subject Research Design. A research design in which a single subject is measured repeatedly during a baseline period (period A), is given a certain treatment and is repeatedly measured during this treatment period (period B), and the treatment is changed, with the client continually measured on the dependent variable during this second treatment period (period C).

AB single-subject Research Design. A research design in which a single subject (client, group, organization, community) is measured on the dependent variable several times during a baseline period before treatment begins and is repeatedly measured on the dependent variable during the treatment period.

Abstract Definition of a Study Variable. A definition of a variable which provides conceptual guidance on the boundaries that are considered fitting for the variable for the present study. It can be likened to a dictionary definition of the variable although it is not required to encompass all territory that others might want to include, but only the conceptual territory that the researcher considers proper for the given study.

Analytic Induction. A method of qualitative inquiry that is designed to test, or refine, a hypothesis. The process begins with a tentative hypothesis and cases are studied in light of that hypothesis, with each case either confirming the hypothesis or suggesting a modification of it.

Assumption. A statement which is not being subjected to assessment in the present study but which must be true in order for the study to provide an accurate inquiry into the research question being examined.

Average Deviation. The average of all deviations from the mean in an array of data. For example, the ages of 24, 26, 28, and 30 would have a mean of 27 (24 + 26 + 28 + 30 = 108 / 4 = 27) and an average deviation of 2 (3 + 1 + 1 + 3 = 8 / 4 = 2).

Bar chart. A chart which depicts the frequencies for the various categories for a variable.

Basic Experimental Research Design. The basic experimental design entails the assignment of people to two groups on a random basis, one group being given the intervention (known as the experimental group) and the other group being excluded from treatment (known as the control group). Both groups of people are measured on the dependent variable before treatment and again after treatment has been completed. The gain in functioning for the two groups is compared to see if the experimental group had a significantly greater gain than the control group.

BA single-subject research design. A research design in which a single subject is measured repeatedly on the dependent variable during the treatment period and during a baseline period which follows treatment.

BC single-subject research design. A research design in which a single subject is measured repeatedly on the dependent variable during a treatment period (period B) and the treatment is changed and the subject is measured repeatedly during the second treatment period (period C).

Causation. The explanation of the reasons that events occur. In research, the concept of causation is treated cautiously because events typically have multiple causes and the pinpointing of causation is difficult.

Celeration Line Method of Statistical Analysis (for single-subject research). A method of statistical analysis for single-subject research in which the baseline trend is not level, i.e., is either ascending or descending. The proportion of recordings of the dependent variable during the treatment period that fall on the favorable side of the trend line is compared to the same for the baseline period to see if the former is significantly greater than the latter. In most circumstances, if you have as many as six treatment recordings and all the treatment recordings are superior to the trend line, you will achieve statistical significance; however, you should consult a statistical test to be sure.

Coefficient. A figure that represents the strength of the empirical relationship between variables. There are various statistical tests which employ the term "coefficient." For example, there is the phi coefficient, the contingency coefficient, the Pearson correlation coefficient, the Spearman rank correlation coefficient, and so forth. The values of such coefficients typically can range from 0 to 1.0.

Comparison Group Design. A research design in which a group of treated clients are measured before and after the intervention and their gains in functioning are compared to the before and after measurements of a group that did not receive treatment. This design is also known as the non-equivalent control group design.

Conclusions. The final major phase of the research process in which conclusions are drawn about the data which were employed in the examination of the research question.

Criterion Validity. A measurement device has criterion validity to the extent that it corresponds to (correlates with) other criteria for observing the concept under study. For example, scholastic aptitude test scores should correlate with college grades if this test has criterion validity. A marital satisfaction scale should be able to predict divorce. One person's self-esteem scale should correlate with another person's self-esteem scale.

Cumulative Frequency. A frequency that includes all those in the present category (reference category) plus the frequency for all categories which come before the present one in the classification scheme.

Cumulative Proportion. The proportion of subjects in the present category plus the proportion of all subjects falling below or above the present category.

Data Analysis. The third major phase of the research process whereby data is analyzed to address the research question.

Deductive. A process of inquiry that begins with theory and moves to observation for the purpose of testing theory.

Dependent Variable. The variable which is believed to depend upon or is caused by another variable, the other variable being known as the "independent variable."

Descriptive Research. Research that describes something with precision but does not attempt to explain it.

Direct Observation. A means of observation in qualitative research in which the researcher is directly observing the behavior of the study subjects.

Disconfirming Evidence. Evidence which is counter to a given explanation of things.

Empirical Relationship. A relationship between variables which can be depicted through concrete measurement devices. An example would be the relationship between gender and salary.

Ethnography. The study of cultures in their natural settings through qualitative research methods.

Evaluative Research. Research that is used to evaluate whether an intervention achieved its objectives.

Exhaustive. Categories for a question on a questionnaire which include a category that fits each potential study subject.

Explanatory Research. Research that is designed to explain something, usually by examining the relationships among a set of variables to see if one offers an explanation of another.

Exploratory Research. Research that is designed to develop knowledge about a relatively unknown phenomenon so that new theory can be developed or new insight can be acquired on the nature of it.

Face Validity. A measurement device has face validity if it appears to knowledgeable persons to be an accurate means of measuring the particular concept it is supposed to measure. This is the least objective of the various methods of assessing validity, but is often the only reasonable alternative for self-developed instruments.

Frequency. The incidence of something, such as the number of females and males in a study sample. There could be, for example, a frequency of 24 females and 21 males in a given sample.

Generalization. The application of knowledge about one group of study subjects to another group of persons.

Grounded Theory. A qualitative research methodology that is designed to develop theory through a highly inductive, but systematic, process of discovery. A major focus is upon the observation of similarities and differences in social behavior across social situations.

History (as a threat to internal validity). When a client improves during the treatment period, it may be because of the treatment, or it may be because of a change in the client's environment, such as obtaining a job, or getting a promotion. History as a threat to internal validity refers to changes in the client's environment which may be the cause of improvement. The comparison group design addresses history as a threat to internal validity because it is assumed that the two groups will be equivalent on history; thus, the superiority of the gain for the treatment group over the gain for the comparison group would be better attributed to the treatment than to history. The AB single-subject design, however, does not address this threat.

Hypothesis. A statement of the expected results of a research study on a given theme based upon theory or explanations derived from existing knowledge. For example, one might hypothesize that males will report higher annual salaries than will females. This hypothesis would be based upon knowledge of sexual discrimination.

Independent Variable. The variable which is believed to cause the dependent variable to be the way it is.

Indirect Observation. A means of observation (measurement) in qualitative research in which the researcher is examining products of behavior such as records or literature as a basis for developing theories or explanations about behavior.

Inductive. A process of inquiry which begins with observations from which theory or generalizations are derived.

Instrumentation. The means used in a study to measure variables.

Internal Consistency. The tendency of items forming a common scale to operate the same way. For example, a self-esteem scale would have internal consistency to the extent that the items on the scale, when treated as separate variables, would be correlated with one another when given to a sample of study subjects. Thus, if John has a higher score than Tom on item 1 on this scale, he would probably have a higher score than Tom on item 2 on this scale as well. If this were *not* the general pattern for items on this scale, then it would *not* be considered to have internal consistency. This situation would suggest that the items on this scale are not measuring the same thing.

Interval. A level of measurement in which subjects are given scores on a scale in which the intervals between each level is equal to the interval between each of the other levels. For example, the temperature of 32 is 1 degree lower than the temperature of 33 which is 1 degree lower than the temperature of 34. This scale is measured in reference to degrees on the scale with each single degree being equal to each of the other degrees.

Interview. A personal encounter between persons in which one person is seeking information from another person. It can take place face-to-face or by way of another mode of personal interaction such as the telephone.

Interview Structure. The extent to which questions for study in an interview have been narrowed or specifically focused. The more specific the focus, the more the interview is structured. The extent to which questions are open-ended. More open questions have less structure.

Levels of Measurement. The hierarchy of measurement for study variables, each level of which provides a different level of sophistication in measurement, and is suitable for different statistical tests. The levels are nominal, ordinal, interval, and ratio, in that order from lowest to highest. A variable measured at a higher level can be treated as though it is measured at a lower level for statistical analysis purposes if necessary. For example, a variable measured at the interval level can be treated as though it is measured at the ordinal level. However, we lose information when we do this, so it is not optimal.

Logic. Whether something makes sense when subjected to careful analysis through the principles of good reasoning.

Maturation. Sometimes people overcome their problems on their own through time and the normal process of growth. This is referred to as maturation, and is one of the most important threats to internal validity. The comparison group design addresses maturation because it compares a treated group with an untreated group, the assumption being that the effects of history would probably be equal for the two groups; thus, the superiority of the treated group's improvement in functioning over the comparison group's gain is normally better attributed to the treatment rather than to history. The AB single-subject design also addresses maturation because the baseline trend is assumed to be an indicator of the progression of maturation; thus, if the client's functioning during the treatment period is significantly better than the projected baseline trend, the client's growth can be better attributed to the treatment than to maturation.

Mean. The average. The mean is calculated by summing the frequencies in a sample of data and dividing the sum by the number of people in the sample.

Median. The mid point in an array of data laid out in numerical order. For example, let's examine the following numbers: 12, 15, 16, 19, 27, 28, 31. The median for this array of data is 19.

Methodology. The second major phase of the research process whereby the study is designed in a manner that adequately addresses the research question.

Mutually Exclusive. Categories for a research instrument which are not capable of overlap such that a study subject could possibly be placed into more than one category among those presented.

Negative Relationship. A relationship between study variables in which *high* values on one variable tend to be associated with *low* values on the other variable (with high values on one being associated with low values on the other). For example, we would expect to find a negative relationship between self esteem and depression, meaning that persons with higher self esteem scores would tend to have lower scores for depression. Thus, if Paul has a higher score for self-esteem than does Jim, he is likely to have a lower score on depression than Jim.

Nominal. The lowest level of measurement. At the nominal level, the attributes of a variable are in categories which have no particular order (such as low, medium, and high). Examples include gender, political party affiliation, and favorite color.

Observation. The measurement of something.

One Group Pretest-posttest Research Design. A research design in which a group of clients are tested on the dependent variable before treatment and again after treatment has been completed. The gain in functioning evidenced by these two tests serves as a measure of the effects of treatment.

Operational Definition of a Study Variable. A definition of a study variable which specifies how the variable will be measured in the present study.

Ordinal. The next level of measurement beyond nominal. Ordinal variables place subjects into categories that are ordered from low to high or most to least, and so forth. The response categories of "agree," "undecided," and "disagree" place respondents into categories of agreement that are ordered from most to least.

p. The letter p is used to designate the estimate of the probability that a set of research data would occur by chance. The designation "p< .05" means that these particular data would occur by chance less than 5 times in 100. The designation "p< .01" indicates that this likelihood is less than 1 time in 100.

Participant Observer. A role in research in which an individual is both a participant in a social process and a researcher of that process.

Pearson's Correlation Coefficient. A measure of the degree of relationship between two variables measured at the interval level. It is designated in research literature with the small letter r (e.g., r = .46). The value of this coefficient can range from a low of 0 to a high of 1.0, and it can be either negative or positive. In other words, possible values include –1.0, 0, and 1.0 and all possible values in between, such as –.21, –.58, –.94, .12, .33, .78, and so forth. Values close to 0 mean that there is little, if any, relationship between the variables.

Phi Coefficient. A measure of the strength of the relationship between two dichotomous variables. It can range from 0 to 1.0, but cannot be negative, because relationships between nominal variables can be neither negative nor positive, because such variables have no order to the categories of the variables. For example, we could not speak of a negative relationship between gender and political party affiliation. To do so would suggest that the categories of these variables are ordered such that male is higher or lower than female.

Pie Chart. A chart that is pie shaped and which depicts the proportions of subjects (or entities) in each category for a variable.

Population. The larger group from which the sample was selected.

Positive Relationship. A relationship between study variables in which high values on one variable tend to be associated with high values on the other variables (with low values on one being associated with low values on the other). For example, we would expect to find a positive relationship between IQ scores and college grades, meaning that persons with higher IQ scores would tend to have the higher grades, while persons with low IQ scores would tend to have the low grades. Thus, if Mary has a higher IQ than Bob, she is likely to have higher college grades than Bob.

Posttest. A measurement of study subjects on the dependent variable after treatment has been completed.

Practical Significance. The extent to which a given set of study findings are noteworthy.

Predispositions. One's preconceived notions of reality. The explanations about our study subject which we take into our study process and which should be open to alteration by the results of our study.

Pretest. A measurement of study subjects on the dependent variable before treatment begins.

Probability. The likelihood of the occurrence of something that is not a certainty. Statistical tests are used to estimate probability and is designated with the letter p.

Probability Sample. A sample that was drawn at random from the specified study population.

Problem Formulation. The first major phase of the research process in which the research question is developed and the research problem is analyzed.

Proportion. The percentage of something, such as the percent of the sample that was female.

Qualitative. A means of observation (or measurement) that is flexible, such as an open-ended question on a questionnaire or direct observation of behavior as it naturally occurs.

Quantitative. A means of observation (or measurement) that is fixed, such as posing a question which places people in discrete categories (e.g., male or female) or gives them a number as a value for the response to the question (e.g. age).

Random Sample. A sample in which each person in the study population had an equal chance of being selected for the sample.

Ratio. The highest level of measurement. Variables measured at the ratio level have all the characteristics of variables measured at the interval level, with the addition that all scores on the scale are based upon a fixed zero point. A practical way to remember this characteristic is to realize that variables measured at the ratio level cannot have negative values, because 0 is the lowest possible value. For example, a person cannot have negative weight, or height, or age.

Reliability. The consistency of a means of measurement. If a scale is reliable, persons will respond to it in a consistent fashion at different points in time.

Research Design. The protocol whereby study subjects are measured on the dependent variable and interventions are administered in evaluative research.

Sample. A portion of a larger entity. In a research study, it pertains to the study subjects from whom data were collected.

Scientific Inquiry. A systematic process of inquiry that is designed to reduce the bias inherent in human observation through the application of both logic and objective measurement of social phenomena.

Single-subject Research Design (also known as single-system design). A research design in which the study subject is treated as a single subject and data is collected on the dependent variable repeatedly for this one subject. While the single-subject design is typically used with a single client, it can also be employed with a single organization or community or group providing that each is treated as a single unit for data analysis.

Social Survey. A means of collecting information from people through questionnaires or interviews in which the information to be collected is specified ahead of time and the questionnaire items for obtaining this information has been developed.

Spearman Rank Correlation Coefficient. A measure of the strength of the relationship between variables measured at the ordinal level. The value of this coefficient can range from 0 to 1.0 and can be either negative or positive.

Standard Deviation. A measure of variance for a distribution. It tells us how much the subjects in a particular sample are similar of different from one another.

Standard Deviation Method of Statistical Analysis (for single-subject research). A means of statistical analysis of single-subject research data when the trend during the baseline period is relatively level. Statistical significance is achieved if the mean for treatment recordings of the dependent variable is two standard deviations better than the mean for the baseline recordings.

Statistical Significance. The likelihood that a given set of study findings would be expected to occur by chance.

Statistical Test. A measure which is used to estimate the likelihood that a given set of study findings would be expected to occur by chance.

Testing (as a threat to internal validity). As a threat to internal validity, testing refers to the effect of being tested. One may develop a sensitivity to the administration of a pretest which may effect the posttest score. This is of special concern if the pretest and posttest deal with knowledge because one may remember items on the pretest when taking the posttest and may have been especially sensitive to this specific piece of information. Thus, it may be this sensitivity rather than the intervention that mostly effected the gain illustrated by the post-test. The comparison group and AB single-subject designs both address this threat. It is assumed that the comparison group would have the same reaction to the testing situation as the treatment group; thus, any differences between the two groups can be better attributed to the treatment than to the effects of testing. For the AB single-subject design, the baseline period establishes a trend that illustrates the effects of testing if there are any. Thus, the superiority of client functioning during the treatment period is better attributed to the intervention than to testing.

Test-retest Reliability. To assess reliability using this method, a group of subjects are measured on the scale at two points in time and the two scores for this same group of persons is correlated. High positive correlations indicate reliability, or consistency.

Theory. In the most simple terms, a theory is an attempt to explain something. Theories can be more or less formal and explicit or more or less sophisticated, but any attempt to explain is a theory, whether or not it is supported by scientific evidence.

Threats to Internal Validity. In evaluative research, a threat to internal validity is something that may be the reason for the client's change in behavior other than the intervention. For example, a change in the client's work situation may be the reason that he is no longer depressed; thus, the treatment may not have caused the improvement in functioning. There are a variety of threats to internal validity, also known as alternative explanations. Among these threats are maturation, history, and testing, which are defined elsewhere on this page. Some research designs do a better job of dealing with certain threats to internal validity than do other research designs. In general, experimental designs which use random assignment of subjects to treatment and control groups do a superior job of addressing the various threats to internal validity.

Treatment Objectives. A statement of the nature of the gain in functioning that is expected for the client of a treatment program. It is a statement of a measured amount of progress toward the accomplishment of broad human goals.

Treatment Period. A period of time during which the client is subjected to the intervention.

t test. A means of determining the statistical significance of data measured at the interval level for either two groups of subjects (t test for independent samples) or a single group of subjects measured at two points in time (t test for paired data). The formula for these two situations is not the same. When testing a directional hypothesis, a t value of 2.0 or greater is significant at the .05 (i.e., $p < .05$) level if the sample size is greater than 5. Slightly lower t values are significant (at the .05 level) with larger samples. Consult a statistical text with a table of t values for further information.

Validity. The extent to which a measurement device truly measures the thing it is supposed to measure. In other words, it refers to the accuracy of a means of measurement.

Variable. Something that varies in the present study. In other words, an entity that takes on more than one value. For example, the variable of gender would be divided into the categories of male and female. A concept is not a variable in a given study unless it is measured in that study and there is some variance in responses. The concept of gender could not be a variable in a study that included only females.

Variance. The extent to which numbers in a set of data are different from one another. The greater the difference from one number to another, the greater the variance. (The term "variance" in statistics has a special meaning. It is the square of the standard deviation.)

Appendix *A*

Developing the Literature Review for a Research Study

The research report should begin with an introduction that provides a succinct statement of the general research theme or question and the purpose of the present study. It normally should be only a few paragraphs in length. The introduction to the study should be followed by a review of the literature. The literature review should provide the knowledge base for the study. It should clarify the nature of the topic through definitions of key terms and should present the reasons that the topic is important for social work. Current research and theory on the topic should be reviewed with a special focus upon that aspect of the general topic that is the target of the present study.

The Importance of Organization

The organization of the paper should provide readers with a logical flow of ideas which keeps them informed of where they are at each place in the body of the text and where you are taking them next. The reader should be introduced to the subject and to the purpose of the paper at the outset. As a part of this introduction, the reader should be informed of what you intend to do with this paper. This point should be made rather early. You shouldn't keep the reader waiting for five pages before you inform them of your purpose.

The paper should be organized into chapters for broad categories such as (1) Introduction, (2) Literature Review, (3) Methodology, and so forth. Chapters should be subdivided into sections that guide the reader through the document. Chapter sections may also be divided into subsections. It is advisable to use transition paragraphs between sections so as to clarify just where you are taking the reader and why.

It is also advisable to use different formats for the headings to help readers understand just where they are in the paper as they examine one section after another. Place major headings in a format that begins each word with a capital and centers the title. Next, align subheads flush with the left margin but set them aside from the text as with the other headings. Finally, if you need subheads within subheads, place them at the beginning of a new paragraph with the topic underlined.

The Literature Review

After introducing the subject and the purpose of the paper, you should provide a literature review that justifies the purpose of the paper and the research questions being pursued. For explanatory and exploratory research, a key question is the justification for the hypotheses that will be presented later. If you are hypothesizing that A and B are correlated, you should provide evidence in your literature review that one should expect this correlation given certain theories or research studies or a logical analysis of the issue.

The literature review should be organized by theme, not by source. You should organize your themes in a logical fashion and present the ideas of various authors around the themes. For example, you should present what various authors have to say about Theme A, then what various writers have to say about Theme B, and so forth. You should not state what John Smith has to say about themes A, B, and C and then proceed to review what Mary Jones has to say about themes A, B, and C, and so forth.

An outline of the literature review section is essential to effective organization. Use an outline to help you lay out this section before you begin writing. After you have written it, go back over your outline and make modifications if necessary, but be sure that you have a sound outline that illustrates the organization of this section. Your initial outline does not need to be as extensive as your final outline after the section is written. Sometimes it is not wise to try to build an initial outline that is too extensive because the experience of writing this section will help you to organize your thoughts; thus, you may want to reorganize your outline as you go through this experience.

The knowledge base employed is a critical factor in the determination of the quality of the literature review. The best knowledge bases are those that are extensive and show evidence of both depth and breadth. The extensiveness of your knowledge base is revealed in the amount and quality of literature research you conduct. There is no generally accepted standard for the number of references for your paper. The adequacy of your knowledge base will depend on the purpose of the study and the availability of literature on your study subject.

Extensiveness is related to the depth of the knowledge base. The depth of the knowledge base is revealed in the type of references consulted. Sophisticated works on research or theory have greater depth than articles that provide one person's practical suggestions on a theme. While the latter is not an irrelevant source, it is not wise to overrely on such sources. Furthermore, a dozen works of depth would be considered more "extensive" than perhaps several dozen of the other type.

The breadth of the literature review is evidenced by the range of the types of sources consulted and the range of the perspectives considered. One should not become so overreliant on one perspective that its weaknesses are overlooked. And you should not become overreliant on sources of a "practical" nature that have no theoretical or empirical base.

Originality

The focus of the paper provides evidence of the researcher's creativity. It should be unique. Thus, overreliance on one source for guidance is ill-advised. The way that you organize the literature is your unique contribution to an understanding of the issue. Needless to say, your focus should be clear to the reader.

Creativity is further indicated by your analysis and criticism of the material explored. Focusing your attention primarily on an uncritical description of a particular program, method, or theory does not show evidence of creativity.

The conclusion section of your literature review is one place where your creativity is best expressed. This section should reveal your conclusions rather than your summary of the conclusions drawn by one of the sources you consulted, even though the latter may be appropriately included in this section. Avoid using direct quotes in this section of the paper—you do not want to give the impression that you cannot say important things in your own words.

Specific Suggestions

Select a Topic with an Accessible Knowledge Base

Some topics simply have not been the subject of much theoretical or empirical work that has been published. Develop a basic bibliography very early in the process so as to examine this issue before it is too late. While it is true that a subject with little previous research is normally considered to be a rich terrain for new research, it is usually not advisable for beginning researchers to tackle such problems. Selecting such a topic does not excuse the researcher from the necessity of securing a knowledge base for the study. Instead, it requires that the researcher be creative in this endeavor by linking the chosen topic to literature in related areas and articulating the connection between the two.

A common mistake is for the student to do a cursory examination of the literature and erroneously conclude that little or no research has been done on the topic. The literature is vast. Before a student is entitled to make such a statement, he or she must undertake at least one computer search of an appropriate literature database. If a student can legitimately say that an on-line search of the Social Work Abstracts database, which contains more than 20,000 entries, generated only three articles with the keywords *aged, rural,* and *schizophrenia,* then he or she is entitled to say that little has been reported in the social work literature on the subject of schizophrenia among the aged in rural areas.

Be mindful of the quality of various sources of information in the literature. Graduate level references are those from scholarly journals such as *Social Work, Social Service Review,* and so forth. While information from newspapers and popular magazines may be necessary in unusual circumstances, they should not be used as major sources of authority on the nature of a problem, how it is defined, or theories about it. These references should only be used as supplementary sources of information. Information from agency policy manuals or reports should be considered in the same way. When you feel that you have adequately surveyed the literature, you should examine the number of relevant references from graduate level sources in order to determine the adequacy of your knowledge base.

You should avoid references to class lectures or workshops when you present your knowledge base. If something important has been said in either of these, you can bet that it has also appeared in a published source. You should find those published sources and make reference to them.

Establish the Importance of Your Topic

Early in the introduction to your paper, it is important to establish the importance of the chosen topic. An example is as follows:

> *Among young people in this nation, there are approximately 500,000 suicide attempts each year, about 5,000 of which actually result in death. These statistics highlight the fact that suicide is the third leading cause of death for persons between the age of 15 and 24 (Morrison, 1987).*

If you begin the introduction with the above statement, it should be followed by brief statements that reveal the major themes of the study, such as, for example, the treatment of suicide or the prevention of it. Then, one should state the purpose of the study.

State the Purpose of Your Study Early in the Paper

The purpose statement should be placed within the first two pages of the paper, preferably the first page. You do not want to hold your reader in suspense too long. On the other hand, it is not best to state your purpose in the first sentence of your paper. You should entice the reader into the subject before laying out the purpose of the study you are presenting. The following is a hypothetical example:

> *Recent studies indicate that many first marriages end in divorce, and the average duration of matrimony is quickly declining. Thus, divorce appears to have become a more acceptable alternative for coping with dissatisfaction in marriages. In light of the short duration of so many marriages, it can be speculated that many of these relationships contained the seeds of their own destruction from the premarital period of the relationship.*

> *Premarital counseling has long been considered an effective means for pre-venting marital disharmony and keeping marriages together for the duration of life. The effectiveness of premarital counseling, however, has not been clearly established. While some researchers have reported success, others have produced conflicting results.*
>
> *The purpose of the study reported in this paper is to examine the effectiveness of one premarital counseling program in the enhancement of marital satisfaction. Several variables considered to be related to marital satisfaction will also be examined to determine if premarital counseling is related to marital satisfaction when other variables are controlled.*

In this example, the problem was presented succinctly and the purpose was stated in the third paragraph. The literature review that follows this introduction will elaborate on various forms of marital counseling, the objectives of such counseling, and the results of studies that have examined the effectiveness of this form of counseling.

Make sure your purpose (or objective) is consistent with what you intend to study. Don't say that your objective is to define the role of social work in working with people who have problem X when you are proposing to study the relationship between knowledge and attitudes about problem X. Don't say that your objective is to examine the relationship between drug abuse and school performance when you are really going to test the effectiveness of an intervention designed to improve the school performance of adolescents at high risk for substance abuse.

Organize Your Literature around Themes, Not Sources

Because you tend to examine the literature source by source, it is tempting to present your literature in this way. In other words, it is tempting to report everything that Smith had to say about the problem and the solutions and the major societal issues involved, and then to report everything that Jones had to say about all these themes. This is wrong! You should organize the literature by themes and present what each source had to say about each of these topics.

Within broad themes, it is also important to organize your information around topics within these themes and to present your literature accordingly. In other words, you should not bounce back and forth between behavioral forms of treatment and psychosocial forms of treatment within the theme of treatment options. Instead, organize the broad theme into topics such as behavioral treatment and psychosocial treatment and present your literature in this way.

Don't Put the Cart before the Horse!

Be sure that you present your literature review in a way that is understandable by the reader. One of the common pitfalls is to refer to an idea or study result before you have adequately explained what the study was all about so the reader can fully understand your reference to it. You should not begin a reference to a study from the literature with a statement such as, "A majority of the 45 students surveyed indicated that they were suffering from a high level of stress." Instead, you should begin the reference with a statement about the nature of the study. For example, you might say: "One study of stress among social work students indicated that a majority of the 45 students surveyed indicated that they were suffering from a high level of stress (Johnson, 19xx)." Information about the nature of the sample is also helpful. Was this study from the students of only one university or several? Was it a random sample or one selected specifically because these persons had complained of having a stressful situation?

Another common mistake is to present the research methodology before the literature review of the problem is presented. The research methodology should flow naturally from the literature review, which sets forth the conceptual framework for your study and discusses what others have theorized or found through research with regard to your topic. In one example, a student presented a rather well-focused research question about the relationship of variable A and variable B and then proceeded to devote almost all of the literature review to the way the study variables had been measured by various instruments. What was most needed was a review of other research on the relationships among the study variables and a justification for the study that was being proposed.

Stick to the Knitting!

In the review of the literature, you should try to draw the big picture within which your study is contained. However, it is easy to "lose the trees for the forest" as well as vice versa. You should be careful not to give equal attention—and certainly not more attention—to variables within this broad picture that are not variables in your own study. You don't want the reader to lose sight of your study variables.

You should also avoid interjecting references to your study throughout the literature review. The purpose of the literature review is to present a knowledge base that supports your study. You will discuss your own study in the methodology section of your paper. The two, of course, must be related.

Develop Headings to Show Your Organization of the Literature

It is useful to use headings to help the reader understand the flow of your organization of the knowledge base in the literature review. It would also be useful to develop your own outline which reveals the subject of each paragraph in your review and how these subjects relate to one another. This will help you to get a handle on how it should be organized because an outline might reveal improper organization.

Use different letter formats for the different types of sections. For example, center major headings, and distinguish subheads from major headings by placing them flush with the left margin. Finally, use underscored titles for subheads within subheads if necessary. In the final case, place the subheads at the beginning of the paragraph rather than separating them from the paragraph as with the other titles. An example of such formatting follows.

An Illustration of Headings and SubHeads for a Research Study

The box below is an illustration of the way one might organize a literature review. It provides only a portion of paragraphs so that the reader can see the general flow of the organization of a particular literature review. An ending with three periods (ellipsis) asks for you to imagine the remainder of that part of the paper.

One final word of caution—it is also possible to use too many headings. You do not need a separate heading for each paragraph. In fact, if a particular subsection contains only one paragraph, you should reexamine the need for headings of such specificity. But it is better to err on the side of too many headings than too few.

Clarity Is the Key

Be sure not to expect the reader to get inside your head when he or she is reading your paper. Be clear. Do not, for example, make a vague reference to "this agency"

The Problem of Child Abuse

In this chapter, the nature and causes of the problem of child abuse will be explored. Because this problem is viewed as a vital priority...

What Is Child Abuse?

Child abuse is defined as...

What Is the Cause of Child Abuse?

Child abuse is viewed by most writers as having multiple causes. One of the perspectives on the causes of child abuse is the psychodynamic perspective. This perspective places emphasis on various aspects of parental behavior and parental pathology. Another perspective is the sociocultural perspective. The sociocultural perspective views child abuse as...

The Psychodynamic Perspective. According to the psychodynamic perspective, child abuse is caused by the following factors: (1) a view by the abusing parent that the abused child is different; (2) unrealistic expectations of the child; (3) stress accompanied by low levels of social support; (4)...

Many abusing parents have expressed concern that the child victim of abuse is different from other children...

Another factor contributing to child abuse are unrealistic expectations of the child...

The Sociocultural Perspective. Contrasting with the psychodynamic perspective of the causes of child abuse is the sociocultural perspective...

---

when referring to your study agency in the middle of the literature review, expecting the reader to realize that you are talking about your study agency. Such a reference would normally be out of place anyway. Your literature review should stick to the literature. You will discuss your own study later. But, of course, your literature review should be relevant to your study.

A common mistake is to say that a given researcher found a relationship between variable X and variable Y, but to fail to clarify the direction of the relationship. Don't take for granted that the reader will know that a discovery of a relationship between marital status and recovery means that people who were married had a better recovery rate.

Another common mistake is to make up acronyms to use throughout the paper because you do not want to repeat the title of something many times. Certain acronyms are appropriate because they are well known. For example, people are now quite aware what AIDS means; however, most people would have trouble remembering that PWA refers to "people with AIDS," even if the author has gone to the trouble to spell this out at the beginning of the paper.

Know When to Use Direct Quotes from the Literature

Be careful not to overdo the direct quotation of material from the literature. You should describe the material in your own words with a reference to the source. Direct quotes should be used for a profound statement or eloquent way of saying something. The following is a good quote:

> *"The chronic consumption of excessive amounts of alcohol, or alcoholism, has both a compulsive character, which hinders rational action, and a devastating effect on various aspects of the lives of its victims. The condition has emerged as one of the greatest public health problems of our world."*

The next example is an inappropriate quote:

> *Several investigators have studied the influence of pretreatment personality.*

The above is a rather routine statement that should be in your own words.

Don't rely too heavily on direct quotes.   If more than one-fifth of your written material is in the form of direct quotations from others, you are in danger of presenting an image of someone who does not know how to say things in their own words.

Don't quote someone who is quoting someone else.   It is tempting to quote Smith who quotes Jones and Bennett and Pearson on a given topic. This is not in good taste. You should go to the original source yourself. If this is impossible, yet the quote is essential to your review, you should indicate that you received the quote from the second source rather than the original source. For example, you can put the information in parentheses after the quote: (Paul V. Jones, as cited in Smith, 1982, p. 23).

Establish the Authority behind What You Say

Be sure that any factual statement is backed by a reference to a source from which the information was obtained. Also, give credit for ideas obtained from your literature sources even when you paraphrase them yourself. Ask yourself, at the end of each paragraph, if you need to give a reference to someone for the idea that you are presenting.

The specification of the reference should be at the end of the idea presented or at the end of the paragraph, whichever comes first. You should present this reference information in such a way that you leave the reader with no doubt about what information is being credited to the particular source. Do not go on for several paragraphs regarding information from a single source without making it clear that all this information is credited to this particular source. If you have such a situation, you could begin by saying something like "According to a theory by Jones (1986), there are two main components of effective treatment for alcoholism.... " You could begin the next paragraph by saying "This theory by Jones proposes that the helping person engage in.... " In this case, you would not need to enter the year in parentheses after the name of Jones because it is clear that you are making a further reference to Jones, who was referenced fully in the paragraph above. However, if you do not refer to this theory again for several pages, you would need to provide the reference information as originally presented with the date along with the last name.

Keep in Mind the Importance of Justification

Throughout your paper, you need to be concerned with the justification of what you say. As noted above, you should give reference information for sources that provide certain information. Do not make statements of fact without such a reference. Also, do not make statements of your own opinions. See, for example, the following statement from one student's paper:

> *Unfortunately, the federal government does not comprehend the fact that it takes money to hire workers to meet an ever growing need for help.*

Such a statement would not be appropriate in a formal paper, although it may be so in other types of papers or documents. It would be quite appropriate, however, to make statements of facts (backed by references) about how much money the government is giving to a program or how it has cut back on funds and so forth. Such statements of facts can do an even better job than your opinion of conveying the message. It would also be fine to refer to opinions of certain writers if it is pertinent to your study and if you provide appropriate reference information.

It is likewise critical that you justify the study that you are proposing. It is tempting to present a literature review about the general theme without providing a clear linkage between the theme and the study you wish to present. Take, for example, one student's proposal to test the effectiveness of the intervention model developed by Alcoholics Anonymous as a treatment of depression in an outpatient mental health center. The question that arises is "why?" Why would someone believe that the AA model would be effective with depression? Just because it works with one problem does not justify its use with another. You might be able to justify this proposal, however, by presenting an analysis of what alcoholics and depressed people have in common and a rationale for why the AA model is especially relevant given this particular similarity.

Using Standardized Instruments for Measuring Study Variables

Standardized instruments are those scales that have been developed by experts in the field and have usually been published. These scales have typically been copyrighted and require permission for reprinting in your work. In other words, you could not reprint the scale in its entirety in your own published article without such permission. Whether you should obtain permission to use such instruments in your own research is less clear. To play it safe, you should obtain permission. However, if an instrument is printed in a reference work in its entirety, the author probably has no problem with your use of the instrument for your own research. If it is a highly commercial instrument such as the MMPI, you will find that it can only be obtained by purchasing copies of the instrument from the copyright holder. You will not find the entire copy of such a test in a book or journal article.

There are many advantages of using established instruments. These instruments have been developed by experts in the field who have a keen understanding of the phenomenon being measured. These persons typically test the instrument for reliability and validity.

You should be cautioned, however, to avoid selecting a standardized instrument that does not do a good job of measuring what you want to measure. Often, you will find that your treatment objectives with your client do not lend themselves to measurement by existing instruments. It is better that you develop your own scale that really measures client progress according to your objectives than to select something that is ill-suited for this purpose or measures a secondary objective rather than the primary one. Do not fall prey to the mistake of selecting an established instrument simply because it is available and will require no work of your own.

Two Key Sources for Social Workers

An excellent source of instruments for social workers is *Measures for Clinical Practice* by Corcoran and Fischer (1987). This book contains descriptions of many instruments that measure social variables ranging alphabetically from alcoholism to verbal aggressiveness. It is conveniently indexed by problem area, so that you can look up a tool by reference to the kind of problem you want to measure. Such problem areas include alcoholism, anger, anxiety, assertiveness, and so forth.

Each instrument is described with reference to its author, the purpose, a general description of what it looks like, norms, scoring, reliability, validity, primary reference, and availability. Each scale is also printed in this book, so you do not have to write to the copyright holder for a copy.

Another key source for social workers is the *Clinical Measurement Package* by Walter Hudson (1982). This package was developed by a professor in a school of social work especially for clinical applications for social workers. Each of these scales provides a five-point scale for responses, ranging from "Rarely or none of the time" to "Most or all of the time." Each scale has twenty-five items with a range of possible scores from 0 to 100, which provides for a convenient basis for interpretation of scores. Each scale has been tested both for reliability and validity and found to be at least adequate for both. There are a total of nine scales in this package:

Generalized Contentment Scale
Index of Self-Esteem
Index of Marital Satisfaction
Index of Sexual Satisfaction
Index of Parental Attitudes
Child's Attitude Toward Mother
Child's Attitude Toward Father
Index of Family Relations
Index of Peer Relations

Several of these scales from the clinical measurement package can be found in the book by Corcoran and Fischer (1987). A few of them are described in the last section of this appendix.

Major Concerns in the Selection of an Instrument

Your first step in selecting an instrument is to develop a clear abstract definition of your variable. In the above-mentioned reference work by Corcoran and Fischer (1987), you will find a number of different scales that deal with anxiety. One is the Achievement Anxiety Test that measures anxiety about academic performance, which is rather different from clinical anxiety, the condition that is typically addressed by clinicians in their mental health practice. Clinical anxiety is measured by the Clinical Anxiety Scale and the Cognitive-Somatic Anxiety Questionnaire, among others. The Cognitive-Somatic Anxiety Questionnaire places a great deal of emphasis on somatic manifestations of anxiety, while the other scale places relatively little emphasis on this expression of the condition of anxiety. In choosing between these instruments, you may wish to ask yourself whether the somatic manifestation of anxiety is your main target.

Two major concerns in the selection of an instrument are reliability and validity. You should remember from your examination of these issues that reliability refers to the consistency of an instrument, while validity refers to its accuracy. An instrument must be reliable in order to be valid, but it could be reliable without being valid. In other words, an instrument could be consistently inaccurate.

You will see reference to different types of reliability and validity in your examination of reports on clinical scales such as the one by Corcoran and Fischer (1987). Some of these are reviewed in the following paragraphs.

> ***Internal Consistency.*** *This means that the items on the scale are correlated with one another. Thus, if John has a higher score than Mary on item (3), he is likely to have a higher score than Mary on item (9). This provides evidence that the items on the instrument are measuring the same thing. There are several formulas for ascertaining the level of internal consistency of an instrument. These include Cronback's alpha, the Kuder–Richardson formula and the Spearman–Brown formula. Generally speaking, if you see a coefficient of .70 or higher for such measures, you have adequate evidence of internal consistency. However, there is no clear rule for judging the adequacy of internal consistency.*

> ***Test-Retest Reliability.*** *This refers to the consistency of an instrument when it is administered more than one time to the same study subjects. If Sue receives a higher score for depression than Martha in the first week in May, you would expect her to receive a higher score than Martha at the end of May (assuming that these people are randomly drawn from a population). If this pattern persists for a study sample, you will find a high correlation between the scores on this depression scale at time one and time two. This would provide evidence of the test–retest reliability of the instrument. Correlations of .70 and higher are normally considered adequate.*

> ***Criterion Validity.*** *This refers to whether the scores on the scale correlate with other variables with which it would be expected to correlate. Forms of criterion validity include predictive validity (whether scores on this scale predict some future event) and concurrent validity (whether scores on this instrument correlate with other means of measuring the same thing). Graduate Record Examination scores, for example, are supposed to predict grades in graduate school. Are GRE scores correlated with graduate school grades? If so, you have evidence of predictive validity. If you and I both develop scales designed to measure depression, the scores of the same group of persons on both of these scales should be highly correlated. This would be evidence of concurrent validity.*

Consruct validity. *Construct validity refers to whether an instrument operates in the manner that would be predicted theoretically. For example, you would
expect that marital happiness and a desire to get a divorce would be negatively
associated. Thus, you would expect to find that marital happiness scores for people
seriously thinking of divorce would be lower than for those who were not giving
this alternative serious thought. Such a finding would be evidence for construct
validity.*

Construct validity also deals with the precision of the instrument in measuring
what it is supposed to measure. You would expect that scores on the XYZ Test of
Research Knowledge would correlate with IQ scores, but you would not expect
this correlation to be higher than a correlation of scores on the XYZ Test with scores
on another test of research knowledge. The latter would suggest that the XYZ Test
is doing a better job of measuring someone's intelligence than their knowledge of
research. An important test of construct validity comes from the study of the correlation of scores on a given instrument and scores on an instrument designed to
measure the social desirability bias. Social scales designed to be self-administered
are vulnerable to the social desirability bias because people might respond to questions on the basis of what they consider to be socially desirable rather than what
they really feel or believe. If scores on the ABC Scale of Self-Esteem are found to
correlate significantly with scores on a scale of social desirability, you have evidence to question the construct validity of the ABC Scale.

The remainder of this appendix is devoted to brief descriptions of selected scales
that appear in the book by Corcoran and Fischer (1987). For more information, you
will need to consult that work.

Selected Instruments

Twelve instruments have been selected from the book by Corcoran and Fischer
(1987). They are briefly described below in order to give you a sample of the kinds
of instruments available for your use. For more complete information as well as a
copy of the scales themselves, you will need to consult the book by Corcoran and
Fischer.

The Clinical Anxiety Scale

This scale was developed by Bruce Thyer to measure the degree of clinical anxiety.
It is especially useful for clinicians who are treating anxiety. Respondents are asked
to respond to each of twenty-five items that depict anxiety, such as "I feel tense" or
"I have spells of terror or panic." Their responses for each statement can range
from a score of 1 (Rarely or none of the time) to 5 (Most or all of the time). This
instrument has excellent internal consistency (coefficient alpha = .94). It has also
been tested for validity. Scores on this instrument were found to discriminate

between people from clinical samples who were known to be experiencing anxiety and samples of people not known to be in need of such treatment.

Assertiveness Scale for Adolescents

This is an instrument designed to measure assertiveness in adolescents from grades 6 through 12. It describes thirty-three different situations that adolescents may encounter, such as feeling that they have been graded incorrectly by a teacher or having someone break in line ahead of them. The respondent is given three options for responses to each situation, one of which is considered to be an assertive response. The other two are either passive or aggressive. A choice is made and the respondent receives one point for each assertive response.

Internal consistency is adequate (.76) while test–retest reliability is quite good (.84). Tests of validity have demonstrated that validity is fair. Correlations with similar instruments were significant but lower than is normal for such tests of validity. Of special importance is the lack of correlation of scores on this test with the Crowne–Marlowe Social Desirability Scale, indicating that people were not responding according to the social desirability bias. This is particularly important in view of the fact that the "good" answers would be apparent to most people.

The Depression Self-Rating Scale

This is a scale that is designed to measure the severity of depression in children between the ages of seven and thirteen. It contains eighteen statements, such as "I feel like crying" and "I feel very lonely," and calls upon individuals to respond to each statement according to how they have felt in the past week. They respond to each statement by marking either "Most of the time" or "Sometimes" or "Never." Some items are reverse-scored because they are positive statements, such as "I am easily cheered up."

Internal consistency and test–retest reliability for this scale have been found to be very good. Validity was supported by results of studies which indicated good correlation between scores on this scale and a similar scale and by evidence that scores on this scale discriminate between children known to be depressed and those not known to be depressed.

The Generalized Contentment Scale

This scale is a part of Walter Hudson's clinical measurement package and can be found in his work on this subject. It is designed to measure nonpsychotic depression. It focuses primarily on affective aspects of clinical depression with statements such as, "I feel downhearted" and "I feel that my situation is hopeless." A total of twenty-five statements are included, some of which are positive statements that must be reverse-scored. The study subject responds on a five-point scale that ranges from "Rarely or none of the time" to "Most or all of the time." Internal consistency has been found to be very high and this scale has also been found to be correlated with other measures of depression. In addition, it has been found to discriminate between people known to be clinically depressed and those not known to be clinically depressed.

Index of Family Relations

This scale is a part of Walter Hudson's clinical measurement package. It is designed to measure family relationship problems. It contains twenty-five statements, such as "My family gets on my nerves" and "My family is an unhappy one." Some items are positive, such as "I think my family is terrific." These items, of course, must be reverse-scored. Study subjects give responses on a five-point scale that ranges from "Rarely or none of the time" to "Most or all of the time."

Internal consistency for this scale has been demonstrated with an alpha coefficient of .95. It has been found to discriminate between those with and without family relationship problems.

Index of Spouse Abuse

This scale is designed to measure the degree of physical and nonphysical abuse that is inflicted on a woman by her spouse or mate. It contains thirty statements such as, "My partner belittles me" and "My partner punches me with his fist." Each of the thirty statements is considered abusive. Subjects respond on a 5-point scale from "Never" to "Very frequently."

This scale has been found to have high internal consistency (alpha = .90), but there is no data on its test–retest reliability. It has been found to discriminate between those known to be in abusive relationships and those not known for this.

Index of Marital Satisfaction

This is another of the many instruments from Walter Hudson's clinical measurement package. It is designed to measure the degree to which a partner in a marriage is having a problem with the marriage. It contains twenty-five statements such as, "I feel that my partner treats me badly" and "I feel that our relationship is empty." Some statements are positive, such as "I feel that I can trust my partner." The positive statements are reverse-scored. Responses for each statement are on five-point scales ranging from "Rarely or none of the time" to "Most or all of the time."

Test–retest reliability and internal consistency have been demonstrated to be excellent. This instrument also has been found to discriminate between those known to be experiencing marriage problems and those not known for this problem.

Adult–Adolescent Parenting Inventory

This is a thirty-two-item scale that is designed to measure parenting and child-rearing strengths and weaknesses for adolescents and adults in four areas:

(1) inappropriate developmental expectations of children, (2) lack of empathy toward children's needs, (3) belief in the use of corporal punishment, and (4) reversing parent–child roles. Subjects respond on a five-point scale, from "Strongly agree" to "Strongly disagree," to such statements as, "Young children should be expected to comfort their mother when she is feeling blue" and "Children learn good behavior through the use of physical punishment." Norms have been developed for scores on this instrument from tests of several thousand people. Internal consistency has been found to be good with alphas ranging from .70 to .86 for different subscales of this instrument. Test–retest reliability has been weaker, especially for some subscales, but adequate overall (.76). It has been extensively tested for validity with very good results. For more information, see S. J. Bavolek (1989).

Hare Self-Esteem Scale

This scale is designed to measure self-esteem in children aged ten and above. It is divided into three subscales: (1) peer self-esteem, (2) home self-esteem, and (3) school self-esteem. Subjects respond to each statement on a four-point scale ranging from "Strongly agree" to "Strongly disagree." Each of the three scales that comprise the overall scale contains ten items. The Peer Self-Esteem Scale contains statements such as, "Other people think I am a lot of fun to be with," while the Home Self-Esteem Scale contains such items as, "My parents try to understand me." The School Self-Esteem Scale includes the statement, "My teachers expect too much of me." Scores can be composed for the individual scales as well as for overall self-esteem.

No information was available on internal consistency, but test–retest reliability for the overall scale was found to be adequate (.74). Correlations were found to be high between scores on this scale and for other scales of self-esteem for children (.83).

The Index of Self-Esteem

This scale is one of those from the clinical measurement package by Walter Hudson. It is designed to measure problems with self-esteem, but is not recommended for use with children under the age of twelve. This scale contains twenty-five items with responses on a five-point scale from "Rarely or none of the time" to "Most or all of the time." Some of the items are, "I feel that people would not like me if they knew me well" and "I feel like a wall flower when I go out." Some items are positive and are reverse-scored so that higher scores indicate lower self-esteem (or more problems with self-esteem). This scale has a clinical cut-off score of thirty, which reflects the line between people who need help with self-esteem and those who do not.

The Index of Self-Esteem has been tested for internal consistency, resulting in an alpha coefficient of .93. A two-hour test–retest reliability examination resulted in a coefficient of .92. It has been found to correlate with scores on a test of depression, as would be expected, and was found to discriminate between clients believed by their clinicians to be experiencing problems with self-esteem and those not identified with this problem.

Index of Sexual Satisfaction

This is another of the measures from Walter Hudson's clinical measurement package. It is designed to measure problems with sexual satisfaction in a relationship. Subjects respond on a five-point scale (from "Rarely or none of the time" to "Most or all of the time") to each of twenty-five statements, such as "My sex life is monotonous" and "I would like to have sexual contact with someone other than my partner." Some items are positive and are reverse-scored so that higher scores indicate problems with sexual relations.

This scale has been found to have internal consistency and test–retest reliability with coefficients in the .90 range. It has also been found to correlate in the expected direction with measures of marital satisfaction and to discriminate between people known to be experiencing sexual problems and those not known for this problem.

Provision of Social Relations

This scale is designed to measure perceptions of the adequacy of social support rather than the structure of social support, which is the focus of some scales on this subject. It contains fifteen statements, such as "I know my family will always stand by me" and " I have at least one friend I could tell anything to." Subjects respond on a five-point scale that ranges from "Very much like me" to "Not at all like me." Higher scores are given for "Not at all like me" so that all positive statements must be reverse-scored in order to derive a score that is higher for higher support. Only two items on this scale are negative statements.

This scale has been found to have good internal consistency (.75 and .87 for coefficient alpha), but no reports of test–retest reliability could be found. It has been found to correlate with the Kaplan Scale of Social Support.

References

Bavolek, S. J. (1989). *Research and validation report of the Adult-Adolescent Parenting Inventory.* Eau Clair, WI: Family Development Resources.

Corcoran, K., and Fischer, J. (1987). *Measures for Clinical Practice: A Resource Book.* New York: Free Press.

Hudson, W. W. (1982). *The Clinical Measurement Package: A Field Manual.* Chicago, ILL.: Dorsey Press.

Appendix C

Writing the Research Hypothesis

The research hypothesis provides a prediction of what you expect to find from your study. This expectation is derived from your knowledge of the subject, which you usually acquire from your literature review. In a broad sense, there are two general types of hypotheses: directional and nondirectional. A directional hypothesis specifies the direction of the relationship (e.g., positive or negative) between the variables, while the nondirectional hypothesis does not.

If you have the basis to predict the direction of the relationship, you should do so in your hypothesis. If you expect to find that males will report higher salaries than females, this expectation would be reflected in your hypothesis, which could be stated as, "Males will report higher salaries than will females." Because the expected direction of this relationship is clear, this hypothesis is directional. In such situations, it would not be appropriate to simply say, "There is a relationship between gender and salary." However, if your literature review suggests that there is a relationship between two variables but the direction of the relationship is not clear, you would use a nondirectional hypothesis such as the last one mentioned. Normally, there is a basis for a directional hypothesis if you have sufficiently reviewed the literature.

The variables named in the hypothesis should be operationally defined. The reader needs to know just how the variables were measured. The operational definition, of course, should be relevant to the abstract definition of the concept reflected by the variable. The abstract definition of a variable provides the type of definition that you might find in a dictionary. It provides conceptual guidance about what you mean by the term. The operational definition specifies how you intend to measure that variable in your study. It is not necessary to specify the scale used in a study in your hypothesis as long as you provide a clear operational definition of that variable in the research methodology section of your report. For example, you could say, "There is a positive relationship between self-esteem and grades in school" rather than "There is a positive relationship between scores on the Self-Esteem Index and grades in school," although either statement would be acceptable. With the former, of course, you would be specifying in your report the specific scale you were using to measure self-esteem, and you would specify how you were collecting information on school grades.

An excellent source of help with the statement of hypotheses is *Writing Empirical Research Reports* by Pyrczak and Bruce (1992). Some of the suggestions which follow are informed by that work.

Pyrczak and Bruce suggest that the specific population be designated in the hypothesis if you expect your findings to be relevant primarily to that group of people. For example, you might say, "Among early adolescents, there is a negative relationship between self-esteem and the extent of the use of drugs." This statement would be relevant if you were only studying early adolescents and your literature review did not address this relationship for other populations.

You should be careful to specify the variables that you are directly measuring in your study rather than other concepts that might be inferred from them. For example, the number of days of training on computers is not the same thing as computer literacy. If you are testing someone's computer literacy, you should use this term in your hypothesis (e.g., There is a positive relationship between computer literacy and willingness to use computers in practice). But if you are measuring days of training, you should refer to days of training in your hypothesis (e.g., There is a positive relationship between days of computer training and willingness to use computers in practice).

If two groups are being compared, both groups should be identified in the hypothesis.   Consider the following hypothesis:

Older social work students will be more anxious about taking a research course.

They will be more anxious than who? It may seem to go without saying that you are going to compare older students with younger students, but this statement is not an acceptable hypothesis. Remember that a hypothesis is a very precise statement and does not follow normally from everyday language. The reader needs to know precisely what you intend to do. Thus, you could say:

Older students will be more likely than younger students to express anxiety about taking a research course.

Hypotheses should be free of terms that are not directly relevant to the variables being measured.   It is tempting to put a lot of unnecessary language in the hypothesis of a research study. Take the example of a study of the relationship between self-esteem and the use of drugs among adolescents. You will measure self-esteem by the XYZ Self-Esteem Scale and the tendency to use drugs by the number of times someone has used drugs in the last month. You have learned from your literature review that an adolescent's willingness to use drugs is theorized to be related to self-esteem, because the drug culture is the only social group available to some adolescents who are socially inept, which will tend to lower their self-esteem. The only admission requirement of the drug culture is the willingness to use drugs. Thus, some adolescents choose the drug-oriented social group rather than have no group. Consider the following two ways to state the hypothesis:

1. *Because some adolescents have no other social group to which to turn for social interaction, they will use drugs so that they will be accepted by the drug-oriented group.*
2. *Among adolescents there is a negative relationship between self-esteem and the use of drugs.*

Is the distinction clear? With regard to the first statement, ask yourself the following:

How is "having no other group to which to turn" being measured in this study?

How is "being accepted by the drug-oriented group" being measured?

As you will recall, there is no provision for the measurement of these variables in your study. You are only measuring self-esteem and the use of drugs. Thus, the second statement is appropriate for your hypothesis and the first is not.

The above principles were not taken directly from the work of Pyrczak and Bruce (1992), but they are in line with the suggestions of these authors. However, the following are a few additional principles from their work that were not addressed by the discussion above:

1. Because most hypotheses deal with the behavior of groups, the plural form should usually be used (p. 4).
2. Avoid using the words *significant* or *prove* in a hypothesis (p. 7).
3. Avoid using two different terms to refer to the same variable (p. 7).

References

Pyrczak, F. & Bruce, R. R. (1992). *Writing empirical research reports*. Los Angeles: Pyrczak Publishing.

Index

youtube

   quant

      categories /#   1) T

                  2) L

   qual   3) T # 1-10

      words

conceptual framework